Said the Prophet of God

The publisher and the University of California Press Foundation gratefully acknowledge the generous support of the Ahmanson Foundation Endowment Fund in Humanities.

Said the Prophet of God

Hadith Commentary across a Millennium

Joel Blecher

UNIVERSITY OF CALIFORNIA PRESS

University of California Press, one of the most distinguished university presses in the United States, enriches lives around the world by advancing scholarship in the humanities, social sciences, and natural sciences. Its activities are supported by the UC Press Foundation and by philanthropic contributions from individuals and institutions. For more information, visit www.ucpress.edu.

University of California Press
Oakland, California

Library of Congress Cataloging-in-Publication Data

Names: Blecher, Joel, 1982– author.
Title: Said the prophet of God : Hadith commentary across a millennium / Joel Blecher.
Description: Oakland, CA : University of California Press, [2017] | Includes bibliographical references and index. | Identifiers: LCCN 2017024233 (print) | LCCN 2017030890 (ebook) | ISBN 9780520968677 (Ebook) | ISBN 9780520295933 (cloth : alk. paper) | ISBN 9780520295940 (pbk. : alk. paper)
Subjects: LCSH: Hadith—Criticism, interpretation, etc.—History.
Classification: LCC BP136.8 (ebook) | LCC BP136.8 .B54 2017 (print) | DDC 297.1/251609—dc23
LC record available at https://lccn.loc.gov/2017024233

Manufactured in the United States of America

26 25 24 23 22 21 20 19 18
10 9 8 7 6 5 4 3 2 1

For Summer

and

for Marc, Sharon, Ian, and Jacob

In a paradox . . . the commentary must say for the first time what has already been said, and must tirelessly repeat what has never been said.

—Michel Foucault

Once a discussion of Bukhārī's chapters began in the Shaykh al-Hind's circle . . . things that had not been heard or read elsewhere seemed to be in the process of being unveiled.

—Manāẓir Aḥsan Gīlānī

Contents

Illustrations

MAPS

FIGURES

TABLES

Note on Transliteration and Conventions

This book has made every attempt to employ English equivalents to Arabic and Urdu words when one exists. This applies to well-known figures, places, texts, and groups, like Muhammad, Osama bin Laden, Mamluk, Córdoba, Gujarat, al-Qaeda, Sunni/Shi'i, Salafi, and the Qur'an. It also applies to common nouns like *hadith, sultan,* and *emir* that are found in English dictionaries. *Hadith* is used in both the singular and the plural, as is English convention. In all other cases, Arabic terms have been written with standardized academic transliteration adapted from the *Encyclopedia of Islam,* 3rd edition, ed. Kate Fleet, Gudrun Krämer, Denis Matringe, John Nawas, and Everett Rowson (Leiden: Brill, 2007-). Plurals, with some exceptions, are typically formed by adding an "s" to the singular, such as *ijāza*s (rather than *ijāzāt*). Texts with both Arabic and Urdu are transliterated according to Arabic transliteration conventions.

For modern figures or groups with Urdu or Arabic names that have been published without standard academic transliterations, I retain their published or popular transliteration as is (e.g., Salahuddin Yusuf rather than Ṣalāḥ al-Dīn Yūsuf; Deobandis and Barelvis rather than Deobandīs and Barilwīs). Likewise, quotations that include Arabic or Urdu terms have been transliterated as is. The first time I mention an Arabic or Urdu name, I give the full name, and in subsequent mentions I use a short name, at which point I dispense with the definite article *al-* (Badr al-Dīn al-ʿAynī, but subsequently ʿAynī). In the notes, which are designed for specialists, the definite article *al-* is retained (e.g.

Nawawī in the text, but al-Nawawī in the notes). However, if the short name includes "Ibn," I usually retain *al-* (e.g., Ibn al-Munayyir, Ibn al-Tīn). Book titles are usually given in shortened form, often replacing *al-* with "the" if it is included in the first word of the title (e.g. the *Muwaṭṭa'*) but longer titles are generally included in the notes.

Dates have been given in both the common era and the Islamic (*hijrī*) calendars up to the nineteenth century, after which only the common era date is given.

Since there are often many different printings and page numberings of hadith commentaries, I frequently append information in the notes about the book and chapter heading in the hadith collection under which a pertinent commentarial discussion can be found. This information is intended to help specialists locate the passage more quickly even if they do not have the precise edition I am citing. This information will appear in the following format: Author, *Book Title,* volume:page number (book title in hadith collection: chapter heading), e.g., al-ʿAsqalānī, *Fatḥ al-bārī,* 12:175 (*Kitāb al-Ḥudūd: Bāb kam al-taʿzīr wa'l-adab*).

Lastly, the following abbreviations have been employed: the *Encyclopedia of Islam,* 2nd edition, edited by P. Bearman, Th. Bianquis, C. E. Bosworth, E. van Donzel, and W. P. Heinrichs, eds. (Leiden: Brill, 1960–2006) will be abbreviated as *EI2,* and the *Encyclopedia of Islam,* 3rd edition, will be abbreviated as *EI3*. The *Encyclopedia of the Qur'an,* edited by Jane Dammen McAulliffe (Leiden: Brill, 2006), will be abbreviated as *EQ*.

Introduction

It was 2009, before the civil war. As the scorching heat of a Damascus summer day gave way to a balmy evening, a friend invited me along to al-Īmān Mosque to hear Shaykh Naʿīm al-ʿIrqsūsī add to his line-by-line commentary on *Ṣaḥīḥ al-Bukhārī*. Grabbing my pen and pad, I accepted. Sunnis popularly hold *Ṣaḥīḥ al-Bukhārī* to be the most reliable collection of hadith—the sayings and practices attributed to Muhammad—and their interpretation of the meanings of the hadith it contains is an event to behold. It was the seventh year of ʿIrqsūsī's commentary, and he was less than a third of the way through explaining the entire work.

At the mosque's threshold, I removed my shoes, and I found a seat on the carpet some sixty feet away from the shaykh. Scanning the room, I made a careful observation of ʿIrqsūsī's students. By my count, nearly eight hundred male students had gathered there. Many local Syrians were in attendance, but a good fraction of his students were from other parts of the Islamic world, particularly Central Asia and Indonesia. Roughly half brought a personal copy of *Ṣaḥīḥ al-Bukhārī* with them. Older students pored over faded editions, filled with marginal notes from prior studies. Younger students brandished sparkling new editions that conveniently included a popular medieval commentary in a smaller font below the main text, and they began adding their own margin notes for the first time. Near the back, some in attendance closed their eyes, counting their prayer beads methodically as they listened to the shaykh explain each hadith. Near the front, students clamored for the shaykh's attention, hoping to prove they could competently answer any question the shaykh might spontaneously pose to them.

While ʿIrqsūsī's periodic slips into Syrian dialect appeared to create an air of improvisation, his commentary was anything but. In one sitting, by capitalizing on the flexibility of the line-by-line commentary to digress into a wide spectrum of detailed discussions, ʿIrqsūsī carefully stitched together citations from hadith commentaries from classical Andalusia, the Mamluk era, and modern India. He also weaved in material from Qur'an commentaries, Islamic legal texts, historical chronicles, and biographies of the Prophet and his companions. With each explanation he exhorted his audience to pious action or elucidated a sectarian, legal, grammatical, historical, or political issue. It took ʿIrqsūsī from the time of the sunset prayer to the evening prayer—about an hour and a half—to recite and explain just three hadith.

The practice of live line-by-line hadith commentary like ʿIrqsūsī's is a fixture of modern Islamic societies. On any given week, one can attend live commentaries on hadith collections in far-flung places, from Baghdad to Britain, Morocco to Malaysia, Pennsylvania to Pakistan, India to Indonesia, and Syria to South Africa to Saudi Arabia. The medium of the hadith commentary is particularly appealing for global audiences in part because the hadith collection's topics range so widely that it allows scholars to expound on almost every subject imaginable: law, theology, governance, manners, mysticism, worship, the Qur'an, history, and the end of time.

And yet, as much as this practice speaks to the broad concerns of contemporary Muslim audiences, it is rooted in a deep history that spans more than a millennium. Scholars of the manuscript tradition have catalogued 232 extant works of commentary just on collections that were first compiled in the classical period.[1] The total number of hadith commentaries is exponentially higher when one takes into account commentaries on popular collections compiled after the classical period.[2]

While academic studies of hadith have illuminated how hadith were transmitted, authenticated, and awarded authority, one vital set of questions has yet to be fully investigated: How did Muslims interpret and reinterpret the meanings of hadith and hadith collections? What aspects of hadith and hadith collections came to require explanation in certain periods, and why? What explains why one hadith commentarial opinion endured while another withered away? When the needs of interpreters' social interests came into conflict with their fidelity to the apparent meaning of the hadith, how did commentators attempt to thread the needle, balancing both sets of concerns? And what were the complex social forces, technologies, times, spaces, and audiences that shaped and were shaped by the practice of commentary on hadith?

This book takes up this set of questions by examining the three key historical periods and locales in which commentary on *Ṣaḥīḥ al-Bukhārī* flourished: classical Andalusia, late medieval Egypt, and modern India. The book closes with an epilogue on contemporary appropriations of hadith commentary by Islamist groups. Throughout, the book tracks continuities and changes that emerged as the commentary tradition moved from the era of manuscripts to the eras of print and video, from eras in which commentators were connected to the ruling elite to eras in which they were distanced from political power, and from eras in which particular textual and institutional authorities were virtually unquestioned to eras in which those same authorities could be challenged. The book argues that the meanings of hadith were shaped as much by commentators' political, cultural, and regional contexts as by the fine-grained interpretive debates that developed over long periods of time.

Why does this book track the cumulative tradition of hadith commentary across a millennium? Like geological processes, certain changes and continuities can be observed only across long periods of time. Some layers of commentary suffered from erosion or were buried under sediment amid historical change. Others, under extreme pressure, morphed into something entirely new. Long-buried layers of commentarial opinions, after sudden moments of rupture, could return to the surface for a new audience to contemplate. Unlike geological formations, social and intellectual forces, rather than natural ones, shaped and reshaped the commentary traditions across time. And unlike sedimentary rock, hadith commentators and their communities could play some role in determining whether their opinions endured or languished.

To this end, broader audiences will find in this book a model for approaching traditions of textual interpretation at the intersection of both social and intellectual history. By documenting how commentaries delivered in a live setting and in writing were conditioned by the interests of their diverse audiences of students, patrons, and rivals, as well as by the affairs of the state, this book challenges the assumption that commentary was merely a derivative and rarefied practice, insulated from the politics of the public sphere. And yet, by giving equal weight to the intellectual stakes of the tradition—such as the cross-generational search for novel solutions to long-standing interpretive problems—this book avoids a common pitfall of recent sociocultural analysis: the reduction of intellectual activity to mere competition over material and social capital. By approaching hadith commentary as a living practice with social and intellectual stakes, this book aims to synthesize new avenues for scholars of history, anthropology, religion, and law who study cultures of reading and textual interpretation.

AN OVERVIEW OF THE HADITH COMMENTARY TRADITION

Traditional accounts hold that in the decades after Muhammad passed away, in the year 10/632, the Muslim community, seeking an example to follow, began to transmit reports—hadith—about what Muhammad and his companions and successors said and did. Source-critical historians disagree about exactly how and when these reports were first collected and brought into circulation and how it was that the authenticity of their transmission was verified. But by the third/ninth century, shifts in Islamic law had elevated the authority of Prophetic hadith. This spurred Muslim hadith scholars (*muḥaddithūn;* s. *muḥaddith*) to produce a number of compilations of what they believed were the most reliable or "sound" (*ṣaḥīḥ*) Prophetic hadith on almost every topic imaginable.

Eventually Sunnis would come to consider six compilations from this period to be canonical, although several others have served in some canonical fashion as well. This process of canonization arguably began in the late fourth and fifth centuries (tenth and eleventh CE), when hadith scholars in Baghdad began to treat two outstanding collections—*Ṣaḥīḥ Muslim* and *Ṣaḥīḥ al-Bukhārī*—as the measure by which others would be judged.[3] Of these two, many Sunni scholars came to argue that the latter was the "soundest" collection of hadith. One indication of this work's importance is that no Islamic text other than the Qur'an has attracted more systematic written commentaries than *Ṣaḥīḥ al-Bukhārī*.

Ṣaḥīḥ al-Bukhārī is a collection of more than seven thousand hadith compiled by Muḥammad ibn Ismāʿīl al-Bukhārī (d. 256/870). The work is divided into roughly a hundred topical books—such as prayer, faith, pilgrimage, knowledge, Qur'an commentary, and jihad—which are themselves subdivided by scores of topical chapter headings. Each hadith in this work consists of a narrative, or *matn,* that was relayed across generations of Muslims by a chain of transmission, or *isnād,* traced to the Prophet himself.

During the first four Islamic centuries, before the canonization of hadith compilations like Bukhārī's gained real traction, many Muslim scholars proceeded as if only popular hadith that contained obscure language, unknown transmitters, or ambiguous legal or theological import required clarification. After all, in many cases, the *matn* of hadith themselves already seemed to explain to readers how the early companions of Muhammad understood his sayings or practices. This stood in contrast to the tradition of Qur'an commentary (*tafsīr*), which had already matured as an encyclopedic and systematic literary genre.

In this way, among the earliest forms of scholarly commentary on collections of hadith were the notes of clarification that hadith transmitters themselves offered as they dictated their hadith collections to their students. Manuscript evidence from an early dictated copy of *Ṣaḥīḥ al-Bukhārī* shows that Bukhārī and his closest student, Yūsuf al-Firabrī (d. 320/932), offered notes to their students in just this way.[4] These notes might have been intended to be marginal but were nevertheless preserved in the central textblock of later recensions of *Ṣaḥīḥ al-Bukhārī* (see fig. 1). As Mamluk-era hadith scholars sought greater textual uniformity, these kinds of notes were removed from the central textblock and were either preserved elsewhere or discarded.

Another form of early commentary on *Ṣaḥīḥ al-Bukhārī* was the thousands of chapter headings by which Bukhārī arranged his collection. Each heading suggested to readers how a particular hadith or group of hadith might be best interpreted and what their legal or theological import ought to be.[5] In some cases, early readers found it clear what point Bukhārī was using his headings to make. In other cases, they found Bukhārī's headings ambiguous or even puzzling. In later periods, these headings sparked their own genre of commentary, as Muslim scholars composed freestanding volumes to explain their meaning. In each of the three periods this book will examine, we will see how commentators either deliberately ignored, responded to, refuted, or gleaned wisdom from Bukhārī's chapter headings.

Alongside dictation notes and chapter headings, a number of notable grammarians and philologists in the third/ninth century began to hone an early genre of "commentary on obscurities of the hadith" (*sharḥ gharīb al-ḥadīth*) that was dedicated to glossing and explaining names and terms in select hadith that were deemed too arcane for lay readers to understand or to pronounce correctly during recitation.[6] In some cases, these works were devoted to elucidating the arcana of a single hadith. The eminent jurist, historian, and Qur'an commentator Muḥammad ibn Jarīr al-Ṭabarī (d. 310/923) produced one such commentary on a single hadith that articulated the ideal qualities of a husband.[7] As the genre developed, these works came to address the more

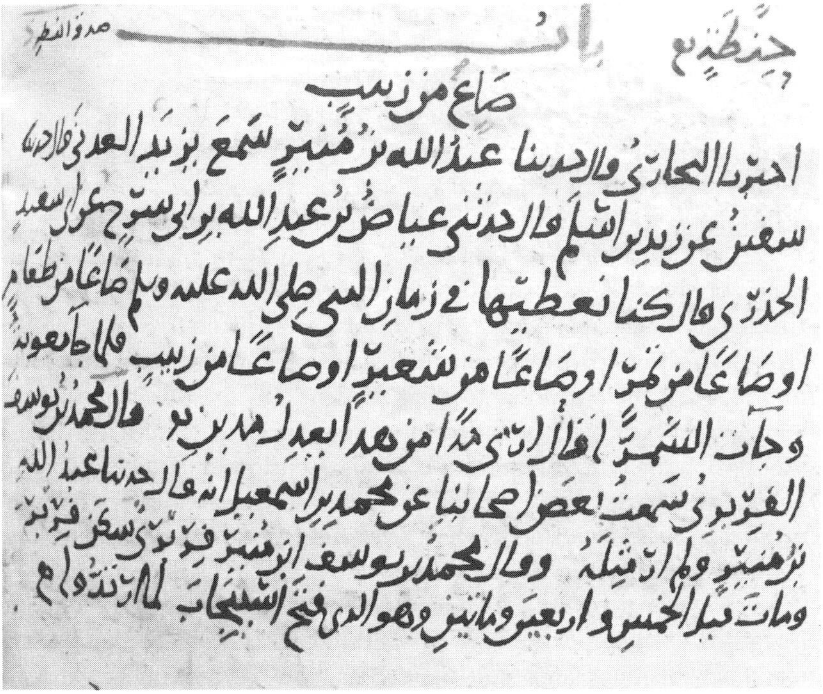

FIGURE 1. The earliest extant form of oral and written commentary on *Ṣaḥīḥ al-Bukhārī:* notes dictated by Bukhārī and Firabrī themselves about the biography and trustworthiness of a hadith's transmitter. These notes, contained in the last three lines of this fifth/eleventh century manuscript folio, are not found in other recensions of Bukhārī's compilation. MS Mingana IA 225, f. 25b. Mingana Collection at the Cadbury Research Library: Special Collections, University of Birmingham. (Author's photograph, published with the permission of the Cadbury Research Library.)

technical issues of language and hadith criticism alongside theological and legal polemics that arose from a large collection of "difficult" hadith (*sharḥ mushkil al-ḥadīth*).[8]

The earliest line-by-line commentary on *Ṣaḥīḥ al-Bukhārī* is often attributed to a Muslim scholar from Central Asia named Ḥamd ibn Muḥammad al-Khaṭṭābī (d. 388/998). Like other early commentators, he offered notes on a selection of hadith that posed legal or theological problems and glossed obscure words rather than the entire work. Recent research has shown that Khaṭṭābī was particularly interested in explaining hadith in a way that would defend the hadith folk from the charge that they had anthropomorphized God.[9] For this reason, his work may be better understood as a theological polemic than the first systematic contribution to the tradition of hadith commentary on *Ṣaḥīḥ al-Bukhārī*.

Beginning in the fourth/tenth century, largely among Mālikī hadith scholars in Andalusia and North Africa, hadith collections themselves came to be understood as worthy of systematic commentary.[10] These commentaries took the form of oral lessons and multivolume written works for use as reference during devotional study, recitation, legal instruction, and legal practice.[11] As Khaṭṭābī had done, early Andalusian commentators also used live lessons and written commentaries on hadith collections to defend their positions on law and theology and to polemicize against the doctrines of their opponents. Although these works were more comprehensive than Khaṭṭābī's, they were not encyclopedic. Often commentators would skip hadith if they did not find their narrative content to be significant. Moreover, they would discuss a hadith's chain of transmission only if it was deemed problematic. In part 1 of this book, I will explore the politics of public commentaries produced among these reading communities, as well as the inner workings and dynamic strategies of the written commentaries they produced.

The regional and temporal center of hadith commentarial activity largely shifted in the seventh through tenth centuries (thirteenth through sixteenth CE) to Egypt and Syria, where the genre of hadith commentary came of age under the patronage of the Mamluk sultanate. *Ṣaḥīḥ al-Bukhārī* was recited and commented upon annually, typically during Ramadan, sometimes in the presence of the sultan, the high court judges, and other members of the civilian elite.[12] A public recitation of and commentary on *Ṣaḥīḥ al-Bukhārī* was frequently called for to respond to social crises.[13] At celebrations honoring the completion of reciting *Ṣaḥīḥ al-Bukhārī*, scholars delivered poems reflecting on the unique blessing (*baraka*) brought about by the act of reading and commenting on the work.[14] In part 2 of this book, I will explore the social and intellectual history of written commentaries and live commentarial performances from this period.

In smaller study circles where the work was recited, hadith scholars of the Mamluk period would have students add new layers of interlinear and marginal notes (*ḥawāshī*) to a manuscript copy of the *Ṣaḥīḥ* each time it was read aloud. In some cases, these many layers of commentarial notes, like a vine wrapping around a tree trunk, overtook the base text (see fig. 2).

Eclipsing the influence of these marginal and interlinear notes were the stand-alone multivolume works of commentary (*shurūḥ*) on the text that came about largely through the efforts of Shāfiʿī hadith scholars (see fig. 3). In this period, commentators not only explicated the contents

FIGURE 2. Folio of *Ṣaḥīḥ al-Bukhārī* (ninth/fifteenth century) with multiple layers and styles of interlinear commentary. MS Amcazade Hüseyin, f. 1a. Süleymaniye Library, Istanbul, Turkey. (Photograph courtesy of the Süleymaniye Library.)

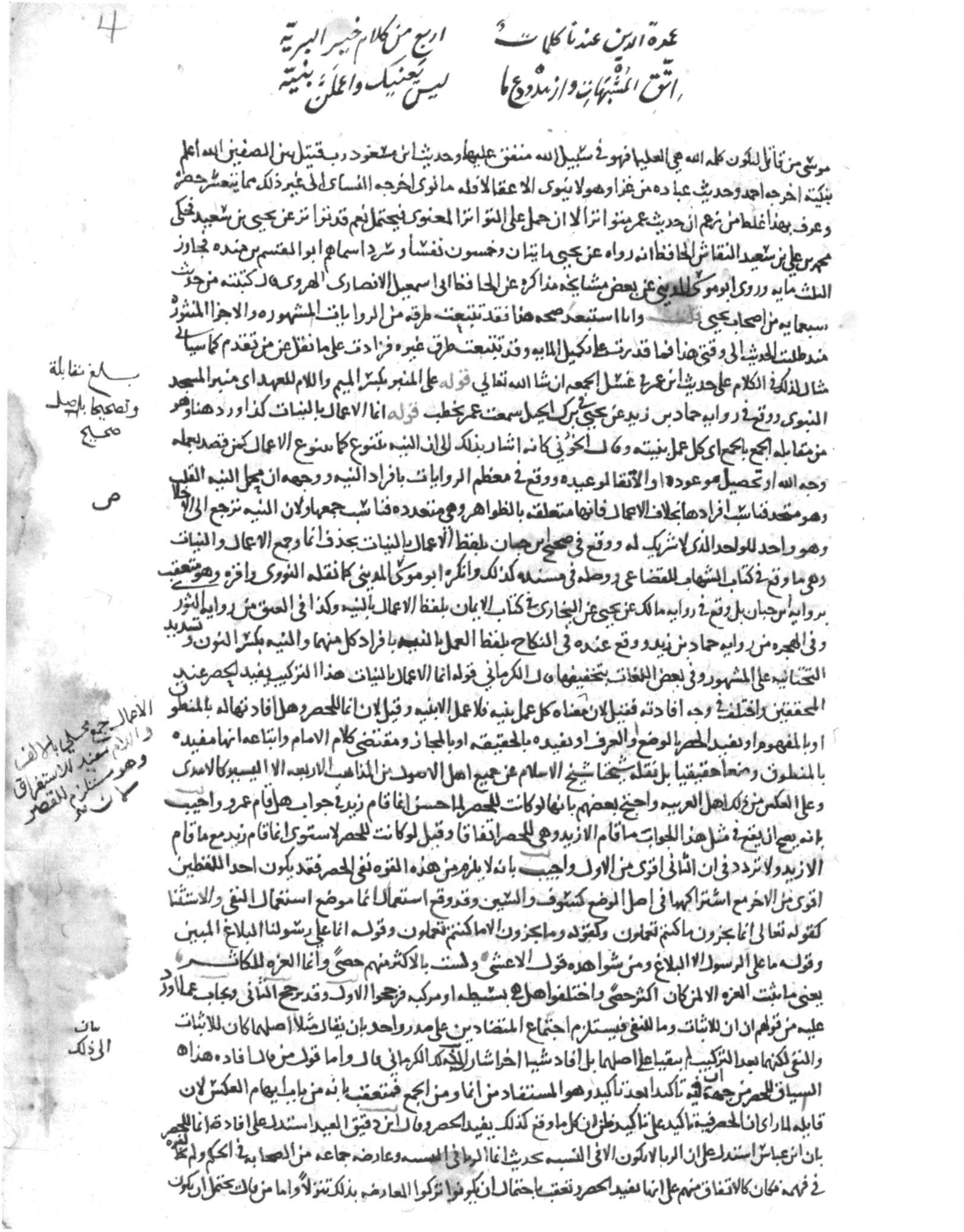

FIGURE 3. Folio of Ibn Ḥajar's *Fatḥ al-bārī*, completed Shawwāl 23, 856 (November 7, 1452), only four years after the death of Ibn Ḥajar, and one of the earliest copies known. A collation note in the margin states that the manuscript was compared with and corrected against a sound *aṣl*, "hand-exemplar." The commentary is centered on the page, with study notes and a poetic couplet in the margins. Only fragments of the base text (*matn*) are included, in the form of lemmata. Islamic Manuscripts, Garrett no. 87Yq, f. 4a, Manuscripts Division, Department of Rare Books and Special Collections, Princeton University Library. (Photograph courtesy of Princeton University Library.)

of hadith collections but also began to include systematic analyses of each hadith's chain of transmission and even the compilations' organization under chapter headings. These stand-alone works, such as Ibn Ḥajar's (d. 852/1449) *Fatḥ al-bārī* (Unlocking the divine wisdom), often took a lifetime to complete and were embedded in a competitive culture of live performance in which patronage, prestige, and legal and theological commitments were at stake.[15] Commentaries on shorter collections, such as topical works of forty hadith, also served to educate general audiences on popular topics such as the principles of Islam, jihad, and Sufism. A number of Mamluk-era hadith scholars made their way to India along trading routes, and hadith commentary began to flourish in India under the rich patronage of sultanates in Gujarat and Bijapur. Meanwhile, under Ottoman patronage, larger works of hadith commentary on important Sunni collections continued to be delivered live in study sessions (*majālis*) and circulated in written form.[16]

While commentary was a substantive component of the earliest Shi'i hadith collections from the outset, systematic commentarial activity on twelver Shi'i hadith collections proliferated in the sixteenth and seventeenth centuries in Persia under the patronage of the Safavids and in the context of Akhbārī and Uṣūlī debates over the status of hadith in Shi'i law.[17] Similar to the role they played in the Sunni tradition, Shi'i commentators used hadith as an opportunity to elucidate and expound upon difficult legal, theological, and mystical concepts and practices.[18] While the tradition of Shi'i commentary on hadith is beyond the scope of this book, I will elaborate on it elsewhere, and its formation and function ought to be a priority of the Islamic commentary studies' research agenda in the coming decades.[19]

Another phenomenon likewise deserving of further attention than can be offered in this book is the issue of gender in early and medieval hadith commentarial culture. While there were a significant number of learned women in early and medieval Islamic history who studied, memorized, and transmitted hadith, there are no records of any systematic commentaries attributed to women.[20] When it came to hearing a hadith from an authority with the fewest degrees of separation to the Prophet, an advanced age often trumped gender. However, as previous scholarship has shown, women were formally excluded from practices of interpretation and disputation in the medieval transmission of religious knowledge generally, though further work may yet shed more light on this discrepancy within hadith studies in particular.[21] In the meantime, however, it may suffice to say that many actors, patrons, and institutions shaping the scholarly culture of the time tacitly or explicitly accepted the discriminatory notion—all too common in many ancient and premodern cultures of learning across the globe—that women were not suited for the arts of interpretation. As a consequence, since commentary has been, until very recently, the domain of men, the works and debates examined in this book are dominated by men, even as some women circulated in their midst.

In the modern era, the practice of hadith commentary continued to thrive, particularly in the Middle East and South Asia, and forms the subject of part 3 of this book. The Deobandi movement, founded in North India in the mid- to late nineteenth century, was especially active in incorporating hadith commentary modeled on the Mamluk-era works into their school curriculum. Modern commentary on hadith not only served as a vehicle for religious polemics and apologetics, as it did in the premodern period, but it also served as a venue for political commentary, both subtle and explicit. Hadith commentaries began to appear in printed translations, notably Urdu, English, and even Indonesian. Although still a minority, a number of female religious authorities who emerged from women's piety movements in the Middle East and elsewhere also began to deliver live commentaries that, as some recent ethnographic work has shown, addressed issues often neglected by male commentators.[22] Moreover, globalization, the rapid expansion of literacy, new technologies, and new media altered the character of the places, times, and audiences of hadith commentary. Although these new technologies have given rise to interpreters who do not have a traditional scholarly genealogy, some neoclassical commentators have also made use of these technologies to compete for audiences and to defend their ideas.

In this vein, ʿIrqsūsī's commentary on *Ṣaḥīḥ al-Bukhārī,* delivered in the classical mode in al-Īmān Mosque, is instructive.[23] As his predecessors had done, ʿIrqsūsī awarded traditional reading certificates (*ijāza*s) to those who attended, but he also made use of novel barcode scanning technology to track those among his unwieldy audience who had actually attended and for how long.[24] Meanwhile, rather than writing down his commentary and circulating it in bound volumes, students set-up two video cameras on tripods to record the event for DVD sales in the bookstore attached to the mosque. The audio from those cameras was sold separately as MP3s on unlabeled CDs (see fig. 4). These audio-visual commentaries appear in bookstores across the city, as well as in YouTube videos for followers and opponents online.

In addition to the systematic commentary in the traditional style, the medium of the video records live improvisation, colloquialisms,

FIGURE 4. Covers of an MP3 and DVD set of Naʿīm al-ʿIrqsūsī's commentary on *Ṣaḥīḥ al-Bukhārī* in Damascus, Syria. The DVD set on the bottom contains seven years of commentary (2002–2009). (Author's photograph.)

entertaining anecdotes, fashion choices, references to current events, and other features not readily visible in the written tradition. In some ways, ʿIrqsūsī's videos offer a faithful return to the rich tradition of live hadith commentary on *Ṣaḥīḥ al-Bukhārī* since the text's inception. In other ways, it is conspicuously entangled in its local social and political moment in a way many written commentaries aspired to transcend.

WHY STUDY HADITH COMMENTARY, AND HOW?

The field of hadith studies has largely overlooked the rich and extensive tradition of hadith commentary (*sharḥ al-ḥadīth*), even as a handful of short articles and book chapters have begun to draw attention to the commentary tradition's value as a key hub of Islamic social and intellectual life over the past millennium.[25] Instead, the field has largely been preoccupied with questions of authenticity, dating, and transmission since the first Orientalists began to study hadith in the nineteenth century.[26] In the last ten years, scholars in hadith studies have advanced the field by investigating the canonization of collections like *Ṣaḥīḥ al-Bukhārī* and *Ṣaḥīḥ Muslim* and how Muslims themselves came to determine the trustworthiness of the hadith and their transmitters over time.[27] These studies and others have also offered sketches of how hadith were later interpreted in broader discourses of law, theology, mysticism, and Qur'an commentary. And yet hadith commentary itself, as important as it was, has remained hidden in plain sight. Whatever the reason for this neglect in the past, this rich interpretive tradition is now ripe for investigation.

A study of hadith commentary not only contributes to the field of hadith studies but can also transform the way students and scholars in disciplines as varied as history, religion, anthropology, political thought, classics, and law make sense of interpretive practices in their social contexts. Combing methods from social history, intellectual history, and social theory, this book poses a multifaceted methodological intervention that brings dimension to the way experience, power, and reason operate and intersect in an interpretive tradition across time.[28]

The first facet of this book's methodological intervention is to challenge the notion that the medium of commentary is merely a derivative and rarefied literary practice. While contemporary theorists in commentary studies have challenged the idea that commentary is intellectually derivative, they still treat it as a phenomenon relegated to the quiet, if crammed, corridors of a written text or a manuscript's margins.[29] Likewise, the swell of scholarly publications by Islamicists on Qur'an commentary (*tafsīr*) has shone a light on the intellectual developments in *tafsīr* as a written tradition but has only begun to fully reckon with the oral dimension of live commentarial performances.[30]

By contrast, this book brings to the fore the way commentary was performed and received during recitation sessions, live debates, and oral lessons in public. Live commentary sessions could thus invite multisensory reading experiences in which audiences and practitioners encountered feats of memory, poetry, elocution, fashion, food, crowded spaces, talismans, ecstatic feelings, and, on rare occasions, apparitions of Muhammad himself. To bring texture to this experiential dimension of the commentary, I will make use of descriptions of live commentary sessions in chronicles; commentarial introductions that address live audiences; biographical dictionaries that describe oratorical performances of hadith commentary; reading notes recorded in manuscript materials collected in university and state libraries in Syria, Turkey, India, Tunisia, the United Kingdom, and North America; memoirs of hadith students; audio and video clips in Arabic, Urdu, and English; Islamic e-magazines; and notes from ethnographic fieldwork undertaken at traditional institutions in Damascus, Syria, and in Hyderabad, India.

These sources lead us to the second facet of this book's methodological intervention: to bring into focus the material and social stakes of the commentary that much of the written tradition attempted to play down, conceal, or transcend. As this book will show, live commentarial performances could serve as arenas for spectacular and destructive contests for wealth and status among rivals in the presence of sultans, high court judges, and broader audiences. Among other things, the material goods and benefits over which commentators competed could include stipends, tax breaks, gifts of food and clothing, and, in some desperate cases, their very survival. The social capital at stake could include, among other things, prestigious judicial and teaching appointments, respect and distinction in the eyes of their colleagues, and rank and influence in the eyes of their larger societies. This methodological gesture answers a recent call for a "sociocultural analysis" of commentarial practices and relates hadith commentary to current conversations among medievalists and anthropologists alike.[31]

However, one danger in introducing sociocultural analysis to commentary studies is that it risks reducing interpretive debates over faith, law, ethics, politics, and practices to mere instruments in the competition for social capital and material resources.[32] After all, if we asserted that the practice of hadith commentary could be sufficiently explained as forums for zero-sum contests over power and capital, would we not be overlooking what commentators and interpreters themselves saw to be so valuable in the practice of hadith commentary?

The answer to this objection leads us to the third and final facet of this book's methodological intervention: we must pay equal attention to the ends internal to the tradition—those *interpretive excellences* only achievable by participating in it—as well as the skills and techniques that commentators master to achieve such ends within the freedoms and constraints of their normative commitments. For instance, one commentator might employ an interpretive strategy to serve his aim of achieving a novel solution to a cross-generational legal or theological puzzle in a way that claims to remain true to the original example of the Prophet.[33] Another commentator might produce an ever-expanding, exhaustive, all-encompassing treatment of a hadith collection, to do justice to the immense range of possible meanings hidden in the Prophet's sayings and practices. Such an encyclopedic project might also serve to better track and maintain the binding consensus of the community, and to keep a check on outlying, weak, or extreme opinions that might harm the integrity of the tradition.[34] Still another commentator might offer students a concise explanation of a hadith collection, thus allowing a student to more quickly access knowledge of the Prophet's example that would have been obscured by an excessively encyclopedic work.[35]

As we will see, commentators often leave unspoken the interpretive excellence their practice yields for them, since they assume their fellow interpreters will be able to appreciate those internal ends without explanation. But when commentators articulate their purpose aloud for broader audiences, they often use a range of Arabic words and phrases to describe it: a "benefit" (*fāʾida*), a "goal" (*qaṣd*), a "use" (*nafʿ*), a "desired aim" (*arab*), among other terms. In all cases, some historical reconstruction on our part will be required to appreciate the nuances of these kinds of achievements.

The way in which lived experiences, power, and interpretive excellences were thickly intertwined in the commentary tradition is typified in one Mamluk-era episode analyzed in chapter 5 of this book. In the shade of the sultan's garden, Ibn Ḥajar sparred with a rival commentator over a prestigious teaching and judicial appointment, as an audience of students enjoyed fruits and sweets. After much posturing, Ibn Ḥajar lamented, "this place is a proving ground," since the scholars were, in his view, overly preoccupied with testing one another in the presence of the sultan. Ibn Ḥajar refused to proceed with his hadith commentary until his audience transformed the space into one in which the listeners could "seek benefit (*istifāda*)" from the wisdom of the hadith.

Once Ibn Ḥajar deemed his students to have taken their places for a lesson, he then clarified the benefits of a hadith that had perplexed students of the past and present on the seven kinds of people who Muhammad said would be guaranteed God's shelter on the Day of Resurrection. While his predecessors cautioned that no more than seven kinds of people would have their salvation guaranteed—a worrying prospect—Ibn Ḥajar drew on his extensive knowledge of other hadith to reason that there were many other kinds of people, beyond the seven, who would also find comfort in God's shade as the Day of Judgment approached. To the delight and awe of his students, Ibn Ḥajar moved between prose and poetry as he delivered his commentary.

For later generations of hadith commentators from late Mamluk Egypt to Modern India, the success of Ibn Ḥajar's interpretation was not measured only by the fact that the sultan ultimately awarded him a prestigious appointment. Nor was it assessed simply on the basis of Ibn Ḥajar's ability to arouse wonder and admiration among his students through his mastery of the arts of memory and poetry. It was also measured by the fact that his interpretative practice opened new avenues for future generations of hadith scholars and students to better understand the meaning of the Prophet's saying and to be faithful to it.

Ibn Ḥajar and many other traditional hadith commentators may well have viewed the ends internal to the tradition to be in conflict with the worldly ends of prestige and power. This book, however, is sensitive to the way that achieving these multiple orders of rewards and excellences sometimes intersected and overlapped in productive and complicated ways. After all, without sufficient patronage or without the respect of fellow commentators, the commentator and his text would simply disappear from the tradition. By the same token, the mastery of certain interpretive techniques and the achievement of certain interpretive excellences could bring both the high esteem of fellow commentators and various material benefits and privileges from those less expert in hadith but willing to confer their patronage. However, in the conceptual framework used in this book, the practice of such techniques and the achievement of such excellences are not understood to be reducible to competition over power or capital. Since they served to motivate Ibn Ḥajar and many other commentators across a millennium, these interpretive excellences are as worthy of study in their own right as the workings of power that were thickly intertwined with them.

For this reason, we might usefully describe hadith commentary as a *social practice,* but one that goes beyond the overly narrow definition used by Pierre Bourdieu and other social theorists, which would reduce these interpretive strategies to competition over capital or power in the final analysis.[36] Bourdieu's notion of a social practice has dominated social histories of Islamic societies for two decades or more, shedding valuable light on the workings of power but leaving us with an impoverished account of the role of normative commitments and experience in motivating human behavior.[37] Instead, this book draws on select aspects of philosopher Alasdair MacIntyre's definition of a social practice: "any complex and coherent socially established cooperative human activity through which goods internal to that form of activity are realized in the course of trying to achieve those standards of excellence which are appropriate to, and partially definitive of, that form of activity."[38] MacIntyre's related concept of a *tradition,* which has become influential in Islamic studies through the work of theorist and anthropologist Talal Asad, also serves our purposes: a living tradition, for MacIntyre, is a social practice extended across long periods of history.[39]

While MacIntyre might agree with Bourdieu and others that practices are socially established in a scene of competing actors and institutions, he also recognizes the way in which these same practices are guided by *standards of excellence* that can only be argued for or maintained through the activity itself.[40] Just as jazz musicians may aim to achieve an original sound by their fellow musicians' standards, commentators may aim to achieve an illuminating interpretation of a text by their fellow commentators' standards. Since these standards of excellence and the techniques used to maintain or surpass them can be contested, they are dynamic over long periods of time. Furthermore, the achievement of excellence according to these standards is related to—but not ultimately reducible to—the social and material rewards that a hit record or a best-selling book might yield.

Since hadith commentary is socially embodied, historically extended, and guided by standards of excellence that are defined by and defining of the practice itself, it would qualify as a *social practice* and as a *tradition* in MacIntyre's technical senses. These terms give us a vocabulary, a conceptual framework, and a cross-generational time scale within which to grasp the commitments and ends that practitioners often claim most animate them, while keeping in full view the textured social and political dynamics at work inside and outside the tradition.

. . .

Where a social historian may see in hadith commentary a veiled mechanism to compete for resources and status, an intellectual historian may see in a hadith commentary a novel attempt to resolve an argument over ethical, legal, or theological norms that extends across generations of interpreters. This book does not view these two approaches as mutually exclusive. On the contrary, this book takes a stereoscopic approach that views the hadith commentary tradition as a social practice in which commentators sought and experienced social and material rewards in their present while seeking to solve intellectual problems that were internal to the tradition across long periods of time.

To this end, this book will tour a range of case studies at the intersection of social and intellectual history to illustrate how and why religious authorities and their audiences participated in the cumulative tradition of commentary. This includes visiting and revisiting—in the multifaceted social and political settings of classical Andalusia, medieval Egypt, and modern India—hadith commentary on issues as varied as the definition of action and intention, the definition of faith, the status of Muhammad's prophethood, the issue of discretionary punishment, those sheltered on the Day of Resurrection, the dressing of the Kaʿba, the prophesized destruction of the Kaʿba, the call to prayer, and the treatment of slaves.

These case studies illustrate the ways that live commentarial performances and written hadith commentaries were the product of multiple and intersecting social and intellectual freedoms and constraints, and that hadith commentaries could serve to both maintain and destabilize institutional orthodoxies.[41] To be sure, interpreters of hadith derived their authority by anchoring themselves among the cumulative layers of past opinions. Yet change and innovation were also valued in the logic of the commentary genre, and they allowed commentators, however subtly or explicitly, to respond to shifts in the political and intellectual landscape over long periods of time. As we will see in the chapters that follow, it was often in the very act of transmitting the archive of past interpretations of the tradition—telling and retelling a hadith's *exegetical history*—that provided the medium for creativity, contestation, and innovation in the present.

PART ONE

Andalusia in the Last Days of the Umayyads

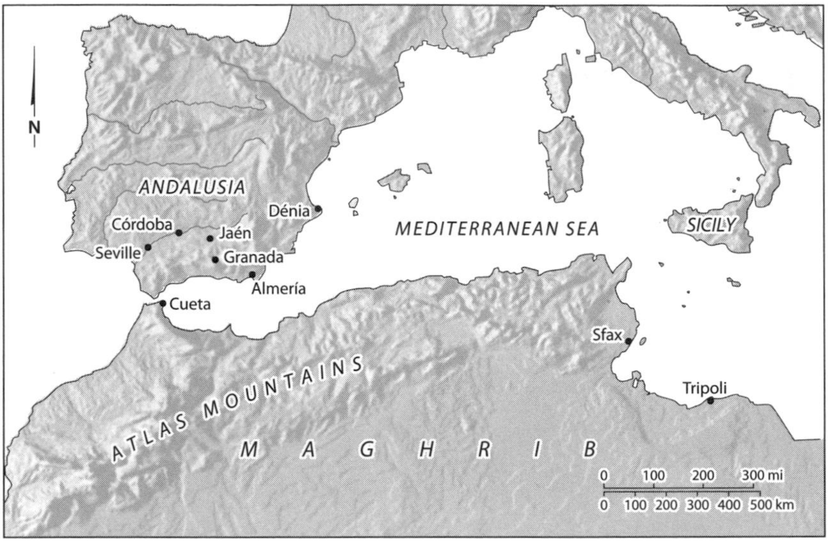

MAP 1. Andalusia and North Africa (Maghrib), ca. the fifth/eleventh century.

CHAPTER 1

The Perils of Public Commentary

If he answered yes, all would judge him, justifiably,
the readiest and most gratuitous of impostors;
if he answered no, he would be judged an infidel.

—Jorge Luis Borges

In the fifth/eleventh century, after having traveled to Mecca to study hadith, an Andalusian scholar returned to the Iberian Peninsula with a report whose plain meaning offered a provocative suggestion: "Muhammad did not write well, but he wrote."[1] For at least a century prior, a powerful and popularly received doctrine had evolved that held that the Prophet's status as "unlettered" (*ummī*) was a miraculous proof of his sincerity.[2] After all, they claimed, an unlettered Prophet could not have been capable of composing the Qur'an. Interpreters pointed to a verse from the Qur'an in which God tells Muhammad, "You did not inscribe it with your right hand lest those who falsify have cause for doubt."[3] A hadith that suggested otherwise required serious explanation.

While many Muslim scholars of the time circumvented this hadith in various ways, Abū al-Walīd al-Bājī (d. 474/1081) chose to take the text at face value: Muhammad did write by hand. But Bājī did not scribble this interpretive impression in the margins of a gloss, where it could easily be forgotten. He offered this reading in public, at a session in which he interpreted hadith for a live audience (*majlis min tafsīr al-ḥadīth*).[4] A local and transregional fiasco followed in its wake, which drew poets, preachers, politicians, and the populace into the fray, some going as far as to say that Bājī had committed a capital offense and to demand that he be held accountable.

For one recent historian, the event marked but one data point within a larger trend of polemical debates about the status of the Prophet during this period, and how they went beyond the restricted circles of hadith scholars, even "spilling over into public demonstrations."[5] But the Bājī affair also offers us rare insight into the dynamics of an early live commentary session on the hadith. Centuries later, live reading sessions on *Ṣaḥīḥ al-Bukhārī* would reach new heights at the citadel in Mamluk Cairo, where readings took place in the presence of the sultan, the chief justices, and the civilian elite. But even at this early date—one of the earliest documented live hadith commentary sessions—the Bājī affair teaches us that live commentaries could serve as a highly visible forum in which standards of excellence as well as material and social rewards were at stake.

By examining the Bājī affair in greater detail, then, I hope to convey a larger historiographical point: reading in Islamic societies, embodied by live performances and handwritten materials, can be rewardingly understood at the intersection of both social *and* intellectual history. After all, the Bājī affair teaches us that while commentators interpreted and debated in order to compete for survival in the everyday scholarly scene, they were simultaneously reading to achieve certain interpretive excellences that were defining of and defined by the cumulative tradition of commentary.

DID MUHAMMAD WRITE BY HAND? A LIVE DEBATE

The story of the Bājī affair begins in the seaside town of Dénia, on the southeastern coast of the Iberian Peninsula, in the latter part of the fifth/eleventh century. This was an era of intense political turmoil in which the Umayyad caliphate in Córdoba sighed its last breath, giving way to an era of party kings.[6] In addition to the political and economic tumult, or perhaps because of it, travel from Iberia eastward to the Near East for study and commerce declined.[7] Dénia was one of some twelve cities across the Iberian Peninsula in which Muslim scholars are known to have studied, taught, and worked, although it was on the periphery. At the time, almost a third of Muslim scholars documented had settled in Córdoba, since it offered relatively greater stability during the unrest.[8]

Hadith had been circulating in the Iberian Peninsula by the third/ninth century, many of which were introduced through legal compendia and collections of traditions, such as Abū Dāwūd's *Sunan* and Mālik's *Muwaṭṭaʾ*, the latter of which held the highest status in the Andalusian context.[9] *Ṣaḥīḥ al-Bukhārī*'s circulation in the Islamic West only preceded the Bājī affair by approximately half a century, as a hadith scholar from Tripoli is credited with the earliest systematic commentary on *Ṣaḥīḥ al-Bukhārī* in the West. Alongside Khaṭṭābī's, it would have been the earliest such work worldwide.[10]

Prior to the fall of the caliphate, a number of Andalusian scholars who traveled eastward for business, study, or pilgrimage returned home having received recitations of *Ṣaḥīḥ al-Bukhārī* on high authority.[11] This fed the growing interest in the science of evaluating hadith transmitters (*ʿilm al-rijāl*) in Andalusia.[12] One hadith scholar from this period who had spent time studying hadith abroad was so devoted to this practice that it was said that Bukhārī appeared to him in a dream in order to settle a technical question on the reliability of a transmitter who had fallen short of the compiler's standards.[13]

Likewise, Bājī, a major voice among Mālikī hadith scholars after the fall of the Umayyad caliphate, had spent years in Mecca immersed in study with some of the greatest living authorities on hadith. One of them was from as far east as Herat, in what would be modern-day Afghanistan.[14] Just as Bājī had returned home, in the middle of the fifth/eleventh century, two of the earliest Andalusian authorities on Bukhārī's collection passed away, al-Muhallab ibn Abī Ṣufra of Almería (d. ca. 435/1044)[15] and his better-known student, Ibn Baṭṭāl of Córdoba (d. 444/1052–53 or 449/1057).[16] Although students were still busy copying and transmitting Muhallab's and Ibn Baṭṭāl's written commentaries on Bukhārī's collection within Andalusia, local audiences no doubt turned to Bājī as the nearest living authority on it. Indeed, Bājī's personal link to the chains of transmission to this collection was so prestigious that his dictation of it to a student was used as the basis for later manuscripts in the Islamic West for the centuries that followed.[17]

Thus Bājī traveled from town to town, including Dénia, teaching, transmitting, and interpreting canonical collections of hadith that he had committed to memory while abroad.[18] Although Bājī never composed a systematic commentary on *Ṣaḥīḥ al-Bukhārī* in writing, his multivolume commentary on Mālik's *Muwaṭṭa*ʾ (The well-trodden path), a legal compendium with even greater stature within the Andalusian context, established him as an enduring authority in the cumulative tradition of hadith commentary.[19]

So one can understand why, in little Dénia, Bājī's live commentary session on hadith from Bukhārī's collection would have been a sight to see and a place to be seen, a high-profile forum in which one's professional reputation could be made—or even broken—and where key theological and intellectual commitments could be challenged or affirmed. Apparently Bājī proceeded smoothly through the live commentary until he arrived at our provocative hadith on the day Muhammad wrote.

According to this hadith, in the year 628, some six years after Muhammad and his companions fled persecution in Mecca and took refuge in Medina, Muhammad was ready to form a pact with his opponents that would permit him and his companions to at last return safely to Mecca and fulfill their duty to perform their pilgrimage. But when both parties convened at Ḥudaybiyya, on the outskirts of Mecca, to put the treaty into writing, a sticking point emerged that threatened to derail the negotiations. The early believers thought the document ought to refer to Muhammad as "God's Messenger." Their opponents maintained that Muhammad should be referred to simply as the son of his father, ʿAbd Allāh. According to this variant of the hadith, Muhammad, no doubt growing impatient as the squabbling wore on, "took the document, and while he did not know how to write well, *he wrote,* 'This is what Muhammad, son of ʿAbd Allāh, agreed upon.'"[20]

When it was time for Bājī to explain this hadith on the Prophet's truce at Ḥudaybiyya in his commentary session in Dénia, a controversy erupted. As a Muslim historian retold it some two centuries later:

> It was said to Bājī, "To whom does the pronoun *he* refer to in the phrase, 'he wrote'"?
>
> Bājī replied, "To the Prophet."
>
> So it was said to Bājī, "He wrote by hand?"
>
> Bājī said, "Yes. Do you not see it stated in the hadith, "The Prophet took the document and while he did not know how to write well, *he wrote,* 'This is what Muhammad, son of ʿAbd Allāh, agreed upon?'"[21]

While a swell of love for the Prophet and the preservation of his example had brought Andalusia's elite and popular audiences to *Ṣaḥīḥ al-Bukhārī,* had a plain reading of the text ironically called the Prophet's extraordinary status into question? The very status that the unbelievers at Ḥudaybiyya had refused to acknowledge?

A Sufi ascetic, Abū Bakr ibn al-Ṣāʾigh,[22] who, either having been present or having heard about the controversial explication afterward, accused Bājī of unbelief on the grounds that claiming that the unlettered Prophet was capable of writing was tantamount to a denial of the authenticity of the Qur'an.[23] As the news spread, so did public denunciations, condemnations, and curses of Bājī in Friday sermons.[24] Preachers and poets alike asked that they and their communities be safeguarded from Bājī. In that vein, the poet ʿAbd Allāh ibn Hind prayed, in verse:

> Keep me safe from the one who gains the world
>   but pays with his afterlife!
> Keep me safe from the one who says, "the Messenger of God wrote!"[25]

In this couplet we can glimpse, in a nutshell, the dialectical tension that would animate hadith commentarial culture well into the modern period: in the arena of the commentary, worldly ends and ends internal to the tradition were at stake, and while both were mutually constitutive, they sometimes appeared to be at odds.

On the one hand, as a public figure with influence, Bājī's performance as a commentator offered him material and social rewards in his everyday life. Bājī was risking all of this and more by doubling down on an unpopular interpretation, risking not only his livelihood but also his very life. And yet, as the poet alludes, Bājī is the one who "gains the world but pays with his afterlife." Perhaps what the poet meant by this was that even notoriety creates an audience and an opportunity to promote one's prestige, consolidate patronage and, as Bājī eventually did, compose and circulate a book, *Taḥqīq al-madhhab* (Verification of the way), in defense of his very survival.

On the other hand, Bājī's reputation meant little if he could not also persuade his audience that he had conformed to certain standards of excellence as they were defined by and defining of the cumulative tradition of commentary. In the immediate aftermath of this commentary session, it appears he failed to persuade his local community that deference to the apparent meaning of an authenticated hadith bolstered one's faithfulness in Muhammad's sincerity rather than compromised it.

News of Bājī's interpretation—and the uproar it caused—soon reached the ear of the emir of Dénia, who appealed for outside help to settle the controversy and restore order.[26] He received answers from Muslim scholarly authorities from Sicily, Iraq, and other parts of the Islamic West and the Islamic East. Although some conceded there was evidence for his position, many others wrote systematic refutations of him and his position.[27]

For his opponents, the only possible way to maintain the Prophet's status as unlettered would have required Bājī to look beyond the apparent meaning of the hadith to the meaning implied (*taqdīr*): one must infer that Muhammad ordered someone else, perhaps his cousin and son-in-law, ʿAlī, to write down the pact by hand.[28] This was not a theory without basis in textual evidence. After all, a variant in *Ṣaḥīḥ al-Bukhārī* reported that Muhammad merely scrubbed out the designation "God's Messenger" in a treaty that Muhammad had ordered ʿAlī to write.[29] Other authoritative collections contain hadith that state more explicitly that Muhammad ordered ʿAlī or someone else to write his name.[30] Despite the availability of these other textual resources, Bājī nevertheless chose to rely on the apparent meaning of the variant that suggested Muhammad himself wrote the pact of Ḥudaybiyya himself. Why? It is to this question we now turn.

A WRITTEN DEFENSE AND A "DOUBLE MOVEMENT"

We have already considered some of the social and material rewards motivating Bājī's choice to rely on this hadith's apparent meaning, but what were his interpretive justifications? Bājī's defense of his interpretation of this hadith filled a lengthy written volume, *Taḥqīq al-madhhab*. I will try, however, to summarize his arguments in two broad categories that are pertinent for our understanding of early hadith commentary.

The first category of intellectual justifications concerned the evaluation of the authenticity of the hadith and the chains of narrators by which hadith were transmitted. While he largely affirmed the authenticity of the variant hadith that stated Muhammad had scrubbed out his name and ordered ʿAlī to emend the treaty, Bājī averred that the phrases "he scrubbed out his name" and "he ordered ʿAlī" were not part of the hadith's sound phrasing.[31] No such questions arose concerning the variant transmitted by Bukhārī that suggested Muhammad wrote by hand. He also pointed to other authenticated hadith that corroborated the idea that Muhammad did not pass away until he learned to read and write.[32] Lastly, he appealed to the authority of a famous hadith scholar with whom he had spent years studying hadith in Mecca, Abū Dharr al-Harawī (d. 434/1043–44). Bājī recalled that Abū Dharr, who was considered one of *Ṣaḥīḥ al-Bukhārī*'s most faithful transmitters, had long asserted that Muhammad wrote at Ḥudaybiyya.[33] Defending his fidelity to this variant of the hadith—and, by extension, his fidelity to the Prophet himself—Bājī was not only competing for his social survival but also championing his commitment to certain standards of excellence internal to the tradition.

Bājī's second broad category of justifications concerned the way that hadith are, in theory, expected to bolster and specify, but never cancel out, doctrines enjoined by the Qur'an. Here, Bājī justified his position using a hermeneutic we might call a *double movement*. While he maintained that Muhammad once wrote, he just as forcefully maintained the doctrine of the "unlettered Prophet."[34] He argued that Muhammad's ability to write at Ḥudaybiyya was among his miracles (*muʿjizāt*), akin—although not on par with—his miraculous ability to recite the Qur'an.[35] He went further, asserting that the doctrine of the "unlettered Prophet" only guaranteed that Muhammad did not know how to read or write prior to the revelation of the Qur'anic verses that said so. It did not preclude the possibility that Muhammad might be able to inscribe a document later in life.[36] In this way, Bājī was attempting to use the authority of the hadith to bolster, rather than challenge, the larger doctrinal orthodoxy. In other words, Bājī's position was more nuanced than the one attributed to him by the poets and popular preachers. He was, so to speak, just as committed to his "afterlife" as they were.

In some ways, Bājī's double move would seem to be a subtle accommodation to his rival—and the rival of many other established Mālikī judges—Ibn Ḥazm of Córdoba (d. 456/1064). Ibn Ḥazm was a key figure in the so-called Ẓāhirī school, and he and others had taken a great interest in the study of hadith transmitters and canonical collections of hadith like *Ṣaḥīḥ al-Bukhārī*.[37] While Bājī famously defended analogical reasoning (or *qiyās*) from Ibn Ḥazm's withering attacks, he did so referencing hadith authenticated by Bukhārī and other canonical collections.[38] In other words, while Bājī maintained preestablished Mālikī positions, he relied on the kinds of hadith that would hold weight with the Ẓahirīs.

Another area where Bājī's and Ibn Ḥazm's interpretive approach shared an inner affinity, despite their public attacks on one another, was their treatment of Bukhārī's sometimes quizzical chapter headings. While some believed Bukhārī's chapter headings contained hidden meanings, later scholars remembered Bājī as one of the harshest critics of such esotericism, claiming that Bukhārī's chapter headings manifested deficiencies in his thought and excessive prejudices.[39] Likewise, Ibn Ḥazm was remembered to have preferred Muslim's *Ṣaḥīḥ* over Bukhārī's on account of the sometimes problematic chapter headings Bukhārī used to organize hadith.[40] In this case, as in the other cited above, both Ibn Ḥazm and Bājī appeared to prefer an unmediated approach to the hadith.

These examples offer an intriguing parallel to the double movement in Bājī's position that Muhammad once wrote at Ḥudaybiyya, especially when we consider the reasonable challenge posed by the Ẓāhirī *apparentist* approach to hadith. We might define this apparentist interpretation as the act of reading an authenticated hadith's apparent meaning whenever possible, even if such a reading ignored established opinions or limited the jurists' ability to assert their own discretion. Ibn Ḥazm, in particular, was a vocal advocate of this approach.[41] While Bājī strived to preserve the established position that Muhammad was an unlettered prophet, he was also attempting to deploy an apparentist mode of reasoning that might have appealed to Ẓāhirīs and other hadith scholars, and to strengthen the orthodoxy against their challenges. Whether these attempts were successful or not, the Bājī affair shows that the rise of collecting and displaying prestigious chains of transmission in Andalusia at this time did not merely bolster one's social status in the newly competitive arena of Andalusian hadith scholars. It also brought new expectations for the way interpreters ought to understand and interpret the content of those hadith.

Bājī's apparentist double movement and his knowledge of hadith may not have been able to persuade all of his contemporary opponents. It did, however, convince observers of later generations that Bājī ought not to be remembered as an unbeliever. After all, he still maintained Muhammad's sincerity as an unlettered Prophet. In the Mamluk period, Ibn Ḥajar found Bājī's position highly speculative, but did not declare him an unbeliever.[42] Likewise, modern South Asian commentator Anwar Shāh al-Kashmīrī (d. 1933) thought that Bājī's position, while misguided, had been sorely misunderstood in his own time. Kashmīrī told of young and zealous Mālikī jurists who sought to hold Bājī accountable for the capital offense of reviling the Prophet (*sabb al-nabī*), and if it were not for a senior scholar who intervened, Bājī would have been executed.[43] The Bājī affair thus became a lesson for Kashmīrī's early modern audiences about the need for qualified religious authority in an age of radical extremes. Kashmīrī would impress this lesson upon his students in his interpretation of other areas of the law as well, as we will see in part 3 of this book.

. . .

There is a bewildering Borgesian beauty in this *mise en abyme:* reading of commentators writing about the public reading of a hadith about whether the Prophet could or could not read and write. As lovely as it may be to contemplate this abyss, we can orient ourselves in it if we understand the Bājī affair as a social practice, in which the competition for everyday social and material rewards was entangled with the achievement of certain interpretive excellences. In other words, the advancement and defense of one's professional reputation among the local and transregional audiences of patrons, rivals, and students was intertwined with the advancement of one's ability to faithfully preserve canonical texts and extend their meanings for present and future audiences.

The material stakes of the outcome of Bājī's defense of his public commentary were stark: his life and his livelihood. But in offering an interpretation of this hadith, he was also striving to reconcile two incommensurable commitments, namely, his fidelity to a sound hadith that reported Muhammad to have once written and his fidelity to the doctrine of the "unlettered Prophet." I have called this hermeneutic a double movement because it ultimately required Bājī to marshal a hadith in service of a theological orthodoxy that, at first glance, it appeared to challenge.

Bājī was speaking not only to readers within his local community but also to Muslim scholarly communities abroad. He appealed not only to multiple audiences within his own time but also to the recent and distant past as well. He interacted with his audiences through oral media, including live recitation sessions and poetry, as well as through handwritten media, such as his lengthy volume defending his position. His commentarial practice was thus one that strived to balance seemingly competing orders of rewards and excellences, as well as one that navigated multiple audiences across space, media, and time.

The Bājī affair, however, offers only a snapshot of the robust community of readers and interpreters of hadith and hadith collections in late and post-Umayyad Andalusia. In the chapter that follows, we will examine in greater depth how this milieu framed the way a different cluster of hadith of legal import were interpreted and reinterpreted across a century. Like Bājī, some of these commentators devised creative strategies to maintain the authority of hadith as they challenged the doctrinal foundations of the most powerful legal institutions of their time.

CHAPTER 2

The Inner World of the Interpretive Tradition

A striking contrast [arises] between the awe of the text, founded on the assumption that everything already exists in it, and the presumptuousness of imposing the truth upon ancient texts.

The commentator . . . always combines both attitudes.

—Gershom Scholem

We have already observed how the spectacle of Bājī's live interpretation of a hadith elicited a controversy in Andalusia and lettered audiences in the wider Islamic world. But the Bājī affair also shined a light on an inner world of commentary, in which commentators developed and exercised fine-grained interpretive strategies to achieve certain interpretive excellences that were defined by and defining of the practice of hadith commentary. We will now dive deeper into this inner world of commentary and fine-grained exegetical reasoning, while keeping in view the complex social context of the Andalusian milieu. As we will see, this inner world refracted and mediated the concerns of an era in which the legal orthodoxy sought to maintain dominance amid the fragmenting Umayyad caliphate and the expansion of hadith scholarship in the Iberian Peninsula. But early Andalusian hadith commentary was concerned with much more than simply propping up or challenging institutional power.

To map in high definition the contours of this inner world of exegesis, I will examine a cluster of hadith in *Ṣaḥīḥ al-Bukhārī* and track their reception among Muslim religious authorities in Andalusia from the fourth to fifth centuries (tenth to eleventh CE). As the cumulative tradition of commentary on these hadith progressed over time, internal debates arose over the limits of legal authority, the authenticity and status of hadith, and the proper methods of textual exegesis. Although exegetes sometimes concealed or ignored broader intellectual shifts—the nascent Ẓāhirī challenge to Mālikī dominance, a growth in the study of chains of transmission, and an interest in Bukhārī's novel editorial choices—these developments shaped both the terms and evolution of these debates.

The case study I have chosen is a cluster of hadith in *Ṣaḥīḥ al-Bukhārī* that Bukhārī placed in a chapter titled "How Much Discretionary Punishment (*ta'zīr*) and Discipline (*adab*)?"* This cluster has been chosen in part because the first three hadith under this chapter heading sparked wide disagreement among scholars within and across time, despite or perhaps because of the clarity of their apparent meaning. By focusing my case study on how these hadith were debated within the cumulative tradition of commentary on *Ṣaḥīḥ al-Bukhārī,* I will shed light on certain interpretive techniques that were uniquely developed and deployed in relation to this particular collection. These techniques tied the meaning of the hadith to Bukhārī's novel organization. Thus, some commentators devised arguments for the interpretation of these hadith that would not necessarily be found in commentary on other compilations of traditions or genres of legal writing. Furthermore, I offer readers an example of a Muslim scholar who debated these hadith beyond the boundaries of the cumulative tradition of commentary on *Ṣaḥīḥ al-Bukhārī.* Future research on the reception of these hadith in other collections, however, would surely further refine our understanding.

Commentaries on *Ṣaḥīḥ al-Bukhārī* would not have had as great a claim on regulating their audiences' behavior as a caliph's decree—or even a verdict from a state-appointed judge. Indeed, commentaries on *Ṣaḥīḥ al-Bukhārī* were never intended to directly rule on particular cases. Nevertheless, as audiences began to take the collection as an authoritative source for hadith, a commentary on it could, along with a constellation of other Islamic discursive traditions, indirectly inform its audiences' behavior or thinking. Commentators often indicated, in both subtle and overt ways, which explanations of Muhammad's sayings and practices

* The word *adab* is typically translated as "refined manners," but *adab* shares a root with *ta'dīb,* which, like *ta'zīr,* conveys chastisement. This latter sense is what later commentators, including Ibn Ḥajar, believe Bukhārī is signaling here, as I will discuss below. I have chosen to translate *adab* as "discipline" since it conveys both senses: excellent training and punishment.

among the cumulative layers of commentary they favored and, indeed, the range of explanations that merited consideration in the first place. Moreover, commentary on *Ṣaḥīḥ al-Bukhārī* could polemicize or influence textual discourses that claimed to regulate behavior in more direct ways.

With these caveats in mind, the following case study is not intended to be a comprehensive study of the juristic reception or application of "discretionary punishment" (*taʿzīr*). Rather, it is simply intended to offer a window into the intellectual stakes of the debates among a sampling of key Andalusian jurists, hadith scholars, and commentators.

RIPE FOR CRITIQUE: THE MĀLIKĪ ORTHODOXY

In order to grasp how the Andalusian milieu might have influenced the interpretation of these hadith, we must first understand that this was a time in which Mālikī jurists dominated the scholarly scene. While there was at least one prominent Ẓāhirī in the judiciary of Córdoba in the mid-fourth/tenth century, even he implemented Mālikī law in his legal practice.[1] In some cases, this Mālikī supremacy was maintained by force rather than persuasion.[2] Nevertheless, all of the known systematic hadith commentators from this period were affiliated with the Mālikī school of law. This is not to say there were no differences of opinion on certain matters.[3] But by the fifth/eleventh century, the era in which Ibn Baṭṭāl and Muhallab lived, commentary on *Ṣaḥīḥ al-Bukhārī* that had bearing on legal matters tended to clarify the Mālikī position using opinions representing other schools of law as a foil.

In our discussion of the Bājī affair, we saw the social pressure to maintain this orthodoxy not only in the political and economic turmoil brought about the dissolution of the Umayyad caliphate, but also in two important and related intellectual developments. The first was the growth of the study of hadith abroad by prestigious chains of transmission that led to the establishment of certificate-granting hadith scholars in Andalusia in the fourth and fifth centuries (tenth and eleventh CE). This trend correlated broadly with the proliferation of Sufism in Andalusia during this time.[4] One outcome of this growth was a renewed seriousness among judges to rely on prophetic hadith as evidence rather than reports attributed to companions of Muhammad (termed "companion reports") or sayings attributed to Mālik ibn Anas (d. 179/796), the eponymous founder of the Mālikī legal approach. To defend themselves from critiques of their opponents, Mālikī jurists strove to find prophetic hadith that could bolster opinions long built on other sources of evidence.

The second and related development was the rise of Ẓāhirism and the challenges posed by interpreting hadith by their apparent rather than implied meaning. The specter of Ẓāhirism that haunted the Mālikīs who wrote commentaries on *Ṣaḥīḥ al-Bukhārī* is difficult to detect. Ibn Baṭṭāl's commentary omits any mention of Ẓāhirī opinions, even though he was living in Córdoba in 418/1027, when Ibn Ḥazm began to teach the Ẓāhirī approach publically in the great mosque of Córdoba and engaged in live debates with adversaries.[5] One hypothesis is that Muhallab's and Ibn Baṭṭāl's commentaries were already completed by that date. Alternately, perhaps Ibn Ḥazm and other representatives of the Ẓāhirī school did not gain sufficient notice in Andalusia to warrant refutation in a commentary until the second part of the fifth/eleventh century, after Muhallab's and Ibn Baṭṭāl's commentaries were put to paper.[6] But one cannot rule out the possibility that Ibn Baṭṭāl and Muhallab knew of the Ẓāhirīs and deliberately chose to exclude them from their discourses rather than refute them.

Yet, even if the early Mālikī commentators on *Ṣaḥīḥ al-Bukhārī* in Andalusia did not directly respond to Ẓāhirism, Mālikism can be read as ripe for critique from within and without by a new generation of hadith scholars who took a greater interest in the authenticity of the prophetic hadith they transmitted and, as a consequence, their apparent rather than intended meaning.[7] While the Mālikīs sought to justify the widest possible judicial discretion in cases involving *taʿzīr*, Ẓahirīs thought judicial discretion to authorize punishments ought to be limited by the apparent meaning of the text: ten lashes and no more. If the Mālikī legal school wanted to maintain its wide judicial discretion in cases of *taʿzīr* and a virtual monopoly on Islamic law in Andalusia amid the economic and political destabilization following the dissolution of the caliphate, it would have to adapt.

THE CASE OF DISCRETIONARY PUNISHMENT

Keeping these local social and intellectual factors in mind, let us turn to the case of discretionary punishment. Three hadith on the limits of discretionary punishment (*taʿzīr*) are listed in *Ṣaḥīḥ al-Bukhārī* in "The Book of God's Forbidden Boundaries (*ḥudūd*, sg. *ḥadd*)" under the chapter "How Much Discretionary Punishment and Discipline (*adab*)?":

1) "One ought not be lashed in excess of ten lashes except in the case of a *ḥadd* among the *ḥudūd* of God."
2) "There is no punishment in excess of ten strokes except in the case of a *ḥadd* among *ḥudūd* of God."
3) "Do not lash in excess of ten whips except in the case of a *ḥadd* among the *ḥudūd* of God."[8]

At first glance, the three hadith appear to be more or less consistent and unambiguous: a maximum of ten lashes for any offenses other than those offenses expressly forbidden by God in the Qur'an (*ḥudūd*).* A second glance suggests a number of questions that might have remained in the minds of Mālikī scholars commenting on *Ṣaḥīḥ al-Bukhārī* in fifth-/eleventh-century Andalusia. How does this text square with Mālik's ruling that discretionary punishment was entirely up to the judge's own reasoned determination (*ijtihād*)? Is *Ṣaḥīḥ al-Bukhārī* so authoritative that Mālik's opinion would be overruled, thus restricting Mālikī judges from authorizing sentences greater than ten lashes? What if someone was not effectively deterred by ten lashes? What if there was compelling textual evidence that Muhammad's companions and successors ordered more than ten lashings for offenses that were not stipulated in the Qur'an as *ḥudūd?* And, by the way, what offenses are defined as *ḥudūd* in the first place?

A second round of questioning would emerge when Mālikī jurists compared the chains of transmission of these three hadith (see table 1). Who is the unknown transmitter of the second hadith? Did ʿAbd al-Raḥmān ibn Jābir hear the hadith on the authority of Abū Burda directly or via his father? Are these inconsistencies serious enough that a judge could disregard these hadith's injunction not to exceed ten lashes? Or is their authenticity guaranteed simply because Bukhārī deemed them authentic enough to include in his *Ṣaḥīḥ* in the first place?

While we do not have detailed anecdotal accounts of live commentary on these hadith and their reception in this early period, we can learn much about how these hadith were interpreted and debated by the earliest commentators and hadith scholars in Andalusia by sifting through the layers of commentary preserved in the works of Ibn Baṭṭāl

* The term *ḥudūd*—literally "limits" or "boundaries"—has a technical meaning in Islamic law: particular offenses stipulated in the Qur'an that were understood as offenses against God. They typically included "unlawful intercourse (*zinā*); its counterpart, false accusation of unlawful intercourse (*ḳadhf*), drinking wine; theft and highway robbery," although a complete list was, as we will see, debated in some quarters. I have left the term untranslated in the hadith above because this technical definition later came under criticism from Mamluk-era jurists. See *EI2*, s.v. "Ḥadd," (B. Carra de Vaux).

TABLE 1 A COMPARISON OF THE CHAINS OF TRANSMISSION OF THE FIRST THREE HADITH CONTAINED UNDER THE CHAPTER ON DISCRETIONARY PUNISHMENT IN *ṢAḤĪḤ AL-BUKHĀRĪ*

Hadith 1	Hadith 2	Hadith 3
Muhammad ↓	Muhammad ↓	Muhammad ↓
Abū Burda ↓	an unknown transmitter from the "helpers" (*anṣār*) ↓	Abū Burda ↓
		Jābir ↓
ʿAbd al-Raḥmān ibn Jābir ↓	ʿAbd al-Raḥmān ibn Jābir ↓	ʿAbd al-Raḥmān ibn Jābir ↓
Sulaymān ibn Yasār ↓		Sulaymān ibn Yasār ↓
Bukayr ibn ʿAbd Allāh ↓		Bukayr ↓
Yazīd ibn Abī Ḥabīb ↓	Muslim ibn Abī Maryam ↓	ʿAmr ↓
Layth ↓	Fuḍayl ibn Sulaymān ↓	Ibn Wahb ↓
ʿAbd Allāh ibn Yūsuf ↓	ʿAmr ibn ʿAlī ↓	Yaḥyā ibn Sulaymān ↓
Bukhārī	Bukhārī	Bukhārī

and the works of later Andalusian and Mamluk-era commentators. What we find is that early Mālikī authorities sought to dismiss one of these hadith on the basis of the unreliability of its chain of transmission and because there were hadith attributed to Muhammad's companions that lent support to the Mālikī position. A Ẓāhirī opponent, Ibn Ḥazm, found a variant of the hadith to be sound and deployed it to advocate against severe or capital punishments for certain offenses. Perhaps anticipating this challenge, Muhallab found a way to maintain both the authority of the hadith and the Mālikī commitment to unrestricted judicial authority in matters of discretionary punishment. He did so by devising an ingenious technique that linked the interpretation of the hadith to the novel organization of *Ṣaḥīḥ al-Bukhārī*.

REFRAMING THE CLASSICAL DEBATE

Ibn Baṭṭāl framed his commentary on these hadith with a much older debate among the legal schools. According to Ibn Baṭṭāl, some of the most respected hadith scholars and jurists from the classical period read the hadith as an unambiguous command not to exceed ten lashes except in the case of an offense against one of God's sanctions (*ḥudūd Allāh*), typically understood to be a short list of offenses stipulated in the Qur'an.[9] These classical scholars included the eponym of the Ḥanbalī school, Aḥmad ibn Ḥanbal (d. 241/855), and his student Isḥāq ibn Rāhwayh (d. 238/853), who was one of Bukhārī's teachers.[10] To corroborate their opinions, Ibn Baṭṭāl pointed to a report that stated that when ʿUmar was serving as the second commander of the faithful, he once ordered the judge and scribe who oversaw the collection of the Qur'an to penalize a man by striking him ten times.[11] Since this corroborating evidence was from a companion report—it was attributed to a companion rather than the Prophet himself—it would have held greater evidentiary weight for Mālikīs than for Shāfiʿī and Ḥanbalī scholars.

The consensus concerning the restriction to ten lashes began to unravel when Ibn Baṭṭāl quoted a companion report that contradicted ʿUmar's practice above. According to this companion report, ʿUmar wrote that twenty was the number of lashes not be exceeded.[12] A quote from the eponym of the Shāfiʿī school seconded the number twenty, because twenty was the fewest number of lashes prescribed for slaves who transgressed God's express prohibition of wine (*khamr*), a number half as severe for free persons, who were held, in theory, to a higher standard of accountability.[13] To this end, representing the Ḥanafī opinion, Abū Ḥanīfa (d. 150/767) and Muḥammad al-Shaybānī (d. 189/805) offered even higher numbers, instructing their students to use their discretion to authorize more than forty lashes, precisely the lowest number of lashes stipulated for a free person who drinks wine.[14] At the outermost limits were two scholars who claimed, at the most, one was permitted to authorize up to seventy-five lashes, although Ibn Baṭṭāl did not bother to explain how they arrived at their position.[15]

Ibn Baṭṭāl ordered the classical opinions in a strategic way that would begin with consensus, highlight areas of disagreement, underline the extremes, and lastly guide the reader to Mālik's opinion, around which the legal orthodoxy in Andalusia orbited: "Discretionary punishment may be greater than those of the *ḥudūd* if the exertion of juristic reasoning brings the imam to it."[16] By placing Mālik's opinion last among the classical authorities, Ibn Baṭṭāl thus indicated which opinion he thought was favorable on the matter, even though Mālik's opinion is a far cry from the apparent meaning of the hadith. Since Mālik never encountered these hadith in his lifetime, Ibn Baṭṭāl thus invoked Mālik's opinion not as a direct commentary on these hadith but as an opinion on the general topic of discretionary punishment.

Despite this strategic reframing of the classical sources, Ibn Baṭṭāl's choice to discuss the classical opinions prior to contemporary ones worked within a broad chronological framework that we might term an *exegetical history*. In other words, Ibn Baṭṭāl constructed a narrative arc of the history of the cumulative tradition that bent toward the eventual affirmation of his legal school. Although we do not typically think of exegesis as a genre of history, there is an important temporal dimension to the presentation of his commentary, one that tracks the development of a commentarial debate across several centuries. It is to the hadith's reception in later centuries he then turned.

AṢĪLĪ AND THE MATTER OF AUTHENTICITY

With the classical debate properly framed, Ibn Baṭṭāl next turned to the opinion of Abū Muḥammad al-Aṣīlī (d. 392/1002), a Córdoban-trained judge of Zaragoza whose family originated on the southern side of the Strait of Gibraltar. During an extended pilgrimage to Mecca, Aṣīlī studied with a well-known hadith scholar from Central Asia, Abū Zayd al-Marwazī (d. 371/982), a student of Bukhārī's closest student, Yūsuf al-Firabrī (320/932).[17] Considering that Aṣīlī was separated from Bukhārī by only two degrees, upon his return to Andalusia in his later years, he propagated the recension of *Ṣaḥīḥ al-Bukhārī* that he received from Marwazī (see fig. 1).[18] Aṣīlī offered technical opinions on the correct transmission of certain hadith and is often cited in Andalusian commentary as an authority on *Ṣaḥīḥ al-Bukhārī*'s correct transmission. Students and copyists well into the Mamluk era and beyond checked their versions against Aṣīlī's, and Mamluk-era commentators cited his opinions as well.[19]

What did Aṣīlī's knowledge of hadith—and *Ṣaḥīḥ al-Bukhārī* in particular—allow him to contribute to the debate over the "ten lashes" hadith? According to Ibn Baṭṭāl, Aṣīlī was of that opinion that "the hadith of ʿAbd Allāh ibn Jābir's chain of transmission was inconsistent (*iḍṭaraba*).[20] Its abandonment (*tarkuhu*) is obligatory on account of its inconsistency, and because the companions and the generation that followed are found to have acted in opposition to it."[21]

TABLE 2 A COMPARISON BETWEEN AṢĪLĪ'S AND IBN AL-SAKAN'S AND OTHERS' CHAINS OF TRANSMISSION OF HADITH 1 IN THE CHAPTER ON DISCRETIONARY PUNISHMENT IN *ṢAḤĪḤ AL-BUKHĀRĪ*

Hadith 1 (Ibn al-Sakan and Others)	Hadith 1 (Aṣīlī)
Muhammad ↓	Muhammad ↓
Abū Burda ↓	Abū Burda ↓
ʿAbd al-Raḥmān ibn Jābir ↓	Jābir ↓
	ʿAbd al-Raḥmān ibn Jābir ↓
Sulaymān ibn Yasār ↓	Sulaymān ibn Yasār ↓
Bukayr ibn ʿAbd Allāh ↓	Bukayr ibn ʿAbd Allāh ↓
Yazīd ibn Abī Ḥabīb ↓	Yazīd ibn Abī Ḥabīb ↓
Layth ↓	Layth ↓
ʿAbd Allāh ibn Yūsuf ↓	ʿAbd Allāh ibn Yūsuf ↓
Bukhārī	Bukhārī

One problem with the chain of transmission for Aṣīlī lay in the possibility that the identity of the transmitter from whom ʿAbd al-Raḥmān ibn Jābir heard the hadith was inaccurately preserved. Did he hear the hadith directly from Abū Burda, who heard it from the Prophet? Did he hear it from his father, who heard it from Abū Burda, who heard it from the Prophet? Or did he hear it from one of the helpers (*anṣār*) in Medina, whose identity was forgotten?

Later scholars from the Mamluk-era remembered that Aṣīlī added to this confusion by transmitting a variant of "hadith 1" in which Ibn Jābir heard the hadith from his father rather than directly from Abū Burda (see table 2).[22] Although Ibn Baṭṭāl did not record anyone who disputed Aṣīlī's doubt, nearly a century later, another Andalusian hadith scholar, Abū ʿAlī al-Jayyānī (of Jaén, d. 498/1105), drew on an alternative recitation—Ibn al-Sakan's—to correct Aṣīlī's, which he speculated may have been incorporated as a scribal error.[23] Nevertheless, Jayyānī agreed with Aṣīlī that the chain of transmission of hadith 1 was discordant (*mukhtalif*).[24] Jayyānī also underscored the other problem with that hadith that Aṣīlī may have been alluding to: the confusion over who heard it from the Prophet—Abū Burda or an anonymous man from among Muhammad's helpers (*anṣār*) in Medina (see table 1).[25] When chains of transmission of the same hadith depart from one another in this fashion and there is no clear reason to favor one chain over another, the hadith may be determined to be weak.[26]

Aṣīlī based his evaluation not only on the reliability of the hadith's chain of transmission but on its content as well. Explicit criticism based on content was not unusual in this period.[27] Yet Aṣīlī's dismissal discloses much about his approach: according to him, this hadith ought to be abandoned not because there was evidence that it contradicted the Qur'an or other authenticated hadith, but because there was evidence that it contradicted the reported actions of Muhammad's companions and successors. That the hadith was authenticated by Bukhārī and included in his compilation was not even considered by Aṣīlī as a reason to accept its authenticity.

BOLSTERING MĀLIKĪ ORTHODOXY AND THE CHALLENGE OF ẒĀHIRISM

Once Ibn Baṭṭāl had planted doubt concerning the hadith's reliability, he sought to build a case for Aṣīlī's claim that the hadith contradicts companion reports. He did this by turning to a well-known Ḥanafī jurist and hadith scholar named Abū Jaʿfar al-Ṭaḥāwī (d. 321/935), who pointed to a companion report that ʿUmar once ordered one hundred lashes for an offense that was not considered one of the *ḥudūd*.[28] This supported Ṭaḥāwī's opinion that "there is no disagreement that discretionary punishment is entrusted to the imam's exertion of juristic reasoning (*ijtihād*), so he can be lenient sometimes and harsh sometimes."[29] By quoting a Ḥanafī authority, Ibn Baṭṭāl drew Mālik's nearly identical ruling into a place of greater overlapping consensus between legal schools. Ibn Baṭṭāl had, moreover, begun to shift the conversation to leniency and severity rather than to determining the fixed maximum number of lashes that would satisfy the law.

Ibn Baṭṭāl then turned to an authority of the Mālikī school of the previous generation in the Islamic East: Ibn al-Qaṣṣār (d. 397–98/1006–8) of Baghdad. Ibn al-Qaṣṣār proffered another companion report in which a scribe was convicted of forging ʿUmar's seal.[30] Forging a seal was a serious crime but was not considered one of the *ḥudūd*. Ibn al-Qaṣṣār reported, however, that in the presence of Muhammad's companions, the scribe was lashed a hundred times, followed by another hundred, followed by another hundred. For Ibn al-Qaṣṣār, the fact that not one of the companions objected to the number of lashings proved that there was consensus that the maximum number of lashings depended on the judge's reasoned discretion. Moreover, the rationale behind this consensus, for Ibn al-Qaṣṣār, is that judges are in the best position to decide what would be an appropriate deterrent. For some, Ibn al-Qaṣṣār suggested, a verbal warning (*kalām*) was all that was required. For others, even a hundred lashes would not deter them.[31] In this way, Ibn al-Qaṣṣār not only expanded the judge's power to choose how many lashings but also intimated that other kinds of penalties, verbal rather than corporal, could be appropriate.

Muhallab arrived at a virtually identical opinion, but he strove to justify it on the basis of the Prophet's example rather than on reports about the early companions, as Ibn al-Qaṣṣār, Ṭaḥāwī, and Aṣīlī did. Muhallab was uniquely positioned to do so by interpreting the three hadith on ten lashes in relation to the other hadith that Bukhārī included under the same chapter heading.

The first of the three other hadith that follow under Bukhārī's chapter heading states that a group of early believers refused to give up a continuous fast (*ṣawm al-wiṣāl*) despite the fact that the Prophet forbade fasting day and night. After the fast came to an end, the hadith states that the Prophet disclosed that he had considered making them fast an extra day, as if to punish them for their disobedience.[32] The next hadith in the chapter states that during the time of the Prophet, those who practiced speculation in the marketplace were punished with beatings. The final hadith states that when a matter was presented to the Prophet, he did not seek reprisal for his own sake, but for God's sake, when what God had forbidden (*ḥurumāt*) was violated.[33]

The connection between the ten lashes hadith and the three hadith that follow in the same chapter is not readily apparent. Yet Muhallab teased out a connection and explained its benefit for jurists:

> Do you not see that the Prophet extended the fast of *wiṣāl* to make an example of them? In just the same way, the imām is permitted to increase a punishment according to his own exertion of legal reasoning (*ijtihād*). In just the

> same way, the successors were beaten for [practicing speculation about] foodstuffs, and the Prophet's reprisal (*intiqām*) for that which God forbade (*ḥurumāt*) was unlimited.
>
> Therefore, it is necessary (*fa-yajibu*) to discipline each person according to his or her disobedience of the Prophet's example (*sunna*) and the willfully disobedient ought to be disciplined more than the ignorantly disobedient. And if there is anything regarding this matter that is a *ḥadd,* disputing it is not allowed.[34]

Reading all six hadith in the chapter side by side, Muhallab argues that the Prophet's own example, rather than companion reports, justified why a judge ought to punish each offender according to his or her particular non-*ḥadd* offense without restrictions. This disciplinary approach was not only permissible but also necessary (*fa-yajibu*). Moreover, in pressing a connection between the hadith on the ten lashes with the hadith on continuous fast, Muhallab used the Prophet's example to justify the jurists' power to choose not only the number of lashings but also the very kind of punishment that would best fit the crime. While Ibn al-Qaṣṣār suggested, without textual evidence, that verbal warnings, in addition to floggings, could function to deter offenses, Muhallab found evidence under the same chapter heading that the Prophet himself considered denying the disobedient food and water as a penalty, rather than flogging. Ibn Ḥajar would later build on this opinion to affirm that the hadith demonstrated the authorization of punishing someone by starvation.[35]

While Muhallab did not make explicit reference to Bukhārī's authority as the compiler, he nevertheless yielded a meaning from the hadith on ten lashes that earlier jurists commenting on the hadith in other legal genres could not. In reading all the hadith in the chapter as mutually illuminating the issue of discretionary punishment, Muhallab simultaneously subscribed to the idea that *Ṣaḥīḥ al-Bukhārī* was an authoritative reference on the Prophet's practice while contradicting the apparent meaning of the three hadith on ten lashes that Bukhārī authenticated. In doing so, he used *Ṣaḥīḥ al-Bukhārī* to affirm a long-established Mālikī orthodoxy.

While the companion reports comfortably demonstrated the Mālikī position, the Prophetic reports in *Ṣaḥīḥ al-Bukhārī* required a greater interpretive stretch or strain to arrive at the same point. In the hadith on continuous fasting, Muhallab did not address the fact that the Prophet never actually implemented the punishment but was reported to have merely considered it. Muhallab also glossed over the fact that the beatings of the food speculators and the Prophet's reprisal for violations of that which God forbade (*ḥurumāt*) were not necessarily unlimited, only unstipulated. Lastly, while Muhallab introduced the idea that judges ought to punish the willfully disobedient with a greater severity than one ignorant of his or her disobedience, it is not entirely clear from where in the above hadith he drew this conclusion.

As the intellectual environment in Andalusia shifted and Mālikīs became vulnerable to criticisms from Ẓāhirīs, proto-Ẓāhirīs, and a burgeoning generation of Andalusian hadith scholars, commentators like Muhallab sought authenticated hadith to help bolster the Mālikī orthodoxy. While Aṣīlī and other prominent Mālikī figures did not think it was necessary to base the Mālikī opinion on the authority of the Prophet, Muhallab did. That Muhallab strained to link the Mālikī position to hadith indicates the urgency and difficulty of the task. Furthermore, that Muhallab appropriated Bukhārī's organization to bolster the Mālikī position suggests *Ṣaḥīḥ al-Bukhārī* functioned for Mālikīs as a unique legal tool in addition to being a measure of authenticity. But once one accepted the ten lashes hadith as a source of law, why not forgo the laborious exegetical rationales and apply the hadith's apparent meaning? This would be the challenge raised by Ibn Ḥazm in the next generation of Andalusian scholars.

While Ibn Baṭṭāl and Muhallab used *Ṣaḥīḥ al-Bukhārī* to justify greater jurisdiction for Mālikī judges in discretionary punishment, Ibn Ḥazm marshaled the hadith on ten lashes authenticated by Bukhārī to narrow judicial authority in his *Ṭawq al-ḥamāma* (Ring of the dove). This was a treatise rather than a commentary, but it is nevertheless instructive for us to read for three important reasons. First, Ibn Ḥazm's opinions on the issue of discretionary punishment were later incorporated into the commentary tradition on *Ṣaḥīḥ al-Bukhārī* among Mamluk-era commentators. Second, Ibn Ḥazm's discussion in *Ṭawq al-ḥamāma* illustrates how hadith from *Ṣaḥīḥ al-Bukhārī* were deployed and received in other legal and textual discourses during this period in Andalusia. Third, Ibn Ḥazm's apparentist approach brings the Mālikī commentators' various approaches into relief, as it illustrates how a hadith scholar in this Andalusian milieu could read the ten lashes hadith to object to rather than to bolster the Mālikī position.

One problem with the Mālikī position, according to Ibn Ḥazm, was that they had a broader definition of *ḥadd* and, by extension, considered a larger number of offenses as capital crimes. In his opinion, the community had only reached consensus on four crimes that could warrant the death penalty: apostasy, adultery, intentional murder, and creating disorder on earth.[36] Otherwise, he asserted, the death penalty ought not to be imposed upon anyone.[37] Ibn Ḥazm disapproved of the approach of those scholars who expanded rulers' power to execute by categorizing a number of other acts as capital offenses.

Sodomy was a key example of the kinds of "capitalized" offenses to which Ibn Ḥazm was alluding.[38] Ibn Ḥazm discussed two companion reports about the first caliph, Abū Bakr. In one, Abū Bakr sentenced a man convicted of sodomy to be beaten to death, and in the other, he sentenced another convicted man to be burned at the stake.[39] More to the point, he was stunned that Mālik was reported to have approved of an emir ordering a man to be beaten to death for merely kissing another man.[40] It may be tempting to suggest, as some have intimated, that Ibn Ḥazm was partly motivated by his own experience with homoerotic desire, an experience documented by Ibn Ḥazm himself in *Ṭawq al-ḥamāma*.[41] It is far more likely that Ibn Ḥazm was motivated by a Ẓāhirī legal approach that advanced a more limited definition of *ḥadd*. While Ibn Ḥazm viewed sodomy as an abomination, in the absence of a definitive prooftext (*naṣṣ*), Ibn Ḥazm preferred to categorize it as a non-*ḥadd* offense that merited a lesser punishment.[42]

Since Mālikī judges had wide discretion in authorizing the leniency or severity of discretionary punishment, merely categorizing sodomy as a non-*ḥadd* offense would not have restricted them from applying the death penalty for it. Thus Ibn Ḥazm went further by limiting discretionary punishment to "ten lashes," on the authority of the third hadith above (see table 1). Ibn Ḥazm's proffering of a hadith authenticated by Bukhārī was, perhaps, an indication of Bukhārī's greater cachet among Ibn Ḥazm's interlocutors. Yet the chain of transmission of the hadith Ibn Ḥazm chose to rely on also shows that he was savvy of criticisms concerning the chains of transmission of the first two hadith. As we saw earlier, the first chain would have been subject to Aṣīlī's and others' critiques that it was problematic or discordant, and the second hadith contained an anonymous transmitter (see table 1). By relying on the third, Ibn Ḥazm was drawing on a source reliable enough to fend off any rivals who might impugn its authenticity. He further remarked that this also happened to be among the opinions expressed by Shāfiʿī, the eponym of a school with which Ibn Ḥazm briefly aligned himself.[43] While it was not his own school's opinion, referencing the Shāfiʿī opinion may have indicated to his opponents that he was not arguing beyond the pale of a cumulative and living tradition of law.

• • •

The early hadith commentarial debate over the ten lashes hadith found in Andalusia and North Africa reflects a number of trends among the early Andalusian commentators. First, Ibn Baṭṭāl devoted the greatest proportion of his commentary to a discussion of prior legal opinions on the hadith. While this cumulative archive of explanations may appear to be a list of opinions passively acquired and transmitted, a close reading shows how a hadith's reception history could also be subtly marshaled to construct a narrative about the hadith's proper interpretation and to bolster the power of one's institution. While Ibn Baṭṭāl could have ordered these layers of prior opinions according to a number of criteria—by discipline, by topic, by region, by alphabetic order—Ibn Baṭṭāl broadly reordered the layers of Muslim scholarly opinions from the earliest to the most recent and, within that, from those opposed to the Mālikīs to those in support of the Mālikīs.

I take this chronological and normative ordering to be a deliberate marker of the genre of commentary, and I have termed it an *exegetical history*.[44] In this way, one of the most productive sites of commentarial construction and deconstruction was the perpetual ordering and reordering of the previous scholarly opinions that had proliferated over time. In other words, hadith commentaries sometimes had as much or more to say about the exegetical history of the hadith than about the hadith upon which it claimed to comment.

Ibn Baṭṭāl addressed peripherally, if at all, any biographical information on the transmitters of the hadith, and he did not linger on the greater historical context in which the hadith occurred or on issues of lexicography, grammar, and rhetoric. He did not subdivide his commentary by discipline (transmitters, rhetoric, grammar, legal benefits), as we will see some later Mamluk commentators do. While Ibn Baṭṭāl offered no explicit or systematic discussion of Bukhārī's novel framework, his teacher, Muhallab, subtly relied on Bukhārī's organization to forward his argument.[45]

While Ibn Baṭṭāl did not systematically discuss the reliability of the chains of transmission, there was, from the time of Aṣīlī to the time of Jayyānī, a burgeoning interest in the chain of transmission as an element in the interpretation and implementation of hadith. Likewise, from the time of Ibn al-Qaṣṣār to Muhallab, there was a shift that pressed jurists to locate their opinions in hadith rather than companion reports as the basis for Mālikī legal positions. This shift correlated with a greater interest in the acquisition and study of chains of transmission that was linked to the development of Sufism in Andalusia and continued to grow even after the fall of the Umayyad caliphate in the West.

Yet Muhallab's interpretation of the ten lashes hadith, like the Bājī fiasco over the hadith that claimed that Muhammad "wrote," illustrated how a Mālikī scholar was pressed into developing an ingenious way of justifying the orthodoxy from which he wrote. Thus, the very same hadith that, for Ibn Ḥazm, radically narrowed the scope of the judiciary's power to authorize severe sentences was flexed by Muhallab to justify unlimited jurisdiction for judges in discretionary punishment.

This is not to say that the ten lashes hadith could mean whatever commentators wanted it to mean. On the contrary, both Muhallab and Ibn Ḥazm had to articulate their arguments within the specific intellectual and social constraints of their era. While Ibn Ḥazm's approach sat most comfortably with the apparent reading of the hadith, it would have been beyond the pale of accepted Mālikī opinion to be incorporated into the institutions that regulated legal thought and practice. By contrast, Muhallab worked within the Mālikī legal orthodoxy to accommodate a greater place for hadith within their interpretive reasoning.

This chapter and the last were not intended to be a comprehensive study of Andalusian hadith commentary, but a gateway into a number of themes pertinent to understanding the dynamics within the social practice of hadith commentary in Andalusia. We have seen how hadith commentary was articulated through both live forums and written media. In both oral and written hadith commentaries, we saw the development of exegetical techniques that could upend or maintain legal and theological orthodoxies or could attempt a double movement that pushed an orthodoxy toward internal change. These exegetical techniques included evaluating sources' authenticity, and ranking and re-ranking some sources over others—such as the Qur'an over hadith, authenticated hadith over questionable hadith, and Prophetic hadith over companion reports and legal opinions from eponymous jurists. Moreover, reading for or against a hadith's apparent meaning and reading with or without the context of other hadith provided by Bukhārī were other strategies that helped commentators settle debates that stretched across near and distant pasts and near and distant regions of the Islamic world.

In sum, over the past two chapters, we have observed how these early commentators struggled over social and material rewards—preserving their livelihoods (or even their lives) or maintaining or challenging the power of legal and theological institutions in a tumultuous era. And we have seen how they struggled to achieve excellences internal to the tradition, such as interpreting the hadith in a way that established an authentic link to the Prophet's example. While this interpretive aim, if achieved, would have surely elevated the social standing and prestige of the commentator, this aim cannot be reduced in our analysis to mere competition over social capital lest we overlook the key norms and standards of excellence that the commentators themselves claimed animated them in their practice.

To be sure, these mutually constitutive orders of material rewards and interpretive excellences overlapped and conflicted in productive ways. Debates over hadith were shaped as much by the commentators' historical context and training as they were by norms that were constitutive of and constituted by the commentary tradition. In the coming chapters, we will return to this case study and others as we examine how reading communities in medieval Egypt and Syria and in modern India amended and elaborated upon this evolving and living tradition of commentary.

PART TWO

Egypt and Syria under the Mamluks

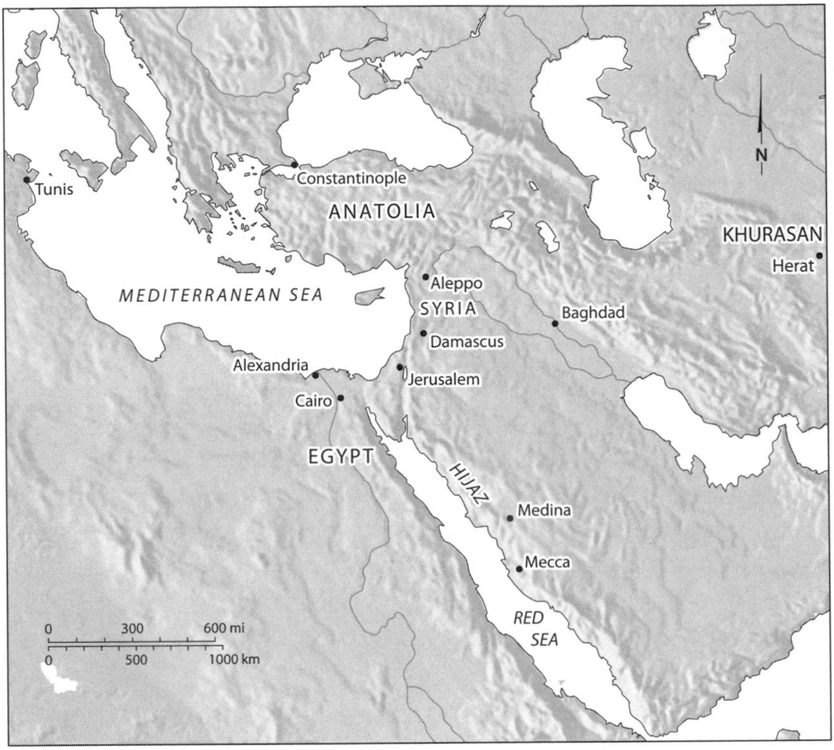

MAP 2. Egypt and Syria, ca. the ninth/fifteenth century.

CHAPTER 3

For Sultans, Students, and Scholars

Reading, far from being an act of abstraction,
is an act of incarnation.
—Ivan Illich

As the social and cultural center of the study of hadith shifted from southern Spain and Central Asia to Cairo and cities in Greater Syria in the Mamluk period, the renowned historian Ibn Khaldūn (d. 808/1406) saw the first attempts at commentary on *Ṣaḥīḥ al-Bukhārī* in Andalusia as insufficient. In his view, those early commentators lacked proper knowledge of the chains of transmission and the biographies of the transmitters. They were also ignorant of the full significance of Bukhārī's quizzical chapter headings. After detailing the many duties an aspiring commentator on *Ṣaḥīḥ al-Bukhārī* must undertake, Ibn Khaldūn lamented, writing: "And whosoever comments on Bukhārī and has not done justice to these [duties] has not done justice (*lam yūfi ḥaqqa*) to the commentary. . . . I have heard from many shaykhs, may God have mercy on them, who say, 'commenting on Bukhārī's text remains an outstanding debt (*dayn*) for the community (*umma*),' meaning that a leading scholar of the community has not fully taken on the requirements of commentary in this sense."[1]

Muslim scholars of the Mamluk period took up the challenge of this debt and attempted to repay it hundredfold. But, like the practice of hadith commentary in Andalusia, exegesis was not an abstract and solitary activity in which a commentator, alone with a sacralized text, interpreted its obscure meanings. Rather, as I will reconstruct in part 2 of this book, the practice of hadith commentary in the Mamluk context was likewise embedded in a communal, competitive, and religious context of manuscript culture and live performances in which social and material rewards as well as the achievement of interpretive excellences were at stake for local and global communities of readers.

One case study I will focus on to explore this broader theme of the social practice of Mamluk-era hadith commentary is the writing of Ibn Ḥajar al-ʿAsqalānī's *Fatḥ al-bārī,* a multi-volume book that Norman Calder called "a work of dazzling scholarship and the most magnificent achievement of exegetical discourse."[2] Ibn Ḥajar's commentary like those of many others, was a quarter-century undertaking. He added to his work in a serial fashion in the presence of students, who helped to copyedit the work. Ibn Ḥajar, like many commentators of his time, was also aware of his local and global patrons, sometimes naming them and praising them in the very text of his commentary. Lastly, Ibn Ḥajar, like many commentators, was acutely aware of his rivals, with whom he sparred over social and material rewards and with whom he argued over religious and interpretive norms.[3]

THE MEDIUM OF COMMENTARY, SHAPED FOR STUDENTS

Students would have been curious about a multitude of aspects of the hadith, so hadith commentators were required to prove themselves masters of a variety of disciplines, including the sciences of hadith, law, theology, Sufism, lexicography, rhetoric, grammar, history, and more. Thus, Muslim scholars in the Mamluk period typically undertook a commentary of a major collection of hadith near the end of their life, after they had studied abroad and accumulated a great number of reading certificates (*ijāza*s), written extensively in related areas, had served as high-ranking judges or advisors—or entertained offers thereof.[4] Ibn Ḥajar was no exception, having begun his commentary after several decades of intensive study and teaching.[5]

Often commentators would complete an independent or conjoined work on language or on the authenticity of select *isnād*s before undertaking a commentary. Ibn Ḥajar did so in an earlier work in which he annotated a description of the chains of transmission contained in *Ṣaḥīḥ al-Bukhārī,* as did Muḥyī al-Dīn Abū Zakariyyā al-Nawawī (d. 676/1277), who composed several major works on transmitters, language, and law prior to preparing a commentary on *Ṣaḥīḥ Muslim.*[6] As a consequence, students could expect these commentators to be competent to draw on a number works, both on the hadith compilation and beyond, to illuminate and elaborate on any given point or aspect of the text. After all, problems in the text of *Ṣaḥīḥ al-Bukhārī* could sometimes be clarified by referencing variant transmissions of a hadith found in other compilations, lexicons, or legal compendia.

While students were attracted to the most prolific scholars, students simultaneously reined in scholastic excesses. Nawawī, in the introduction to his commentary on *Ṣaḥīḥ Muslim,* spoke of his longing to write an "expansive work, a work stretching to more than a hundred volumes, without repetition or pointless expansion."[7] The obstacle to this commentarial indulgence, for Nawawī, was "the weakness of aspirations, the paucity of seekers, and fear that such a book would have no market, students being little inclined towards long books."[8] Similar to the dialectic we saw in Andalusian commentarial culture, Nawawī weighed his responsibility to serve the needs of the market against his desire to devote himself entirely to the never-ending work of interpreting a sacralized text, producing volume after volume over many years. In this case, Nawawī had his cake and ate it too: he resigned himself to writing a "midsize commentary" (*sharḥ mutawassiṭ*) but nevertheless produced a ten-volume work.[9]

Despite Nawawī's characterization of them as unmarketable, these unfinished or unfinishable commentaries served an important marketing function. As a commentator's prior publications did, unfinished commentaries were a profound signal of the depth of his capacity to comment and the sincerity of his devotion to the study of hadith. In 808/1405, Ibn Ḥajar, a close reader of Nawawī's and a follower of the Shāfiʿī legal school, began a commentary on another renowned compilation of hadith, Tirmidhī's *Sunan,* for the students who attended his lessons at the school attached to the Shaykhūniyya, a Sufi residence (*khānqāh*) in Cairo. He never finished the commentary, but he did leave a mammoth teaching outline of the work, which his biographer, Sakhāwī, touted as the size of an entire volume.[10] Sakhāwī did not view the unfinished commentary as a failure, but a signal to audiences about the Ibn Ḥajar's untapped commentarial resources.

Drawing largely on his work with European sources, the literary theorist Hans Gumbrecht suggests one limit common to commentators: the width of the margins, a most severe constraint.[11] Gumbrecht's archetypical commentators are driven to fill them to the brim, even exceeding them at times—spilling over into the headers and footers and, sometimes, between the lines of the base text. While this may have been true for the inclusion of marginalia and glosses (*ḥawāshī*) in compilations of hadith, it was not true for the line-by-line commentary (*sharḥ*) under discussion here. The commentaries of Ibn Ḥajar and his predecessors, going back at least to the early Córdoban commentator Ibn Baṭṭāl, were laid out in the center of the page. Commentators would include only lemmata, the fragmentary phrases from the base text that were relevant for explication. Ibn Ḥajar toyed with the idea of including the base text but decided against it, reasoning that it would make his commentary too long (see fig. 3).[12] Including the base text of a major hadith compilation in the same volume as a line-by-line commentary would not enter the mainstream until the technology of print made it more cost effective to do so in the nineteenth and twentieth centuries.

Untethered from the restrictions of the margins or the added weight of including a base text, Ibn Ḥajar's commentarial limit was the span of his life and his capacity to write. According to Ibn Ḥajar's own description of composing *Fatḥ al-bārī,* at first the writing process was overwhelming. As he had done with his previous commentarial effort, on Tirmidhī's *Sunan,* Ibn Ḥajar confessed that he had filled an entire volume with commentary on just a short selection of the compilation, to the point that he dreaded the exhaustion of finishing his commentary in such a way.[13] Ibn Ḥajar, echoing a previous comment made by Nawawī, claimed to recalibrate his approach and aimed to compose a midsize commentary (*sharḥ mutawassiṭ*). Nevertheless, he wrote continuously over the course of twenty-nine years and produced a thirteen-volume work.[14]

Ibn Ḥajar composed the first quarter of this midsize commentary on *Ṣaḥīḥ al-Bukhārī* by dictation. This took approximately five years, from 813 to 818 (1410 to 1415 CE). Following this period, Ibn Ḥajar took greater control over the physical labor of writing the commentary, dropping the dictation sessions.[15] Since we know that Ibn Ḥajar wrote by candlelight, he probably wrote before dawn or after dusk, but we do not know for certain what company, if any, he kept as he wrote.[16] Nevertheless, as he composed his written document at night, he continued to contemplate and shape his understanding of *Ṣaḥīḥ al-Bukhārī* in the presence of his students during his ongoing meetings with them.[17] He would add to the document little by little during informal meetings with students, as well as once every week, probably on a Thursday, during a larger meeting for the study of *Ṣaḥīḥ al-Bukhārī.*[18]

In these larger meetings, the outline or draft of Ibn Ḥajar's commentary would have been read aloud by an assistant, almost always Ibn Ḥajar's longtime companion and highly skilled reader, Burhān al-Dīn Ibrāhīm ibn Khiḍr (d. 852/1448).[19] The precision of Ibn Khiḍr's pronunciation was highly respected among Muslim scholars in Cairo, no doubt enhancing *Fatḥ al-bārī*'s gravitas at this early stage of the commentary process. In fact, Sakhāwī notes that Ibn Khiḍr's reading performances maintained their superior quality despite the fact that Ibn Ḥajar's handwritten outlines composed by candlelight could be very difficult to read.[20] As he read the text, Ibn Khiḍr would have paused regularly, to allow Ibn Ḥajar to intervene with fuller commentary and the audience to join the discussion with questions and comments.[21]

How much input his students had in explicitly shaping the commentary is a difficult question to answer with any precision. Of the many voices included in the commentary, the one voice conspicuously absent is that of the student. There is no anonymous or rhetorical questioner prompting the commentator, as is found in influential works of other Islamic scholars.[22] The various instances of the phrases "if you were to say" (*in qulta*) or "if one said" (*in qāl*) in Ibn Ḥajar's commentary tend to reflect the potential objections of other commentators rather than a transcription of an inquisitive student's question.

Nevertheless, students were heavily involved in the process of copyediting the written copies of *Fatḥ al-bārī*. Ibn Ḥajar reported that in 818/1415, his most proficient students gathered around him and persuaded him to begin the process of writing down the rest of the commentary on quires of paper (*kurrās*) so they could assist him in editing it.[23] After Ibn Ḥajar had written the commentary down on paper, a student would read it aloud to a companion sitting opposite him, scrutinizing the draft and proofreading it for errors.[24] Each volume was subject to this slow process until the entire commentary was pronounced complete in the winter of 842/1438. The completion of the commentary was celebrated with a rich feast, costing five hundred dinars, or nearly 3.8 pounds of gold.[25] This feast was more expensive than fifteen of the fifty-five camel-loads of spices that Ibn Ḥajar left when he died.[26]

Although the work was formally declared finished, Sakhāwī pointed out that Ibn Ḥajar continued to add to the work for ten years following its "completion" (*farāgh* or *khatm*), until his death in 852/1449.[27] In this sense, Ibn Ḥajar never considered the work of his commentary truly finished. Ibn Ḥajar's feeling of incompletion, despite having penned some thirteen volumes over twenty-nine years, was not a personal idiosyncrasy. It is in line with what theorist Hans Gumbrecht has argued is the principal drive toward *copia* in the figure of the commentator. For Gumbrecht, commentators write endlessly to anticipate, but never fully anticipating, the questions of students.[28] But we can detect another important audience-oriented motivation at work here, consistent with a larger *topos* in commentarial introductions: Ibn Ḥajar's account of coming up against his physical limitation to comment—and facing the risk of incompletion—signaled to students that his mental ability to comment exceeded his physical ability to do so.

A GIFT TO RULERS FROM THE EAST AND THE WEST

Ibn Ḥajar would have been accountable to political patrons who requested volumes of the work as it was underway. This would have included the Mamluk sultan, who changed several times over the course of the writing of the commentary, from al-Muʾayyad Shaykh (r. 814–24/1412–21) to Barsbāy (r. 825–41/1422–38) to Jaqmaq (r. 843–57/1438–53), as well as transregional patrons, who sought copies of the work more than ten years prior to its completion.[29] Rulers would have heard of Ibn Ḥajar's *Fatḥ al-bārī* through their domestically appointed judges and scribes who had studied *Ṣaḥīḥ al-Bukhārī* with Ibn Ḥajar in Cairo.[30] This was the case with Zayn al-Dīn ʿAbd al-Raḥmān al-Birishkī (d. 839/1435–36), a Mālikī judge from Tunis, who was permitted to transcribe a third of *Fatḥ al-bārī* to present as a gift to the Tunisian ruler Abū Fāris (r. 796–837/1394–1434).[31] Likewise, Shams al-Dīn Muḥammad ibn al-Jazarī (d. 833/1429), a native of Damascus who was captured by Tamerlane (r. 771–807/1370–1405) and brought to serve as a judge at the Timurid court, copied part of the work as a gift for Tamerlane's successor, Shāh Rukh (r. 807–50/1405–47).[32] Shāh Rukh was later given a complete copy.[33] This was no minor gift, as *Fatḥ al-bārī* was reported to have been sold for three hundred dinars, nearly 2.3 pounds of gold.[34] A mosque janitor from this period would have needed to save his entire monthly salary of three hundred copper dirhams for more than thirty years in order to afford it.[35]

Of course, this was a period in which distinguished copies of *Ṣaḥīḥ al-Bukhārī* itself could fetch high prices from collectors among the political elite. In 832/1420, a copy of *Ṣaḥīḥ al-Bukhārī* transmitted by Ibn ʿAsākir (d. 571/1175–76) in Damascus by one of the more prestigious chains of transmission was sold to an emir for fifteen hundred dinars, nearly 11.25 pounds of gold (see fig. 5). Our poor janitor would have needed to save over two or three lifetimes' of his salary sweeping mosques to make a higher bid.

Unlike the students in attendance, whom Ibn Ḥajar never explicitly identified in his written commentary, political patrons were mentioned

FIGURE 5. An ownership statement dated Jumādā al-Ūlā 19, 823 (June 1, 1420), indicating the sale of a collectors' copy of *Ṣaḥīḥ al-Bukhārī* to an emir, Naṣr Allāh ibn ʿAbd al-Laṭīf al-Shakirlabī, for the price of 1,500 dinars. 1904Y, f. 2a. Manuscripts Division, Department of Rare Books and Special Collections, Princeton University Library. (Photo courtesy of Princeton University Library.)

by name. They were not named frequently, but any mention is significant, since invoking the names of sultans and potentates was unprecedented in the genre of commentary. A search of *Fatḥ al-bārī* reveals that Ibn Ḥajar mentioned al-Muʾayyad Shaykh by name in his discussion of four hadith, and he mentioned Ashraf Barsbāy and Shāh Rukh in his discussion of one hadith. It is worth noting that Ibn Ḥajar cultivated a particularly close relationship to al-Muʾayyad Shaykh, attaining a level of trust and influence he was never able to replicate with al-Muʾayyad Shaykh's successors, although he was appointed Shāfiʿī chief justice under Barsbāy and also served intermittently under Jaqmaq.[36]

Ibn Ḥajar often invoked al-Muʾayyad Shaykh's name when he explained hadith that reference the repair, maintenance, and decoration of the Kaʿba. The Kaʿba was a symbolic site of transregional politics, and in the midst of his commentary concerning a hadith on the cloth draped over the Kaʿba (*kiswa*), Ibn Ḥajar took time to narrate the hadith's exegetical history and how it was applied by each governor who controlled Mecca throughout Islamic history to Ibn Ḥajar's own day.[37] When his description arrived at the Mamluk period, Ibn Ḥajar provided details on the endowment (*waqf*) of the cloth used to drape the Kaʿba and even praised al-Muʾayyad Shaykh's appointment of a colleague to oversee the *kiswa*'s beautification.[38] When recounting an exegetical history of another hadith, one on the destruction of the Kaʿba, Ibn Ḥajar noted that al-Muʾayyad Shaykh took an interest in repairing the Kaʿba, and he prayed that God would facilitate al-Muʾayyad Shaykh in such maintenance.[39]

Ibn Ḥajar commended al-Muʾayyad Shaykh when discussing a hadith that pertained to the politics of pilgrimage and transportation to Mecca. And concerning a hadith regarding the path the Prophet took when entering and leaving Mecca, Ibn Ḥajar noted that al-Muʾayyad Shaykh had cleared the path the Prophet was said to have taken: the higher route descending from the mountain of Kadāʾ in the direction of Mecca's cemetery.[40] Al-Muʾayyad Shaykh was not the first ruler to have undertaken this task, and Ibn Ḥajar compared him favorably with renowned figures from the Umayyad and ʿAbbāsid periods who had also cleared the path. Lastly, Ibn Ḥajar praised al-Muʾayyad Shaykh when discussing a hadith that pertained to the pulpit (*minbar*) in Medina. Al-Muʾayyad Shaykh had sent a new pulpit to Medina, and Ibn Ḥajar prayed that God might thank him for it.[41]

Barsbāy did not receive as high marks from Ibn Ḥajar. Near the end of his systematic explication of the hadith on the *kiswat al-Kaʿba,* Ibn Ḥajar tells us of a dispute that arose between Shāh Rukh and the sultan Barsbāy over who had the honor of dressing the Kaʿba.[42] The biographical sources can help clarify this case, which, as it turns out, was an important incident, and Ibn Ḥajar was personally involved. According to Sakhāwī, Shāh Rukh pleaded with Barsbāy to allow him to dress the Kaʿba to satisfy a vow (*nadhr*) he had made.[43] After refusing him several times, Barsbāy sought to halt Shāh Rukh's requests by acquiring a favorable legal opinion from the leading jurists in Cairo. Ibn Ḥajar ruled in favor of Shāh Rukh, despite the pressure of the other jurists, who issued *responsa* in favor of Barsbāy.[44] That Ibn Ḥajar later gave Shāh Rukh a complete copy of *Fatḥ al-bārī* over Barsbāy's objection should thus come as little surprise.[45] The dispute between Barsbāy and Shāh Rukh may explain the pattern of Ibn Ḥajar's mentioning of political figures when discussing hadith on the Kaʿba. These were matters upon which Ibn Ḥajar had advised the sultan, as legal counsel.

But Ibn Ḥajar's willingness to mention his patrons in his discussion of certain hadith makes the omission of their names in other places all the more interesting. Ibn Ḥajar did not mention political figures when he commented on overtly political hadith, such as hadith that mention a "just ruler" or "disobedience to the ruler." Perhaps Ibn Ḥajar was too cautious or too indebted to the political elite to measure individual rulers against the theoretical ideals presented in the hadith. But Ibn Ḥajar's commentary on hadith that concerned Mecca and Medina show there was no generic prohibition against discussing politics or the political application of certain hadith, even in the premodern period. There was a time and a place for it, and the discussion of politics and patrons was appropriate when explaining some hadith, but not others.

RIVALRY, INNOVATION, AND ACCUSATIONS OF PLAGIARISM

Because commentary sessions were performed for live audiences, students could take notes and share them with rival commentators who were working in other parts of the same city. If commentators used their rivals' works in their own, they were expected to conform to authorized practices of attribution, which, if transgressed, could amount to intellectual theft, an accusation that could diminish a commentator's reputation in the eyes of his colleagues. To be clear, this intellectual theft was not related to the more nuanced conceptions of literary borrowing that was discussed by Arab literary critics in treatises on the "thefts" (*sariqāt*) of motifs and phrases among litterateurs and poets.[46] Rather, the concern articulated by commentators, including Ibn Ḥajar, was about maintaining the intellectual integrity of their social practice. While our own conception and regulation of plagiarism is surely different than that of the Mamluk period, borrowing without attribution was far from a positive commentarial practice. Unattributed borrowing may not have been an academic violation that could be enforced with some kind of disciplinary action by administrators or patrons, nor was it a copyright violation in which a suit could be brought before a judge's court. However, unattributed borrowing reflected very poorly on a scholar's reputation in the eyes of his peers.

The most memorable example is an accusation of plagiarism that developed between Ibn Ḥajar and ʿAynī as they wrote their commentaries on *Ṣaḥīḥ al-Bukhārī*.[47] Although Ibn Ḥajar and ʿAynī both intermittently served as chief justice for their respective legal schools during the composition of their commentaries, it should be noted that Ibn Ḥajar's position as the Shāfiʿī chief justice was more powerful than ʿAynī's in the Ḥanafī school in both practical and symbolic ways.[48] The Mamluk ruling elite's Turkic origins associated them with the Ḥanafī school, but they recognized the Shāfiʿī school as the dominant one.[49] Noteworthy for our purposes was the fact that the Shāfiʿī chief justice typically had the honor, during Ramadan, of commenting on *Ṣaḥīḥ al-Bukhārī* at the citadel, in the presence of the sultan, the emirs, and other members of the scholarly and judicial elite. Thus, we should expect that ʿAynī's and Ibn Ḥajar's commentarial rivalry would be driven in part by the asymmetry of their positions and their competition over legal jurisdiction, political influence, and social capital.[50] Evidently, the acrimony became so unworkable that ʿAynī and Ibn Ḥajar were summarily dismissed from their chief judgeships on the basis of accusations that they "would not cease fighting, or [ever] agree, such that the interests of Muslims were lost between them."[51]

The rivalry between ʿAynī and Ibn Ḥajar was ripe from the very outset. In the winter of 820/1418, a moment when each scholar's commentary on Bukhārī was still in note form, the two openly lampooned one another by trading barbs in the form of couplets.[52] ʿAynī had been appointed to teach hadith at the now famous mosque complex built by al-Muʾayyad Shaykh near Bāb Zuwayla in Cairo. Al-Muʾayyad Shaykh ordered the construction of new minarets on the complex that would dominate the cityscape in a conspicuous display of the sultan's power and piety. After construction was completed, however, one of the minarets displayed a perilous tilt, an embarrassment for the sultan and a safety hazard for the neighborhood and the construction workers. Bāb Zuwayla was closed for a month while workers demolished the minaret.[53] Meanwhile, the poets of Cairo mocked the fiasco mercilessly, and couplets concerning the leaning minaret proliferated.[54] Ibn Ḥajar himself felt prompted to weigh in with a couplet of his own:

The mosque of our protector, al-Muʾayyad, was glorious—
its minaret radiated grandeur and grace!
It says, as it stands aslant, "Be gentle,
for nothing is more ruinous to my beauty than the evil eye (*al-ʿayn*)!"[55]

The final line was widely received as a pun on ʿAynī's name, on account of the rivalry between the two scholars and ʿAynī's occupational link to the complex, both as an educator and as the appointed supervisor of pious endowments (*nāẓir al-aḥbās*) under the sultan.[56] In Ibn Ḥajar's own recounting, however, he disavowed any such ill intentions, asserting that "any person who has a sense of propriety (*ādāb*) knows that [the lines] were not [composed] for him."[57] However, among those who shared that perception was ʿAynī himself, and we can imagine that ʿAynī would not have looked upon Ibn Ḥajar's pronouncement about ʿAynī's sense of propriety kindly. ʿAynī chose to respond in kind, cutting Ibn Ḥajar with an insulting pun of his own at the end of the second couplet:

The minaret was unveiled as a beauteous bride,
and its decay was destined by God's decree!
They say it was caused by the evil eye [*ʿayn*],
but I say: "That's mistaken."
Nothing caused its ruin except the shoddy stone [*ḥajar*]! [58]

In our Twitter age, similarly populated by political celebrities obsessed with their reputations, it is not difficult to imagine the potential for two short lines to spark a very public spat. Poetic praise (*madīḥ*) or poetic insult (*hijāʾ*) from the lips of a distinguished authority could hold great sway in shaping one's reputation. Moreover, taunting by rhyming couplet made the verbal jab easy to remember and quick to circulate.

The historian Ibn Asbāṭ (d. ca. 926/1520) would remember the exchange more dramatically, fancifully restaging it as a verbal skirmish in the presence of the sultan.[59] While Ibn Asbāṭ or his source concocted this new element, there is a sense in which the modified narrative remains faithful to the high political stakes of such a quarrel unfolding in full view of the public eye. Keep in mind that if a scholar like ʿAynī or Ibn Ḥajar could be credibly linked to the fall of a minaret, by neglect or by superstition, it would be disastrous for his career. In fact, several decades later, Ibn Ḥajar was indeed forced from an appointment as chief justice because he had neglected to repair a minaret that fell, causing several casualties.[60]

ʿAynī began his own commentary, *ʿUmdat al-qārī* (Reliance of the reciter), in 820/1417, some three years after the completion of the first quarter of Ibn Ḥajar's work.[61] Ibn Ḥajar and ʿAynī shared students, who went back and forth between their lectures. Some of these students made notes in Ibn Ḥajar's commentarial sessions as Ibn Ḥajar was in the process of writing *Fatḥ al-bārī*. Ibn Ḥajar claimed that those students then shared their notes with ʿAynī, who incorporated them into his work without attribution. Indeed, Ibn Ḥajar documented in an unfinished two-volume work called *Intiqāḍ al-iʿtirāḍ* how ʿAynī often challenged Ibn Ḥajar's opinions and interpretive approaches while frequently repeating verbatim Ibn Ḥajar's words, phrases, and whole sentences on almost every page without proper attribution.[62]

Of course, in the process of compiling, it is assumed that some basic or agreed-upon information will typically be recycled without a source and without summarizing or paraphrasing. The choice of which lemmata to comment upon, for example, is so tralatitious that commentators are expected to duplicate the lemmata of their predecessors without conscious consideration. If a commentator includes information and does not attribute the phrase to a particular shaykh or source, this may mean that the commentator did not even regard the item as a unique and arguable opinion (*qawl*) but simply as an agreed-upon fact and therefore permissible to recycle verbatim.

When a commentator wants to attribute an opinion to another commentator in order to refute or defend it, he writes, "he said" (*qāl*). He might also cite another's opinion because it is unique or has some peculiar benefit. A commentator typically writes, "one of the commentators said" (*qāl baʿḍ al-shāriḥīn*) when he does not know to whom he should attribute the opinion, the opinion is shared by someone who is not well known or not worth mentioning to his students or readers as a source, or the opinion offered is generic.[63] But when ʿAynī advanced or criticized the well-known opinions of his rival, Ibn Ḥajar, he also employed the anonymous phrase "one of the commentators said" (*qāl baʿd al-shāriḥīn*). Why?

In their competition for patrons, we might speculate some combination of the following possible explanations: ʿAynī did not care to gift Ibn Ḥajar with any undue attention, he meant his omission to wryly diminish Ibn Ḥajar as an authority worth including by name, or that he sought to conceal his reliance on Ibn Ḥajar's commentary in the making of his own. A more generous explanation would be that ʿAynī wanted to disparage Ibn Ḥajar's opinion but leave his good name intact. Or perhaps ʿAynī was hesitant to appear overly aggressive toward a living colleague. While ʿAynī explicitly addressed a less-advanced audience than Ibn Ḥajar's—his digressions on introductory topics of Arabic language and Islamic law clue us in to this point of fact—the wry critique implied in the omission would not have been lost on Ibn Ḥajar or on those students in his audience who would have recognized the anonymous opinions as Ibn Ḥajar's.

In Ibn Ḥajar's *Intiqāḍ al-iʿtirāḍ* (Objection to the opposition), a reply to ʿAynī's extensive criticisms of his work, Ibn Ḥajar stated simply that ʿAynī waited until *Fatḥ al-bārī* was nearly finished to undertake the bulk of his commentary and that he borrowed material from *Fatḥ al-bārī* through one of Ibn Ḥajar's students who had a copy.[64] Ibn Ḥajar stopped short accusing him of theft (*sariqa*), a harsher term, and instead suggested that ʿAynī plagiarized, using the term *istiʿāra,* which can mean "borrowing," "adopting" or "taking on." Ibn Ḥajar then used a longer and more technical phrase: *yanquluh^u ilā sharḥih^i min ghayr an yansubah^u ilā mukhtarʿih^i* (transferring it to his commentary without attributing it to its originator).[65] But the condemnation is clear, especially with Ibn Ḥajar stressing, by contrast, the creative task of the commentator as an "originator" (*mukhtariʿ*).

In addition to polemicizing against ʿAynī, Ibn Ḥajar highlighted passages in which ʿAynī duplicated Ibn Ḥajar's *Fatḥ al-bārī* word for word.[66] It is hard to imagine that Ibn Ḥajar's strategic reply would have been effective unless an exposé of ʿAynī's borrowing was a serious cause for embarrassment. Several chief justices and commentators of the time also weighed in on these charges of plagiarism, siding with Ibn Ḥajar.[67] Ibn al-Mughulī (d. 827/1423), the chief justice for the Ḥanbalī legal school, with his usual flare, came down particularly harshly against ʿAynī, in addition to criticizing ʿAynī's grammar.[68]

But these competitions over prestige and status were intertwined with competitions over exegetical norms, for instance, arguments over how best to interpret *Ṣaḥīḥ al-Bukhārī* and to what degree an ideal commentator ought to be expected to be critical of precedent and prior authorities in his interpretation of the text. Ibn Ḥajar alerted his audience to the fact that he was not afraid to challenge his predecessors, sometimes stridently, such as when he had the temerity to point out Nawawī's reliance on a scholar who had miscalculated the number of hadith in each chapter of *Ṣaḥīḥ al-Bukhārī* and had thus miscalculated the number of hadith in *Ṣaḥīḥ al-Bukhārī* altogether.[69] While the intended target is probably still ʿAynī, who cited Nawawī uncritically, Ibn Ḥajar goes on to complain of tralatitious commentarial practices in general: "I wanted to take a count [of the number of hadith in the *Ṣaḥīḥ*] in order to show that many of the hadith scholars and others slack off by relating (*naql*) the discussions of their predecessors, adhering to them as followers (*muqallidūn*). The earliest commentators are not perfect or flawless. Still, they follow them blissfully supposing so."[70]

The appearance of a commentary's repetition of previous scholarly opinions buttressed a commentator's interpretive privilege, and, as a result, Muslim scholars of this period were often cautious to appear innovative.[71] It is significant, then, that Ibn Ḥajar's authority is partly grounded in his explicit valuation of innovation and internal criticism within the social practice of commentary.

Ibn Ḥajar's complaints over failed attribution were not limited to ʿAynī's borrowing of his own work. He also took aim at many commentators on *Ṣaḥīḥ al-Bukhārī* and on other works who borrowed from others without proper attribution. According to Ibn Ḥajar, Ibn Jamāʿa (d. 733/1333), a Shāfiʿī chief justice, had taken his commentary on Bukhārī's chapter headings from Ibn al-Munayyir (d. 683/1284), adding little original material but still alleging that the commentary was his own.[72] Likewise, Ibn al-Mulaqqin (d. 804/1401), according to Ibn Ḥajar, had merely compiled a number of commentaries in the first part of his commentary, and he based the second part of his commentary on the commentaries of Ibn Baṭṭāl and Ibn al-Tīn al-Ṣafāqisī (d. 611/1214), claiming it was his own, but adding little original to it.[73] Others were less restrained and accused Ibn al-Mulaqqin of outright theft (*sariqa*).[74] In any event, according to Ibn Ḥajar, Ibn al-Mulaqqin's commentary was itself borrowed by later scholars without proper attribution.[75]

There is evidence that plagiarism did not arise only because of the openness of live sessions but also because scholars were transitioning, in this period, to reading outside of the teacher's reading session (*qirāʾa bi-nafsih*) with greater frequency.[76] A plagiarism dispute that seemingly arose from "reading on one's own" cropped up among Muslim scholars of the latter ninth/fifteenth century. The fiasco began when the renowned commentator Shihāb al-Dīn al-Qasṭallānī (d. 923/1517–18) quoted an opinion that al-Suyūṭī (d. 911/1505) had previously quoted. Suyūṭī maintained that Qasṭallānī had not read the opinion directly in the primary source but had found it in Suyūṭī's work, without acknowledging this.[77] Suyūṭī was so offended that he would not relent with his accusations until he received an apology in person.[78]

Although Suyūṭī did author a text on plagiarism, he was a notorious egotist, and we can imagine that injury to his pride may have been of greater concern than commentarial integrity.[79] After all, Suyūṭī himself was charged with cribbing a work on hadith by Sakhāwī, who claimed that Suyūṭī had stolen his material from one of Sakhāwī's live lessons.[80] That said, Suyūṭī was remembered to have asserted that "one's learning is blessed only when one mentions its source."[81] Suyūṭī saw God's blessing in action—his own "work spread to people in every county," while Sakhāwī's work "has not even left his house."[82] In a reversal of the commentarial dialectic we have observed thus far, for Suyūṭī, success on the book market did not detract from his integrity as a commentator but was a confirmation of it. Whether one agrees with Suyūṭī or not, this anxiety over conventions of attribution signals a competitive commentarial culture in which scholars sought to protect the fruits of their intellectual labor from theft both during the live sessions and after, as their written texts made the rounds.[83]

It is not difficult to find examples of textual practices in which it is acceptable to cite uncritically or to reference without attribution. Indeed, the liberal borrowing of motifs and phrases among classical Arab litterateurs and poets, like the citation standards of contemporary American "recombinant" novelists, are an excellent illustration of a literary culture that celebrates unattributed references.[84] But Ibn Ḥajar's valuing of critical attribution laid claim to how commentary ought to be practiced. The accusation of uncritical attribution was not only entangled in rivalries over patronage and prestige but also reflected an argument over the interpretive norms that were constitutive of the practice itself.

. . .

A close examination of the chronicle literature and the commentaries themselves teach us that Mamluk-era multivolume works of hadith commentary were delivered as a series of performances in the presence of students, patrons, and rivals. For students, commentators needed to prove their mastery of multiple disciplines, as well as display their pious devotion to preserving the legacy of the Prophet by aspiring to an endless commentary, one unconstrained by margins, and one only reluctantly constrained by the crudeness of the book market and the finality of death. In this way, most commentators framed their predicament as a dialectical conflict between worldly ends—producing a complete and marketable book—against ends internal to the tradition. The latter entailed continually sacrificing one's time to God and the Prophet through the study of hadith and perpetually aspiring to free the community from their "debt" of ignorance, regardless of the book market.

While any mention of patrons was virtually absent from the Andalusian commentarial context, patrons are praised by name in the text of Mamluk-era exegetical works. In one rare case, a current global political dispute between a commentator's two patrons over a ritualized practice—dressing the Kaʿba—became fodder for his exegetical material. In these cases, local and global historical context directly influenced the way a hadith was interpreted. Having a patron to praise or relay news about was itself a marker that one's commentaries were prestigious enough to be the object of a collector's desire.

Since major commentators on *Ṣaḥīḥ al-Bukhārī* of the Mamluk era sometimes held powerful political positions—Ibn Ḥajar and Badr al-Dīn al-ʿAynī were chief justices for their respective legal schools and supervised pious endowments, including mosque complexes—it is clear that their rivalries were sparked, in part, by competition over material and social rewards. It is tempting to likewise read accusations of plagiarism between commentators as a dispute over a primitive conception of intellectual property. But a close examination of commentarial introductions shows that interpretive ends and the maintenance of standards of excellence were also at stake in these debates. Intellectual innovation in the social practice of commentary was vital, and "borrowing without attribution" was defined as inimical to its practice.

CHAPTER 4

Rivalry and Revision in the Manuscript Age

I never saw anybody who wrote a book, and did not say the next day: If this would be changed, it would be better.

—al-Baysānī

Despite the fact that multivolume works of exegesis composed in the Mamluk period were often written across several decades, such works have often been treated largely as static representations of an author's thought.[1] Perhaps this is because our own scholarly culture's roots in philological work and the field's continuing need for critical editions have driven our fascination with the *aṣl,* the definitive hand-exemplar.[2] Or perhaps it is because a number of works strive to achieve the effect of "completion," smoothing over the rough edges that inevitably emerge in any compositional process. But a substantial intellectual work is not only a representation of an author's *vision;* it is also necessarily a representation of an author's *revision.* By mining archives that are littered with Mamluk-era material artifacts of works in progress—as some scholars in Mamluk studies have already begun to do—we can bring these stories, which sit at the intersection of social and intellectual history, to light.[3]

In order to explore the broader theme of revising exegesis in the manuscript age, I will continue to focus on the case of Ibn Ḥajar's *Fatḥ al-bārī,* that veritable gem of Mamluk intellectual history. What were the social and intellectual challenges and considerations that came into play as this work was revised in the context of Mamluk scholarly culture? While in the previous chapter we gained an understanding of the composition process of *Fatḥ al-bārī* from narrative sources like biographical dictionaries and authorial prefaces, an examination of new manuscript evidence can yield new insights into the development of Ibn Ḥajar's magnum opus and the composition of exegetical works more broadly in the context of the Mamluk period.

EARLY VERSIONS OF IBN ḤAJAR'S *FATḤ AL-BĀRĪ*

While I was digging through copies of *Fatḥ al-bārī* at the manuscript library attached to the Süleymaniye mosque in Istanbul in the summer of 2014, one in particular caught my eye: a partial copy shelved under "Mahmud Paşa 79." There, in the colophon, a scribe claimed the work was dictated to him by Ibn Ḥajar in 822/1419, roughly ten years before parts of the work were first commissioned by potentates of Transoxania and Tunisia, twenty years before the entire work was pronounced "complete" at a *khatm* in 842/1438, and thirty years before Ibn Ḥajar's death in 852/1449 (see fig. 6).[4] Mahmud Paşa 79 begins by commenting on chapters of the *adhān* (call to prayer) and concludes by commenting on the *zakāt* (alms tax), which corroborates Ibn Ḥajar's own account that he had largely composed about a third of the work by 822/1419 and had dictated portions of it to students.[5]

Adjacent to the colophon, a margin note indicates that additions (*zawāʾid*) were incorporated into this copy in 850/1446, based on a version transmitted by Ibn Ḥajar's longtime companion and distinguished recitation assistant, Ibn Khiḍr.[6] Rather than being destroyed or discarded, as many holograph drafts were,[7] or preserved as is for posterity, a later hand updated the early dictated copy with Ibn Ḥajar's additional passages. It must have been seen to have had some practical or symbolic value, likely as a source for future copies or as a reference work that could be modified as Ibn Ḥajar updated his copy. Both the colophon and the audition statement—certifying that the text had been reviewed against an authorized copy—adjacent to it pray that God keep and preserve Ibn Ḥajar's life, corroborating the fact that Ibn Ḥajar was alive at the time the colophons were recorded.

The note does not stipulate that Ibn Khiḍr's copy was an exemplar (*aṣl*), and as we will see, the *zawāʾid* only partly reflect the recension preserved in modern printed editions.[8] In effect, this manuscript, Mahmud Paşa 79, preserves not one but two early versions of *Fatḥ al-bārī*.

Who was the scribe who received *Fatḥ al-bārī* years in advance of rulers in the Islamic east and west? Apparently a mid-level bureaucrat and an aspiring scholar named Ibn al-Miṣrī.[9] The full name given in the colophon is Muḥammad ibn Abī al-Ḥayāt al-Khiḍr ibn Abī Sulaymān Dāwūd

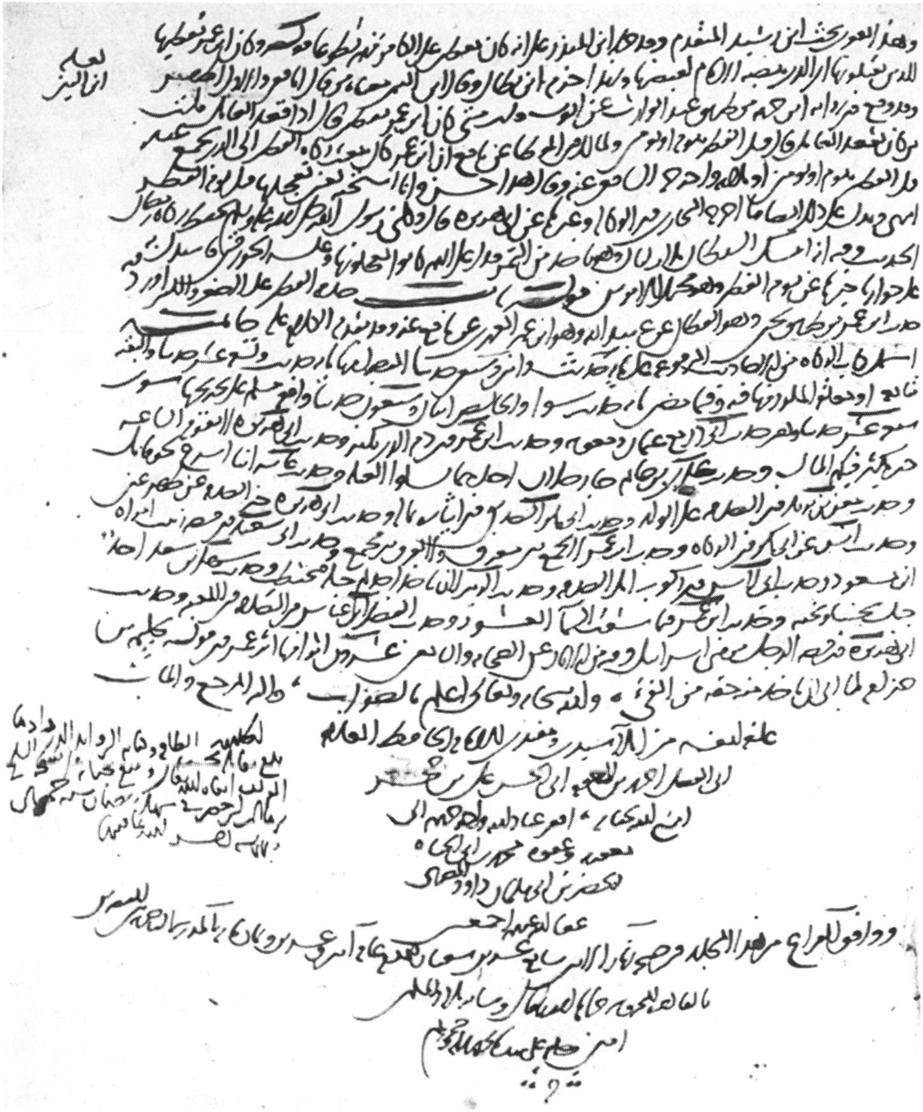

FIGURE 6. The colophon of this copy of *Fatḥ al-bārī* states that the work was copied "from the dictation" of "al-Imām al-Ḥāfiẓ" Abū al-Faḍl Ibn Ḥajar and that the volume was completed during the last hour before dawn on Monday, Shaʿbān 17, 822 (September 18, 1419). The audition statement adjacent to the colophon testifies that the copy was collated with elaborations (*zawāʾid*) that the author (i.e., Ibn Ḥajar) added to it according to a copy of Shaykh Burhān al-Dīn Ibn Khidr in Ramadan of 850 (November or December 1446). MS Mahmud Paşa 79, folio 137a. Süleymaniye Library, Istanbul, Turkey. (Photo courtesy of the Süleymaniye Library.)

al-Miṣrī, and we are fortunate that Ibn Ḥajar happened to write his obituary. According to Ibn Ḥajar, Muḥammad ibn al-Khiḍr ibn Dāwūd, also known as Shams al-Dīn and Ibn al-Miṣrī, was born in Aleppo around 768/1366–67 and died in Jerusalem in 841/1437–38.[10] He grew up studying with a number of reputable scholars in Greater Syria, after which he settled in Cairo for a time and performed scribal work at the chancery (*dīwān al-inshāʾ*) at the pleasure of a high-ranking minister for the military (*nāẓir al-jaysh*). Ibn al-Miṣrī then traveled to Jerusalem, where he was appointed shaykh at the madrasa al-Bāsiṭiyya. Most significantly for our purposes, the obituary states that Ibn al-Miṣrī had written down Ibn Ḥajar's dictated commentary on *Ṣaḥīḥ al-Bukhārī*.[11] Ibn al-Miṣrī's early dictated copy shelved as Mahmud Paşa 79 must be that very copy that Ibn Ḥajar mentioned in the obituary.

Where and for whom did Ibn al-Miṣrī copy Ibn Ḥajar's dictation of *Fatḥ al-bārī*? The colophon states that it was completed at the madrasa named for al-Nāṣir Muḥammad ibn Qalāwūn (al-Nāṣiriyya), in Bayn al-Qaṣrayn, a neighborhood of Cairo lodged between two Fatimid-era palaces.[12] The copy was made for Ibn al-Miṣrī's private use (*ʿallaqahu li-nafsihi*).[13] A lack of formality of the handwriting suggests as much, as any scribe in the service of the chancery would surely be capable of calligraphy more consistent with professional conventions.

Note that I use the phrase "early dictated copy" here rather than "draft," since the technical terms *naskh* (copy) and *min imlāʾ* (from dictation) were used in the colophon and the audition statement to describe the manuscript rather than *musawwada* (draft), which would better describe a rough draft composed in the author's own hand. That said, to suggest a better but still imperfect analogy, we might think of this early dictated copy less like a rough draft that was polished into a final copy and more like an advance copy of a first edition that was later expanded and revised for a second and then a third edition. Nevertheless, it should be clear that this document offers us a rare opportunity to see both the social and intellectual considerations pertaining to the revision of *Fatḥ al-bārī* over the course of its composition. Indeed, this manuscript can shed light on at least three layers of revisions and additions that *Fatḥ al-bārī* underwent.

To offer a rough idea of these additions quantitatively, we can compare the number of words in a sampling of text from the early dictated copy—say, the first three folios—with the total number included in printed editions that are based on later recensions of *Fatḥ al-bārī*.[14] While the sample from Ibn al-Miṣrī's copy contains 2,185 words, for instance, the printed editions contain 2,979 words, which means that 794 words were added later. More research needs to be done to refine this picture, but based on this limited sample, which appears consistent with my preliminary findings in other samples, roughly 25 percent (26.66 percent) of the final version did not appear in the earliest version. In other words, for every three words that Ibn Ḥajar dictated in 822/1419, he would add one more by the time he passed away in 852/1449.

On the one hand, a 25 percent change may seem of great consequence. Indeed, even a 1 percent change over the course of the work's composition could be qualitatively significant. On the other hand, *Fatḥ al-bārī* was already such a long work, by Ibn Ḥajar's own concession.[15] If roughly three-quarters of *Fatḥ al-bārī* were ready for the "final" exemplar in 822/1419, what made Ibn Ḥajar return to these earlier chapters, years later, to add more? Having established that this manuscript, Mahmud Paşa 79, is indeed an early dictated and later revised copy of Ibn Ḥajar's *Fatḥ al-bārī*, the next question we must ask is: what kinds of revisions and expansions did *Fatḥ al-bārī* undergo, and why?

STRATEGIES OF REVISION AND EXPANSION

Ibn Ḥajar revised *Fatḥ al-bārī* in serial iterations over long periods of time in response to his predecessors' work and that of his rivals. These revisions and additions operated at two levels: to prove the superiority of Ibn Ḥajar's work amid the politics of a competitive scholarly scene while simultaneously championing hermeneutic norms that Ibn Ḥajar believed best preserved the meaning of the hadith. In sum, these revisions and additions stood to offer the commentator both social rewards as well as the achievement of interpretive excellences internal to the practice of commentary. To shed light on this process, I will briefly examine and analyze an example from each of the three observable layers of revisions and additions.

The first layer includes the changes made when the dictation was checked by audition and collation, soon after it was first copied. This layer consists of interlinear cancellations and marginal corrections that match the handwriting in the body of the text. Ibn al-Miṣrī, who was known as Shams al-Dīn, signs an audition statement telling us as much.[16] In this layer, however, we find more than just minor corrections to scribal and dictation errors, although there are plenty of those as well. But we sometimes see a reconsideration of Ibn Ḥajar's interpretation of a hadith or his predecessors' understanding of it.

Consider, for instance, Ibn Ḥajar's analysis of a hadith on the "seven [types of believers] who will be shaded" on the Day of Resurrection. Among those seven types are those who maintain chastity stating "I fear God," and those who remind themselves of God through practicing *dhikr,* repeatedly uttering his name. In the early dictated copy, Ibn Ḥajar quotes a previous commentator, Muḥammad ibn Yūsuf al-Kirmānī (d. 786/1384), who groups these seven types into three broad categories: those who are saved by obedience to God "by the tongue," "by the heart," and "by the body."[17] But Kirmānī never fully explained how each of the seven types, including the chaste and the practitioner of *dhikr,* are distributed into these categories.

Enter Ibn Ḥajar. He first proposes that the type of person Kirmānī means by obedience to God "by the tongue" is "the one who says 'I fear God'" (*al-qāʾil innī akhāf Allāh*) and remains chaste. In the collation, however, Ibn Ḥajar cancels this statement and substitutes it with the notion that obedience through the tongue means "the one who utters [the name of God repetitively] in remembrance" (*al-dhākir*).[18]

These two explanations are so different that they cannot be a scribal error. What, then, accounts for the change? While Ibn Ḥajar's initial solution is technically correct—the chaste person utters "I fear God" with his or her tongue—there is an astute logic behind Ibn Ḥajar's cancellation and substitution. On further reflection, uttering "I fear God" is not the main point for Ibn Ḥajar, but rather the maintenance of one's chastity (*ʿiffa*), and thus that aspect of the hadith fits better in the category of obedience to God through the body. Meanwhile, uttering God's name in remembrance can only be placed in the category of obedience to God through the tongue. Yet Ibn Ḥajar's confusion reveals an ambiguity that may arise from Kirmānī's categories themselves. The tongue, after all, acts in the service of the body. But Ibn Ḥajar's correction nevertheless maintains Kirmānī's distinction between a speech act and a bodily act, glossing over any overlap between to the two. Although Ibn Ḥajar could have eschewed Kirmānī's categories altogether, he either could find no better alternative or found them useful enough to keep.

While it may be easy to characterize those exegetes who quote past authorities as a signal of repetition or intellectual stagnation, the first layer of revisions from this marked-up early dictated copy of *Fatḥ al-bārī* clearly indicates the extent to which exegetes sometimes considered and reconsidered the commentary of their predecessors.

REVISING FOR RIVALS

The second layer is visible in the hand of an anonymous scholar or scribe who recorded Ibn Ḥajar's additions (*zawāʾid*) in the margins almost twenty-eight years after the work was first dictated, eight years after the work was declared "complete" at the *khatm,* and two years before Ibn Ḥajar passed away. As stated above, these additions were included on the basis of comparing Ibn al-Miṣrī's early dictated work against a copy belonging to Ibn Ḥajar's distinguished recitation assistant, Burhān al-Dīn ibn Khiḍr, in the year 850/1446. Although Ibn Khiḍr's copy reflected the text at a much later date, it was not a final exemplar. This means that the marginal additions were based on yet another copy of the text, which later must have undergone further revision.

Although we do not know the identity of the collator who inked these additions in the margins, we can rule out a number of prime suspects. Our anonymous collator was working nine years after Ibn al-Miṣrī passed away, so it could not have been him. We can also out rule out Sakhāwī or Ibn Ḥajar himself, whose distinctive handwriting does not resemble that of our collator's.[19] One possibility, although it is purely speculative, is that it was Ibn al-Miṣrī's son Khiḍr, a learned scholar in his own right, who updated *Fatḥ al-bārī* after he inherited the work from his father.[20] And yet, if this were so, one might have also expected Ibn al-Miṣrī's son to have signed his contribution.

One clear pattern in this second layer is Ibn Ḥajar's additional references to other hadith collections that he neglected to mention in the first layer. I will walk through this layer in more detail, because it reflects the project that ultimately distinguished Ibn Ḥajar's genius as a commentator: to explain a hadith by reference to another hadith (*sharḥ al-ḥadīth bi'l-ḥadīth*).

To take one illustrative example from the early dictated copy, Ibn Ḥajar discusses a hadith in the "Book of Friday Prayers" (*Kitāb al-Jumʿa*) that claims that it was the third caliph, ʿUthmān, rather than the Prophet, who instituted an additional call to prayer (*adhān*) in the marketplace of Medina prior to Friday prayers. The practice of an additional call to prayer on Fridays, which was said to have been described by the son of the second caliph, ʿUmar, (d. 73/693) as "an innovation (*bidʿa*)," generated many differences of opinion over its origin and permissibility.[21] After explaining each of the lemmata, Ibn Ḥajar briefly discusses what he thought Bukhārī intended to prove by including this hadith in his *Ṣaḥīḥ* under the heading "The Friday Call to Prayer."[22] But he does not discuss the controversial origins of the practice, a staple discussion in other commentators' exegetical histories of this hadith.

In the marginal note added nearly three decades later, however, we see that Ibn Ḥajar has included an entirely new section, under the heading "Two Notes of Caution (*tanbihān*)" (see fig. 7).[23] Here we find Ibn Ḥajar addressing the issue of origins forthrightly. He references three additional hadith: one that suggests the practice was actually initiated by the second caliph, ʿUmar; a second that reports that no one, not even ʿUthmān, instituted the practice of an additional call to prayer in Medina's marketplace; and a third report that claims that Ibn ʿAbd al-Malik redefined the status and location of an additional call to prayer.[24] In all three cases, Ibn Ḥajar offers withering criticism of the trustworthiness and plausibility of each hadith's chain of transmission. In the case of the third hadith, he goes so far as to scold other commentators of *Ṣaḥīḥ al-Bukhārī* for even troubling to include such an untrustworthy hadith, as he could find no pious ancestors (*salāf*) who transmitted it, and he deemed its content incongruous with the prima facie meaning of the hadith.[25]

Although Ibn Ḥajar leaves the commentators he wishes to criticize unnamed, by process of elimination, it must have been his contemporaries Ibn al-Mulaqqin and Badr al-Dīn al-ʿAynī, who were the only notable scholars who included these three hadith in their commentaries.[26] That Ibn al-Mulaqqin and ʿAynī agreed with Ibn Ḥajar's opinion that it was indeed ʿUthmān who instituted an additional *adhān* is beside the point. The clear message, underlined by the fact that Ibn Ḥajar returned to this passage to add the two notes of caution, is that his contemporaries should not have included untrustworthy material just for the sake of including it.

In this way, we can reconstruct a micro-narrative about Ibn Ḥajar's thought process in crafting this section. In Ibn al-Miṣrī's early dictated copy, Ibn Ḥajar omitted any mention of those three hadith, perhaps indicating their unworthiness through his silence. Norman Calder, in discussing the genre of *tafsīr,* described this activity as "scholarly exclusion" and framed it as an inevitable reaction to the "danger" of an "unmanageably large" accumulation of layers of commentarial opinions over time.[27] In the later copy, Ibn Ḥajar, presumably after reading his colleagues' work in which these three hadith were included without reproach, decided it was part of his charge to include those hadith, if only to unequivocally reject them.

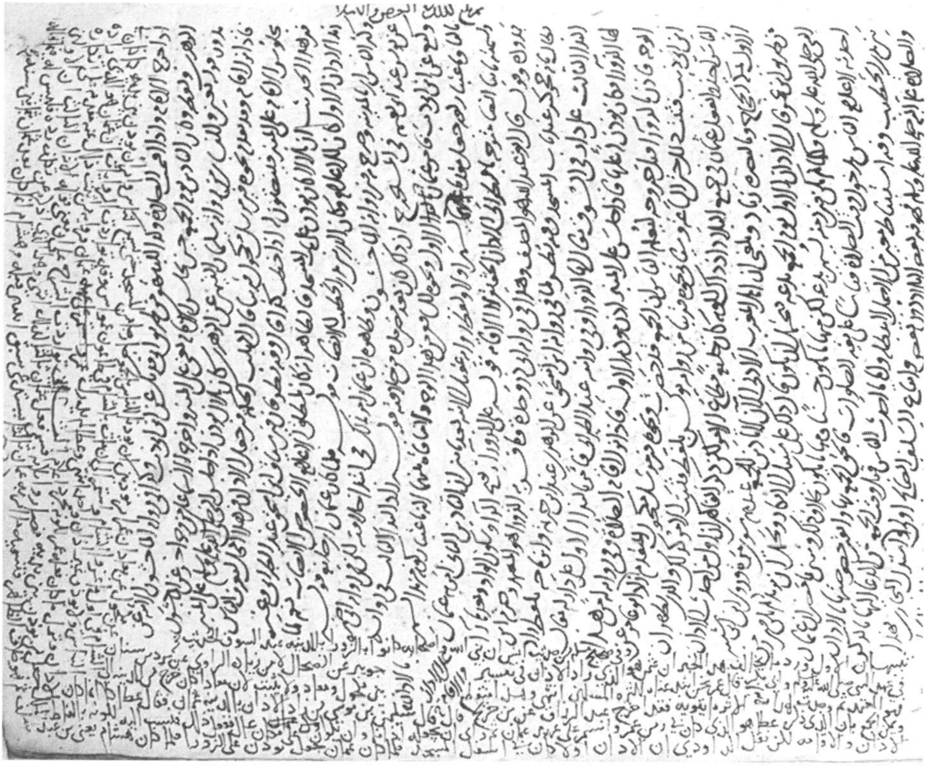

FIGURE 7. "Two Notes of Caution (*tanbīhān*)" addresses unnamed commentators who included hadith of dubious origin in their work. The *tanbīhān* spirals across the bottom and left margins in this image of a folio rotated once counterclockwise. MS Mahmud Paşa 79, folio 317a. Süleymaniye Library, Istanbul, Turkey. (Photo courtesy of the Süleymaniye Library.)

Ibn Ḥajar's practice of including additional references, then, was not only a quantitative matter that would prove to a competitive scholarly community that his commentary was more comprehensive than anyone else's, although this was surely a factor. Nor was it simply a mark of his living devotion and piety, a hadith scholar who sacrificed all the time and energy he could muster to clarifying the mission of God's Prophet, although this was also surely a factor. But what was at stake here for Ibn Ḥajar in making his revision was a certain commentarial hermeneutic—one he helped to define as *sharḥ al-ḥadīth bi'l-ḥadīth*—a hermeneutic that imbricated social rewards *and* interpretive excellences: if the hadith to which a commentator refers are to have any persuasive claim to influence an audience's social behavior, their authenticity must first be judged to be sound.

TRACES OF AN INTELLECTUAL RIVALRY

The final layer in Ibn al-Miṣrī's early dictated copy consists of later interpolations that can be observed by comparing this copy with one based on the exemplar that was circulated after Ibn Ḥajar's death. We do not know precisely when these later additions were composed. One possibility is that they are contemporaneous to the second layer (ante-850/1446), but that the anonymous editor of the second layer omitted them by accident. This explanation is plausible where the changes amount to minor additions and alterations that had been overlooked by the anonymous collator of the second layer. However, there are frequently critical lines and long passages of commentary that are included in printed editions that are not indicated either in Ibn al-Miṣrī's version or the version used by the anonymous collator in 850/1446. In these cases, it is hard to believe that our anonymous collator would have neglected to incorporate these passages while diligently including others.

Since we know from narrative sources that Ibn Ḥajar continued to add material during the ten years that followed the work's "completion" (*khatm*),[28] a more plausible conjecture is that the additions in the second layer reflect the state of *Fatḥ al-bārī* at the time of the *khatm* but do not reflect any changes that Ibn Ḥajar made in the last decade before his passing in 852/1449. In any event, we can posit firmly that our third layer consists of further changes made to *Fatḥ al-bārī* after the copy of Burhān al-Dīn ibn Khiḍr used by our anonymous collator was first put to paper. That said, these further changes did not necessarily occur after 850/1446 (the date the second layer was added), as the anonymous collator of the second layer may have been updating Ibn al-Miṣrī's copy with an already out-of-date version of *Fatḥ al-bārī*.

As I argued in the previous chapter, Ibn Ḥajar suspected that some of the students who copied early dictations of *Fatḥ al-bārī* shared their notes with ʿAynī. Thus, in Ibn Ḥajar's estimation, ʿAynī's commentary on *Ṣaḥīḥ al-Bukhārī* used an early dictated copy of *Fatḥ al-bārī* as a source for material to plagiarize and criticize. Not one content to sit on his heels, Ibn Ḥajar composed a written response to ʿAynī's criticisms in *Intiqāḍ al-iʿtirāḍ*.[29]

An example of one of their many intellectual disputes was Ibn Ḥajar's explanation for why Bukhārī used the obscure phrasing *al-adhān mathnā mathnā* in the chapter heading "Doubling the Call to Prayer," when there is no hadith authenticated by Bukhārī that uses this phrasing. In Ibn al-Miṣrī's early dictated copy of Ibn Ḥajar's commentary,

Ibn Ḥajar solves this problem in the following way: "The wording of this chapter heading is established by a hadith that can be attributed to the Prophet (*marfūʿ*). Abū Dāwūd and al-Nasāʾī found a corroborating chain of transmission for it (*akhrajahu*). Ibn Khuzayma and others authenticated it with the hadith of Ibn ʿUmar."[30]

This may seem like a minor point of phrasing. However, interpreting Bukhārī's quizzical chapter headings (*sharḥ tarājim al-Bukhārī*) was another key way in which Ibn Ḥajar had distinguished the genius of his commentary. Since Ibn Ḥajar was referencing other hadith in order to explain the phrasing in the hadith (*sharḥ al-ḥadīth bi'l-ḥadīth*) both of the interpretive strategies Ibn Ḥajar most prized were being put to the test.

But Ibn Ḥajar's first attempt at an explanation, in this case, leaves something to be desired. If one consults the hadith of Ibn ʿUmar in Abū Dāwūd's collection and others, one finds a completely different wording: instead of *mathnā mathnā*, one finds that the *adhān* in the time of the Prophet was described as *maratayn, maratayn.*

Ibn Ḥajar must have realized this passage in *Fatḥ al-bārī* needed more work, because in the third layer of additions, one can see that he had included new information and an important qualification: "The wording of this chapter heading is established by a hadith of Ibn ʿUmar that can be attributed to the Prophet (*marfūʿ*). Abū Dāwūd al-Ṭayālisī recorded it in his *Musnad.* He says in it *mathnā, mathnā*. It is also found in [the collections of] Abū Dāwūd and al-Nasāʾī. Ibn Khuzayma and others authenticated it, but worded it in the following way: *maratayn, maratayn.*"[31]

Here Ibn Ḥajar lives up to his reputation. The revised version clarifies that a different Abū Dāwūd, Abū Dāwūd al-Ṭayālisī (d. 204/819), transmitted the hadith by a chain of transmission in which Ibn ʿUmar recalled that the *adhān* in the time of the Prophet was *mathnā, mathnā*. In this version, he makes clear that the other Abū Dāwūd, Abū Dāwūd al-Sijistānī, along with others, narrated the hadith of Ibn ʿUmar with a different expression: *maratayn, maratayn.* The hidden benefit that Ibn Ḥajar wanted students of hadith to take away was that Bukhārī was tipping his cap (or his turban, if he wore one) to the authority of the phrasing *mathnā, mathnā*.

Enter ʿAynī. According to Ibn Ḥajar in his *Intiqāḍ al-iʿtirāḍ,* ʿAynī took issue with Bukhārī's title and Ibn Ḥajar's interpretation of it, stating, "This is not the pronunciation of the hadith being referenced (*laysa lafẓ al-ḥadīth al-madhkhūr*)," but that instead it should be pronounced, on the basis of a hadith from the *Sunan* of Abū Dāwūd, *maratayn maratayn.*[32]

This rubbed Ibn Ḥajar the wrong way. He speculated that either ʿAynī read a copy of *Fatḥ al-bārī* in which the quote from Abū Dāwūd al-Ṭayālisī was missing or ʿAynī thought that Abū Dāwūd al-Ṭayālisī and Abū Dāwūd al-Sijistānī were the same person.[33] Proceeding as if it were the latter, Ibn Ḥajar gave ʿAynī a stern lecture about the difference between the two Abū Dāwūds, and for repudiating an erudite point.[34]

Although we do not know what copy of *Fatḥ al-bārī* ʿAynī had in his possession, the discovery of Ibn al-Miṣrī's early dictated copy in which the reference to Abū Dāwūd al-Ṭayālisī is missing lends a point in ʿAynī's favor. If ʿAynī indeed read an early copy of *Fatḥ al-bārī,* one similar to Ibn al-Miṣrī's—which seems overwhelmingly likely, given Ibn Ḥajar's own account that ʿAynī obtained early dictation notes from one of Ibn Ḥajar's students—then ʿAynī can hardly be faulted for criticizing Ibn Ḥajar's interpretation. Although ʿAynī distinguished his commentary on *Ṣaḥīḥ al-Bukhārī* through his use of rhetoric, grammar, and language rather than his knowledge of other hadith, as Ibn Ḥajar did, ʿAynī surely knew enough about hadith to know the difference between Abū Dāwūd al-Ṭayālisī and Abū Dāwūd al-Sijistānī. In this case, ʿAynī's only shortcoming was that he did not know that a hadith contained in Abū Dāwūd al-Ṭayālisī's *Musnad* employed the phrasing *mathnā, mathnā.* But even Ibn Ḥajar missed this point in 822/1419, as Ibn al-Miṣrī's early dictated copy clearly preserves.

There is an intriguing epilogue to this story that raises fresh questions about the way in which Mamluk-era scholars read and responded to one another's work. If one relies on modern editions of ʿAynī's *ʿUmdat al-qārī* that are based on a later manuscript recension,[35] rather than Ibn Ḥajar's description of ʿAynī's commentary in *Intiqāḍ al-iʿtirāḍ,* one is surprised to find the text free from any criticism of Ibn Ḥajar or his work. ʿAynī made no mention of Abū Dāwūd, neither al-Sijistānī nor al-Ṭayālisī. And he made no mention of *maratayn maratayn.* Instead, he offered, as was typical of his approach, a linguistic explanation for the obscure phrase. This suggests that ʿAynī read Ibn Ḥajar's critique of him and revised his own work accordingly. Compare, for instance, ʿAynī on the chapter of *mathnā mathnā* according to Ibn Ḥajar's *Intiqāḍ al-iʿtirāḍ* (1) and according to printed editions of *ʿUmdāt al-qārī* (2):

> (1) [Mathnā mathnā] is not the pronunciation of the aforementioned hadith. Rather, as Abū Dāwūd related on the authority of Ibn ʿUmar: "The *adhān* was doubled [*maratayn maratayn*] during the time of the Prophet of God."[36]

> (2) This chapter mentions in it the doubling (*mathnā mathnā*) of the *adhān. Mathnā mathnā* is repeated in this way in the recitation of [*Ṣaḥīḥ al-Bukhārī*] of al-Kushmihānī. According to other recitations it is a single *mathnā.* And *mathnā mathnā* is derived from the same root as *ithnayn ithnayn* (two two).[37]

The evidence gives one the distinct impression that Ibn Ḥajar and ʿAynī must have been reading and responding to one another's works in progress and made revisions accordingly, knowing their readers would be judging them against one another. It also shows just how difficult it was for authors to control the text of their works once they had been dictated, even if they were circulating as private copies among a very limited readership. In other words, whether authors liked it or not, these early dictated works in progress exerted influence, and one could be held accountable for what one dictated in an early copy. The experience of reading and writing in Mamluk intellectual culture could thus involve circulating and competitively responding to works in progress prior to and sometimes even after a work was declared complete.

. . .

Even though I have shown that Ibn Ḥajar was motivated to revise and re-revise *Fatḥ al-bārī* out of a desire to compete with rivals, this is only a partial understanding of commentary as a social practice. An examination of the three layers of additions in Ibn al-Miṣrī's early dictated copy of *Fatḥ al-bārī* sheds light on Ibn Ḥajar's interpretive and religious aims to better preserve the meaning of the Prophet's legacy.

Concerning these normative commitments, it is worth considering three concluding points that are distinctive to the composition of exegetical works, especially in a culture that canonized *Ṣaḥīḥ al-Bukhārī.*

First, as we will see in the next chapter, the practice of reading *Ṣaḥīḥ al-Bukhārī* was a cyclical one, with recitations performed at the citadel during Ramadan, in the presence of the sultan.[38] We should therefore be unsurprised that Ibn Ḥajar returned to add more and more to his commentary on it, even in the years and decades following his early dictation of the text to Ibn al-Miṣrī.

Second, like many exegetes of canonized and sacralized texts, commentators viewed the act of explaining *Ṣaḥīḥ al-Bukhārī* as a task that would extend beyond their lifetime.[39] As micro-debates made apparent by a close analysis of the many layers added to this early dictated copy of *Fatḥ al-bārī* show, Ibn Ḥajar was guided by a piety that drove him to continually tease out new benefits from the Prophet's sayings and practices, as well as by a rigorous commitment to maintaining the soundness of the hadith of scholars who compiled and interpreted them. Death, ostensibly willed by God, surpassed the *khatm* as the true moment at which the scholar's commentary was at last brought to an end.

Third, scholars were commenting on a traditionally transmitted text not only for themselves and their contemporary readers but also for audiences in the near and distant future. The future Ibn Ḥajar may have hoped for was one in which the day of resurrection was around the corner, but he was clearly preparing for the long haul. Since nearly five hundred years separated Ibn Ḥajar and al-Bukhārī, it is not unreasonable to expect that Muslim scholars might still be debating the origins of a hadith or the phrasing of a chapter heading five hundred years in the future. Indeed, they did and they do. To this end, *Fatḥ al-bārī* was revised and elaborated upon for decades with the knowledge that nothing like it had ever been produced,[40] and because it might have to sustain the community as a monument for centuries to come.

Nevertheless, as valuable as this monument has been, the new evidence from Ibn al-Miṣrī's early dictated copy shows scholars how much there is to learn if we look past the artifice of a monumental work's completeness. In his book *Patterns of Intention,* Michael Baxandall wrote:

> Cezanne had said, and Picasso later quoted him with approval as saying, that every brushstroke changes a picture. The point they were making was not that a finished picture will look different if even one brushstroke is removed or changed. They meant that in the course of painting a picture, each brushstroke will modify the effect of the brushstrokes so far made, so that with each brushstroke the painter finds himself addressing a new situation. . . . This effect is very powerful, however clearly the painter has in mind a final character.[41]

Baxandall was discussing Picasso's process, but this idea can enrich our analysis of works in progress in the manuscript age. The power of recognizing a commentary and its revision as a serial performance is that it allows us to bring a stereoscopic "relief to the process."[42] We are no longer limited to seeing and analyzing a work retrospectively from the moment of completion, when the exegete finally declared that the work approximated what he had intended to complete. Instead, we can reconstruct the exegete's intention forward as he first began to solve an old question. With each word dictated and each explanation inked on paper, new riddles, new debates, and new ambiguities emerged, both for him and his readership.

In other words, to view *Fatḥ al-bārī* as a single, coherent text is to subscribe to the artifice of completion and singularity of intention that any *khatm,* if properly performed, retroactively crystallizes. This artifice of a "completed" work is itself worthy of contemplation, not just for convenience sake, but also because the artifice of a "completed" work is an authoritative and powerful representation of an author's thought at an important moment in time. But this artifice is also contingent on concealing and excluding the complicating and densely layered stories of how a "completed" work came to be.

As new evidence from Ibn al-Miṣrī's early dictated copy shows us, the rich life of debate in the Mamluk scholarly scene is hidden in plain sight in the lines of *Fatḥ al-bārī.* At stake in the life of this debate were both the social rewards, in which Ibn Ḥajar was a fearsome competitor, as well as the achievement of certain interpretive ends and the adherence to certain standards of excellence, in which Ibn Ḥajar's strategies for preserving the meaning of the Prophet's authenticated sayings and practices evolved over time.

CHAPTER 5

Oratory in the Shade of the Sultan's Garden

This place is a proving ground, not a place of seeking benefit.

—Ibn Ḥajar

Commentators not only attacked one another from the safety of their written texts but also face-to-face during commentary sessions on *Ṣaḥīḥ al-Bukhārī* in the presence of the political and judicial elite at the citadel during Ramadan. Live debates on *Ṣaḥīḥ al-Bukhārī* were spectacular and sometimes destructive contests in which rival commentators argued over law, terminology, and chains of transmission in the presence of students, patrons, and colleagues. That commentary was delivered live meant that stratagems of the body—including fashion, elocution, and other markers of ethnicity—worked alongside signs of encyclopedic memory and world travel to persuade a diverse audience of one's power within the scholarly scene and one's faithfulness to the Prophet's example. William Blake may have aphorized that "the road of excess leads to the palace of wisdom," but for the Mamluk-era commentators, the road of excess just as surely lead to the palace of the sultan.

As the first part of this chapter will show, these live commentaries often occurred and recurred at annual recitation sessions, in which impromptu debate among high court judges would bubble up over the clarification of a technical term or word. Moreover, the space of the citadel reminds us that commentaries were not relegated to the mosque or the madrasa but were embedded in political institutions and their spaces. In examining accounts of clashes between rivals, I will be less concerned with determining the victor than with how commentators constructed oral strategies to fend off rivals.

In the latter part of this chapter, I focus on a rare episode that took place in the sultan's garden, over fruit and sweets—a more intimate setting for live commentary on hadith. A chronicle of Ibn Ḥajar al-ʿAsqalānī's tells of this afternoon discussion in the shade of the sultan's garden, prompted by a Cairene student's curiosity about the contradictory logic of a hadith from *Ṣaḥīḥ al-Bukhārī*. Ibn Ḥajar used the impromptu live commentary to embarrass his rival, Shams al-Dīn al-Harawī, and to impress his patron, al-Muʾayyad Shaykh. While Ibn Ḥajar stated that deriving religious benefit (*istifāda*) from knowledge in the live commentary sessions was the ideal, his conspicuous commitment to *istifāda* in the garden session ironically served as a key credential in the pursuit of his patron's favor and, as a consequence, a judicial and teaching appointment. In a rare crossover, Ibn Ḥajar retells this anecdote of the garden session in his written explication of the same hadith in his multivolume written commentary, *Fatḥ al-bārī*, but there he engages in an interpretive practice with radically different stakes. By juxtaposing these accounts of the live commentary with the text of the written commentary, I will strive to make visible the political and social conditions that make a commentary possible without losing sight of what normative commitments and beliefs were of grave concern in determining the meaning and application of these texts.

DEBATING *ṢAḤĪḤ AL-BUKHĀRĪ* AT THE CITADEL, LIVE

Since *Ṣaḥīḥ al-Bukhārī*, in its material, oral, and aural form, functioned apotropaically as a source of *baraka* and as an authoritative source for Islamic legal, ethical, and theological norms, the ruling elite in the Mamluk period naturally recognized that by patronizing recitation sessions of *Ṣaḥīḥ al-Bukhārī*, they gained prestige as "guardians of the faith."[1] As Konrad Hirschler observed, "the most prominent example for Egypt was certainly the ritualized recitation of Bukhārī's ḥadīth collection during the month of Ramadan that gained in importance from the eighth/fourteenth century onwards."[2] Under al-Muʾayyad Shaykh, the recitations doubled in length, beginning in the month of Shaʿbān and ending in Ramadan.[3]

The Ramadan sessions at the citadel were highly formal events, usually attended by the sultan, the four chief justices of the Sunni legal schools, the emirs, and a who's who of the scholarly elite. As I described in chapter 3, there was typically a recitation assistant of some renown who would read the text aloud alongside the commentator, pausing to allow time for the commentator to elucidate important matters. While seating arrangement is important at any formal or political event, it would have been especially important at a commentary session such as this, where the sharpest students and most prestigious scholars would sit nearest to the commentator on the recitation, typically the Shāfiʿī chief justice, facilitating aural clarity and heightening their potential to interact with the recitation's commentator through questions or comments.[4]

These recitation sessions became sites for clamorous debates among rival interpreters over social capital, material resources, and the standards of excellences internal to the tradition. Since the sultan and the emirs would have been expected to attend, the rectorships, judicial appointments, stipends, tax benefits, and gifts of clothing and food that they routinely doled out were on offer for a truly excellent live performance. For a particularly bad performance, wealth and status could also be taken away. But live debates also served as arenas for the achievement of interpretive excellences internal to the tradition: first, those ends that could be achieved through the craft of commentary itself (such as a skilled performance in the arts of memory, oratory, and argument), and second, those excellences that could be achieved through maintaining or deriving legal and theological norms of pertinence to daily practice and belief.

Ibn al-Mughulī (d. 827/1423), the chief justice for the Ḥanbalī legal school, frequently engaged scholars in these recitation environments.[5] He had, after all, distinguished himself in Syria by memorizing commentaries, studying at the feet of an esteemed commentator on Bukhārī's *Ṣaḥīḥ* from the previous generation of Muslim scholars, Ibn Rajab al-Ḥanbalī (d. 795/1392) of Baghdad and Damascus.[6] Scholars like Ibn al-Mughulī who had memorized commentaries would be at an advantage to offer impromptu commentary of their own as they locked horns with rivals.

One such spontaneous commentarial debate involving Ibn al-Mughulī at a Ramadan recitation session of *Ṣaḥīḥ al-Bukhārī* occurred at the citadel in 826/1423.[7] According to Ibn Ḥajar's account of the affair, "the crowd was very numerous" and had hastened to the lower palace on Sultan Barsbāy's order.[8] An argument broke out between Ibn al-Mughulī and Ibn al-Dayrī, a rector at the Muʾayyadiyya madrasa and a former Ḥanafī-trained judge in full view of the sultan, the entire Mamluk court, and the civilian elite. A Turkish speaker, Barsbāy may not have had a sufficient mastery of Arabic to understand these debates, but he did understand when a commotion had gotten out of hand. He promptly relocated the session to the higher palace, with a more exclusive guest list of scholars, officials, and judges. The move apparently failed to quell the ruckus, as the debaters "were scolded many times, but they were not restrained."[9] So the session was returned to the lower palace so that the sultan might view them remotely from a balcony, away from the noise. The sultan would "sit among them quietly, not moving a hand or a leg."[10] In the end, the sultan chose to dismiss and replace the reciter, rather than either of the judges who fiercely debated the recitation. While the subject of these discourses was neither recorded nor circulated, and nor did Ibn al-Mughulī himself use this material to write any commentaries on *Ṣaḥīḥ al-Bukhārī,* such debates serve as a window onto an important part of the culture in which more formalized oral and written commentaries emerged.

This anecdote suggests that commentarial debates could be difficult to regulate. To the extent that they exposed rifts between the scholarly elite, such debates were depicted as subversive to the power of the sultan, who is presented as seeking a spectacle of stability, not contestation. It is an open question whether this is an accurate representation of the sultan's aims in holding these commentary sessions or a projection of a politically anxious chronicler. It is also an open question how much of the commentary session the sultan could understand.[11] Instead, the sultan is often portrayed in anecdotes of commentarial sessions on *Ṣaḥīḥ al-Bukhārī* as a silent or mostly silent arbiter, letting commentarial feuds heat up, intervening only if they reached a rolling boil. Nevertheless, his power to shape these sessions was undeniable. He could appoint and dismiss reciters, include and exclude students, and choose or alter the site for the recitation. Scholars and students were thus aware of their physical proximity to the sultan and even his slight body language, the stillness or movements of his hands or legs and any subtle messages they might have conveyed.

THE HARAWĪ AFFAIR: SCANDAL AND FRAUD ON THE HIGH COURT

Ibn Ḥajar relays an account of another clamorous debate, one that arose five years earlier in Ramadan 821/1418, when a controversial figure named Shams al-Dīn al-Harawī (d. 829/1426) was serving his first of two terms as the Shāfiʿī chief justice (*qāḍī al-quḍāt*) in Cairo, the most powerful judgeship on the high court. Harawī was ultimately imprisoned on charges of embezzlement and corruption and only narrowly avoided calls for his execution.[12]

We know very little about Harawī's scholarly biography before he arrived in the Mamluk Sultanate. No sources in Arabic mention any of Harawī's teachers, with the exception of Sakhāwī, who, in a late and uncorroborated account, claimed that Harawī learned hadith at the foot of the renowned legal commentator, exegete, theologian, and grammarian Saʿd al-Dīn al-Taftāzānī.[13] We do know that he was born in Khurasān and may have been part of Tamerlane's circle before he fled west to Anatolia and then Greater Syria, looking for judgeships and rectorships.[14] Harawī was thus part of a moment of "mass exodus,"[15] when many scholars from Transoxania fled the chronic instability brought about by Tamerlane's military excursions.[16]

For some of Harawī's biographers, neither Harawī's appearance nor his facility with language was harmonious with Cairene society. According to the renowned Cairene historian Maqrīzī (d. 846/1442), who employed the term *ʿajam* polemically as a term for non-Arab in his writings, Harawī used to ride and walk the streets of Cairo with "the look of an *ʿajam,* wearing an open fur mantle (*farjiyya*) on his breast, and his turban had tassels drooping to his left. And he conducted himself in his coverings in a way improper for judges, with little knowledge of the parlance of the country (*muṣṭalaḥ al-balad*) or the customs of the people in Egypt (*ʿādāt al-nās bi-Miṣr*)."[17]

Maqrīzī took a personal fascination with Harawī's apparel, tracking the evolution of his costume over the course of his career: as chief justice, "he wore a *jubba* [a large gown or *thawb*], with a large turban with tassels drooping to his shoulders"; as the sultan's secretary (*kātib al-sirr*), he wore "a little ribbed round turban, losing the tassel and wearing a neckband around his neck," as was the style of the scribes.[18] Worse still was that Harawī began "dressing in gold silk," two materials that were so luxurious they were unbecoming of a scholar and, according to his own Shāfiʿī training, considered unlawful to wear.[19]

Despite Maqrīzī's horror with Harawī's crimes of fashion, another serious criticism was the fact that Harawī would not address the sultan directly, as was customary, but through a spokesperson, because of Harawī's lack of fluency in Arabic.[20] Maqrīzī wrote, "If he wanted to speak, it was with great difficulty. He began to talk a little, laboring greatly. Then he would speak incorrectly (*yatakallam bi-ʿujma*)."[21] Maqrīzī also reported that the sultan received an anonymous note that, in addition to criticizing Harawī's corrupt dealings, his relationship to Tamerlane, and his ignorance as a scholar, lampooned his knowledge of Arabic.

For other biographers, Harawī's looks were not disagreeable, only his accent. Ibn Ḥajar wrote that Harawī was "a portly shaykh, tall, with a white beard and handsome looking. But his language was halting."[22] Ibn Taghrībīrdī, who made remarks identical to Ibn Ḥajar's on Harawī's good looks, made similar comments as Maqrīzī regarding Harawī's linguistic abilities: "To be sure, [Harawī] did not know the Egyptian convention (al-iṣṭilāḥ al-miṣriyya) and was not fluent in Arabic discourse, as was typical for the non-Arabs (a'ājim)."[23] But Ibn Taghrībīrdī also sympathized with Harawī, testifying to the hostilities between the two groups at that time. He explained that Harawī was ineffective during his two terms as Shāfiʿī chief justice, "because of the disgust of the descendants of the Arabs (awlād al-ʿarab) toward him, as was often evident between the awlād al-ʿarab and the a'ājim."[24] But we should keep in mind that Ibn Taghrībīrdī was not without his own prejudices. Ibn Taghrībīrdī, of Anatolian origin, was himself ridiculed for being non-Arab and lacking eloquence in Arabic.[25] Moreover, Harawī was a friend of his father's.[26]

In preparing for his recitation and commentary of Ṣaḥīḥ al-Bukhārī at the citadel, Harawī gave his aged reading assistant, Shams al-Dīn al-Jibtī (d. 825/1422), a handwritten copy of a certificate (ijāza) authorizing him to recite the Ṣaḥīḥ to the audience, from beginning to end, documenting each link in the chain of transmission of the recitation of Ṣaḥīḥ al-Bukhārī from Harawī to the compiler, through the renowned and oft-referenced recitation of Abū al-Waqt.[27] Jibtī was expected to read out Harawī's chain of transmission from the certificate after the introductory supplicatory prayers had been uttered, prior to beginning the recitation and commentary proper. This practice was a key way commentators justified their authority to interpret Ṣaḥīḥ al-Bukhārī in the first place, and possessing a certificate was not merely a formality but might put one at a clear interpretive advantage over other commentators. Jibtī, who was learned in the sciences of the transmission of hadith, was certain Harawī must have fabricated it (ikhtalaqa fī al-ḥāl).[28]

A number of Jibtī's rivals, Ibn Ḥajar and Sakhāwī among them, collected a number of documents and reports of Harawī's chain of transmission (isnād) to Abū al-Waqt's recitation of the Ṣaḥīḥ, some which they were careful to state were jotted down in Harawī's own handwriting.[29] After careful examination, they conjectured that Harawī had added names of obscure transmitters with implausible ages or, in another case, had copied it directly from the introduction to the widely circulating commentary on Ṣaḥīḥ al-Bukhārī by Kirmānī. The insinuation was that Harawī, having read the commentary of Kirmānī on his own in manuscript form, deceptively authorized himself to transmit the recitation of Abū al-Waqt as if he had heard it from an authority, when he actually had not.

Jibtī was presented with a dilemma when he was handed Harawī's *isnād*. On the one hand, reciting Harawī's fraudulent chain of transmission would have devalued Jibtī's reputation as well as the currency of genuine certificates for a community that viewed them as guarantors of scholarly authority. On the other hand, Jibtī was hesitant to overstep the boundaries of his social status as a reading assistant to expose his superior outright in plain view of the sultan. To resolve the issue, Jibtī feigned that he forgot to bring the handwritten copy of Harawī's certificate to the commentary session, and he stated simply to the audience that he would be reciting "by a chain of transmission to *Ṣaḥīḥ al-Bukhārī*," leaving it ambiguous whose chain of transmission it was and whether the chain of transmission was genuine.[30] In this case, Jibtī struck a balance between social survival and a commitment to the standards of excellence in the practice of commentary.

In theory, the sultan and his chief justices would have been expected to attend each of Harawī's sessions at the citadel. In practice, however, al-Muʾayyad Shaykh was absent often enough that Ibn al-Mughulī broke with etiquette as well, playing hooky.[31] As with any ceremonial affair, the absences did not go unnoticed, and the sultan's private secretary, Naṣir al-Dīn al-Bārizī (d. 823/1420), inquired into the judge's truancy. The Ḥanbalī judge confessed to Bārizī that he despised Harawī and had nothing but contempt for Harawī's knowledge of hadith.[32] Recognizing, perhaps, that Harawī's perceived incompetence was trying the patience of such influential members of the court, Bārizī urged the sultan to allow Harawī's main rival, Jalāl al-Dīn al-Bulqīnī—a former Shāfiʿī chief justice whom the sultan had recently removed from power—to attend Harawī's commentary sessions in the citadel. This action persuaded Ibn al-Mughulī to return to the commentary session, but it also set the stage for the elderly and prolific Bulqīnī to plot a late-in-life comeback to retake the Shāfiʿī chief judgeship.[33]

Bulqīnī had been unhappy to learn of his dismissal from the judgeship, but he had been livid when he found out that his replacement was Harawī.[34] In contrast to Harawī, Bulqīnī was perceived by his colleagues as a genuine authority on *Ṣaḥīḥ al-Bukhārī*. He had authored various works on the science of authenticating hadith, including a commentary on Ibn al-Ṣalāḥ al-Shahrazūrī's (d. 643/1245) classic and comprehensive textbook *al-Muqaddima fī ʿulūm al-ḥadīth* (Introduction to the sciences of hadith). Bulqīnī was also praised for conserving, in a commentary of his own, helpful notes from Ibn al-Mulaqqin's commentary at the citadel during the latter half of the eighth/fourteenth century, especially on the transmitters of hadith, as well as for adding many insights that had not previously been included in works of commentary on *Ṣaḥīḥ al-Bukhārī*.[35] In addition to this, Bulqīnī had produced a widely read commentary on the chapter headings of *Ṣaḥīḥ al-Bukhārī*, an innovative genre whose pertinence to the craft of commentary was gaining much more respect among scholars and their audiences. By accepting Bārizī's invitation to attend the recitation and explanation of *Ṣaḥīḥ al-Bukhārī* during Ramadan and in such a politically important space—the citadel, in plain view of Cairo's political and judicial elite—Bulqīnī had found the perfect arena in which to challenge Harawī's authority for the most prestigious judgeship in the land.

According to Ibn Ḥajar's account, Bulqīnī sat right between Harawī and the Mālikī chief justice.[36] The sultan and the other chief justices would have been seated nearby. Ibn Ḥajar records that it was Bulqīnī's ally, Ibn al-Mughulī, a Ḥanbalī judge on the high court, who struck first, challenging Harawī in vigorous debate (*yujārīhi*) on technical points of law and hadith, leaving Harawī stuttering and speechless.[37] To fill the silence, he then defied Harawī by teaching the session concerning each hadith as it was read and reciting commentarial opinions from memory in a competitive fashion (*yataḥaddā bi-dhālika*).[38]

As a matador's sword follows the lance of the picador, Bulqīnī's interrogation followed his Ḥanbalī ally's. Bulqīnī pressed Harawī on problems and controversies raised by the hadith, drilling him on technical points and the responses and complexities raised by scholars on those points. Harawī was enraged and responded by shouting brashly.[39] Although Ibn Ḥajar did not record the content of their argument, his description nevertheless communicates a number of the standards of excellence that were at stake in the tradition. Among them, adhering to the best practices of authenticating hadith, applying legal reasoning properly, and demonstrating a mastery of past scholarly debates concerning hadith. Harawī, in Ibn Ḥajar's account, also failed to display a proficient memory, an understanding of the technical debates concerning hadith, and the ability for swift oratory in Arabic.

Apart from these standards of interpretive excellence, a number of social and material rewards were also stake, most notably, the most powerful judgeship in Mamluk Egypt. In Ibn Ḥajar's narrative, Bulqīnī had effectively exposed Harawī in full view of the sultan. Ibn Ḥajar reports that the sultan's leg had grown numb from sitting, so he withdrew to an upstairs area overlooking the commentary session, leaving no opportunity for Harawī to salvage his damaged reputation. Despite this, Harawī was not tossed out for another six months, but when he was finally sacked, Bulqīnī was reinstated as the Shāfiʿī chief justice.*

Harawī not only failed to meet the qualifications for a hadith scholar that had been defined and redefined by his contemporaries within the social practice of commentary, but he had also been accused of fabricating his credentials. That he nevertheless attained positions in which he was responsible for the instruction of knowledge is evidence that successful or underwhelming performances in oral competitions—as they were regulated by the standards of the hadith scholars—did not necessarily correlate with material rewards or sanctions.

However, Harawī's interpolation as a foreigner through markers of dress, habit, elocution, and scholarly networks did offer subtle advantages and disadvantages over the course of his scholarly career. He was not unique in this regard. Qimmanī, a scholar who was among the descendants of Arabs (*awlād al-ʿarab*), used his political connections to wrangle the consolation prize of a lucrative tax break, despite his shortcomings in the competitive scholarly scene.[40] The Harawī affair thus conveys a complicated story about the relationship between the basic qualifications of live performance, as defined by the hadith scholars, and the cultivation of political connections and social networks in the attainment of teaching and judicial appointments.

Michael Chamberlain has argued that the scholarly elite of the Mamluk period gained and traded in social capital in order to compete for academic appointments and the favor of the Mamluk military elite.[41] Anne Broadbridge has built on Chamberlain's observations to show how ʿAynī and Ibn Ḥajar "maneuvered for proximity to patrons and favorable material and financial rewards."[42] Yet the perceived winners of the live debate, according to standards constructed by the hadith scholars, were not always those who won material and social capital. The sultan's seemingly arbitrary power to appoint and dismiss judges—and the

* Al-Harawī's performance was so inadequate for Ibn Ḥajar that Ibn Ḥajar was surprised that it took a full six months for al-Harawī to be replaced. Ibn Ḥajar chronicled the other scholarly transgressions of al-Harawī during this six-month period: he was attacked for committing gross errors in his legal *responsa,* and he was again exposed by the other chief justices in the presence of the sultan for citing an invalid opinion and falsely attributing it to al-Thaʿlabī's *tafsīr.* See al-Sakhāwī, *al-Ḍawʾ al-lāmiʿ*, 4:108ff.; al-ʿAsqalānī, *Inbāʾ al-ghumr,* 7:310–11.

power of special relationships cultivated by certain scholars and social networks—would complicate any historically reductive explanation of the debates over *Ṣaḥīḥ al-Bukhārī* as merely sites for the exchange of social and social capital. Even the limited role played by regional displacement and culturally constructed ethnic identities conditioned the reception of certain interpreters in the live spaces in which their voices were heard and their bodies seen. In many cases, no amount of knowledge displayed in these sessions could be exchanged for material rewards or for mobility within a social structure.

IN THE SHADE OF THE SULTAN'S GARDEN

Up until this point, the anecdotes I have discussed provide a glimpse into the competitive environment in which premodern commentaries were first made public. I have also shed light on commentarial motives, the bases of commentarial authority, and commentators' relationships with their students, rivals, and patrons, all of which shaped the form and function of the commentary in fundamental ways. But did these live environments shape the explanation of a particular hadith in an explicit and direct way?

To answer this question, I will translate and analyze an account from a chronicle of Ibn Ḥajar's that tells of an impromptu commentary session in the intimate setting of the garden of the sultan al-Muʾayyad Shaykh. In this session, which took place well before the completion of *Fatḥ al-bārī*, Ibn Ḥajar offers commentary on a hadith found in *Ṣaḥīḥ al-Bukhārī* in part to discredit his rival for the sultan's favor. I will compare the autobiographical narrative of Ibn Ḥajar's impromptu live commentary with his explication of the same hadith found in his written commentary, *Fatḥ al-bārī*.

It was the heat of summer, Rabīʿ al-Ākhir 818 (June 1415), three years before Harawī's meltdown at the recitation session at the citadel. Harawī had just arrived at al-Muʾayyad Shaykh's court in Cairo. Aware that al-Muʾayyad Shaykh was vetting him for the high court judgeship, Harawī claimed that he had memorized the *Ṣaḥīḥ*s of Bukhārī and Muslim, in addition to twelve thousand hadith.[43] After a morning of raucous scholarly debate, Harawī, Ibn Ḥajar, al-Muʾayyad Shaykh, and others from the scholarly and judicial elite enjoyed sweets and fruit in the afternoon in a secluded part of the garden attached to the sultan's residence. A reciter incanted a phrase from the Qur'an, Sūrat al-Raʿd, verse 35: "the food of paradise is everlasting, as is its shade."[44] One scholar,

Nūr al-Dīn al-Talwānī,[45] wondered how there could be everlasting shade in paradise. "Shade cannot be without light," he reasoned, "and heaven has no sun or moon!"[46] Some of the scholars in attendance grappled with the puzzle, consulting authenticated hadith that mention otherworldly shade, especially a famous hadith mentioned in *Ṣaḥīḥ al-Bukhārī:* "There are seven kinds of people whom God will shade in his shade on the day when there is no shade but his shade."[47] The narrative continues:

> Ibn Ḥajar asked, "Is there anyone among you who remembers in addition to the seven, an eighth type of person?"
>
> They replied, "No."
>
> Ibn Ḥajar said, "Not even this one who claims that he memorized twelve thousand hadith?" He gestured to Harawī, who was silent.
>
> One of them said to him, "Have you memorized an eighth?"
>
> Ibn Ḥajar said, "Yes, I know an eighth and a ninth and a tenth. But more amazing than this is that in the *Ṣaḥīḥ* of Muslim—which Harawī claims to have memorized in its entirety—there is an eighth for the aforementioned seven."
>
> It was said to him, "Acquaint us with that hadith, so that we may derive benefit from it."
>
> Ibn Ḥajar replied, "This place is a proving ground, not a place of seeking benefit (*istifāda*). If you rearranged this to be a place of seeking benefit, then I would acquaint you with it."
>
> After that, Ibn Ḥajar collected what was mentioned on the subject and imparted more than ten in addition to the seven mentioned in the hadith. Abū Shāma versified the seven famous types in two famous lines of poetry. And Ibn Ḥajar collected seven more—mentioned with good chains of transmission—and versified them in two lines of poetry. Then he collected a third group of seven—while saying their chains of transmission—and versified them in two other lines of poetry.
>
> And the session broke for the evening prayer. When the scholars wanted to take off, Ibn Ḥajar said to the sultan, "Your eminence, I accuse Harawī of owing me a debt!"
>
> "What's that?" the sultan replied.
>
> "Twelve thousand hadith." The sultan smiled and left.[48]

This live lesson contained not only food but also humor and style. We can glimpse how Ibn Ḥajar might have interacted with his colleagues and students. From a sensual experience of tasting the food and enjoying the shade to the versification of chains of transmission, the conversation meandered through a variety of questions and multiple genres of texts. The ideal hadith scholar, modeled by Ibn Ḥajar, was expected to be so masterful he could play in the intertextuality of multiple genres of Islamic religious literature, moving from the Qur'an to a well-known hadith, then a less well known hadith, their chains of transmission, and finally to the extemporization of verse that might aid the memory of students and advance the circulation of these hadith.

While adeptness at poetry is not one of the explicit qualifications required of hadith scholars, such a skill was a marker of elite status, and handling such literary requests could have been understood to be an implicit part of the job of a hadith scholar. The movement from technical questions of hadith to poetry would thus not have been unusual for Ibn Ḥajar or the culture from which he emerged. The grandson of Shāh Walī Allāh, Shāh ʿAbd al-ʿAzīz al-Dihlawī (d. 1239/1824), recalled a correspondence in which Ibn Ḥajar was asked a question about the trustworthiness of an *isnād* in verse, and Ibn Ḥajar responded spontaneously in verse, describing the *isnād* and grading it in poetic meter. Again, the spontaneity of his response highlighted his memory and facility with language.[49] Ibn Ḥajar was not unprecedented in this skill. Shams al-Dīn al-Mawṣilī (d. 774/1372), a Shāfiʿī scholar of the generation prior to Ibn Ḥajar's, composed verse on the authenticity of the hadith contained in an abridgment of Qāḍī ʿIyāḍ's (d. 544/1149) popular compilation *Mashāriq al-anwār* (The source of light).[50]

While Ibn Ḥajar's autobiography is well known for its dry, impersonal, and, at times, self-deprecatory narrative of his study of hadith, this passage is anything but.[51] Ibn Ḥajar's punch line to the sultan about the debt he was owed was meant to malign Harawī's trustworthiness. But it would be the sultan who ultimately paid the debt. Al-Muʾayyad Shaykh instructed his private secretary to reinstate Ibn Ḥajar as the shaykh at the Baybarsiyya, since Ibn Ḥajar had earlier been ousted by another rival "who wrongly wrested it away from him."[52] Ibn Ḥajar's successful live performance was thus linked to his winning of a prestigious judgeship.

That Ibn Ḥajar won an appointment returns us to the commentarial dialectic we observed first among the Andalusian commentators and then among the early Mamluk commentators. When Ibn Ḥajar was asked to prove his own memory, he said that he would not recite and transmit hadith in an examination setting, but only if the setting was one of students seeking benefit (*istifāda*). For Ibn Ḥajar, one ought not recite hadith for the sake of showing off or passing a test, even if it may appear he was doing exactly that, but only in the service of explaining the Prophet's guidance to the community. Just as Ibn Ḥajar was dialectically bound by the need to interpret *Ṣaḥīḥ al-Bukhārī* endlessly and the need to complete his commentary, he was likewise bound to compete for appointments while explicitly refusing to compete for them.

I initially hypothesized that there would be no evidence for a direct correlation between the intimate garden session and the content of *Fatḥ al-bārī*. The genre constraints of a systematic written commentary, I assumed, focused on explicating the biographies of the transmitters, grammatical questions, and legal matters. A written commentary, after all, is supposed to be a timeless encounter with a hadith, insulated from mundane local events, even if commentaries are structured by those events in fundamental ways. Studying a written commentary might equip one for a live contest in the garden, but not the other way around.

However, upon consulting *Fatḥ al-bārī,* I found, to my surprise, that Ibn Ḥajar retold the story of the garden session in his commentary on the same hadith. The hadith's *matn* and part of Ibn Ḥajar's commentary are translated here:

> [There are] seven [kinds of people whom] God will shade in His shade on the day when there is no shade but His shade:
>
> [1] A just imam.
> [2] A youth raised worshipping his lord.
> [3] A person whose heart is attached to places of prayer.
> [4] Two people who love one another for the sake of God, meeting and parting for the sake of that [love].
> [5] A man who is pursued by a woman of nobility and beauty, and states [in refusal] "I fear God."
> [6] A person who gives charity, concealing it so that his left hand knows not what his right hand spends.
> [7] A person who remembers God in seclusion and his eyes overflow with tears.[53]

Ibn Ḥajar comments:

> [After a discussion of the narrator and variants]
>
> [al-Bukhārī's] statement: "Seven"
>
> Its apparent meaning is the singling-out of the aforementioned seven with the aforementioned reward.
>
> Regarding that reward which was obtained, [the commentator] al-Kirmānī addressed the concept of obedience, either in service to God or in service to human beings.
>
> The former is by the tongue through "the one who remembers (*al-dhākir*)"; by the heart and that is "the one attached to the places of worship"; by the body, and that is the "youth raised worshipping his lord."
>
> The latter is, at a general level, [performed by] the "just [imam]." At an individual level, [it is performed] by the heart, which is "loving [another for God's sake] or [performed] through [expenditure of] money, which is "charity"; or [performed] by the body, which is "chastity (*al-ʿiffa*)."

The learned Abū Shāma ʿAbd al-Raḥmān ibn Ismāʿīl [d. 665/1266] put the seven into verse, according to what Abū Isḥāq al-Tanūkhī recited to us on the certified authority of Abū al-Hudā, Aḥmad ibn Abī Shāma, who heard on the authority of his father in his phrasing saying:

Said the Prophet chosen by God, there are seven
whom the Generous God will shelter in His shade

a loving friend, a chaste man, a youth, a charitable person
a weeper, one who prays, and the imam in his justice

Located in the hadith of Abū al-Yasar in the *Ṣaḥīḥ* of Muslim [ibn al-Ḥajjāj] by a chain of transmission attributed to the Prophet (*marfūʿ*) is "Whosoever provides [financial] aid to the hard-up, or writes off a debt, God will shelter him in His shade on the day in which there is no shade but His shade." And these two attributes are not included in the previous seven. This is evidence that the number is not to be understood in the literal sense.

And I tossed this issue to the scholar Shams al-Dīn ibn ʿAṭāʾ al-Rāzī, known as al-Harawī, when he came to Cairo and alleged that he had memorized the *Ṣaḥīḥ* of Muslim. I asked him in the presence of the sovereign al-Muʾayyad on this matter and other [attributes that lead to God's shade] but he did not recall anything. After that, I sought, one after another, the aforementioned hadith that were similar in [listing other attributes that make a person worthy of God's shade], and it exceeded ten attributes. Among those I selected seven reported by excellent chains of transmission, and versified them into couplets supplementing Abū Shāma. They are:

add to the seven: shading a war hero and aiding him
and granting a reprieve to the hard-up and lightening his load

and aiding a debtor, and supporting a slave working to free himself
and the merchant who is honest in words and deeds[54]

Manuscript evidence indicates that in later versions, Ibn Ḥajar returned to this passage to add more material, quipping a second verse and citing a hadith transmitted by Abū Hurayra with a weak chain of transmission.[55] Ibn Ḥajar found and grouped another set of seven, versified another couplet, and yet another. The final couplet, Ibn Ḥajar noted, is sourced in weak hadith. Lastly, he added, "I mentioned all of these in *al-Amālī,* and I sectioned it off in a part which I titled, 'Knowledge of the Attributes Leading to the Shade.'"[56]

Prior to comparing these two versions of the garden session, I would first like to reiterate how rarely a live event made its way into the explication of a hadith in Ibn Ḥajar's *Fatḥ al-bārī.* The stated impetus for Ibn Ḥajar's explication of this hadith was his rival's coming to Cairo and alleging the authority to comment in the presence of the sultan. Ibn Ḥajar explicitly mentioned not only the name of his rival but also that of his own patron. The competition between Ibn Ḥajar and Harawī, in the presence of the sultan in Cairo, thus explicitly and directly changed the way this hadith was explicated for scholars and students of hadith over time.

A comparison between these two accounts illuminates some key differences between the chronicle genre and the commentary genre. While Ibn Ḥajar's chronicle offers drama, humor, colloquialisms, and references to food, the commentary is, by comparison, rather dry. Even mention of the garden and the time of day are omitted. Harawī and al-Muʾayyad Shaykh are there, but peripherally. Gone is the sensory, the taste of the food and the relief of the shade that inspired the intellectual curiosity of the students. Gone is the test, the competition for powerful appointment, and gone is the smile of the sultan, who apparently got the joke.

While much is lost in the translation from history to commentary, much is also gained. Ibn Ḥajar offered a summary of Kirmānī's commentary on the hadith, as well as Abū Shāma's couplet versifying it, by a chain of transmission to the poetry. We also hear the exact couplets he formulated, their chains of transmission, and the grades of the chains' authenticity, all of which he omitted in the chronicle. The commentary account is still intertextual, but its intertextuality is reoriented: while the verse from the Qur'an that supposedly sparked this debate has been left out, in its place we find attention devoted to the commentarial work of Kirmānī.

What this comparison brings into greatest relief, however, is a commentator's engagement with the hadith's exegetical history, a different causal, spatial, and temporal order, with thoroughly different stakes. In the written commentary, Ibn Ḥajar critiqued commentators who might read the seven to be saved on the Day of Resurrection as a limit: there were literally no more than the seven kinds stipulated in the hadith. The seven types are intended to be moral exemplars: a chaste man, a just ruler, one who prays, and so on. The fact that Ibn Ḥajar offered an explanation for the hadith that extends the possible number of attributes was not only meant to display the superiority of his memory in a competitive environment where an appointment was at stake but was also meant to open up the canon (indeed, it opened up heaven!) for present and future students justifiably concerned about who will be sheltered on the Day of Resurrection. Drawing on his memory, Ibn Ḥajar showed that many other kinds of people beyond the seven will be sheltered: a war hero, an honest merchant, a benevolent lender, and many others. In other words, this hadith's interpretation was not only about the power struggles among scholars over who will be appointed the most powerful chief justice in Egypt. It was also entangled in a debate over norms definable only in relation to the traditional practice of commentary that are no less pressing: on what basis can one determine how many kinds of people will be protected on the Day of Resurrection?

This explanation greatly influenced other Islamic texts, affecting commentaries on other collections of hadith and spawning its own literary genre. Jalāl al-Dīn al-Suyūṭī would go on to quote Ibn Ḥajar's *Fatḥ al-bārī* verbatim regarding Harawī in his commentary on the hadith that contained the attributes leading to God's shade in his commentary on another famous compilation, the *Muwaṭṭaʾ* (The well-trodden path) of Anas ibn Mālik.[57] Moreover, Suyūṭī then wrote a book, *al-Khiṣāl al-mūjibah lil-ẓilāl* (The traits needed for the shade), in which he collected seventy such attributes, later abridging it.[58] He later had to defend himself from the accusation of stealing material from Sakhāwī, who had collected eighty such attributes.[59] Even the twentieth-century South Asian commentator and glossator Muḥammad Zakariyyā al-Kāndhlawī (d. 1982) continued to summarize these growing lists of attributes, although he no longer felt required to mention Ibn Ḥajar's initial interaction with Harawī in the presence of the sultan.[60] Through his interpretation of this hadith, Ibn Ḥajar thus provided an avenue for future generations of scholars to overcome the limits set by the canon.

Does this comparison clarify what Ibn Ḥajar meant when he stated to Harawī and his colleagues, "This place is a proving ground, not a place of seeking benefit"? Ibn Ḥajar may have been invoking the commentarial dialectic that pits commentary to gain a social reward against commentary to realize an interpretive aim—getting a teaching or judicial appointment versus extending the applied meaning of the Prophet's legacy for the benefit of present and future audiences.

Yet the production of this dialectic itself is entangled in the politics of commentary. Ibn Ḥajar can be read as a social critic in so far as he excoriated the fact that right-intending and benefit-oriented hadith commentators were not always those who were appointed by the sultan. According to Ibn Ḥajar, this was partly because individuals who were not practitioners of commentary controlled the appointment of commentators and could take matters external to the traditional practice of commentary into consideration when making an appointment.

Even if, or especially if, this anecdote is skewed in favor of Ibn Ḥajar's own interests, it tells us that the construction of the hadith commentator in this period was far more complex than we previously understood it to be. It was not only built on his collection of quantitatively documented credentials, such as reading certificates (*ijāzas*). It was also intertwined with his cultivation of political networks and his ability to persuade a living and easily divided inexpert audience who witnessed live debates of *Ṣaḥīḥ al-Bukhārī* and read written explications of its meaning.

. . .

In the preceding chapters, I made use of sources that might offer a snapshot of the day-to-day times, spaces, actors, and institutions that shaped and were shaped by the process of commentary. Indeed, the site of commentarial authority was not relegated to the quiet surfaces of the written commentary but was performed by living people in the limits of space and time. The medium of the written commentary—its length, form, and rhetorical strategies—reflected and inflected the times and spaces in which commentaries could be performed live for audiences. The competition we observe in commentarial writings, such as quarrels over unattributed borrowing, can often be linked to the reality that patrons and rivals would be present in the live sessions.

Since live sessions conspicuously displayed these commentators' regional identities through marked differences in dress, elocution, and training, the construction of regional, social, and cultural identity may also play a larger role in the construction of interpretive authority than previously assumed. After all, the migration of scholars—for both the rewards of study, prestige, and appointments and the protection offered by political asylum—often brought scholars from diverse regions of origin to the shared space of the hadith commentary.

Possessing a good memory is not linked to a particular region or a culturally constructed ethnicity. This quality is, at least in theory, open to anyone willing to cultivate the art of memory. But it was not the possession of memory alone upon which commentarial authority relied. Commentators needed to be able to transmit and display their memory to an audience of patrons, rivals, and students, in contexts in which audiences had specific culturally constructed expectations of how one's memory ought to be displayed. Hadith commentators were thus expected to thrive in a live environment in addition to composing written texts.

And yet the social practice of hadith commentary could not have only been a site in which commentators' bold personalities clashed in competition over patrons, prestigious appointments, and circulation among transregional audiences. If that were so, it would reduce the arguments over the explication of hadith to mere quarrels over power and material wealth and would diminish our understanding of why hadith were worth arguing about in the first place.

To that end, this chapter showed that realizing interpretive ends, such as deriving benefit (*istifāda*) from hadith, was also at stake in this social practice. The excellence of extending the legal or theological application of *Ṣaḥīḥ al-Bukhārī* for present and future audiences, while contingent on power or social capital, is not reducible to it. These kinds of excellences can only be defined and attained by the performance of excellence as it would have been recognized within the living practice of commentary itself. After all, commentators' ability to give more persuasive explications of *Ṣaḥīḥ al-Bukhārī*, a text that made normative claims on the audiences who heard them, could, alongside other discursive and non-discursive motivators, work to shape how audiences chose to act.

To take this one step further, interpretive excellences were defined in relation to a wholly different conception of time and space than they would be in a historical chronicle. This conception of time, an exegetical history, foregrounded people, texts, and ideas who never encountered one another in a live lesson in the sultan's garden on a sunny afternoon. In this way, commentary on *Ṣaḥīḥ al-Bukhārī* was not merely a proving ground for the superiority of memory, but a reason-giving practice, a debate about the text's normative claims on a community that stretched across time and space, one that was circumscribed by legal and theological institutions, but also helped to constitute them.

CHAPTER 6

Gatekeepers of the Law

Before the Law stands a gatekeeper . . .

—Franz Kafka

In a lecture delivered in 1970, Foucault attempted to describe the way in which discourses of knowledge are ordered. One principle he observed was that "none shall enter the order of discourse if he does not satisfy certain requirements or if he is not, from the outset, qualified to do so."[1] Foucault referred to this principle as *raréfaction,* in which "societies of discourse" circulate texts and ideas "in a closed space, distributing them only according to strict rules."[2] Historically, only after absorption of these strict rules through prolonged apprenticeship with a master would a student learn the "secret" that the text concealed and thus become initiated into the group.[3] What is so harrowing about Kafka's short story "Before the Law," quoted in the epigraph, is that the gatekeeper to the law, an authority with a "black Tartar beard," never grants the desperate seeker admission.[4] It is the principle of raréfaction run amok.

The first part of this chapter examines the way in which Ibn Ḥajar's and ʿAynī's disparate intellectual genealogies admitted them into these closed "societies of discourse" and justified their authority to comment on hadith and to contemplate their legal implications. In doing so, it illustrates the way that the mastery and deployment of intellectual techniques and the achievement of interpretive excellences could intersect with the competition over social and material rewards. In the second part of this chapter, I revisit a case study we examined in part 1 of this book: a hadith on discretionary punishment (*taʿzīr*) contained, among other places, in *Ṣaḥīḥ al-Bukhārī.*

LICENSE TO COMMENT: SCHOLARLY AND TEXTUAL GENEALOGIES

Shāfiʿīs' interest in obtaining reading certificates and knowledge of the chains of transmission of hadith and canonical collections was not merely to attain prestige or appointments.[5] It was also rooted in the promise that such training would yield a stronger explication of hadith relative to one's predecessors and rivals within the tradition.

Nawawī, a Shāfiʿī, was the first commentator to emphasize the importance of knowledge of the chain of transmission as both a license and a technique with which to explain *Ṣaḥīḥ al-Bukhārī.* Nawawī included a lengthy prolegomenon surveying the sciences of authenticating hadith in order to cultivate in his students and readers an appreciation for the function of chains of transmission. He then repeated the chain of transmission between himself and, in his opinion, the most reliable transmission of *Ṣaḥīḥ al-Bukhārī.* Two degrees separated Nawawī from a chain of transmitters that included a well-known transmitter named Abū al-Waqt, who himself was separated by two degrees from Bukhārī's close student Firabrī.[6] Nawawī described this chain of transmission as the most famous in Syria and went on to quote Firabrī himself, who boasted, "among the ninety thousand men who had heard *Ṣaḥīḥ al-Bukhārī,* there was none who could match me in narrating it."[7] For Nawawī, explaining the chain of transmission did not merely enhance his prestige as a commentator. It also provided him with an interpretive tool that could explain the hadith contained therein in ways earlier commentators could not. Moreover, if Nawawī could help students understand how Bukhārī had guaranteed the authenticity of each hadith in the *Ṣaḥīḥ,* perhaps the normative authority of the *Ṣaḥīḥ* would be elevated.

While Ibn Ḥajar affirmed his predecessors' opinion that Firabrī was the most reliable, he found the boast that Firabrī was peerless among "the ninety thousand men" to be baseless.[8] Rather than rest his genealogy solely on one transmission, Ibn Ḥajar claimed to invent something new in the presentation of his genealogy: prior to beginning his commentary, he presented every single chain of transmission, by certification (*ijāza*) or audition (*samāʿ*), between himself and Bukhārī.[9] The result was a mammoth genealogical tree, naming over 150 Muslim scholars involved in four major branches and many smaller branches of transmitters between Bukhārī and himself.[10] In selecting a chain of transmission he generally favored over others, Ibn Ḥajar looked past Abū al-Waqt's chain of transmission that Nawawī had relied on in favor of Abū Dharr's, which was transmitted directly on the authority of not one but three of Firabrī's students.[11]

While Ibn Ḥajar claimed to have invented something new with respect to documenting his genealogy to *Ṣaḥīḥ al-Bukhārī*, there were precedents in the scholarship on other canonical collections. For example, Ibn Khaldūn's lectures on Mālik's *Muwaṭṭa'* included a highly detailed description of his numerous links to what had been considered, by his contemporaries' consensus, the most reliable chain of the transmission of the *Muwaṭṭa'*.[12] Whether or not Ibn Ḥajar modeled his own genealogical display on Ibn Khaldūn's, Ibn Ḥajar was still unique in treating *Ṣaḥīḥ al-Bukhārī* in this way. That Ibn Ḥajar departed from the tradition in favor of a more meticulous way of preserving the multiple chains of transmission to *Ṣaḥīḥ al-Bukhārī* demonstrates that innovations and challenges to the commentary tradition could be justified during this period as long as they persuasively served the greater good of preserving *Ṣaḥīḥ al-Bukhārī*.

Ibn Ḥajar sought to hear the complete text from so many scholars for more than prestige or blessings (*baraka*). His greater knowledge of other transmissions placed him in a better position to recognize a number of textual variations or corruptions that emerged as scholars transmitted Bukhārī's text. Variations among transmissions of *Ṣaḥīḥ al-Bukhārī* were so common that copyists employed standardized abbreviations to mark disagreements among the well-known recitations in the margins as they copied the text by hand.[13] Still, audiences would have been left wondering which reading was preferred, and Ibn Ḥajar's scholarly genealogy thus enhanced his ability to derive benefit from the collection.

To take one example, we can examine Ibn Ḥajar's commentarial discussion of the chain of transmission of the first hadith in *Ṣaḥīḥ al-Bukhārī*, which begins "actions are by intentions." While the consensus of the majority of recitations states that the hadith "was narrated to us by (*ḥaddathanā*) Yaḥyā ibn Sa'īd,"[14] Abū Dharr remembers that the hadith was stated "on the authority of (*'an*) Yaḥyā ibn Sa'īd." This is a technical difference, but an important one: most hadith scholars consider *'an* to be a less authoritative mode of transmission than *ḥaddathanā*. Some of the commentators Ibn Ḥajar cited argue that Bukhārī intentionally chose to begin his collection with this particular chain of transmission because of the absence of "*'an*," while others argue that Bukhārī had wanted to begin his work with a chain of transmission that included every possible mode (*ʿan, ḥaddathanā,* "reported to us" [*akhbaranā*] and "heard" [*samāʿ*]) to instruct students that all modes were authoritative. Even though Abū Dharr was the outlier, Ibn Ḥajar preferred it over the others, and thus he used his knowledge of the various chains of transmission to settle the point.[15] Moreover, Ibn Ḥajar's inclusion of the recitation of Abū Dharr limited the explaining power of those among his contemporaries who did not have as direct access to it.

While the Mālikīs and Shāfiʿīs played a formative role in commenting on *Ṣaḥīḥ al-Bukhārī* from the fourth to the seventh centuries (tenth to thirteenth CE), Ḥanafīs were relative latecomers. They began studying and commenting on *Ṣaḥīḥ al-Bukhārī* in earnest in the eighth/fourteenth century, with unfinished commentaries begun by Quṭb al-Dīn al-Ḥalabī (d. 735/1335)[16] and ʿAlāʾ al-Dīn ʿAbd Allāh al-Mughulṭāy (d. 762/1361),[17] but even then, some Ḥanafīs could barely veil their "contempt for transmission-based scholars."[18]

While ʿAynī followed Ibn Ḥajar's lead by including a scholarly genealogy of the transmission of the *Ṣaḥīḥ* between himself and Bukhārī in the introduction to *ʿUmdat al-qārī,* students of Ibn Ḥajar would have noticed right away that ʿAynī had heard far fewer narrations of the work.[19] Moreover, ʿAynī was missing the recitation that Ibn Ḥajar set apart from the rest, the recitation from Abū Dharr on the authority of three of Firabrī's closest students.[20] The fact that ʿAynī was compelled to "borrow" Nawawī's introduction wholesale indicated that Ḥanafī sources on *Ṣaḥīḥ al-Bukhārī* and the science of authenticating hadith were lacking.[21]

Differences between ʿAynī and Ibn Ḥajar and their respective training could also be found in the weight they accorded to certain kinds of evidence and sources. Commentators' fluency with the privileged interpretive techniques of their respective schools signaled the authority of their opinions not only through the prestige they derived by their affiliation with a legal school but also because their legal school offered unique strengths in explicating hadith relative to their rivals.

For example, ʿAynī and Ibn Ḥajar took different approaches when trying to make explicit what they believed was the implied meaning (*ithbāt al-muqtaḍā*) of a hadith. While both consulted variant hadith or Qur'anic verses, as well as the rhetorical sciences (*balāghah*), both schools tended to weigh some sources over others. Consistent with his general attempt to explain hadith by referencing other hadith (*sharḥ al-ḥadīth bi'l-ḥadīth*), Ibn Ḥajar preferred to research how an ambiguous phrase or term was employed in other hadith to clarify what meaning was implied.[22] Meanwhile, ʿAynī claimed expertise in rhetoric and language, reserving sections of his commentary to discuss each of the three major subfields of eloquence (*bayān*), "notions" or "motifs" (*maʿānī*), and embellishment of style (*badīʿ*).

In spite of these clear departures in training, we should, however, be cautious about drawing too sharp a boundary around legal identity. Of course, legal polemics flared up at numerous traditional flash points, such as the permission of usury, the permissibility of legal loopholes (*ḥiyal*), the proper pronouncement of supplicatory formulae (*bismillah, taṣbīḥ*), and others.[23] But while it may have been relevant for the elite commentators of the Mamluk court, historian Yossef Rapoport has argued that, for the Mamluk era, "there is practically no evidence of factional partisanship along school lines outside the community of legal practitioners."[24] Going further, he argued that "[judges] were not community leaders nor were they appointed as representatives of social groups; their main obligation was to apply their school's doctrine."[25] It was also not unheard of for some judges to change their legal affiliation.[26]

Moreover, as *Ṣaḥīḥ al-Bukhārī* came to be revered symbolically and recognized as an authoritative source for hadith across the legal schools, so came the need for commentary that appealed to the concerns of multiple schools of law. This is not to say that there was "prejudice against prejudice" such as that which theorist Georg Gadamer saw in ascendance in Enlightenment Europe.[27] However, a commentary could be discredited if it was perceived to be too partial to a single legal school, not least because it alienated opponents in competing schools. Ibn Baṭṭāl's commentary on *Ṣaḥīḥ al-Bukhārī* was perceived to be inadequate in this regard, and Kirmānī took him to task for overly asserting the Mālikī position.[28] Likewise, Ibn Ḥajar critiqued Ibn Rajab al-Ḥanbalī's commentary on *Ṣaḥīḥ al-Bukhārī* for expressing excessive zeal (*al-taʿaṣṣub*) for the Ḥanbalī position.[29] Ibn Ḥajar himself would later suffer the criticism that his interpretations were overly favorable to Shāfiʿī opinions by a number of Ḥanafī scholars in modern South Asia.

While these kinds of criticisms may have served to bolster enduring feuds between legal schools, they may have also pushed commentators to contemplate the proper balance between their broadening commentarial readership and the idiosyncrasies of their legal school's approach. To that end, as Norman Calder has pointed out in the case of Nawawī's commentary on the *Ṣaḥīḥ* of Muslim ibn al-Ḥajjāj (d. 261/875), commentators sometimes employed subtler methods to bend the meaning of the hadith in favor of their legal school's opinions even as they addressed broader audiences.[30]

Thus far I have argued that a commentator's scholarly genealogy and legal training were factors in establishing their authority to explain hadith. They were not the only such factors but, as I have shown in previous chapters, two among many at work in the complex social and intellectual matrix of Mamluk scholarly culture. But I have also suggested throughout that genealogy and legal training were factors that both freed and constrained how Muslim scholars exercised their authority to interpret hadith on issues of law. To better illustrate this latter proposition, we will now examine a case study of commentarial reception on a controversial hadith with legal implications.

DISCRETIONARY PUNISHMENT, REVISITED

We first examined the reception of a hadith on discretionary punishment (*ta'zīr*) among the early Andalusian commentators in part 1 of this book. Its reception now bears reexamination within the Mamluk commentarial context. While the Andalusian hadith scholar Aṣīlī could counsel his readers to disregard the hadith on the basis of its chain of transmission's unreliability and its content's incompatibility with companion reports—which were used in bolstering his school's position—*Ṣaḥīḥ al-Bukhārī*'s stature in the Mamluk period left representatives of multiple schools unable to deny, in the final analysis, the hadith's reliability. Jonathan Brown recounts the following warning issued by Ibn Ḥajar to scholars who sought to discount hadith on the basis of their content rather than on the trustworthiness of their chains of transmission: "For if people open that door to rejecting *ḥadīth*s it would be claimed that many *ḥadīth*s from the *Ṣaḥīḥayn* [Bukhārī's and Muslim's *Ṣaḥīḥ*] were false, but God most high and the believers have refused to let this happen."[31] Ibn Ḥajar, according to Brown, suggested that scholars must instead "try to reconcile this material and not dismiss it."[32] In other words, these Mamluk-era commentators would have to devise strategies that maintained the authority of the hadith while subtly bringing the meaning of the text into line with their own normative commitments. At the same time, we also begin to see discontent from some quarters with those who accorded too much authority to rarified juristic opinions.

One final note of caution before we proceed. Readers may be tempted to draw a causal relationship between commentarial discussion of judicial discretion to the enactment of judicial discretion. But the

Mamluk-era appointment of four chief justices not only in Cairo but also in other cities in the sultanate permitted each school to remain internally consistent and predictable in their legal rulings while allowing for some modicum of flexibility in rulings. The case of discretionary punishment (*taʿzīr*) illustrates this point: the Mamluk political elite were reported to have "frequently referred cases requiring discretionary punishment (*taʿzīr*) to Mālikī" judges.[33] Moreover, the Shāfiʿī jurist Tāj al-Dīn al-Subkī (d. 771/1370) was reported to have approved of such a practice, even though his own school placed greater restrictions on judicial discretion.[34] Nevertheless, this case still has a great deal to teach us about how commentators justified their authority to comment and how they exercised that authority within the arena of commentarial debate.

We will begin with Ibn Ḥajar's commentary on the hadith that claimed the Prophet had said that "one ought not be lashed in excess of ten lashes except in the case of a *ḥadd* among the *ḥudūd* of God."[35] While the early Andalusian commentator Ibn Baṭṭāl began with a discussion of the legal benefits, Ibn Ḥajar began with a discussion of Bukhārī's chapter heading, followed by an extremely detailed discussion of the reliability of the chains of transmission and their transmitters and debates concerning their authenticity. This in part reflects Ibn Ḥajar's greater interest and training in chains of transmission.

After Ibn Ḥajar compared the chains of transmission in *Ṣaḥīḥ al-Bukhārī* to six other chains of transmission from the *Mustakhraj* of Abū Bakr Aḥmad al-Ismāʿīlī (d. 371/981–82),[36] he summarized the gist of the debate, which circled around the following contradiction, among others: one chain of transmission in *Ṣaḥīḥ al-Bukhārī* recalled that the Prophet made the statement within earshot of a transmitter named Abū Burda, who relayed it to another transmitter named Ibn Jābir. A second chain was transmitted that did not recall whom Ibn Jābir heard the hadith from. A third chain of transmission maintained that the Prophet made the statement in front of Abū Burda, who first relayed it to Ibn Jābir's father, Jābir, who then relayed it to Ibn Jābir:

1. Ibn Jābir ← Abū Burda ← Muhammad
2. Ibn Jābir ← Unknown ← Muhammad
3. Ibn Jābir ← Jābir ← Abū Burda ← Muhammad

The hadith scholar known for evaluating the chains of transmission in canonical collections, ʿAlī ibn ʿUmar al-Dāraquṭnī (d. 385/995), favored the first chain of transmission, while many other hadith scholars continued to favor the third chain.[37]

Aṣīlī, if you recall, some four centuries earlier, judged the hadith's chain of transmission as too inconsistent to be used as a source of law (see tables 1 and 2). Ibn Ḥajar did not have that luxury. Instead, he rebuffed Aṣīlī by appealing to the status of Bukhārī and Muslim as guarantors of authenticity: "the two shaykhs [i.e., Bukhārī and Muslim] agreed on its soundness, and they are the pillar of soundness (*al-ʿumdā fī al-taṣḥīḥ*)."[38] For Ibn Ḥajar, the only uncertainty hinged on whether Ibn Jābir was trustworthy (*thiqa*). But since both Bukhārī and Muslim included him in their collections, the hadith was declared to be "sound" (*ṣaḥīḥ*). In any event, it was not impossible, according to Ibn Ḥajar, that Ibn Jābir could have heard the hadith in one phrasing directly from Abū Burda and then heard it with a slightly different phrasing on the authority of his father. In this way, both chains could be accurate, and the disagreements among the hadith critics would in no way undermine the soundness of the hadith and, by extension, of Bukhārī's and Muslim's *Ṣaḥīḥ*.*

While Ibn al-Mulaqqin, a Shāfiʿī jurist in Cairo who preceded Ibn Ḥajar with a commentary on *Ṣaḥīḥ al-Bukhārī* of his own, recorded an overview of the hadith's chain of transmission, he mainly compiled a list of other collections in which the same or similar hadith appears and by what chains of transmission it appears in those collections.[39] But Ibn al-Mulaqqin provided no final analysis of his own on the reliability of the hadith, as Ibn Ḥajar later did.

Having dispensed with any concerns his audiences may have had regarding the hadith's reliability, Ibn Ḥajar then turned to addressing any ambiguities in the meaning of the hadith. Rather than focusing on the issue of the precise number of lashes, as Ibn Baṭṭāl did, Ibn Ḥajar

* Another Shāfiʿī commentator of the period, Muḥammad ibn ʿAbd al-Dāʾim al-Birmāwī (d. 831/1428) chose to limit his discussion to the *isnād*, and he urged the reader to consult a work of law (*fiqh*) if curious about the legal technicalities of *taʿzīr*. He stated that the fact that there was a companion who was unknown (*ibhām*) does not detract from the authenticity of the hadith, since (a) the companions are assumed to be trustworthy, and (b) it is likely that Abū Burda is the identity of the unknown companion. The reason that Bukhārī has two chains of transmission, one linking Abū Burda directly to ʿAbd Raḥmān and one linking him to ʿAbd Raḥmān via Jābir (ʿAbd Raḥmān's father), was because ʿAbd Raḥmān genuinely heard it both from his father and from Abū Burda. Birmāwī cited no authorities to ground his opinions, and he acknowledged no debate over the *isnād*'s authenticity. Muḥammad ibn ʿAbd al-Dāʾim al-Birmāwī, *al-Lāmiʿ al-ṣaḥīḥ bi-sharḥ al-Jāmiʿ al-ṣaḥīḥ*, Garrett Collection MS 2372Yq, Princeton Univerity Library, no fol. (Kitāb al-Muḥāribīn min ahl al-kufr wa-ridda: Bāb Kam al-taʿzīr wa'l-adab).

instead addressed the definition of the *ḥudūd* (s. *ḥadd*) in the phrasing of the hadith. According to Ibn Ḥajar, its apparent meaning (*ẓāhiruhu*) was the technical one employed by jurists to describe penalties for the offenses against God specified in the Qur'an. This technical meaning was itself the subject of debate, and Ibn Ḥajar enumerates Ibn Ḥazm's dissent on the status of certain crimes without explicitly naming him.[40]

In writing his exegetical history of this hadith, Ibn Ḥajar preserves a debate over the meaning of the term *ḥudūd* that had erupted between the iconoclastic Ḥanbalī scholar Ibn Taymiyya and one of Ibn Ḥajar's predecessors as chief justice of the Shāfiʿī school, Ibn Daqīq al-ʿĪd (d. 702/1302). Ibn Daqīq al-ʿĪd argued in favor of what he said was the hadith's "apparent" meaning: a judge could only authorize punishments with more than ten lashes but only in cases of the *ḥudūd,* understood to be the short list of penalties expressly stipulated in the Qur'an. Ibn Taymiyya, however, held that Ibn Daqīq al-ʿĪd's "apparent" meaning backprojected a definition of *ḥudūd* that had been constructed by later jurists (*fuqahāʾ*) rather than the meaning the Prophet originally intended.[41] What the Prophet meant by *ḥudūd,* he contended, was anything forbidden by God (*ḥurumāt*) or any disobedience (*maʿṣiya*) regarding the law, great or small.

What had appeared as a continuity over time for Ibn Daqīq al-ʿĪd and his predecessors was represented as a discontinuity by Ibn Taymiyya. On this originalist position, only those acts that are not expressly associated with disobedience to God are limited by the ten lashes hadith. For instance, a father could not discipline a misbehaving child in excess of ten lashes.[42] In this way, even a judge who saw the ten lashes hadith as an authentic source of law could, like the Mālikīs, sentence the offender in excess of ten lashes, as long as the act fell broadly into the category of that which was forbidden by God.

When clarifying an ambiguity in a hadith, Ḥanbalīs, like the Shāfiʿīs, preferred to cite prooftexts from the Qur'an and hadith. Ibn Taymiyya thus chose to draw on four prooftexts from the Qur'an (2:229, 65:1, 2:187, and 4:14) in order to bolster his broader definition of the *ḥudūd.* In order to defend Ibn Daqīq al-ʿĪd—and by extension, the Shāfiʿī school—Ibn Ḥajar curiously took the grammatical approach rather than return with another volley of prooftexts. Supporting Ibn Daqīq al-ʿĪd, Ibn Ḥajar pointed out that the hadith's meaning rests on an implied understanding (*taqdīr*) that it is possible to distinguish between different kinds of disobedience (*maʿṣiya*), greater and lesser (*kabīra* and *ṣaghīra,* respectively). The greater, for Ibn Ḥajar, was the exception that can exceed ten as stipulated by Qur'anic prooftexts.[43] If the definition of the *ḥudūd* were extended to include all manner of offenses against God, both greater and lesser, it would obviate the need for the exception in the ten lashes hadith in the first place, since, in the two Shāfiʿīs' opinion, there are no criminal offenses outside of those two categories.[44] In other words, it would make the exception the rule.

The disagreement between the two Shāfiʿīs and the two Ḥanbalīs demonstrates that even for scholars who took the "no more than ten lashes" hadith to be an authentic source of law, interpretive resources were available to expand the power of the jurists to authorize severe or even lethal sentences for a broad number of crimes. Nevertheless, Ibn Daqīq al-ʿĪd and Ibn Ḥajar chose a more restricted reading of the text that was consistent with the opinions of their legal school.

As I stated earlier, the Mamluk context was one in which the political elite were reported to have "frequently referred cases requiring discretionary punishment (*taʿzīr*) to Mālikī" judges, knowing that Mālikīs would be at greater liberty to authorize severe sentences, even the death penalty.[45] Ibn Ḥajar's critique of the Mālikī-trained jurists' practice is palpable, as he concludes with a quote from a Mālikī judge named Abū Jaʿfar al-Dāwūdī (d. ca. sixth/twelfth century).[46] Dāwūdī was often reported to have held that the hadith never reached Mālik and, as a consequence, Mālik viewed non-*ḥadd* offenses to be at the judge's discretion.[47] Ibn Ḥajar, however, expanded on Dāwūdī's statement to suggest that had the hadith of "no more than ten lashes" reached Mālik, Mālik would have turned away from his initial opinion and be required to act on its basis.[48] The Mālikī's liberal discretion, as Ibn Ḥajar would have it, was grounded neither in the hadith nor in the thinking of Mālik himself.

While ʿAynī may have used other moments in his commentary to attack Ibn Ḥajar and polemicize against the Shāfiʿī position, the discussion of discretionary punishment does not appear to be one of them. Although one can certainly find opinions of some Shāfiʿīs siding with Ḥanbalīs by favoring a limit of ten, and some Ḥanafīs siding with Mālikīs by favoring an unlimited number, most of the Shāfiʿīs and Ḥanafīs can be found somewhere in the middle: the number can exceed ten in some instances, but it should not exceed the lowest number stipulated for a *ḥadd* offense. Nevertheless, ʿAynī's exegetical history of the hadith closes with the Ḥanafī opinion articulated by al-Ṭaḥāwī (d. 321/933): the imām has the power to deliver severe or more lenient sentences according to his best judgment (*ijtihād*).[49] While ʿAynī had ruled expressly against his own school in favor of the apparent meaning of a hadith in other forums, in this case, he sided with his school.[50]

Otherwise, ʿAynī's commentary was largely in agreement with Ibn Ḥajar's. ʿAynī did not delve into the sciences of rhetoric as he did earlier in his commentary. In fact, he did not contribute any analysis or opinion genuinely his own. When ʿAynī states "my opinion is (*qultu*)," he simply delivers an unattributed summary of Ibn Ḥajar's opinion, even preserving much of Ibn Ḥajar's phrasing: "ʿAbd al-Raḥmān is trustworthy (*thiqa*). . . . The two shaykhs [i.e., Bukhārī and Muslim] agreed on its soundness, and they are the pillar concerning the sound (*al-ʿumdā fī al-ṣaḥīḥ*)."[51] Likewise, regarding the debate over the definition of *ḥadd,* ʿAynī offered an unattributed summary of Ibn Ḥajar's discussion of Ibn Daqīq al-ʿĪd and Ibn Taymiyya, omitting any of their names and framing their opinions under the speculative "it is said (*qīl*)."[52]

One notable difference is that the second wave of early Andalusian commentators had a larger voice in the layers of ʿAynī's *ʿUmdat al-qāri* than they did in Ibn Ḥajar's *Fatḥ al-bārī.*[53] ʿAynī deployed Dāwūdī as earlier commentators had deployed him: simply to state that the hadith under discussion never reached Mālik and nothing more.[54] These choices are more likely an accidental product of ʿAynī's compositional process than a deliberate emphasis on early Mālikī scholarship on *Ṣaḥīḥ al-Bukhārī.* ʿAynī likely borrowed from a commentary on *Ṣaḥīḥ al-Bukhārī* that had been influenced by Mālikī sources, probably Mughulṭāy's. Since the " no more than ten lashes" hadith is located in the final third of *Ṣaḥīḥ al-Bukhārī,* which many commentators left unfinished, contributing new material would have required great ingenuity on the part of anyone who aspired to do so. Yet, as we will see in part 3, ʿAynī's *ʿUmdat al-qārī* did not need to be ingenious to be revived as the reference of choice among certain circles of Deobandi hadith scholars in early modern and modern South Asia. Many of these students sought the comfort of a commentator who identified as Ḥanafī over one who identified as Shāfiʿī.

• • •

To return to the metaphor of Kafka's gatekeeper, what permitted one to stand guard to the door of the hadith corpus in the Mamluk period? To be sure, there was a diversity of informal markers of one's bona fides—including one's memory, one's ability as an orator, and one's proximity to patronage—but I have also illustrated how a commentator's disciplined mastery of and genealogical connection to a canonical collection became an important prerequisite to commentary in the late Mamluk era. Moreover, a subtler marker of authority was a commentator's conspicuous mastery of the rarified rules and procedures of a given legal approach. For Ibn Ḥajar, a Shāfiʿī, knowledge of the chains of transmission informed his link to the *Ṣaḥīḥ* as well as his legal approach to it. For ʿAynī, a Ḥanafī, his expertise in the sciences of rhetoric was, for his students, qualification enough.

But commentators' genealogies as hadith scholars and training as jurists were not merely symbolic credentials, intended to rarify knowledge and exclude certain people from access to it. Their training also played a role, within the complex social and intellectual matrix of the Mamluk scholarly scene, in shaping the way commentators interpreted canonical collections and the hadith contained therein. The case of discretionary punishment is an illustrative example. In that case, both Ibn Ḥajar and ʿAynī framed and reframed the exegetical history of the hadith to affirm the opinions of their respective legal schools. Moreover, Ibn Ḥajar marshaled his training as a hadith scholar to bolster his case.

In a counterpoint offered by the iconoclastic scholar Ibn Taymiyya, we observed what might be called a challenge to scholastic *raréfaction* in favor of what he claimed was the hadith's original meaning. The stakes were life and death, at least in theory, as Ibn Taymiyya's broader interpretation of the hadith authorized judges to approve of far more severe sentencing, even capital punishment. While Ibn Ḥajar's commentary quickly dispensed with Ibn Taymiyya's opinion, the overall challenge to the orthodoxy of the traditional legal schools in shaping the interpretation of hadith would resurface among vocal reformers during the early modern period in the Middle East and South Asia, as we will see as we return to this case study in part 3.

In every generation since they were first collected, certain hadith contained in collections such as *Ṣaḥīḥ al-Bukhārī* have posed legal, theological, political, or ethical challenges to certain constituents of Muslims. In each period, some Muslim thinkers have turned to the science of transmitters (*ʿilm al-rijāl*) to exclude or cast doubt on a hadith they opposed on moral or political grounds. For hadith scholars, however, the use of this science in such a way was (and remains) frowned upon. The task, then, for Mamluk-era commentators, was a double movement: to maintain the authority of *Ṣaḥīḥ al-Bukhārī* as a guarantor of authentic hadith, while simultaneously reconciling the meaning of controversial hadith with the multiple and sometimes conflicting needs of their present. Whether they succeeded or failed has not been my primary concern. Rather, I have been trying to uncover the kinds of intellectual resources they marshaled in undertaking this intricate two-step.

In that vein, the chapter that follows explores the development of a distinctive interpretive strategy that rarified knowledge but also functioned in the service of this exegetical double movement. This extraordinary method brought commentators and their audiences to the very thresholds of the text.

CHAPTER 7

Mysteries of the Thresholds

Rather than a boundary or a sealed border,
the paratext is a *threshold.*

—Gérard Genette

Ṣaḥīḥ al-Bukhārī is divided into roughly a hundred topical books which are themselves subdivided by thousands of topical chapter headings (*abwāb*) under which Bukhārī arranged hadith in no predictable order. In many books, these chapters contain just one or two hadith. Chapter headings can reference phrases from other hadith or Qur'anic verses, or they can address legal and theological issues. Sometimes the same hadith, or a variant of it, appears in multiple chapter headings. Strangely, it is sometimes unclear what relationship there is between the hadith and the chapter headings under which they are contained. Stranger still are those chapter headings that contain no hadith at all.

Literary theorists and textual scholars in the West have taken an interest in analyses of chapter headings, titles, and other paratextual elements for some time. In his book on the subject, *Seuils* (Thresholds), Gérard Genette wrote that paratexts constituted "a zone between text and off-text, a zone not only of transition but of transaction: a privileged place of pragmatics and strategy, of an influence on the public that—whether well or poorly understood and achieved—is at the service of a better reception for the text and a more pertinent reading of it (more pertinent, of course, in the eyes of the author and his allies)."[1]

Rather than conceiving of titles as a perfunctory border or the last barrier a reader must past to get to the content of the book, Genette argues that titles, headings, or "paratexts" play an important role in the way a book is interpreted. They are thresholds (*seuils*), strategically crafted by an author or an editor to shape a readers' understanding on their way in, around, and out of the text.

The analogy of a threshold is particularly apt for our discussion of Bukhārī's chapter headings, or *abwāb*. In Arabic, *abwāb* can mean "chapters," "titles," or "rubrics," but it can also mean "doors," "gateways," or "thresholds." Moreover, resonating with Genette's notion of the paratextual threshold as a place of transaction, "a privileged place of pragmatics and strategy," some Mamluk-era commentators argued that Bukhārī's chapter headings promised the disclosure of the "secret essence" (*sirr kawn*) of *Ṣaḥīḥ al-Bukhārī*.

While many early Andalusian commentators viewed these chapter headings as an example of deficiencies in need of correction, Mamluk-era commentators found in them an opportunity to claim to be faithful to Bukhārī's compilatory goal (*qaṣd*) while simultaneously deriving contemporary meanings from the text. These commentators came to access the compiler's intentions by parsing the relationship of the headings to one another, to the hadith categorized under them, to the abbreviation (*ikhtiṣār*) of certain hadith, and to the repetition (*tikrār*) and placement of certain hadith under them.

Ignaz Goldziher offered one of the earliest and most enduring accounts of these "thresholds."[2] He briefly evaluated the specific function of the *Ṣaḥīḥ*'s chapter headings, inferring that the headings were relevant to interpretation from the outset and that they functioned to serve Bukhārī's own editorial interests.[3] Then, citing the transmitted opinions of Muslim scholars, Goldziher posited that Bukhārī composed his chapter headings first, and then filled in the relevant hadith later.[4] He argued that the fact that some chapter headings were left without any hadith listed under them served as proof of this theory. For Goldziher, the chapter headings "afford Bukhārī ample opportunity to mold the opinion of the reader towards his view on the practical application of the particular hadith."[5] In some cases, this limited commentators' interpretations.[6] But in many other cases, it created new opportunities for commentators to subtly marshal what they believed were Bukhārī's intentions in the service of their and their audiences' interests.

To this end, rather than attending to what Bukhārī himself may have meant by his chapter headings, as previous studies have done, I will focus on what interpretive value later commentators and their audiences accorded to them.[7] In doing so, I will argue that including Bukhārī's chapter headings as objects of analysis limited, on the one hand, the number of people qualified to interpret the meaning of the text as well as the freedom with which commentators had in revising it. On the other hand, the inclusion of the headings also created new ways in which commentators could achieve certain interpretive excellences and acquire certain social and material rewards. By analyzing the chapter headings, they could at once affirm their own prestige, expand their authority over the compilation, and bring the text's meaning and symbolism closer into line with their communities' legal and theological commitments.

A LOOK BACK: EARLY COMMENTARY ON THE THRESHOLDS

As we observed in part 1 of this book, the documentary record in the first two centuries following *Ṣaḥīḥ al-Bukhārī*'s compilation suggests that the value of interpreting the *Ṣaḥīḥ*'s chapter headings was, at the most, a contested one. Even for those who thought it was a valuable interpretive technique, the question of whether Bukhārī's intention (*qaṣd*) was fully expressed in these "thresholds" or required the alterations of an expert remained an open question.

Early hadith scholars from Central Asia like al-Khaṭṭābī (d. 388/996) of Bust or Abū Bakr Aḥmad al-Ismāʿīlī (d. 371/981–2) of Jurjān expressed confusion about the link between the hadith and the chapter headings under which Bukhārī had organized them, and took the liberty of altering the arrangement of Bukhārī's text.[8] For example, failing to understand the connection between the first hadith, "actions are by intentions," and its heading, "How Revelation Began," both hadith scholars declared that Bukhārī had originally intended the hadith to be a preface. This opinion allowed them to resituate the hadith on intention prior to its chapter heading rather than as the first hadith under that heading. A lack of textual uniformity among recitations and codices in this early period may partly explain the extent to which these scholars felt free to exercise such editorial discretion.[9] It is important to note, however, that they were not choosing between multiple variants of the text, but adding one of their own, and in a conspicuous place.

This is not to say that Khaṭṭābī and Ismāʿīlī discounted Bukhārī's compilatory aims. Rather, the text of the *Ṣaḥīḥ*, as they inherited it, was left unfinished. Thus an expert was required to make the necessary modifications to fully realize the compiler's aim. These modifications served to clarify the text to its earliest students, as well as to strengthen the consistency of the text in the face of attacks from sectarian opponents.[10] Yet, as we saw in the example above, and as we will see in examples to come, Khaṭṭābī exhibited a subtle interpretive reliance and concern with *Ṣaḥīḥ al-Bukhārī*'s framework, as well as with other issues unrelated to sectarian disputes. Since, as Tokatly notes, Khaṭṭābī was writing during a time in which it was not necessary to expound on the chapter headings to the same degree of detail as later commentators, it may be significant that Khaṭṭābī bothered referencing or relying on the titles at all.

As we saw in part 1, for Andalusian scholars, Mālik's *Muwaṭṭa*ʾ held a higher station, and it was Bukhārī's methods of authentication rather than the text of his compilation that was valued.[11] These scholars were thus operating in an environment in which textual uniformity was looser, and they felt at some liberty to modify the text in certain cases. When encountering a chapter heading that lacked hadith under it, Córdoban scholar Ibn Baṭṭāl glossed over the lacuna by linking the heading with the one that followed it, altering the received transmission of *Ṣaḥīḥ al-Bukhārī* by treating the two as if they were one.[12] At the same time, however, Ibn Baṭṭāl began offering some notes and reflections on the relationship between the chapter headings and the meaning of the hadith.[13]

Ibn Baṭṭāl's teacher, Muhallab ibn Abī Ṣufra, subtly relied on Bukhārī's organization of hadith under the headings to devise new justifications to maintain the orthodoxy of the Mālikī position. But Muhallab, in other parts of his commentary, openly took Bukhārī to task for placing a hadith under a heading that did not provide any evidence for that heading.[14] Like Khaṭṭābī, however, neither Muhallab nor Ibn Baṭṭāl offered a systematic method for analyzing the chapter headings, which would earn them the rebuke of later observers.[15]

The record in the first two centuries following *Ṣaḥīḥ al-Bukhārī*'s compilation suggests that the value of interpreting the Bukhārī's chapter headings was, at most, a contested one. Even for those who thought it was a valuable interpretive technique, the question of whether Bukhārī's goal (*qaṣd*) was fully expressed in the chapter headings remained in doubt. Some experts went as far as to make alterations in the text, because they believed it to be required to fully realize the compiler's original aims. As *Ṣaḥīḥ al-Bukhārī*'s canonical status deepened in the Mamluk period, readers' reception of the *Ṣaḥīḥ*'s headings became a subject worthy of contemplation, which, in turn, contributed to the process of canonization itself.

THE RISE OF ESOTERIC READINGS OF BUKHĀRĪ'S CHAPTER HEADINGS

By the seventh/thirteenth century, Nawawī legitimated the chapter headings as an analyzable feature of *Ṣaḥīḥ al-Bukhārī* by presenting an overview of them in the introduction to his unfinished commentary on the work. Nawawī's interest in these "thresholds" may be traced to his earlier commentary on another highly ranked compilation of hadith from the third/ninth century, *Ṣaḥīḥ Muslim*. The compiler of that work, Muslim ibn al-Ḥajjāj (d. 261/875), in contrast to Bukhārī, originally transmitted it without any chapter headings. Nawawī thought chapter headings could illuminate the meaning or legal importance of the hadith, so he added his own, and then commented on them.[16] As an indication of their popularity, many of Nawawī's chapter headings were later circulated in copies of Muslim's *Ṣaḥīḥ* without explicit attribution to Nawawī's commentary, as if they were part of the original text. Likewise, Nawawī divided his popular compilation of hadith, *Riyāḍ al-Ṣāliḥīn* (Gardens of the righteous), and each strategically titled chapter served as a shorthand reference for a hadith's interpretation.

With respect to *Ṣaḥīḥ al-Bukhārī*, Nawawī emphasized the chapter headings' reflection of the compiler's goal to guide readers in the use of the *Ṣaḥīḥ* as a legal reference, and he neglected to include opinions that might contradict that or show that analyzing the Bukhārī's headings was ever a disputed issue.[17] Marshaling Bukhārī's chapter headings as evidence, Nawawī simply stated that "no one can come close to matching [Bukhārī] in precision of hadith and his derivation of subtleties of law."[18] Considering the depth of the controversy on this matter, the omission of any objections was surely deliberate.

The Alexandrian Nāṣir al-Dīn Ibn al-Munayyir (d. 683/1284), a Mālikī jurist, went one step further than Nawawī, a contemporary of his. Ibn al-Munayyir was among the first to recognize that the ambiguities and disputes over Bukhārī's titles were not a problem to be edited out or glossed over, but rather an opportunity to justify and expand the role of the contemporary interpreter as mediator between the text and the community. In the introduction to his commentary, *al-Mutawārī ʿalā Abwāb al-Bukhārī* (The concealed through Bukhārī's thresholds), the earliest surviving work devoted specifically to explaining

Bukhārī's chapter headings, Ibn al-Munayyir laid out an argument for his interpretive authority over several pages, prior to making even one mention of Bukhārī or his compilation. In highly stylized prose, Ibn al-Munayyir narrated a history of Islamic revelation that necessitated that the door of further elaboration of Islamic law (*sharīʿa*) be "open to our era." He continued: "Thus God makes [those] worthy of [the *sharīʿa*] in each age, upholding in its affairs, as a treasurer to its secrets. They disseminate its jewels, and they clarify its inner and outer meanings. They treat the disorders of each field (*faṣl*) [of law] with the precise wisdom connected with that field [of law]."[19]

Pushing against the idea that only the early generations following Muhammad could discover new benefit from the sources of Islamic law, Ibn al-Munayyir argued that in each age there is an enduring task to fulfill. Moreover, while modern readers might consider preservation, clarification, and distinction as a barrier to intellectual innovation, Ibn al-Munayyir presented these activities as the key to the secrets of Islamic law.

To address the concerns of those in his legal school who might have disagreed with him, he pointed to an oft-quoted (if misattributed) opinion of Mālik ibn Anas that states that judges ought to adapt rulings in light of changing circumstances.[20] This can be found with slightly different wording in Mālik's *Muwaṭṭaʾ*: "Fatwas (legal *responsa*) have to be brought about for people according to what immoralities they invented" ("tuḥdathu lil-nās fatāwā bi-qadr mā aḥdathū min al-fujūr").* Ibn al-Munayyir then related his lengthy preamble to the task of explaining *Ṣaḥīḥ al-Bukhārī*: "The goal of this introduction is [to say] that when Imām Abū ʿAbd Allāh Muḥammad ibn Ismāʿīl al-Bukhārī placed in his book the law (*fiqh*) that the chapter headings contained, and he adorned the necklaces in those chapters with jewels of meaning . . . useful points from those goals rose to the surface. [Some] useful points remained hidden, and confusion [arose] concerning what was concealed, so [there are] those who circle around [without understanding] or flee [from difficulty]."[21]

In the context of the introduction and the quote from Mālik, it is clear that Ibn al-Munayyir thought that contemporary interpretive authorities still had an active role to play in negotiating between Bukhārī's text and its meaning for the community in two ways. First,

* I translate *aḥdathū* as "they invented" since Ibn al-Munayyir seems to suggest that the quote can be used as a prooftext to encourage new rulings and is an indication of the principle of *al-maṣāliḥ al-mursala*. Even though it is not phrased as a command to students, Ibn al-Munayyir reads the quote as if it were a command-less proverb with jussive force, such as "the early bird catches the worm."

scholars discerned between the apparent and the esoteric meanings of the text. Second, scholars made sense of the esoteric meanings for their own era. In fact, according to Ibn al-Munayyir, some of the justifications for Bukhārī's chapter titles could not be fully understood until the arrival of a new era.

For Ibn al-Munayyir, the case of the palm pith (*jummār*) is but one illustrative example of this disclosure of Bukhārī's titles over time. Ibn al-Munayyir argued that even though a chapter heading legislating the permissibility of eating and selling *jummār* would have been obvious to the point of redundancy in Bukhārī's own era, he speculated that Bukhārī had foreseen that a debate about its permissibility could have arisen in a later era, so he included the chapter heading for future readers. Sure enough, Ibn al-Munayyir observed that a debate among his contemporaries had emerged concerning the permissibility of *jummār*'s sale and consumption.[22] He wrote, "when I pored over a chapter heading of Bukhārī, its miracle (*karāma*) appeared to me after some three hundred years, may God have mercy on him."[23]

Another function of the chapter headings, which he listed later in his introduction, further exemplifies this idiosyncratic commitment to new rulings: if a heading and a hadith appear to blatantly contradict each other, Bukhārī is merely highlighting that the issue is open to debate and requires the exertion of jurists' independent reasoning with reference to the foundational sources (*ijtihād*).[24]

Like Nawawī, he assumed that Bukhārī's chapter headings were laden with intentional meanings. Unlike Nawawī, and a step further into esotericism, he assumed that Bukhārī intended some of his titles' meanings to be kept secret from a lay reader and even from some misguided experts. While Nawawī edited out any misgivings by his predecessors, Ibn al-Munayyir acknowledged that past scholars had expressed doubts about the meaning of these "thresholds." Summarizing the reception history of the titles up to his time, he wrote, "Some say [Bukhārī] passed away and did not polish the book and did not organize the chapters. Some say deficiencies [in the chapters] were introduced by the copyists and their hastiness and [by] the transmitters and their corruption. Some say [Bukhārī] missed the mark in legal derivation (*istidlāl*)."[25]

Ibn al-Munayyir's impressions of the early commentators are consistent with my observations of the Andalusian commentators in part 1. These early commentators held that the chapter headings were probably arbitrary, and even if they were intentional, they did not merit interpretation. After rehearsing fellow Mālikī jurist Abū al-Walīd al-Bājī's disparagement of the interpretation of Bukhārī's chapter headings at length, Ibn al-Munayyir adduced just one citation to counter the long history of opposition to interpretation of the chapter headings: a short quote from his grandfather, Manṣūr ibn Abī al-Qāṣim, who held that "two books whose *fiqh* are in their chapter headings are Bukhārī's book on hadith, and Sībawayh's book on grammar."[26] Thus the opposing view was dismissed.

In the context of a canonical culture that revered Bukhārī and his collection, a short quip may have been more than adequate to vanquish the opinions of early commentators on the *Ṣaḥīḥ*. Alternatively, Ibn al-Munayyir's scholarly reputation may have been enough to legitimize his method, since he was described by a contemporary as one of the two scholars of whom Egypt could be proud.[27] Judging from the ornate vocabulary with which he decorated his introduction and from his dexterity with puns, we may also comfortably view him as a skilled belletrist among the jurists of his period.

One possible attraction for students of Ibn al-Munayyir's approach was access to esoteric knowledge. At the close of his introduction, he described Bukhārī's chapter headings as the "secret essence" (*sirr kawn*) of *Ṣaḥīḥ al-Bukhārī*.[28] In the midst of commenting, he often reminded readers of his promise to instruct them in the chapter headings' "hidden meaning" (*al-ramz al-khafī*).[29] The possibility of disclosing concealed knowledge became a recurring theme in the social practice of commentary on the *Ṣaḥīḥ*. Commentators did not, however, promise esoteric knowledge of God or of the Prophet's inspiration. Instead, they offered backstage access to the hadith scholar's craft. With expertise in hadith, law, and theology, Ibn al-Munayyir must have appeared perfectly positioned to grant students access to this kind of hidden knowledge.

Beyond justifying his authority to explain *Ṣaḥīḥ al-Bukhārī*, Ibn al-Munayyir exercised this technique, the disclosure of the chapter headings' secrets, to advance an Ashʿarī theological reading of the *Ṣaḥīḥ*.[30] The chapter headings, in their ambiguity, are particularly well suited for such an end.[31] For instance, his Ashʿarī position on the hotly debated divine attributes becomes apparent in his reading of titles from Bukhārī's "Book of Unity (*tawḥīd*)" that contain Qur'anic verses that reference those attributes, including Qur'an 51:58, 20:39, and 54:14.[32]

Another example is his discussion of the relationship between the first hadith, "actions are by intentions," and its chapter heading, "How Revelation Began." Ibn al-Munayyir implied that Bukhārī was suggesting that the Prophet's revelation was contingent on God having endowed him with sincere intention. According to Ibn al-Munayyir, this refutes the position that Muhammad earned his own prophethood, a belief he attributed to some Muslim philosophers and certain Neoplatonic Sufi orders. Such a belief stands in particular opposition to the Ashʿarī school's conception of the divine will and determinism.[33]

One final example of Ibn al-Munayyir's theological readings of Bukhārī's chapter headings occurs in his discussion of a hadith contained in the "Book of Pilgrimage." The heading referenced a Qur'anic verse that said, "God made the Kaʿba a sacred house, as an enduring support for humankind (*qiyām^an lil-nās*)"[34] paired with a hadith that foretold its destruction by "one who has little stick-legs from Ethiopia."[35] Why did God tell his community that he created the Kaʿba as an enduring place of safety while simultaneously disclosing to his messenger that the Kaʿba would one day be destroyed? Ibn al-Munayyir explained, using the determinist language of a committed Ashʿarī theologian, that God had made the Kaʿba to be a place of safety "during the time which he willed." If God willed, he could allow it to be destroyed during the time "of the little stick-legged one," and, if he so willed, return it to humanity.[36] In this way, the problem was resolved in a way that served Ibn al-Munayyir's theological commitments.

In sum, while Ibn al-Munayyir honored *Ṣaḥīḥ al-Bukhārī* as a complete work in which the compiler's intentions were worthy of contemplation, he was not restricted by his reverence. On the contrary, the very technique that he developed to explain the compiler's original intentions opened new possibilities for contemporary interpretation.

Other scholars followed in Ibn al-Munayyir's footsteps, bringing his work to the orthodoxy of the Mamluk court. Ibn Jamāʿa (d. 733/1333), the successor to Ibn Daqīq al-ʿĪd (d. 702/1302) as Shāfiʿī chief justice in Cairo, composed a work on the chapter headings of *Ṣaḥīḥ al-Bukhārī*. Following Ibn al-Munayyir, he refuted some anonymous opinions that, according to him, ignorantly dismissed the meaning of those ambiguous chapter headings that had resulted from textual corruption as the work was copied and transmitted. Moreover, like Ibn al-Munayyir, he went on to outline a number of legal functions that the chapter headings fulfilled.[37]

One exception proves the rule. A scholar from the Islamic West, Ibn Rushayd al-Sabtī of Cueta (d. 721/1321) remained more cautious than Ibn al-Munayyir with respect to the pertinence of Bukhārī's chapter headings but nevertheless devoted a work solely to understanding them. He wrote, concerning the first hadith, "actions are by intention," that "too much has been made of the relationship between the chapter heading and the hadith, and every [commentator] offers an opinion based on his own perspective."[38] While he may have agreed with earlier commentators who cast doubt on the possibility of understanding the chapter headings, he did not follow them in taking the liberty of altering the text of *Ṣaḥīḥ al-Bukhārī* in order to make it appear more coherent.[39] A shift in the canonical culture surrounding the text had closed it off from such radical modifications.

DOING JUSTICE TO THE COMMENTARY

Exemplifying the broad appeal of attending to Bukhārī's chapter headings in the latter part of the eighth/fourteenth centuries, Ibn ʿUrwa al-Zaknūn (d. 837/1434), a Damascene Ḥanbalī, in his eighty-five volume commentary on the *Musnad* of Ibn Ḥanbal, explicitly rearranged the *Musnad* in accordance with the chapter headings of Bukhārī's *Ṣaḥīḥ*.[40] Without a large comparative study, it is not possible to describe what kind of interpretation of Bukhārī's titles Zaknūn's reorganization represents. Nevertheless, it indicates a determined effort to standardize other hadith scholars' compilations not only by Bukhārī's criteria of authenticity, as Jonathan Brown has demonstrated, but also by his chapter headings.

The rocketing importance of the chapter headings is attested in another anecdote from the latter part of the eighth/fourteenth century. Ibn Khaldūn, the renowned historian from the Islamic West, crystallized the demand for expertise on the matter of Bukhārī's titles in a rare description of the necessary qualifications of a commentator on the *Ṣaḥīḥ:* "Regarding Bukhārī['s *Ṣaḥīḥ*], the highest ranked [among hadith compilations], people found it difficult to explain and [they found] its manner ambiguous, since they lacked [the requisite] knowledge of its numerous chains (*ṭuruq*) and its transmitters (*rijāl*) from the people of the Ḥijāz, Syria, and Iraq, as well as knowledge of their statuses and the differences of scholarly opinion about them. Moreover they needed the utmost comprehension in his chapter headings (*tarājim*)."[41]

Ibn Khaldūn went on a lengthy excursus on this final prerequisite unique to interpreters of the *Ṣaḥīḥ:* "utmost comprehension" of Bukhārī's chapter headings. In particular, they needed to be able to understand Bukhārī's inclusion of chapter headings without hadith and apparent contradictions between some chapter headings and those chapters' contents. Ibn Khaldūn devoted more time and space to the importance of understanding Bukhārī's chapter headings than to any other qualification, detailing at length the purpose and method of such an interpretation, as well as the source of his own instruction in this method.[42] One could not have, according to him, "done justice to the commentary" without it.[43] Again, this view represents a marked change since the early reception history of *Ṣaḥīḥ al-Bukhārī,* when early commentators from Andalusia were doubtful of what could be made of the chapter headings. Nearly five centuries after the text's compilation, interpretation of Bukhārī's chapter headings had come to serve as the sine qua non of authoritative commentaries on it.

One example to which Ibn Khaldūn drew his audience's attention is the one we examined earlier in the context of Ibn al-Munayyir's approach: the hadith that foretold the Kaʿba's destruction linked, by Bukhārī, to a Qur'anic verse that guaranteed the Kaʿba's protection.[44] What could Bukhārī have meant by linking these two statements? While Ibn al-Munayyir saw this as God's power to will as he pleases, an expression of Ashʿarī theological determinism, the solution Ibn Khaldūn learned from his teachers was different. Bukhārī, according to Ibn Khaldūn, intended the Qur'anic verse to mean that God made the Kaʿba a place of safety by law rather than by divine decree. The latter is fixed, but the former is a command that can be transgressed, including by a "stick-legged one." Thus, he explained, Bukhārī included the chapter heading to instruct a student on this distinction, and, presumably, the obligation of Muslims to keep the Kaʿba safe.[45]

Ibn Khaldūn's perspective is particularly revealing because he was not writing as a practicing commentator on *Ṣaḥīḥ al-Bukhārī,* but as a historian with a peripheral interest in commentaries on the *Ṣaḥīḥ.* His lessons on interpreting Bukhārī's chapter headings were taught to him in Fez by his teacher, Abū Barakāt al-Ballafīqī (d. 771/1370),[46] who had studied *Ṣaḥīḥ al-Bukhārī* at the foot of the Andalusian judge Abū ʿAbd Allāh Ibn Bakr (d. 741/1340).[47] These were learned scholars, but neither was a commentator with an enduring written work on the *Ṣaḥīḥ.* Perhaps for this reason, as his editor and translator Franz Rosenthal points out, Ibn Khaldūn may have even misremembered some of the details of his teachers' lesson.[48] Nevertheless, we find Ibn Khaldūn's student, Ibn Ḥajar, arriving at a similar opinion on a corresponding puzzle in his magnum opus, as it was composed decades later. Whether or not Ibn Khaldūn relayed their lessons accurately, they still attest to the rise of scholarly interest in Bukhārī's chapter headings, even for those on the periphery of the field.

Ibn Ḥajar came closest to addressing Ibn Khaldūn's demand for scholars to better explain Bukhārī's chapter headings. In fact, for Ibn Ḥajar,

Bukhārī's collection was not only the most authoritative source of hadith, but it also served as an authoritative hadith commentary. That is, Bukhārī's chapter headings, and his choices in arrangement, abbreviation, and repetition, serve to frame, critique, and comment on the hadith contained in the *Ṣaḥīḥ*. While the Andalusian scholar Ibn Ḥazm preferred the *Ṣaḥīḥ* of Muslim ibn al-Ḥajjāj over Bukhārī's, in part because Bukhārī's chapter headings created interpretive problems, Ibn Ḥajar preferred Bukhārī's over Muslim's, in part because of the intellectual challenge posed by the headings.[49] By including the chapter headings as the key to understanding the hadith contained in *Ṣaḥīḥ al-Bukhārī*, Ibn Ḥajar enshrined this once marginal exegetical technique as a part of mainstream Sunni thought.

According to Ibn Ḥajar, the first major function of an ambiguous chapter heading was to sharpen the intellect—and here he echoed Ibn al-Munayyir—by encouraging one to uncover hidden meanings in the text.[50] The other functions that Ibn Ḥajar listed largely treat issues of legal interpretation. For Ibn Ḥajar, an ambiguous heading allowed Bukhārī to suspend judgment and leave a ruling as an open question. It could also explain an ambiguous hadith in a profitable way or could be explained by an ambiguous hadith in a profitable way.[51] Additionally, Ibn Ḥajar observed several functions of an unambiguous chapter heading. A chapter heading on the surface may seem unambiguous but may bear a subtle meaning when one reflects on its relationship to the hadith under it.[52] A chapter heading may also refute an opponent's position, break a reader's assumptions, or provide a judicial ruling.[53]

For Ibn Ḥajar, rearranging a chapter heading or altering it, as early commentators unknowingly or knowingly did, significantly altered Bukhārī's intended meaning. This is why Ibn Ḥajar, following Ibn al-Munayyir, expressed frustration at commentators who hypothesized that Bukhārī did not finish his *Ṣaḥīḥ*. Of course, conceiving of the *Ṣaḥīḥ* as an unfinished text would not allow interpreters like Ibn Ḥajar and Ibn al-Munayyir as great a claim in explaining the intent of the compiler and the meaning of the work. If one accepts Ibn Ḥajar's and others' premise that Bukhārī's chapter headings bear hidden and subtle meanings, the position of the layperson becomes precarious. How could one hope to approach the *Ṣaḥīḥ* without an astute guide?

To take one example of an earlier commentator criticized by Ibn Ḥajar for manuscript alteration, let us examine a passage in the Andalusian commentator Ibn Baṭṭāl's commentary on the "Book of Pilgrimage."[54] According to Ibn Ḥajar, Ibn Baṭṭāl's recension, through will or neglect, reconciled a lacuna in the manuscript by joining two Qur'anic verses (14:35 and 5:97) under a single chapter heading. In Ibn Ḥajar's opinion, based on his knowledge of the *Ṣaḥīḥ*'s transmission, each verse was its own chapter heading, and the chapter heading that referenced 14:35 ought to be transmitted without a hadith under it. Ibn Ḥajar then went on to speculate what hadith Bukhārī may have intended to place in the gap, and he pointed the reader to a later section in which he would comment on that hadith.[55] Absence, for Ibn Ḥajar, was presence. And presence warranted interpretation, not alteration.

Another example of Ibn Ḥajar's speculative method can be seen in his commentary on the first hadith. Why, many commentators asked, was a hadith that began "actions are by intentions" placed under the chapter heading "How Revelation Began?"[56] Ibn Ḥajar inferred that Bukhārī chose to place this hadith under "How Revelation Began" because it was transmitted by a chain of scholars that began with his teacher al-Ḥumaydī (d. 219/834) who was from Mecca, and the revelation began in Mecca.[57]

That may have shed some light on the relationship between the hadith and the chapter heading, but why did Bukhārī choose to place this hadith first under that heading? Why not lead with some other hadith, whose content better matched the topic advertised in the heading? Ibn Ḥajar explained that Ḥumaydī was from the Prophet's ancestral tribe, the Quraysh, and that Bukhārī was applying a principle grounded in another hadith that enjoined the Muslim community to be led by a Qurashī.[58]

As clever as this interpretation was, it was not accepted by all. In response, ʿAynī, Ibn Ḥajar's rival, belittled the explanation as speculation: "This question is worthless."[59] While their personal and political differences can explain this harshness, ʿAynī offered a well-considered intellectual objection to back it up. He demurred that this hadith might apply to leadership in prayer and perhaps leadership in governance (*al-imāma al-kubrā*), but it did not necessarily apply to the placement of a transmitter in a hadith compilation.[60] Although we can only imagine Ibn Ḥajar's reply, it would no doubt have reinforced the importance of interpreting the chapter headings.

Returning briefly to our case study on discretionary punishment (*taʿzīr*), the choice of organization is among the first major differences between Ibn Ḥajar's commentary and early Andalusian commentators. Ibn Ḥajar's discussion of the chapter heading, "How Much Discretionary Punishment (*taʿzīr*) and Discipline (*adab*) [is authorized]?" which previous commentators had not explicated, linked *taʿzīr* to its root, ʿA-Z-R. He then addressed its lexical definition and usage in the Qur'an 2:12.[61] More importantly, he suggested that Bukhārī phrased the chapter as a question in order to indicate that there was a difference of opinion on this matter. In other words, for Ibn Ḥajar, Bukhārī did not pose the question rhetorically, assuming that the hadith categorized under the chapter provided the agreed upon answer. Rather, Bukhārī acknowledged a level of disagreement on the issue.[62]

Ibn Ḥajar did not always read Bukhārī's chapter headings sympathetically. One example of this can be found in Ibn Ḥajar's treatment of Bukhārī's lengthy chapter heading in the "Book of Faith (*īmān*)" that begins "The Chapter of Jibrīl's Question to the Prophet concerning faith (*īmān*), submission (*islām*), and filial piety (*iḥsān*)." The heading preceded one of the best-known hadith on the fundamental duties of Islam.[63] Ibn Ḥajar suspected, on the basis of this chapter heading as well as earlier hadith included in the "Book of Faith," that Bukhārī saw no nuanced distinction between *islām* and *īmān*. The implications of this position, which Ibn Ḥajar attributes to Bukhārī's own partisan reasoning,[64] are of great theological and legal consequence: without a finer-grained sensitivity to the differences between these two terms, one might conclude that one's religion was complete with faith alone, without the performance of good works. Even though Bukhārī did not explicitly claim this, the conflation of these two terms "is the gist of his language" for Ibn Ḥajar.[65]

In a lengthy excursus, Ibn Ḥajar respectfully argues that while Bukhārī is correct that *islām* and *īmān* have overlapping meanings and are sometimes used interchangeably when discussed in isolation, their meaning ought be understood as complimentary rather than synonymous, especially when both terms are mentioned together in the same statement. The proof, for Ibn Ḥajar, is the very text of the hadith mentioned in the heading that appears to distinguish between the two terms.

While earlier examples showed how Ibn Ḥajar and other commentators extended charity to Bukhārī, here Ibn Ḥajar had just done the opposite: he extrapolated Bukhārī's intentions from the chapter heading in order to respectfully push back against Bukhārī's interpretation and to bring the meaning of a hadith concerning the very definition of Islam into line with the mainstream opinion of Mamluk-era jurists.[66] Even within the context of the canonical culture of the Mamluk period, Bukhārī was not immune to some measure of internal criticism.

MYSTERIOUSLY MISSING WORDS

Typically, scholarly characterizations of the culture of hadith scholars in which the *Ṣaḥīḥ* emerged emphasize the precision and fidelity with which hadith were memorized and transmitted. Some hadith scholars were so insistent on this fidelity that they would even transmit a hadith that had blatant grammatical errors, lest some hidden meaning be lost for later interpreters.[67] Goldziher wrote of Bukhārī as one of the exemplars of this tradition, describing his scholarly practice's "slavish exactness."[68] It is surprising, then, to learn that Bukhārī frequently abbreviated or truncated some of the hadith he compiled, often without providing any indication he had done so. Commentators of the Mamluk period used commentary on Bukhārī's chapter headings to point to these other moments in which Bukhārī's editorial fingerprints could be seen.

As for the function of Bukhārī's choice of abbreviation, Ibn Ḥajar suggested two benefits. First, he speculated that Bukhārī wanted to show multiple chains of transmission of the same hadith without repeating them in full, which would lengthen an already lengthy book. Second, Bukhārī wanted readers to focus on one particular meaning over others.[69] Again, Ibn Ḥajar's hermeneutic required that the *Ṣaḥīḥ* include meaningful abbreviations, just as it did ambiguous chapter headings, ensuring the readers would require the expertise of commentators to understand the work.

A question over Bukhārī's abbreviating of hadith arose when commentators encountered the first hadith, "actions are by intention." This widely circulating hadith was typically recited with the following phrasing: "Actions are by intention, and every person receives what he intends. Whoever's migration (*hijra*) was for the sake of God and his messenger, his migration was for the sake of God and his messenger. Whoever's migration was aimed toward gaining the world or marrying a woman, his migration was for whatever he migrated."[70]

But the first hadith of Bukhārī's compilation is transmitted in the following way: "Actions are by intention, and every person receives what he intends. Whoever's migration was aimed toward gaining the world or marrying a woman, his migration was for whatever he migrated."[71]

Why, the commentators asked, is the "God and his messenger" phrase missing from the middle of the text? The commentators consider a number of options to unlock "the secret (*sirr*)" of this omission. Was it a scribal error in need of correction, as early commentators supposed? Or was it that Bukhārī narrated exactly what he heard from Ḥumaydī, and that narration did not include "God and his messenger"? Was it that ʿUmar himself made the omission on the pulpit for his own purposes? One scholar, al-Dāwūdī (d. 402/1011), noted that the *Musnad* of Ḥumaydī, compiled by transmitters other than Bukhārī, includes the full text of the hadith. This means that the omission could have only come from Bukhārī himself.[72]

Earlier commentators, as we saw in part 1, took the liberty of altering the arrangement of Bukhārī's text, declaring that Bukhārī must have intended the abbreviated hadith to be part of a preface—a threshold of the text, but not yet the text itself.[73] Ibn Ḥajar, by contrast, claimed that Bukhārī deliberately removed "God and his messenger" in order to underline a particular meaning of the hadith. Ibn Ḥajar asserted that Bukhārī sought in his omission to convey the sincerity of his intention, fearing he would appear arrogant in his piety by invoking God and his messenger in the first hadith.[74]

This debate was related to commentators' conception of the *Ṣaḥīḥ* as complete or incomplete, and whether or not it was legitimate to abbreviate a hadith without indicating that one had done so to one's audience. Both Ibn Ḥajar and early commentators were thus arguing, across time, over how to realize the same interpretive end—fidelity to Bukhārī's intentions, and by extension, fidelity to the normative content of Muhammad's sayings and practices—but they had come to different conclusions.

To be sure, a singular and unified version of the *Ṣaḥīḥ* would always elude hadith scholars. By Ibn Ḥajar's time, however, commentators assumed the *Ṣaḥīḥ,* taken as a composite of its authoritative textual variants, to be virtually complete and intentional, and it was no longer possible to maintain fidelity to Bukhārī's intentions by correcting or revising the original text without providing evidence for that correction in an authoritative recitation. As a consequence, Ibn Ḥajar chose to frame Bukhārī's omission as a commentary on the meaning of the hadith rather than as a mistake or evidence of scribal tampering. Again, as Ibn Ḥajar had it, Bukhārī's compilation was not merely a reference work for hadith, but was itself an interpretation of those hadith. Yet Bukhārī never explicitly indicated whether the omission was intentional or, if it was, what meaning he intended by it.

Ibn Ḥajar's solution to the secret of Bukhārī's omission has often been repeated by later commentators in their recounting of the exegetical history of the hadith. This repetition does not necessarily indicate continuity, however. Just as the same hadith produces a diversity of responses in different social and historical contexts, the same interpretation of that hadith produces various responses in different contexts. When Ibn Ḥajar presented his solution to the "secret" of Bukhārī's abbreviation of the first hadith in his compilation, it represented an imaginative solution to a difficult and long-debated problem, to the applause or disgust of his contemporaries. When contemporary shaykh Naʿīm al-ʿIrqsūsī repeated Ibn Ḥajar's solution in his twenty-first-century live commentary on the *Ṣaḥīḥ,* it was simply stated as a well-known fact, not to be scrutinized or reopened, not even worth attributing to a source, to the applause or disgust of his contemporaries.[75]

. . .

In taking into account the social and material rewards as well as the achievement of interpretive excellences at stake in the practice of hadith commentary, there is little doubt that the commentators' growing interest and analysis of *Ṣaḥīḥ al-Bukhārī*'s chapter headings is linked to the deepening culture of canonization in the Mamluk period. After all, it is only when texts are accorded canonical status that their fringes, paratexts, and thresholds become worthy of extended interpretation within a given scholarly culture. But in what ways did these new interpretive strategies affect the social practice of interpreting the work? Did this effect of canonization constrain commentators or free them to interpret the work in light of their own considerations?

Philosopher Moshe Halbertal, when considering a similar question of the Jewish interpretative tradition on the Talmud, answers it in the following way: "Canonizing a text results in increased flexibility in its interpretation, such as the use of complex hermeneutical devices of accommodation to yield the best possible reading. This phenomenon conflicts with the restrictive impulse of canonization itself, an act which creates boundaries and in many cases censors other texts and prevents them from becoming canonical."[76]

Likewise, we find that new interpretive freedoms and new interpretive restrictions emerged as the *Ṣaḥīḥ* reached new heights in the Mamluk period. On the one hand, including the chapter headings as objects of analysis created novel opportunities for commentators to maintain the authority of the *Ṣaḥīḥ* while making it speak to their present. In some cases, the relationship between the chapter headings and the hadith contained therein were ambiguous enough that Bukhārī's intention was understood to have conformed to several commentators' diverse social and intellectual interests across time and space.

On the other hand, the extraordinary reverence for the *Ṣaḥīḥ* limited the freedom that commentators had in revising problems in the text. While the commentators and hadith scholars we examined in part 1 of this book had the liberty to rearrange and fuse Bukhārī's chapter headings when encountering textual problems, later commentators discouraged and were discouraged from such practices. Moreover, requiring a rarified knowledge of the chapter headings of *Ṣaḥīḥ al-Bukhārī* as a prerequisite to commentary limited the number of people and texts that could serve as authorities on the meaning of the *Ṣaḥīḥ*.

The "thresholds" of *Ṣaḥīḥ al-Bukhārī* thus became an area of contestation in which social capital, material resources, and excellences internal to the tradition could be achieved. When Muslim scholars employed commentary on the thresholds to justify their rarified authority to comment, they were competing for status in a learned society. But their struggles to understand the thresholds of the *Ṣaḥīḥ* were not reducible to struggles over power and prestige in Mamluk society. As they competed for social and material rewards, they also saw the technique of interpreting *Ṣaḥīḥ al-Bukhārī*'s chapter headings as way to create a stronger intellectual link between the present and the compiler's original intentions and, by extension, the legacy of God's messenger.

The struggle to explain Bukhārī's chapter headings would return again with new vitality among reading communities in modern South Asia, who saw it as a vehicle to unveil "new knowledge" to students, and they responded in "ecstasy" and "awe." In that way, commentary that saw every aspect of the text worthy of explanation spoke across time to future generations of students curious about the *Ṣaḥīḥ*. But the interpretation of Bukhārī's thresholds came into their own in the Mamluk period, striking a chord with the trend toward encyclopedism of that particular age. But encyclopedism was not without its counterpoint: a commentarial movement toward concision that reined in scholastic and interpretive excesses. It is to this counterpoint we now turn.

CHAPTER 8

The Art of Concision

Excess invites boredom.

—al-Zarkashī

Jalāl al-Dīn al-Suyūṭī (d. 911/1505) grew up in the shadow of a generation in Cairo that produced some of the most elaborate multivolume commentaries on the hadith.[1] To suggest something of an analogy, one might say that the late Mamluk period was for Cairene commentary that the late Baroque period was for Roman architecture. Commentary was not the only genre of Islamic literature of the era that flooded quires with ink, but it was an influential one.[2] During his childhood, Suyūṭī witnessed the passing of two great masters of commentarial excess, Ibn Ḥajar and ʿAynī, both of whom, as we have seen, produced competing commentaries on *Ṣaḥīḥ al-Bukhārī* that far surpassed any hadith commentary prior in terms of volume and detail, and expanded the range of hermeneutic techniques and resources used in the practice of hadith commentary.

Suyūṭī's hadith commentaries turned away from this aesthetic of excess toward one of extraordinary breadth and concision. Nevertheless, Suyūṭī's gloss on *Ṣaḥīḥ al-Bukhārī,* called *al-Tawshīḥ* (The adorned), was among his most popular works and was known to have circulated among audiences in North Africa, the Arabian Peninsula, and West Africa throughout the 880s (late 1470s and early 1480s).[3] Likewise, his commentaries on the collections of Ibn Māja and Nasāʾī were among the first attempts ever to systematically comment on those works.[4] His commentary on *Sunan Nasāʾī* attracted a supercommentary by an eminent and influential hadith scholar who was active two and a half centuries after Suyūṭī's death.[5] These works have also enjoyed a vibrant afterlife in contemporary print.[6]

Despite their enduring success, Suyūṭī once described his commentaries on *Ṣaḥīḥ al-Bukhārī* and *Ṣaḥīḥ Muslim* as texts "for which comparable works have been composed, and a very learned person could produce its like," and his commentaries on Ibn Māja and Nasāʾī as works he "started then lost interest in, having written only a little."[7] Despite the fact that these works did not, by Suyūṭī's own reckoning, meet the standards of excellence for their originality or virtuosic comprehensiveness, what explains their purpose and their success in their own time and beyond? The answer lies in understanding a different standard of excellence—or better yet, a standard of value—that Suyūṭī strived to meet in his commentary: "usefulness without toil" (*al-nafʿ bilā taʿab*).[8]

SHIFTING READING CULTURES AND SLIMMER VOLUMES

After the passing of Ibn Ḥajar and ʿAynī, the production of elaborate commentaries did not come to a halt. Indeed, one of Suyūṭī's own competitors, Shihāb al-Dīn al-Qasṭallānī produced an enduring commentary on *Ṣaḥīḥ al-Bukhārī* that not only combined the works of Ibn Ḥajar, ʿAynī, and their predecessors but also surpassed them in terms of its preservation of the multiple recitations of the *Ṣaḥīḥ*.[9] Indeed, Suyūṭī's first attempts at hadith commentary conformed with the grander displays encyclopedism modeled by Ibn Ḥajar. His early treatment of Mālik's *Muwaṭṭaʾ*, for instance, surpassed its predecessors in terms of detail and the preservation of the multiple recitations of the work.[10] But by the end of his life, Suyūṭī practically boasted of his ability to comment on Aḥmad ibn Ḥanbal's tremendous *Musnad* in a single volume.[11]

There were some early indications of a countering trend among audiences that sought more abbreviated commentary, at least in Cairo. While recitations and live commentary of *Ṣaḥīḥ al-Bukhārī* in the presence of the sultan had customarily spanned two months during the days of al-Muʾayyad Shaykh,[12] in Suyūṭī's adult life they had all but ceased. Only after an earthquake struck Egypt in 875/1472 were readings of *Ṣaḥīḥ al-Bukhārī* revived at the citadel for the sultan, but even then they lasted but a single month.[13] Regular dictation of hadith in other venues in Cairo vanished, and both Suyūṭī's and Sakhāwī's attempts to reestablish the practice fizzled.[14] It would be at least another century until manuscript evidence and narrative sources suggest that live commentary on *Ṣaḥīḥ al-Bukhārī* had been revived at study sessions (*majālis*) in Ottoman Syria and Yemen.[15] Suyūṭī tells us in his autobiography that his earliest commentaries on hadith collected by al-Shāfiʿī and Abū Ḥanīfa emerged from a series of live lessons at the madrasa of the Shaykhūniyya and other venues for live gatherings.[16] However, there is little evidence that his serial commentaries on the six canonical collections emerged in concert with live sessions, so it may be safest to assume they did not.

Suyūṭī's own training reflects this trend, as he viewed live commentary in a far less glamorous light than the previous generation of hadith scholars. As Suyūṭī scholar E. M. Sartain pointed out, Suyūṭī famously preferred learning hadith from books rather than audition. The latter had fallen, in his opinion, under the direction of "common people, rabble, women, and old men."[17] Although Suyūṭī studied some collections of hadith with a number of teachers, it is difficult to determine what influence, if any, these studies had on his commentarial practice.[18] Suyūṭī once attended a lesson on hadith from Ibn Ḥajar, but he was no more than a toddler at the time.[19]

One clear inspiration, however, was Badr al-Dīn al-Zarkashī (d. 794/1392). Suyūṭī modeled his Qur'an commentary, *al-Itqān,* on Zarkashī's *Burhān,* so it may come as little surprise that Suyūṭī's hadith commentary, *al-Tawshīḥ,* was modeled on Zarkashī's *al-Tanqīḥ*—the very name of his work echoes Zarkashī's.[20] Zarkashī, in the introduction to *al-Tanqīḥ,* whose title suggests careful review and paring down, wrote that "excess invites boredom. . . . I hope that this dictation will spare the toil of checking, investigation and reading."[21] This marked a departure from the commentarial encyclopedism articulated a century earlier by Nawawī, who longed to write an "expansive work, a work stretching to more than a hundred volumes, without repetition or pointless expansion."[22] In this way, Zarkashī's gloss would have lacked the prestige of these more elaborate commentaries that conspicuously signaled to audiences the depth of the commentators' capacity to comment and the commentators' willingness to risk exhaustion and even commercial failure in devotion to studying hadith.

The *Tanqīḥ*'s content initially received mixed reviews. Ibn Ḥajar penned a corrective gloss on it and the Alexandrian Mālikī judge Badr al-Dīn al-Damāmīnī (d. 827/1424) wrote a commentary on *Ṣaḥīḥ al-Bukhārī* that unequivocally criticized it, sometimes unfairly.[23] Damāmīnī drew heavily on the form of the *Tanqīḥ* while claiming to correct its many grammatical, morphological, and linguistic errors. Most damning, for Damāmīnī, was Zarkashī's errors in the transmission of hadith. Damāmīnī's work was somewhat longer than Zarkashī's and circulated in Egypt, Yemen, and India, where Damāmīnī traveled for teaching and study.[24]

Nevertheless, Zarkashī's shorter work was more pragmatic, and Suyūṭī no doubt recognized its power for reciters and students who, as ample manuscript evidence collected from the period shows, incorporated snippets of it into the margins of their copies of *Ṣaḥīḥ al-Bukhārī*. In spite of its flaws, Zarkashī's work was ideal for quick reference, its comments fit comfortably on the periphery of a hadith collection's base text, and it sought to provide no more and no less than any reciter needed to know, whether sight reading or preparing to recite from memory. The fact that so many eminent scholarly authorities read and responded to the *Tanqīḥ*—including not only Ibn Ḥajar and Damāmīnī but also Muḥammad al-Birmāwī (d. 831/1428), Zakariyyā al-Anṣārī (d. 926/1520), and Shihāb al-Dīn al-Qasṭallānī (d. 923/1517–18)—is a testament to its wide circulation.[25] It was, to the applause of some and the jeers of others, a source for the hadith commentarial sound bites of its day.

Suyūṭī wrote, in the introduction to the *Tawshīḥ*:

> [This commentary on *Ṣaḥīḥ al-Bukhārī*] runs along the way of the notes of Imām Badr al-Dīn al-Zarkashī, called *al-Tanqīḥ*. It contains benefits and additions that the reciter and listener need concerning:
>
> - correct phrasing
> - commentary on obscure words (*tafsīr gharībihi*)
> - clarification on variants in chains of transmission (*ikhtilāf riwayātihi*)
> - additions to a hadith that are not mentioned in the path (*ṭarīq*) [contained in *Ṣaḥīḥ al-Bukhārī*].
> - a chapter heading whose phrasing comes from a hadith attributed to the Prophet (*marfūʿ*)
> - connecting a chainless (*taʿlīq*) hadith whose full connection is not given in *Ṣaḥīḥ al-Bukhārī*
> - identifying unknown persons
> - [rectifying] problems of syntax
> - reconciling controversies[26]

"In this way," Suyūṭī wrote, "nothing is missing from the commentary except legal derivation (*istinbāṭ*). I am determined to compose a book in this fashion on all of the six books [of hadith] to gain *usefulness without toil and achieve the desired aim without fatigue*."[27]

The list of nine aspects of the collection to be explained is indeed modeled on Zarkashī's. One notable point of confusion that Zarkashī explicitly clarified in the text that Suyūṭī did not was the esoteric relationship between each hadith and the chapter heading under which Bukhārī had placed it. As we saw in the previous chapter, this technique had grown in popularity throughout the Mamluk period and even began to generate its own genre.[28] While esoteric commentary on Bukhārī's chapter headings is related to legal derivation (*istinbāṭ*), a task Suyūṭī perhaps thought was better left to the reader, it is not synonymous with it. As we will see, however, Suyūṭī does include discussion of both Bukhārī's chapter headings and his opinion on the legal derivation of the hadith, albeit infrequently. In other words, Suyūṭī, as Zarkashī did before him, left the number of aspects of hadith that earlier scholars had believed merited explanation largely intact, diminishing only the volume and frequency with which he believed they merited it.

STRATEGIES OF INCLUSION AND EXCLUSION IN SUYŪṬĪ'S WORK

Although Suyūṭī's *Tawshīḥ* was theoretically modeled on the *Tanqīḥ*, it was far from a supercommentary on it. In fact, in order to succeed in his aim of providing the audience with a reading experience that was useful but free from toil, Suyūṭī chose to exclude most of the commentary tradition he inherited, including many of Zarkashī's clarifications.[29] Ironically, Suyūṭī excluded so much that the work's most recent editors could see no way to maintain the aims Suyūṭī promised in the introduction other than by adding a dense layer of footnotes to fill in much of what Suyūṭī excluded. While this may help repackage the *Tawshīḥ* for modern audiences, it obscures the fact that Suyūṭī's contribution to the cumulative tradition of commentary was, in some sense, his strategic omissions. The point, for Suyūṭī, was not to offer commentary on nine aspects for every hadith he discussed, but only when a problem rose to a level at which commentary would have practical value.

This is especially clear when discussing issues concerning the interpretation of Bukhārī's chapter headings and Bukhārī's abridgements (*ikhtiṣār*) of select hadith. As I showed in the last chapter, the technique of disclosing the esoteric meaning of the *Ṣaḥīḥ* through Bukhārī's sometimes quizzical headings and abridgements was first brought into the mainstream by Ibn Ḥajar's commentary *Fatḥ al-bārī*.[30] Suyūṭī, however, had little patience for the grander theories proposed by

Ibn Ḥajar to harmonize apparent inconsistencies in Bukhārī's chapter headings.

For instance, in the first hadith, "actions are by intentions," from which Bukhārī omits a key phrase, Suyūṭī excludes Ibn Ḥajar's creative attempts to discern Bukhārī's intention in making the apparent abridgement and instead states that Bukhārī conservatively transmitted the hadith from his teacher in the way he heard it.[31] Similarly, in the second hadith, Suyūṭī omits any mention of Ibn Ḥajar's critical attempt to explain its link to the chapter heading. Instead, Suyūṭī quotes the early hadith scholar Abū Bakr Aḥmad al-Ismāʿīlī (d. 371/981–82), who openly questioned what relevance the hadith could have had.[32] Whether or not one agrees with Suyūṭī's approach, these examples illustrate cases in which Suyūṭī was not arbitrarily abridging his predecessors but thought carefully about what exclusions benefited his audience—based on what he believed they practically needed to know—even at the cost of creating an impression of consensus on matters upon which there were ongoing debates among scholars.

And yet, at many other moments, the reasoning behind many of the exclusions is not entirely clear. In an unusually extended digression on the exegetical history of decorating of the Kaʿba with a *kiswa,* Suyūṭī borrows heavily from Ibn Ḥajar's *Fatḥ al-bārī* to chronicle the practice since it was first recorded. Strangely, while Ibn Ḥajar tracked the practice up to his present era—the ninth/fifteenth century—Suyūṭī quotes a source that halts the narrative a century earlier.[33]

Likewise, when discussing the report about "a little stick-legged Ethiopian" who will demolish the Kaʿba at the end of time, Suyūṭī indicates to his readers that the hadith reported by Aḥmad ibn Ḥanbal contained the additional information that "no one will live long after that."[34] But this is only a part of what predecessors, such as Ibn Ḥajar, informed their readers that Aḥmad ibn Ḥanbal added: "no one will live long after that, and they will be the ones who loot its treasure."[35] In this case, the omission appears arbitrary. Even in the name of maintaining brevity, the erasure saved only a line or a few lines of space on a folio's page.

Suyūṭī sometimes presented a truncated version of a legal debate that would give readers a far different impression of the field than Suyūṭī's predecessors would have given them. Consider, for example, Suyūṭī's comments on the hadith of the treaty of Ḥudaybiyya, in which the phrasing, taken literally, suggested that Muhammad wrote the treaty himself by hand. Suyūṭī wrote, "a group takes this literally, and they allege that [Muhammad] wrote by hand. Others are of the opinion that he ordered someone to write it."[36] Suyūṭī's characterization opened the door to contemporary debate where none really existed. After all, only a handful of scholars have ever argued that the hadith should be taken literally. Among them was Abū al-Walīd al-Bājī, a Mālikī jurist who preceded Suyūṭī by five centuries, and who, as we saw earlier, was taken to task locally and transregionally for appearing to call into question Muhammad's status as an "unlettered Prophet" (*nabī ummī*).[37] Unlike Ibn Ḥajar, Suyūṭī's *Tawshīḥ* gives us no sense of the contemporary proportions or stakes of the debate, and Suyūṭī offers no opinion of his own to guide the reader on the more favorable or favored interpretation.[38] Again, it is not clear what interpretive principle is guiding these omissions.

One way of gaining insight into the process by which Suyūṭī composed the *Tawshīḥ* is to examine the frequency and diversity of Suyūṭī's citations from other sources over the course of the work. While readers find a great number and variety of sources cited in the opening book, which discusses the chapter heading "How Revelation Began," by the middle of the "Book of Faith" and even more so in the "Book of Knowledge," the diversity and frequency of sources cited begins to narrow substantially. About a third of the way through his commentary, in the "Book of Festivals," Suyūṭī's citations are sparse by comparison, providing only clarifications on pronunciation and pointing the reader to variant transmissions of the hadith.[39] Although it could be a coincidence that the hadith that Suyūṭī believed required greater elaboration happened to be near the beginning of the work, it could also be a deliberate technique that Suyūṭī employed to demonstrate himself as a repository of knowledge at the beginning of the work, which would allow him to rest on his laurels in the body of the work. Notable exceptions to this trend of narrowing the diversity and frequency of his citations are his commentaries on popular hadith such as the "hadith of Jibrīl" and the closing hadith on glorifying God (*taṣbīḥ*).[40] These two hadith have traditionally attracted dense layers of commentary. This is a small indication that Suyūṭī was acutely aware of the interests of his audience and was careful to include greater layers of commentary on more well known hadith.

Sometimes Suyūṭī suggested readers consult other works of his for further reading. In his relatively extended commentary on the hadith concerning "the seven who will be shaded" on the Day of Resurrection, he not only mentions a volume he wrote on this subject but also suggests that the reader refer to his discussion on the same hadith in his commentary on the *Muwaṭṭa'*.[41] At another point, he encourages readers to consult his commentary on *Ṣaḥīḥ Muslim,* even though he drafted his commentary on *Ṣaḥīḥ al-Bukhārī* prior to his commentary on *Ṣaḥīḥ Muslim.*[42] This important clue tells us that Suyūṭī later went back and revised his work, adding notes such as this one. This self-citation goes both ways. In his commentary on *Ṣaḥīḥ Muslim,* when Suyūṭī encounters the "hadith of Jibrīl," rather than repeat himself, he simply instructs readers to consult his *Tawshīḥ* for more information.[43] In fact, Suyūṭī directs readers to the *Tawshīḥ* five times in the first two volumes of his commentary on *Ṣaḥīḥ Muslim,* suggesting that this earlier work was still very much on his mind as he began his commentary on *Ṣaḥīḥ Muslim.* Before one labels this practice as yet another example of Suyūṭī's shameless self-promotion[44]—and it may very well be that—in the context of Suyūṭī's principle of "usefulness without toil," it is also a subtle acknowledgment that some readers might seek to toil in greater layers of commentary than Suyūṭī believed was practically necessary.

A CONCISE APPROACH TO DISCRETIONARY PUNISHMENT

What did Suyūṭī do when faced with a controversial hadith that most of his predecessors believed required more elaborate commentary to be of practical use? In other words, when the toil of excess was useful, how did Suyūṭī balance the need for practical value against the goal of exegetical concision?

To shed light on this question, I will examine the same hadith from Bukhārī's heading on the limits of discretionary punishment (*taʿzīr*), that generated so much controversy in the previous chapter and among the early Andalusian commentators in part 1: "One ought not be lashed (*lā yujladu*) in excess of ten lashes (*jaladāt*) except in the case of [violating] a boundary (*ḥadd*) among the boundaries (*ḥudūd*) of God." Much was at stake in the interpretation of this hadith, and most found it difficult to be concise. In light of its complexity, how did Suyūṭī thread the needle within the constraints of his historical context and in light of his exegetical ideal to achieve "usefulness without toil"? Suyūṭī comments in the *Tawshīḥ:*

> Most people [of knowledge are of the opinion that] it is permissible to go beyond [ten strokes]. They respond [to critics] that [say] this [hadith] was abrogated by the consensus of the companions.
>
> In my opinion, [the hadith] was not abrogated but that the hadith conveys a preference, not a requirement.[45]

First, what has Suyūṭī excluded from the hadith's exegetical history? Despite his promise in his introduction, Suyūṭī does not make any mention of early debates over the unknown transmitter, which I discussed in chapters 2 and 6. This may be tied to Suyūṭī's and his audience's belief that Bukhārī's rigorous standards in evaluating hadith simply guaranteed the authenticity of the hadith. Nor does Suyūṭī mention either the debates among the classical legal authorities over the acceptable number of lashes or the more recent debate provoked by Ibn Taymiyya that challenged the juristic definition of *ḥadd,* and Ibn Ḥajar's reasoned response to it. This indicates that, at the very least, defending his predecessor or the Shāfiʿī school was not of primary concern to Suyūṭī or his imagined readership, which he may have hoped would be broader than his legal school affiliation. He also left out the only thing Zarkashī left in—the correct pronunciation of the Arabic for "lashes."[46]

But what did Suyūṭī add to the cumulative tradition of commentary? While he affirms the authenticity of the hadith, he characterizes the limit of ten lashes as a preference rather than a requirement, which would permit judges, on occasion, to exercise their full discretion.[47] In this way, he offers a new solution, one that allows his multiple audiences to have their cake and eat it too. And yet Suyūṭī remains silent about the basis on which he distinguishes preference from requirement. He offers no grammatical justification, no prooftexts, no traditional opinions to support his own. In other words, this case lays bare a paradox at the heart of Suyūṭī's approach: he makes the hadith useful to the largest audience while ironically omitting more than might be necessary to justify that use.

Lastly, let us compare this discussion with Suyūṭī's commentary on the *Ṣaḥīḥ* of Muslim ibn al-Ḥajjāj that also contains this hadith. In this work, we find Suyūṭī offer the following comment on the ten lashes hadith: "[Aḥmad ibn Ḥanbal] and some of our contemporaries take this hadith at face value. They say going beyond ten strokes is not permitted. And those who permit it respond, 'The hadith is abrogated.' The interpretation of some of the Mālikīs is that the hadith was specific to its time, because [ten strokes] sufficed the wrongdoers among them."[48]

Here Suyūṭī includes additional information on what groups are at the extremes: the Ḥanbalīs on one side and the Mālikīs on the other. But rather than hearing Suyūṭī's own opinion at the end, we hear the justification he claimed the Mālikīs used to bolster their position. This hadith, he claimed they argued, was specific to an earlier time, when ten lashes sufficed. By ending with this Mālikī justification, perhaps Suyūṭī was subtly deferring to the Mālikīs, whom the political elite also deferred to on this matter. Alternatively, the absence of Suyūṭī's opinion in this work could mark a change in Suyūṭī's approach. Perhaps he believed it was now up to the audience, not the commentator, to come up with their own verdict after hearing the opinions of the two extremes.

In his commentaries on later collections, like Abū Dāwūd's and Ibn Māja's, Suyūṭī skips over this hadith entirely. Even if we take these later commentaries to be unfinished drafts, as Suyūṭī once described them, it is curious that he would have skipped over this hadith, when he had already formulated opinions on it in two of his previous works. His treatment of discretionary punishment, then, suggests that, at the least, working within the same generic constraints of concision, he never fully settled the question of how much commentary was too much and how little was too little.

. . .

In our own scholarly tradition, we often measure ourselves by our claims to interpretive originality and comprehensiveness. We also project those measures into the past, seeking out that which was most original and comprehensive in the work of scholarly hadith of the Middle Ages. To be sure, the appreciation of an original and comprehensive scholarly contribution is one defining feature that we share with Suyūṭī's scholarly tradition. After all, in Suyūṭī's own estimation of his oeuvre, he placed at the top those works that "nothing comparable has been composed in the world, as far as I know." Of each one, he said that his contemporaries could not "produce its like due to what that would require of breadth of vision, abundance of information, effort, and diligence."[49] But even by his own estimation, most of his scholarly output was not included in this category. If not by originality or encyclopedic excess, then, how were the successes of these works measured? Suyūṭī's "usefulness without toil," I have argued, was one such measure. But useful for whom? And did he succeed?

Suyūṭī was enamored of neither the intellectual elites of his day nor those "common people, rabble, women, and old men" who claimed intellectual or religious authority.[50] Suyūṭī's audience, then, was a group of educated readers—many of whom lived abroad—who were neither aspiring experts nor laypeople. This was an audience who had little time to pore over the encyclopedic hadith commentaries but still sought a guide to clarify the canonical collections' conspicuous difficulties. For this market of readers, practicality and ease of use, rather than originality and comprehensiveness, was most valued.

By modeling his work on Zarkashī's *Tanqīḥ,* Suyūṭī hoped that those who consulted the *Tawshīḥ* and his serial commentaries on other key collections would come away knowing, among other things, how to pronounce and identify obscure words and names and the important variants contained in other collections, and they would be aware of any major scholarly controversies. In some cases, Suyūṭī pared down the commentary tradition he inherited strategically, keeping denser commentary on more popular hadith, and excising commentary that served esoteric debates. In other cases, his choices to abridge or omit appeared arbitrary. A close examination of the case of Suyūṭī's commentary on discretionary punishment shows the degree to which Suyūṭī himself toiled to strike the right balance between concision and elaboration as he came face-to-face with a paradox inherent in the task of composing a commentary that was both pragmatic and brief: excess can obscure a useful point, but some points require elaborate explanations to be useful.

While I endeavored earlier in the book to understand the excellences of encyclopedism that was paradigmatic of Mamluk-era hadith commentaries on *Ṣaḥīḥ al-Bukhārī,* Suyūṭī's practice of concision calls our attention to a counter-paradigm. In a period of virtuosic comprehensiveness, Suyūṭī strived to make a user-friendly hadith commentary, one that struck a balance between inclusion and exclusion, between making a point and leaving the reader without one. In doing so, scholars such as Suyūṭī were not only competing for social and material rewards, prestige and commercial success in the book market—although they were indeed doing that—they were simultaneously invested in achieving interpretive aims that they believed ought to be defining of the tradition, even if they did not meet the standards of excellence their fellow commentators set in terms of originality and detail. In the case of Suyūṭī's commentary on *Ṣaḥīḥ al-Bukhārī,* "usefulness without toil" was the interpretive aim he sought and sometimes struggled to achieve.

PART THREE

Early Modern India and Beyond

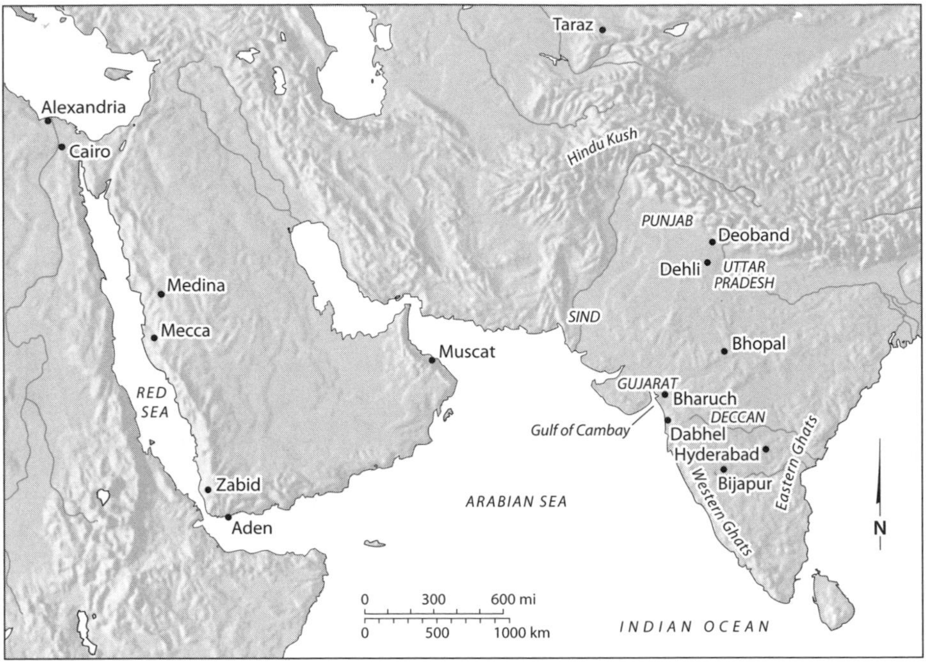

MAP 3. India and the Arabian Peninsula, ca. the nineteenth century.

CHAPTER 9

Trustees across the Ocean

Gujarat to Deoband to Bhopal

Thousands of miles intervene between us and them,
nevertheless, the unity of purpose has removed
all geographical distances.

—Qāḍī ʿAbd al-Raḥmān, Dār al-ʿUlūm Deoband

As early as the eighth/fifteenth century, Egyptian hadith commentators and their texts had made their way to India by way of well-trodden pilgrimage and trade routes down the Red Sea, around the southern coast of the Arabian Peninsula, and across the Indian Ocean to the Gulf of Cambay.[1] It is in this context of long-distance trade that we can best understand anecdotes of seafarers who claimed that packing *Ṣaḥīḥ al-Bukhārī*'s heavy volumes on their ship could protect them from harm.[2] Although Muslims of diverse genealogies had continuously traded and settled in India since the early Islamic conquests, what attracted this new generation of Egyptian hadith scholars to travel eastward may be partly linked to larger political shifts in northwest India in the late seventh/fourteenth century.[3]

As the Delhi sultanate began to lose hold of its provinces, it appointed a new governor, Muẓaffar Khān, to the coastal province of Gujarat to quash a nascent rebellion and push back the influence of the Rajput armies to the north. While Muẓaffar Khān succeeded, Delhi itself was sacked by Tamerlane, and the last of the sultanate's Tughluq rulers fled to Gujarat for refuge. After a series of political intrigues, poisonings, and prison breaks, Muẓaffar Khān himself established an independent sultanate in Gujarat at the turn of the ninth/fifteenth century.[4] What inadvertently emerged from this tumultuous and violent series of events was a century of generous patronage for Muslim learning in the

Gujarati sultanate that attracted religious authorities to move there from abroad.[5]

In fact, there may be no potentate in Islamic history more grandly immortalized in a commentary on *Ṣaḥīḥ al-Bukhārī* than Muẓaffar Khān's successor and grandson, Sultan Aḥmad Shāh (r. 814–46/1411–42).[6] It was to this Gujarati sultan, who was himself a poet, that Damāmīnī, the Mālikī-trained hadith commentator from Alexandria we met in the previous chapter, dedicated his written commentary on *Ṣaḥīḥ al-Bukhārī,* called *Maṣābīḥ al-Jāmiʿ* (Lights of the collection). Although Damāmīnī composed the commentary while in Zabīd, Yemen, he offered pages of unreserved praise and flattery for the sultan with couplets, belletristic rhetoric, and countless exaltations and epithets, such as "Caliph over the Creation" and "Sultan of the Imams of the World."[7] Damāmīnī joined the sultan's court in Gujarat in 820/1417, and there he continued to write and teach on issues of law and language at the service of the sultan.[8]

Likewise, the Gujarati Sultan Maḥmūd Shāh (r. 863–917/1458–1511), who was known for his zeal in politically addressing external and internal threats to the reigning Islamic orthodoxies, exhorting circumcision, and prohibiting the use of interest or usury (*ribā*) among his soldiers, attracted to the court another Egyptian hadith scholar: Wajīh al-Dīn Muḥammad (d. 919/1513), a Mālikī-trained judge who had studied with Ibn Ḥajar's student Sakhāwī in Mecca.[9] Wajīh al-Dīn's reputation as an authority on hadith grew to the point that the sultan nicknamed him "Master of the Hadith Scholars" (*Malak al-Muḥaddithīn*).[10] In addition to teaching Islamic law and hadith, Wajīh al-Dīn also served on the court's treasury.

Although illiterate, Sultan Maḥmūd Shāh dabbled in hadith commentary himself, having become familiarized with some of the debates through his translator.[11] In an anecdote recorded by a tenth-/sixteenth-century historian in Persian, the sultan was said to have disagreed with scholars who doubted the authenticity of a hadith in which God paralyzed a child because he interrupted the Prophet's prayer.[12] The sultan was said to have reasoned that, on the basis of the text's content, its chain of transmission, and its corroboration by other prooftexts, the hadith was authentic and ought to be included in legal reference works as evidence that cursing others was permissible in the service of God.[13]

Whether this anecdote of the sultan wading into legal and exegetical debates is apocryphal or not, it speaks volumes about the perceived value of interpreting hadith in the Gujarati political and religious environment. The Gujarati sultan, in contrast to the silent Mamluk sultans, was represented here as active in the debates of the hadith commentators. While not an expert, he was shown to be savvy to the importance of authorizing the hadith on the basis of its chain of transmission and finding corroborating evidence to tease out its meaning. But by seeking to include the hadith in the legal curriculum, Sultan Maḥmūd was also represented as suggesting that verbal and physical violence was in store for those who distract one from the worship of God. In the context of Maḥmūd Shāh's intermittent competition and conflicts with non-Muslims and intra-Islamic heterodoxies within and along their borders, the polemic against those groups seems barely veiled.

Maḥmūd Shāh's successor, Sultan Muẓaffar Shāh II (r. 917–38/1511–25), also cultivated a companionship with a migrant hadith scholar: Jamāl al-Dīn al-Baḥraq (d. 930/1524), a student of Sakhāwī's, who had emigrated from Ḥaḍramawt in Yemen.[14] A later historian recorded that Baḥraq was so close to the sultan that jealous competitors at the court poisoned him.[15] Most pertinent to our study, the sultan was said to have granted a supplicant land revenues (*jāgīr*) from the district of Bharuch and a high-ranking political appointment (*amīr*) in exchange for a copy of Ibn Ḥajar's *Fatḥ al-bārī* that had once belonged to Wajīh al-Dīn.[16] According to one historian, it was the first copy of *Fatḥ al-Bārī* to have entered Gujarat.[17] Other anecdotes of Muẓaffar Shāh II's commitment to hadith abound. After hearing a hadith that those who memorized the Qur'an would be sheltered on the Day of Resurrection, he was said to have fully devoted himself to the undertaking.[18]

Although the sources do not offer any detailed descriptions of commentaries on hadith in India at this time, the work of a historian who migrated from Gujarat from Yemen in 975/1567 can offer some insight into the form, function, and value of live and written commentaries on *Ṣaḥīḥ al-Bukhārī* within the complex social and intellectual horizon of Muslim scholars traversing the Indian Ocean. The work, *al-Nūr al-sāfir* (The traveling light) of ʿAbd al-Qādir al-ʿAydarūs (d. 1038/1628), was intended to chronicle the events and obituaries of notable Muslim scholars in the tenth/sixteenth century, as Ibn Ḥajar and Sakhāwī had done for the preceding centuries.[19] Alongside news of earthquakes, drownings, and wars, ʿAydarūs recorded the "event" of the arrival of Ibn Ḥajar's *Fatḥ al-bārī* in Yemen in 901/1495. *Fatḥ al-bārī* was one "of the signs of God all Mighty," purchased by a Yemeni sultan from the Banū Ṭāhir and brought to centers of learning in Zabīd and then Taʿizz.[20] Ibn Ḥajar's written commentary had become a character, as it were, in the history of the Indian Ocean, migrating toward centers of power and learning as scholars of the time did.

This character of *Fatḥ al-bārī* made a second appearance in a highly detailed description of the live recitation and study sessions (*majālis*) on *Ṣaḥīḥ al-Bukhārī* at a mosque in Zabīd in 948/1545.[21] The sessions were led by ʿAbd al-Raḥmān ibn Ziyād al-Maqṣarī (d. 975/1568), who, ʿAydarūs observed, had cultivated audiences in Mecca, Medina, Yemen, India, and Ethiopia. In these sessions, scholars and students studied *Ṣaḥīḥ al-Bukhārī* from beginning to end in a period of three months: Ramadan and the two months that preceded it. While ʿAydarūs did not mention the number or names of the scholars and students present, he took care to note that roughly forty copies of *Ṣaḥīḥ al-Bukhārī* were present in the audience, as well as a copy of Ibn Ḥajar's *Fatḥ al-bārī*. Apparently, the sessions were so moving that Ibn Ziyād al-Maqṣarī claimed he saw the Prophet in attendance with his "naked eye."[22] As the sessions came to a close in Ramadan, a celebration took place that largely resembled the gatherings at the citadel in Mamluk-era Cairo a century earlier. ʿAydarūs reported that the political and judicial elite, as well as people of all kinds from the Zabīdī general public came together, partying and reciting poetry to commemorate the event.

Thus, in ʿAydarūs's idealized representation of the commentary session, reading and explaining hadith was a multisensory act, involving the eye, the tongue, and the ear. It was remembered, moreover, as a collective act in the broadest possible sense: in addition to the general public and a diverse community of scholars and seekers, transregional and transtemporal objects and visions were described as being in attendance.

Eager to emulate their counterparts in Zabīd and Cairo, scholars native to India also began to compose commentaries on canonical hadith collections in the tenth/sixteenth century. The first such work on *Ṣaḥīḥ al-Bukhārī* was ʿAbd al-Awwal al-Ḥusaynī al-Zaydpūrī's (d. 968/1560) *Fayḍ al-bārī* (Abundance of the divine wisdom).[23] Zaydpūrī studied hadith in Mecca and Medina, after which he returned to Aḥmadābād in Gujarat, sometime before 941/1524, as an expert in hadith.[24] Although no manuscript of his work has survived, the commentary nevertheless influenced later students native to India, who combined his commentary on *Ṣaḥīḥ al-Bukhārī* with those of his Mamluk predecessors.[25]

In the ninth to eleventh (fifteenth to seventeenth) centuries, a rich culture of hadith scholars also began to flourish beyond the coastal districts of Gujarat, in part because of the robust patronage of Deccan sultanates like the Bahmanīs and the ʿĀdil Shāhīs. Nawras Ibrāhīm

ʿĀdil Shāh II (r. 988–1037/1580–1627) in Bijapur had a copy of *Ṣaḥīḥ al-Bukhārī* and as well as a copy of *Fatḥ al-bārī* in his library, stamped with his seal.[26] When his predecessor, ʿAlī ʿĀdil Shāh (r. 965–88/1558–80) began the construction of the Jāmiʿ mosque in Bijapur, he imagined a grand but austere structure in the style of other Shi'i mosques of the Deccan during the period.[27] When Nawras finished the construction, he was reported to have inscribed hadith from canonical collections on the excellences of the rightly guided caliphs and other close companions of the Prophet.[28] Nawras's patronage of scholarship on and deployment of *Ṣaḥīḥ al-Bukhārī* would have been a loaded symbol, marking a brief turn to Sunnism for the ʿĀdil Shāhīs.[29]

In the period up to the early twelfth / late eighteenth century, commentary on canonical works like *Ṣaḥīḥ al-Bukhārī* continued in India under the Mughals. Although scholarly networks between India and the Arabian Peninsula remained strong, practitioners native to India began to develop their own scholarly legacies. We know of at least five other large commentaries on *Ṣaḥīḥ al-Bukhārī* that were produced by Indian-born scholars, each titled in a way that rhymed with *Fatḥ al-bārī*, indicating their engagement with the cumulative tradition of commentary that reached back to Mamluk Egypt and Syria.[30] Meanwhile, students readily gleaned insights from slimmer works of commentary on *Ṣaḥīḥ al-Bukhārī* produced by twelfth-/eighteenth-century South Asian luminaries such as Shāh Walī Allāh's (d. 1175/1762) single-volume commentary on Bukhārī's chapter headings and Muḥammad Ḥayāt al-Sindī's (d. 1165/1751) skinny but influential gloss on the *Ṣaḥīḥ*.

Through this brief survey of the cumulative commentary tradition on *Ṣaḥīḥ al-Bukhārī* in premodern Indian scholarly culture, we can see how centers of patronage in Gujarat and the Deccan and centers of learning in Egypt and the Arabian Peninsula animated the transregional movement and exchange of scholars and texts across the Indian Ocean. Chronicle sources suggest that hadith commentary was a multisensory, transregional, and transtemporal social and intellectual practice in which Mamluk-era figures like Ibn Ḥajar al-ʿAsqalānī and his students served as idealized exemplars. At its zenith, the commentary session was described as a space in which the Prophet himself could appear. While Gujarati patrons were memorialized in commentators' dedications, impressing their seal on collectible copies of commentaries, the prestige, legitimacy, and social capital their patronage afforded them was only part of the story. Political patrons were also portrayed as having been genuinely invested in preserving and acting upon the meaning of the hadith, significant in a context in which Muslim scholars viewed the Prophet's legacy in India to be under threat from within and without.

A NEW GENEALOGY OF HADITH COMMENTATORS IN COLONIAL INDIA

As European colonial power expanded in the nineteenth and early twentieth centuries, the Islamic world as a whole witnessed tremendous changes that are difficult to understate. The diverse Muslim community of British India was no exception, and it experienced the deepening influence of colonial rule on their political, military, legal, educational, commercial, financial, religious, and cultural institutions.[31] Secularization, new technologies, and new languages transformed the freedom and constraints of social and intellectual practices in these multiple spheres of human activity. The influence of colonialism must have also been psychological, and historian Francis Robinson has even argued that Muslims in British India began to view themselves as "selves" situated in the world in revolutionary ways.[32]

Within this colonial context, a diverse landscape of traditional and modernist Islamic reform movements emerged, including the Deobandis, the Barelvis, the Ahl-i Hadith, the Ahmadiyya, and the Aligarh Movement.[33] Since a comprehensive treatment of each of these groups and their diverging relationships to hadith commentary is not possible within the scope of this book, I will focus my analysis on a number of key figures from the Deobandi movement and the Ahl-i Hadith, as well as their texts, their contexts, and their commentarial strategies.

The Deobandis were founded by a reformist group of Ḥanafī scholars who founded a school in the North Indian locale of Deoband in 1866. While other scholars have undertaken far more detailed studies of the Deobandis,[34] my aim here is to tease out some of the key elements of their social and intellectual history vital to understanding the complex context in which commentaries on *Ṣaḥīḥ al-Bukhārī* and other hadith collections emerged.

The premodern hadith commentators in Egypt and Gujarat enjoyed the rich patronage of the political and military elite. In the case of Ibn Ḥajar and some of his colleagues, they were themselves wealthy merchants and traders. Likewise, the Deobandi scholars and staff descended from the Mughal elite (*ashraf*) and relied on the support of elite Muslim landowners, civil servants, government officials, military officers, merchants, teachers, judges, and religious authorities.[35] Furthermore, these

Deobandi scholars linked up with transregional networks to address readers across the Indian Ocean, as Anwar Shāh al-Kashmīrī, a leading figure in the Deobandi school, found patrons for his commentary on *Ṣaḥīḥ al-Bukhārī* among merchants in the Muslim South Asian diaspora in South Africa.[36] Nevertheless, the power of these elite networks of patrons had been diminished under colonial rule, when compared to the ostentatious wealth of elite families in the Mughal era. Perhaps this helped spur the largely unprecedented move on the Deobandis part to cultivate local support from humble "villagers, craftsmen and agriculturalists."[37]

While their Gujarati and Mamluk counterparts were directly appointed by the state to serve as judges, treasurers, and scribes, the Deobandi scholars had far less access to the political and judicial power of the state. Their biggest donors may have worked within British institutions of power, but the early Deobandi commentators served as rectors and teachers in Deobandi schools. In a way, this freed commentators on *Ṣaḥīḥ al-Bukhārī* to address politics more overtly, since the colonial administrators would not have been present in the commentary sessions. Kashmīrī incorporated his anticolonial politics in his explanations of hadith, and there are even moments in which those politics appeared to lead him to contradict the apparent meaning of the hadith.[38]

Ironically, or inevitably, the Deobandi movement adopted many of the technologies and organizational patterns introduced by the British colonial bureaucracy. While, in the premodern period, the locus of knowledge rested in the personal authority of the hadith commentator, and qualifications were recognized with a lesser degree of formality, schools affiliated with the Deobandi movement reflected the British model: an institution serving as the locus of authority, with a hierarchical staff that shepherded students through a sequential and degree-granting curriculum with exams.[39] Whether students attended a Deobandi school in Gujarat or Uttar Pradesh, a certain level of organizational and pedagogical predictability could be expected.

Also patterned on Western cultural practices was the adoption of print technology. While far less expensive and less time-consuming than copying manuscripts by hand, print was mass reproduced with mechanical but impersonal efficiency, in contrast to the idiosyncrasies of handwritten texts expressly imbued with the personal authority of a copyist and an authorized teacher.[40] Nevertheless, even in the context of the fragmentation of personalized authority that was brought about by European models of bureaucratized institutions and print culture, the Deobandis found ways to construct and maintain the aura of a qualified religious scholar and exegete, and students' connection with his presence. In this way, they could claim to have preserved a connection with their past even as they and their audiences experienced major cultural transformations in their present.

One way Deobandis constructed the authority of the hadith commentator was by linking scholarly genealogies to exemplars from an idealized "Arab" past. There was a sense among the Deobandis that Indian Muslims—and Kashmīrī himself—had inherited the mantel of the Arab hadith scholars. Muḥammad Yūsuf al-Banūrī (d. 1977), a student of Kashmīrī's, prior to listing a genealogy of hadith scholars of South Asia after the Mamluk period that lead up to Kashmīrī, wrote:

> When, from the middle of the tenth century of the Hijra [sixteenth century CE], the sciences of *ḥadīth* were overtaken by weakness in the Arab lands, and the eternal sunna of Allah—as expressed in His statement, "and if you turn away, He would replace you with a people other than you . . ."[41]—came true, this privilege [of attending to *ḥadīth*] passed from the people of these [Arab] lands to its [new] carriers and trustees in the lands of India.[42]

Here Banūrī affirmed that Indian scholars and Arabs are distinct groups and that Indian scholars, at this point in history, were entitled to some interpretive privilege over the Arabs. But the boundary between the groups was blurred by the fact—or myth—that Kashmīrī's ancestors hailed from Baghdad.[43] To be sure, as we have seen, there were transregional links between the hadith scholars and commentators of South Asia, the Arabian Peninsula, and Mamluk-era Cairo. But Deobandi scholars chose to emphasize that the link between these two reading communities was articulated as one of a lineage through blood, not merely scholarly genealogy.

Constructing a genealogical link to the "Arab lands" appealed both to their own imagination and the imagination of the British colonial officials.[44] Members of another Deobandi-related late nineteenth-century reform movement, called Nadwat al-ʿUlamāʾ, were known to have complained about their students: "If an Arab comes their way, they would not be able to converse with him in Arabic for five or ten minutes."[45] Nadwat al-ʿUlamāʾ encouraged their students to become proficient in writing and speaking Arabic and even to dress and dine "in the manner of Arabs" and to consume Arab news media.[46] Even though Persian and Urdu were the dominant languages of North Indian Muslims in the nineteenth century, it was in Arabic that the most distinguished and comprehensive commentaries were written and circulated.[47]

These commentaries were also indicative of a reversal from the premodern flows of knowledge and patronage in the Indian Ocean, as interpretations of hadith were now being produced in India and sent to Arabic-speaking audiences in the West.

Kashmīrī's live lessons were delivered in a mixture of Arabic and Urdu, but his students wrote them down and published them in Arabic.[48] While the display of eloquence in Arabic would have been a basic expectation for the continued employment of premodern hadith commentators, this modern Indian commentarial display of virtuosity in Arabic is somewhat startling, since it would have come at the expense of book sales and understanding among the mostly Urdu-speaking and Urdu-reading audiences.[49] The desire to reach these non-Arabic speaking audiences weighed on Kashmīrī to the point that he also encouraged his students to write commentaries in Urdu and English in addition to Arabic.[50] Eventually they did, although those books, at least in the study of hadith, were less rigorously edited and systematically organized.[51] Nevertheless, displaying memory and eloquence in classical Arabic came to serve as "a mark of religious authority and cultural authenticity" for Deobandi hadith scholars and religious authorities in general, as it had been for the premodern hadith scholars.[52]

The emphasis on the display of memory and eloquence in Arabic points to another way Deobandi hadith scholars constructed a connectedness with the past: emulating the live performances of commentary in the premodern eras. The increase in literacy, which was brought about by the establishment of British secular schools and the availability of affordable texts in print, would, at first glance, seem to obviate the need for live readings. After all, students could now read books without a teacher present. And yet, even though the spectacles of the Ramadan sessions in the citadel of Mamluk Cairo and ʿAydarūs's Zabīd were a distant memory, oral dictation of Deobandi hadith scholars' commentary to students remained an important part in the production of printed commentaries. As Anwar Shāh al-Kashmīrī had, Rashīd Aḥmad Gangohī (d. 1905) delivered lessons regularly on *Ṣaḥīḥ al-Bukhārī* at the madrasa in Deoband he helped to found. These lectures were written down by a close student and were later published as a multivolume work with a printed reading certificate (*ijāza*).[53]

One reason for this was that live performances allowed room for a multisensory and social experience. The memoir of a student of the renowned Deobandi hadith scholar and anticolonial revolutionary Maḥmūd Ḥasan (d. 1920), known as Shaykh al-Hind, offers an evocative account of such a performance, in which the very act of commentary on the tradition opened the door to new knowledge and sparked a transformative and ecstatic experience:

> Once a discussion of Bukhari's chapters began in the Shaykh al-Hind's circle, a particular state would overcome him. The listeners, too, seemed to be in awe. It was as if the entire group was in ecstasy. . . . New information, new knowledge—things that had not been heard or read elsewhere—seemed to be in the process of being unveiled. . . . Once the study of Bukhari had begun . . . both the heart and mind thrived on this nourishment—one not found in any work of logic, philosophy, belles-lettres, or any other discipline. I can't speak for others but, so far as I am concerned, I felt that I was being transformed both outwardly and inwardly.[54]

Although none of Shaykh al-Hind's students claimed to have seen the Prophet in attendance at the live session with his naked eye, as had been reported at a commentary session in ʿAydarūs's tenth-/sixteenth-century Zabīd, his students felt a similar kind of awe as this new knowledge was "unveiled."

The value of "new knowledge" in Shaykh al-Hind's commentary suggests that in the same breath that Indian scholars displayed their genealogy to idealized exemplars rooted in the "Arab lands," they also sought to surpass them. According to the memoir of a student of Shaykh al-Hind, the appeal of studying with the shaykh was his ability to open the door to new knowledge of "the secret consonance" of Bukhārī's chapter headings.[55] He writes:

> Just as the question of how particular Qur'anic verses relate to one another is a matter of the Qur'an's great [but elusive] wisdom, so too is the case with how the titles of Bukhari's chapters relate to the chapters' contents: the secret of their consonance lies in the very appearance of their dissonance. . . . Perhaps from the day Bukhari's work was introduced into scholarly circles, people have been busy trying to solve this puzzle. What they have thought about over the course of a thousand years is preserved in their books, though the more discerning have always recognized that the scholarly community owes it to Bukhari to provide a better solution to this problem than has been offered so far. For all the other achievements of Ibn Ḥajar's comprehensive commentary on Bukhari, this aspect has remained in need of further discussion. . . . [Shah] Wali Allah opened new avenues towards the understanding of this problem. And the Shaykh al-Hind was the legatee of the new approach.[56]

For Shaykh al-Hind's student, *Fatḥ al-bārī* may have been comprehensive, but it was not and could not be the final word in the cumulative tradition of commentary. The very hermeneutic that distinguished Ibn

Ḥajar in the eyes of his own students is seen to have come up short for the Indian hadith scholars since Shāh Walī Allāh. While Shaykh al-Hind's student claimed his teacher was following in the footsteps of Shāh Walī Allāh in approaching the text in innovative ways, Shāh Walī Allāh himself would have hesitated to describe his approach as "new," insofar as he largely followed Ibn Ḥajar's commentary on Bukhārī's chapter headings.

We see this double movement toward continuity and change in the case of Kashmīrī's relationship to Ibn Ḥajar al-ʿAsqalānī. Biographers sought to play up his comparison to Ibn Ḥajar and other Mamluk-era hadith scholars in terms of memory and precision.[57] As his Mamluk-era predecessors' were, the caliber and quantity of Kashmīrī's reading certificates for *Ṣaḥīḥ al-Bukhārī* were praised and reprinted in full in the introduction to his commentary on the work.[58] Of course, Kashmīrī himself spoke of his extraordinary admiration for Ibn Ḥajar's commentary on *Ṣaḥīḥ al-Bukhārī*.[59] But for all his admiration, Kashmīrī found Ibn Ḥajar's *Fatḥ al-bārī* in need of further commentary for a different reason: Ibn Ḥajar was biased toward the Shāfiʿī legal school.[60] In a colonial age in which the continued vitality of the legal schools was being questioned from within and without, commentary on *Ṣaḥīḥ al-Bukhārī* was incorporated as a capstone course into the Deobandi curriculum in part to show that it was in harmony with Ḥanafī norms.[61] For this reason, Kashmīrī could not simply abridge Ibn Ḥajar's *Fatḥ al-bārī* but had to contribute new interpretations that could marshal the text in the service of the Ḥanafī legal positions. In this sense, while Kashmīrī was concerned with defending his legal tradition, he also saw an important place for a qualified jurists' mental exertion (*ijtihād*) upon the foundational sources to achieve that goal.[62]

In this environment, ʿAynī's commentary prospered and, in some cases, eclipsed Ibn Ḥajar's in the Deobandis' exegetical histories of the hadith collection.[63] In his preface to Kashmīrī's commentary, Muḥammad Yūsuf Banūrī elevated ʿAynī as a reference by listing the Ḥanafī commentaries on *Ṣaḥīḥ al-Bukhārī* prior to mentioning Ibn Ḥajar's *Fatḥ al-bārī*. Likewise, *Intiqāḍ al-iʿtirāḍ*, the text that Ibn Ḥajar had hoped would expose ʿAynī as a plagiarist, was described by Banūrī as Ibn Ḥajar's sectarian refutation of ʿAynī's Ḥanafī refutations of *Fatḥ al-bārī*.[64] Banūrī did not consider patronage, clashing egos, or scholarly integrity to be at stake in their conflict, only the advancement and defense of their respective legal schools.

Thus, the complex social and political matrix of British India upended traditional Muslim sources of patronage, calling into question the traditional technologies and structures of their legal and religious authority and distancing Muslim scholars from political power. But within these new constraints, reformist Muslim scholars maintained a multisensory connectedness to an idealized past that they simultaneously claimed to preserve and improve upon. The British colonial context likewise brought them into conversation with new audiences in India and the broader Islamic world, and it pressed them to consider the foundational sources anew and to write and think more freely about issues of politics than their predecessors. Let us then turn to a case study on the issue of discretionary punishment in order to examine how Kashmīrī's commentary on *Ṣaḥīḥ al-Bukhārī* achieved certain interpretive excellences internal to the tradition, while simultaneously speaking to the political and social interests of new audiences of the colonial context.

RECASTING DISCRETIONARY PUNISHMENT IN A DEOBANDI COMMENTARY

By 1870, the British's systematic and structural secularization of Indian society had effectively relegated Islamic law and Islamic legal education to the private sphere and had created secular courts and schools to compete with them. In some cases, they eclipsed them altogether.[65] This was not done by an overnight abolition of Islamic legal authority, but through a complex political and intellectual process of reflection, appropriation, accommodation, translation, and codification of Islamic legal texts.[66] What emerged was a hybridized code called Anglo-Muhammadan Law. In the process, the British Privy Council often appeared to wield arbitrary power in approving, overruling, including, or excluding the frameworks, procedures, vocabularies, and resources constitutive of the new legal code when it was not in harmony with British legal, moral, and political values.[67] With respect to our case study on discretionary punishment (*taʿzīr*), in his 1903 digest of Anglo-Muhammadan Law, Barrister Roland Knyvet Wilson wrote that worse than "the specifically ordained punishments for certain offences—crucifixion or impalement for rebellion, stoning or scourging for adultery, amputation for theft, scourging for slander and wine-drinking . . . [was] the wide scope left for magisterial caprice in regard to *tazir,* or discretionary punishment, in all the very numerous cases for which no *hudd,* or specific penalty, is provided [*sic*]."[68]

While amputations and stoning may have stoked fear in the popular British imagination, it was the "wide scope left for magisterial caprice" in cases of discretionary punishment that most concerned this British legal specialist. Wilson addressed none of the debates and none of the limits placed on discretionary punishment that we have closely tracked in this book. Rather, Wilson viewed the issue of discretionary punishment as unpredictable, leaving too much authority to the judgment of a person.

But the process by which Anglo-Muhammadan Law came about was not entirely unidirectional. In some cases, Deobandi religious authorities worked with the British to help make the law reflect the best of the dynamic values, opinions, and procedures of the diverse Islamic legal tradition.[69] Other Deobandi scholars, like Kashmīrī, placed some modicum of external pressure on these processes, if indirectly, through the medium of the hadith commentary. Kashmīrī's commentary, along with others, would have worked to shape some Indian Muslims' expectations about the proper religious, cultural, political, and legal functions of the hadith and the dynamism of the differing layers of opinions that the Privy Council found too complicating to include. Kashmīrī also argued for the necessity of the kind of judicial discretion that British legal practitioners found deeply disconcerting. Kashmīrī's explanations of the hadith on discretionary punishment in *Ṣaḥīḥ al-Bukhārī* should thus be read in a context in which his primary goal was not to regulate a current practice, but to serve as a counterpoint to competing claims of legal authority from within and without.

While Kashmīrī did not comment on every single hadith in *Ṣaḥīḥ al-Bukhārī,* he did offer a unique explanation of the hadith that claimed the Prophet had exhorted believers not to "lash in excess of ten whips except in the case of a *ḥadd* among the *ḥudūd* of God."[70] Like Ibn Baṭṭāl's commentary on *Ṣaḥīḥ al-Bukhārī* from the last days of the Umayyad period in Andalusia, Kashmīrī began with an exegetical history of the classical opinions on the hadith. But rather than capture the range of early opinions across the legal spectrum, Kashmīrī limited his discussion to the Ḥanafī opinions on the matter.[71]

The classical Ḥanafī opinions, in Kashmīrī's framing, were largely divided between two camps. First, he mentioned those who thought that discretionary punishment ought to be limited to thirty-nine lashings, one less than the most lenient of the *ḥadd* penalties sanctioned by God in the Qur'an. Second, he mentioned those who held discretionary punishment to be unlimited. For the second camp, Kashmīrī cited

Ḥanafī scholars like Abū Yūsuf, Ṭaḥāwī, and Abū Ḥanīfa.[72] The last of these authorities, whom Kashmīrī reverentially referred to as "our Greatest Imam," permitted judges to authorize executions for non-*ḥadd* offenses if they so reasoned.[73]

Kashmīrī favored the view that there was no limit on *taʿzīr* on the grounds that exceeding ten lashes had been established by other hadith, although he does not say which hadith or evaluate their provenance.[74] But Kashmīrī added an important stipulation, which may have been assumed by previous commentators but was never explicitly stated: only the pious who fear God's limits and who preserve the ordinances of the law by heart (*yaḥfaẓ awāmir al-sharīʿa*) can issue legal rulings on the basis of this view.[75] In other words, even though Kashmīrī affirmed, against the apparent meaning the hadith, his legal school's opinion that gave unlimited discretion to the interpreter, he restricted its practical application to a privileged and discerning few. Thus, for Kashmīrī, the general public did not have carte blanche to carry out executions on a whim.

Was there a basis for Kashmīrī's worry that the general public would deliver severe punishments without proper training? Kashmīrī may have simply been concerned with an overzealous husband or father taking the law into his own hands, beating his spouse or his child abusively. However, the fact that Kashmīrī needed to assert the privilege of a traditionally trained expert in the first place subtly acknowledges a landscape in which new technologies and educational institutions had allowed general audiences to acquire Islamic literacy outside the careful control of traditional institutions and methods of learning, and with potentially hazardous consequences. Kashmīrī's retelling of the Bājī fiasco, in which a senior scholar intervened to save Bājī from the public's demand for his execution after he claimed that the Prophet wrote, is consistent with this broader contemporary concern.[76]

Kashmīrī addressed another contemporary concern in his discussion of what seemed like a banal point: why the Mamluk-era Shāfiʿī chief justice Ibn Daqīq al-ʿĪd failed to explicitly mention his opponent, Ibn Taymiyya, by name. Kashmīrī hypothesized that Ibn Daqīq al-ʿĪd was among the great Sufi saints (*awliyāʾ Allāh*) of his time and did not want to utter Ibn Taymiyya's name because he had harsh views concerning matters of Sufi saints.[77] Whether this reading of Ibn Daqīq al-ʿĪd's motives is accurate or not, it nevertheless connects the Deobandis' contemporary polemics against certain practices of visiting Sufi shrines to a conception of the Mamluk-era past. The very utterance of Ibn Taymiyya's name in the context of Sufi saints would have been a dog whistle for Kashmīrī's audiences in Deoband and across the Indian Ocean.[78]

Kashmīrī's discussion of the ten lashes hadith thus spoke to contemporary concerns about the enduring legitimacy of Ḥanafī-trained scholars in a colonial era in which Muslim scholars' legal authority was diminished by Anglo-Muhammadan Law and by an increasingly literate public. But in addition to these social and political factors, Kashmīrī's commentary also attempted to achieve certain interpretive excellences by answering intra-Muslim polemics within and across time: hinting at past and present polemics against the status of Sufi saints and asserting over and against those past and present exegetes who maintained the apparent meaning of the hadith that judges had unlimited discretion in cases of *ta'zīr.*

THE AHL-I HADITH CRITIQUE IN THE AGE OF PRINT

While the Deobandis went beyond the patronage of the elite, Ṣiddīq Ḥasan Khān (d. 1890), the principal figure behind another Sunni reform movement in India, the Ahl-i Hadith ("the People of the Hadith"), largely relied upon the aristocratic support of the princely state of Bhopal.[79] Once penniless, Ḥasan Khān had "free access to eight official printing presses and a team of court scholars, which included some Yemenis" through his marriage to Shāh Jahān Begum (r. 1868–1901).[80] The fact that the Ahl-i Hadith and the Deobandis found common cause in opposing certain saint-shrine visitation practices, and that both traced their scholarly genealogies to the luminary tenth-/sixteenth-century Shāh Walī Allāh, did not prevent stark disagreements in their approach to Islamic law and its derivation.[81] In fact, the Ahl-i Hadith sought to extinguish the authority of the traditional legal schools like the Ḥanafīs altogether, which it viewed as a corrupting "innovation" (*bid'a*) that postdated the Prophet and the rise of Islam.

The Ahl-i Hadith's critique of traditional legal authority may also find its roots in nineteenth-century scholarly networks around the Indian Ocean. Ṣiddīq Ḥasan Khān, like many other Indian Muslim hadith scholars of the time, claimed the influence of 'Abd al-Ḥaqq Banārasī (d. 1870). Banārasī had brought to India the iconoclastic ideas of his teacher, Muḥammad al-Shawkānī (d. 1834), with whom Banārasī had studied in Ṣan'ā', Yemen. Not only did Shawkānī seek to dissuade jurists from following the opinions of a single legal school (*taqlīd*), he also condemned those who adhered blindly to the opinions of their legal school as committing an unlawful innovation (*bid'a*).[82] For Shawkānī, the only legitimate opinions were those of a capable jurist who exerted himself fully to discover the law in the foundational sources (*ijtihād*). And yet, for all his bombast against the authority of the legal schools, with respect to the interpretation of *Ṣaḥīḥ al-Bukhārī,* Shawkānī felt limited by Ibn Ḥajar's *Fatḥ al-bārī.* When Shawkānī's students asked him to comment on *Ṣaḥīḥ al-Bukhārī,* Shawkānī quipped, "there is no going (*hijra*) after the *Fatḥ,*" a pun on a well-known hadith from the *Ṣaḥīḥ,* "there is no migration (*hijra*) after the conquest (*fatḥ*) [of Mecca]."[83]

Ṣiddīq Ḥasan Khān recounted Shawkānī's refusal in the introduction to his commentary on an abridgement of the *Ṣaḥīḥ,* adding, "if this is the reply from a distinguished master, and one who obtained the ability of *ijtihād,* then how would someone like me, helpless, and of lowly aptitude" undertake the challenge of commenting on the *Ṣaḥīḥ?*[84] Rather than try to improve upon Ibn Ḥajar, as Kashmīrī and Shaykh al-Hind attempted to do, Ṣiddīq Ḥasan Khān's first goal was merely to edit and distribute printed editions of *Fatḥ al-bārī.*[85] Previously, *Fatḥ al-bārī* had been virtually inaccessible in Delhi, with sections of a hand-written copy scattered in three places.[86] Ṣiddīq Ḥasan Khān's printed editions of the work, the first of their kind, thus significantly broadened the work's accessibility.

Later, Ṣiddīq Ḥasan Khān produced his own short commentary on *Ṣaḥīḥ al-Bukhārī,* which was called *ʿAwn al-bārī* (Comfort of the divine wisdom). This work, out of deference to the comprehensiveness of *Fatḥ al-bārī,* was effectively a strategic abridgment of Ibn Ḥajar's commentary. But Ṣiddīq Ḥasan Khān further limited the authority of his own text by publishing it in the margins of Shawkānī's famous commentary on a collection of hadith compiled by the grandfather of Ibn Taymiyya.[87] Hand-written margin commentaries produced in a traditional setting would always have responded to the base-text itself, but a base-text with a supercommentary on a completely separate, albeit related, text could only have been imagined in an era of print (see fig. 8).

One function of coupling these two separate commentaries in this way was that a purchaser of the text would have acquired two works in a single transaction, and the reader could easily cross-reference between them. But the credibility of Bukhārī's and Ḥasan Khān's comparatively even-tempered explications must have bolstered the authority of Shawkānī's more audacious work. While Shawkānī boldly condemned adherence to any single legal school's opinions in the center of the page, Ḥasan Khān subtly purged *Fatḥ al-bārī* of any overt Shāfiʿī recommendations in the narrow corridors of Shawkānī's margins.[88]

عجب الذنب (فيه يركب الخلق) ولمسلم ٦٠ من طريق همام عن أبي هريرة ان فى الانسان عظما لا تأكله الارض أبدا

مسعود المذكور فيه متمسك لمن يجوز للامام والحاكم ومن صلح ان يقيم الحدود اذا علم بذلك وان لم يقع من فاعل ما يوجبها اقرار ولا قامت عليه البينة به وقد خالف فى أصل حكم الحاكم بعلمه مطلقا شريح والشعبي وابن أبى ليلى والاوزاعى ومالك وأحمد واسحق والشافعى فى قول له فقالوا لا يجوز له ان يقضى بعلمه مطلقا وقال الناصر والمؤيد بالله فى قول له والشافعى فى قول له أيضا انه يجوز للحاكم ان يحكم بعلمه فى كل شئ من غير فرق بين الحد وغيره وذهبت العترة الى أنه يحكم بعلمه فى الاموال دون الحدود الا فى حد القذف فانه يحكم فيه بعلمه ويدل على ذلك ما أخرجه البخارى تعليقا ان عمر قال لعبد الرحمن لو رأيت رجلا على حد فقال أرى شهادتك شهادة رجل من المسلمين قال أصبت ووصله البيهقى ويؤيده حديث لو كنت راجما أحدا بغير بينة لرجمتها فى قصة الملاعنة وقد تقدم فان ذلك يدل على ان النبى صلى الله عليه وآله وسلم قد علم زناها

(باب ما جاء فى قدر التعزير والحبس فى التهم)

(عن أبى بردة بن نيار انه سمع النبى صلى الله عليه وآله وسلم يقول لا يجلد فوق عشرة أسواط الا فى حد من حدود الله تعالى رواه الجماعة الا النسائى * وعن بهز بن حكيم عن أبيه عن جده ان النبى صلى الله عليه وآله وسلم حبس رجلا فى تهمة ثم خلى عنه رواه الخمسة الا ابن ماجه) حديث أبى بردة مع كونه متفقا عليه قد تكلم فى اسناده ابن المنذر والاصيلى من جهة الاختلاف فيه وقال البيهقى قد أقام عمرو بن الحرث اسناده فلا يضره تقصير من قصر فيه وقال الغزالى صححه بعض الائمة وتعقبه الرافعى فى التذنيب فقال أراد بقوله بعض الائمة صاحب التقريب ولكن الحديث أظهر من أن تضاف صحته الى فرد من الائمة فقد صححه البخارى ومسلم وحديث بهز بن حكيم حسنه الترمذى وقال الحاكم صحيح الاسناد ثم أخرج له شاهدا من حديث أبى هريرة وفيه ان النبى صلى الله عليه وآله وسلم حبس فى تهمة يوما وليلة وقد تقدم الاختلاف فى حديث بهز بن حكيم عن أبيه عن جده قوله لا يجلد روى بفتح الياء فى أوله وكسر اللام وروى أيضا بضم الياء وفتح اللام وروى بصيغة النهى مجزوما وبصيغة النفى مرفوعا قوله فوق عشرة أسواط فى رواية فوق عشر ضربات قوله الا فى حد المراد به ما ورد عن الشارع مقدرا بعدد مخصوص كحد الزنا والقذف ونحوهما وقيل المراد بالحد هنا عقوبة المعصية مطلقا لا الاشياء المخصوصة فان ذلك التخصيص انما هو من اصطلاح الفقهاء وعرف الشرع اطلاق الحد على كل عقوبة لمعصية من المعاصى كبيرة أو صغيرة ونسب ابن دقيق العيد هذه المقالة الى بعض المعاصرين له واليها ذهب ابن القيم وقال المراد بالنهى المذكور فى التأديب للمصالح كتأديب الاب ابنه الصغير واعترض على ذلك بأنه قد ظهر ان الشارع يطلق الحدود على العقوبات المخصوصة ويؤيد ذلك قول عبد الرحمن بن عوف ان أخف الحدود ثمانون كما تقدم فى كتاب حد شارب الخمر وقد ذهب الى العمل بحديث الباب جماعة من أهل العلم منهم الليث وأحمد فى المشهور عنه واسحق وبعض

الشافعية

فيه يركب يوم القيامة قال أى عظم قال عجب الذنب وهذا الحديث عام يخص منه الانبياء لان الارض لا تأكل أجسادهم وقد ألحق ابن عبد البر بهم الشهداء والقرطبى المؤذن المحتسب قال ابن الجوزى قال ابن عقيل لله فى هذا سر لا نعلمه لان من يظهر الوجود من العدم لا يحتاج الى شئ يبنى عليه ويحتمل ان يكون ذلك جعل علامة للملائكة على احياء كل انسان بجوهره ولا يحصل العلم للملائكة بذلك الا بابقاء عظم كل شخص ليعلم انه انما أراد بذلك اعادة الارواح الى تلك الاعيان التى هى جزء منها ولولا ابقاء شئ منه لجوزت الملائكة ان الاعادة الى أمثال الاجساد لا الى نفس الاجساد (قوله عز وجل الا المودة فى القربى) أى ان تودونى لقرابتى منكم أو تودوا أهل قرابتى (عن ابن عباس رضى الله عنهما قال ان النبى صلى الله عليه) وآله (وسلم لم يكن بطن من قريش الا كان له فيهم قرابة فقال الا ان تصلوا ما بينى وبينكم من القرابة) فحمل الآية على ان تودوا النبى صلى الله عليه وآله وسلم من أجل القرابة التى بينه وبينكم فهو خاص بقريش ويؤيده ان السورة مكية وأما حديث ابن عباس عند ابن أبى حاتم قال لما نزلت هذه الآية قل لا أسألكم عليه أجرا الا المودة فى القربى قالوا يا رسول الله من هؤلاء الذين أمر الله

FIGURE 8. Page 60 from volume 7 of the 1880 Būlāq edition of Shawkānī's *Nayl al-awṭār* a commentary on Majd al-Dīn Ibn Taymiyya's *Muntaqā al-akhbār,* with Ḥasan Khān's *ʿAwn al-bārī,* a commentary on *Ṣaḥīḥ al-Bukhārī* in the margins.

Although Ṣiddīq Ḥasan Khān enjoyed the patronage of the princely state of Bhopal, he may not have had any greater power than the Deobandis in shaping the Privy Council's position on discretionary punishment (*taʿzīr*). In fact, many of his ideas were met with the British suspicion that he espoused views identical to those of the Wahhābīs, a central Arabian reform movement. Despite some similarities between their ideas, Ṣiddīq Ḥasan Khān objected to this characterization.[89]

Ṣiddīq Ḥasan Khān and Kashmīrī came to opposite conclusions on the issue of discretionary punishment (*taʿzīr*). While Kashmīrī concluded that a qualified judge ought to have unrestricted authority in discretionary punishment, Ṣiddīq Ḥasan Khān averred that judges ought to be restricted to the apparent meaning of the hadith: ten lashes for non-*ḥadd* offenses and no more. Since Ṣiddīq Ḥasan Khān's own discussion of discretionary punishment consists of an abridgement of Ibn Ḥajar's explanation of the ten lashes hadith in *Fatḥ al-bārī*, we do not have any views unique to Ḥasan Khān to analyze. Rather, we will have to examine what Ṣiddīq Ḥasan Khān chose to include and what he chose to omit in his abridgment of Ibn Ḥajar's work.

If you recall, Ibn Ḥajar read Bukhārī's question in the chapter heading "How Much Discretionary Punishment?" as an indication that the issue of discretionary punishment was open to debate.[90] Ṣiddīq Ḥasan Khān's omission of any discussion of the chapter heading ironically functioned to close the text in this regard. While Ṣiddīq Ḥasan Khān acknowledged that there was genuine disagreement among the legal schools concerning discretionary punishment, in the final section in his commentary, as we will see, he obviated the need for such disagreement. Likewise, the disagreements over the authenticity of the hadith's chains of transmission are virtually absent. Ḥasan Khān stated little more than the fact that these hadith had been authenticated by both Bukhārī and Muslim, as well as by the four *Sunans* of Abū Dāwūd, Tirmidhī, Nasāʾī, and Ibn Māja.[91] The time in which the debate over the authenticity of these hadith was relevant must have, for Ṣiddīq Ḥasan Khān, long passed.

Ṣiddīq Ḥasan Khān did include a discussion of the disagreement between Ibn Daqīq al-ʿĪd and Ibn Taymiyya over this hadith. However, while Ibn Ḥajar referred to the latter in his commentary simply as "Ibn Taymiyya," Ḥasan Khān inserts a reverential title into Ibn Ḥajar's quote: "Shaykh al-Islām Ibn Taymiyya."[92] Part of the reason Ṣiddīq Ḥasan Khān chose to include this discussion was that his readership would have been particularly curious to hear of Ibn Taymiyya's position on this hadith, since he was greatly admired as a Mamluk-era proponent of the kinds of reforms Shawkānī and the Ahl-i Hadith thought were badly needed in their eras.

Ḥasan Khān also summarized Ibn Ḥajar's exegetical history of the classical jurists' opinions. What is most significant in this aspect of Ḥasan Khān's abridgement, however, is that he did not tilt toward one particular school's position. In fact, he excluded the very opinion Ibn Ḥajar thought ought to be "relied upon" (*al-mu'tamad*): Nawawī's dissent that the majority did not rule on its basis. In this way, Ṣiddīq Ḥasan Khān strategically assured his readers that there was a consensus that the hadith ought to be treated as a source of law, even if it bucked the opinion of one's legal school.[93]

Although Ḥasan Khān brought into greater relief aspects of *Fatḥ al-bārī*'s discussion of discretionary punishment that resonated with the legal principles of the Ahl-i Hadith, he was far more restrained than he would have been if he had built his commentary directly on Shawkānī's discussion of discretionary punishment. While Ḥasan Khān simply omitted Ibn Ḥajar's reliance on Nawawī's opinion, Shawkanī included it only to promptly denounce it outright: "a just man must not prop up the opinions of one person against the utterance of the Prophet of God."[94] Ḥasan Khān, as I pointed out earlier, considered himself "helpless, and of lowly aptitude" in comparison to Shawkanī, and his more limited rhetoric may be a reflection of that modesty. While some biographers and opponents remembered Ḥasan Khān as unskilled, tactless, and aggressive, his power to persuade lay precisely in his ability to make the commentary tradition speak the conclusions of the Ahl-i Hadith without explicitly saying so or polemicizing against rival opinions.[95]

At the level of composition, Kashmīrī's commentary was, in many ways, far more open than Ḥasan Khān's. While Kashmīrī defended the Ḥanafī school, he offered unique and novel responses to the interpretive tradition and its best application in the present. Ḥasan Khān, by contrast, in spite of his admiration for those who bucked reliance on traditional authorities, limited himself to speaking through the words of a Mamluk-era paragon of hadith scholars and clung to the apparent meaning of the ten lashes hadith. In both cases, the preservation of Mamluk-era commentarial opinions was not merely a qualification of their authority but also a medium of innovation and normative debate.

• • •

Patronage in the Gujarati sultanate and the Deccan in the ninth/sixteenth century animated scholarly movement and migration between

India and centers of learning in Egypt and the Arabian Peninsula. The practice of hadith commentary, which had reached baroque-like heights in Mamluk Cairo, thus found a robust afterlife in India, first among migrant scholars and then among Indian-born and Indian-trained hadith scholars in the tenth to twelfth (sixteenth to eighteenth) centuries. A migrant chronicler writing in tenth-/sixteenth-century Gujarat reminisced of live commentarial performances on *Ṣaḥīḥ al-Bukhārī* in Yemen that rivaled the celebrated performances at the citadel in Mamluk Cairo. Material objects and super-sensory visions were part of this experience, as a witness noted that a copy of Ibn Ḥajar's *Fatḥ al-bārī* was among the books at the performance and claimed that he saw the Prophet himself in attendance.

Meanwhile, Gujarati sultans recognized the prestige, legitimacy, and other forms of social capital at stake in the commentary tradition and generously gave land revenues and wealth in order to support it. In exchange, they acquired distinguished Mamluk-era written commentaries on hadith for their libraries and earned laudatory dedications with exaltations that were unsurpassed in the history of the genre. At the same time, some patrons recognized the ends internal to the tradition and how they might be achieved within certain standards of excellence. One Gujarati sultan was remembered to have directly weighed in on a debate over a hadith loaded with symbolism for piety-minded Muslims. Reasoning with fine-grained exegetical methods, the Gujarati sultan's contribution to the debate was remembered to have resulted in the hadith's inclusion as an authentic source of law in a widely circulating legal compendium. Even if this portrait is overly flattering, it shows the extent to which hadith commentators in India saw the fortunes of their scholarly legacy intertwined with the fortunes of political life.

In the nineteenth and twentieth centuries, the complex social and political matrix of colonialism in India upended hadith commentators' historical sources of patronage, called into question the traditional technologies and structures of their legal and religious authority, and distanced them from political power. Figures from diverse reformist movements turned to the medium of hadith commentary as one way to respond to and mediate the expansion of British colonial power in all spheres of life, including law and education. Reformist commentators thus adopted some British technologies and frameworks while maintaining a living connectedness to an idealized Mamluk-era and "Arab" past they simultaneously claimed to preserve and improve upon. Colonialism may have brought new constraints and new competitors to traditional religious authorities, but it also brought hadith commentators into conversation with new audiences in India and the broader Islamic world, pressing them to consider the foundational sources anew and to write, speak, and think more freely about issues of politics than their predecessors. The resulting experience, at least for some students attending the hadith commentary sessions, was ecstatic and transformative.

In the case of discretionary punishment, an issue that was of graver consequence to a colonial legal expert than the more popular British polemics against amputation for theft and stoning for adultery, representatives from the Deobandi school and the Ahl-i Hadith recast the meaning of the hadith to opposing ends. For Kashmīrī, judges should be accorded the greatest possible discretion. For Ṣiddīq Ḥasan Khān, judges ought to be limited by the hadith: ten lashes and no more. One should not conclude, however, that hadith could mean whatever best suited the hadith scholars' social and political interests. While Kashmīrī was attuned to the fragmentation of traditional religious authority in the colonial context and the polemics concerning Sufi-shrine visitation practices, he also was bound to defend the opinions of the legal school he inherited. Likewise, Ṣiddīq Ḥasan Khān, whose critique of legal school authority was shaped by the social, historical, political, and sectarian factors in his contemporary context, was also bound by his exacting commitment to the hadith's apparent meaning and spoke largely through the voice of earlier masters in Mamluk-era Egypt and the Arabian Peninsula.

In both cases, preserving the opinions of authorities from Egypt and the Arabian Peninsula was not merely a requirement that commentators needed to fulfill in order to speak credibly to their present audiences and to assert their diminishing power and authority in the colonial context. Rather, in the very act of reordering, abridging, and repeating Mamluk-era commentaries, nineteenth- and twentieth-century commentators synthesized new ideas to connect their present audiences with their conception of the past.

CHAPTER 10

Lost in Translation

Arabic to Urdu to English

The degree of the historical sense of any age may be inferred from the manner in which this age makes *translations* and tries to absorb former ages and books.

—Friedrich Nietzsche

In order to reach broader audiences at home and abroad, South Asian commentators in the twentieth and early twenty-first centuries began to publish commentaries in Urdu and English in greater numbers. The authors of these translations employed many of the strategies that Arabic-language commentators employed to construct their authority and their commentaries: they deployed Arabic literary conventions, defended their legal schools, rooted written commentaries in live performances, and traced their living genealogies to religious authorities and spaces in the Arabian Peninsula and the Arab Middle East. They also continued to turn to the medium of commentary to accommodate and respond to new challenges and opportunities that arose in their social, political, and historical contexts. These translations wove in references to modern life, including new developments in science and technology.

Historically, the audience of commentaries on *Ṣaḥīḥ al-Bukhārī* was made up of those already initiated into the tradition. But in an age of mass literacy, some of these translations began to broaden their imagined audience even to non-Muslims, including religious and secular opponents as well as potential converts. By the twenty-first century, the new media of television and online videos allowed anyone, in theory, to peek into a contemporary commentary session.

This chapter will examine this theme of translation and shifting audiences in two parts. In the first part, I will analyze an English translation of *Faḍl al-bārī* (Bounty of the divine wisdom) by a Deobandi hadith scholar from the generation that followed Kashmīrī: Shabbir Aḥmad ʿUthmānī (d. 1949). Notes from his live Urdu commentaries were posthumously edited and published in Urdu and English in the mid-1970s in Pakistan. As we will see, ʿUthmānī enshrined himself in a transregional and transtemporal genealogy of traditional interpreters, defended the Ḥanafī school, and contributed new ideas to an internal debate over the meaning of Islam and faith. How was this commentary transferred from the master's lips to the printed page over the course of roughly thirty years? And how did ʿUthmānī maintain a connection with a traditional past while opening up to wider audiences in India and beyond, in the West?

In the second part, I will examine the work of a contemporary Urdu commentator on hadith in Hyderabad, India, named Muḥammad Khʷāje Sharīf. I will draw on ethnographic observations of his lessons and close readings of his texts to understand how his commentary navigated and emerged from the spaces, times, audiences, technologies, intellectual debates, and syncretic cultural milieu of twenty-first-century Hyderabad. In concluding, I will attempt to tease out broader comparative insights between these two cases, as well as the cases we examined in the preceding chapters.

CONSTRUCTING ʿUTHMĀNĪ'S AUTHORITY

After Anwar Shāh al-Kashmīrī passed away in 1933, a scholar from the next generation of Deobandi students emerged as an exegete of the Qur'an and hadith: Shabbir Aḥmad ʿUthmānī. Born in 1886, his father was of some means, having been employed as deputy inspector of schools, and was learned in Urdu literature.[1] As a child, ʿUthmānī was initiated as a student in the Dār al-ʿUlūm in Deoband and began studying Persian. As a teenager, he began his course of study in Arabic.[2] During that time, he studied with a number of scholars, including Shaykh al-Hind Maḥmūd al-Ḥasan, the expert hadith scholar and commentator whom we met in the preceding chapter.[3] After completing his studies, ʿUthmānī began his teaching career at Deoband and then moved to a branch of Dār al-ʿUlūm in Dabhel, Gujarat, where he developed his early commentaries on the Qur'an and *Ṣaḥīḥ Muslim*. Following Kashmīrī's death, a fifty-year-old ʿUthmānī returned to Deoband to deliver his lectures on *Ṣaḥīḥ al-Bukhārī* and *Sunan Tirmidhī*.[4] He would return to Dabhel in the last decade of his life in part because the political situation in colonial India at Deoband had grown untenable, as pro-independence students and scholars like ʿUthmānī faced the threat of arrest.[5]

Thus ʿUthmānī's biographers, in introducing his commentary on *Ṣaḥīḥ al-Bukhārī*, remembered and praised him not only for his immense learning and his scholarly genealogy but also for his political activities. His model in this regard may have been his teacher, Shaykh al-Hind, who was both a hadith scholar and an anticolonial revolutionary, serving over three and a half years of imprisonment in Malta for his role in the so-called Silken Letters Movement, an armed and international conspiracy against the British.[6] Although ʿUthmānī was not involved in that movement, he did participate in the Indian nationalist party called Jamʿiyyat al-ʿUlamāʾ-yi Hind and even served as their representative to the first king of the third Saudi state, ʿAbd al-ʿAzīz Āl Saʿūd.[7] This underlines not only the importance of continued connections between the Arabian Peninsula and Muslim scholars in India but also the mutual interdependence of political and religious networks.

ʿUthmānī was also important to the Pakistan movement. While Muslim scholars like Abū ʿAlāʾ al-Mawdūdī vocally criticized the idea of the creation of Pakistan, fearing it would be a secular state in Islamic garb, ʿUthmānī saw potential. He inaugurated the first session of the National Assembly on the day of Pakistan's independence with a verse from the Qur'an and was appointed to hoist the flag in the presence of Muhammad Ali Jinnah, the founder of Pakistan, on Independence Day.[8] But his participation was not merely at symbolic inaugurations and flag hoistings. After partition, ʿUthmānī's support was critical to the passing of the so-called Objectives Resolution, which helped to Islamize the nascent Pakistani constitution. ʿUthmānī pleaded with the Constituent Assembly for "the establishment of Islamic law" as "the final objective," even if this goal was achieved gradually, through phases.[9] This was a marked departure from Jinnah's vision for Pakistan that, much to the dismay of many Muslim scholars, envisioned a secular homeland in which "Muslims would cease to be Muslims, not in the religious sense, because that is the personal faith of each individual, but in the political sense as citizens of the State."[10] Whether or not one agrees with his student's bold assessment that ʿUthmānī was among "the front-rank architects of Pakistan"[11] is beside the point: ʿUthmānī's authority as a commentator on *Ṣaḥīḥ al-Bukhārī* was linked with his students' memory of him as an icon in the founding of Pakistan.

FROM URDU LECTURE TO ENGLISH PRINT

Since ʿUthmānī had composed popular commentaries on the Qur'an and *Ṣaḥīḥ Muslim*, Kashmīrī asked him to compose a major commentary on *Ṣaḥīḥ al-Bukhārī* along the same lines.[12] When ʿUthmānī began to deliver his commentary in Urdu at Deobandi madrasas in northern India and Gujarat in the mid- to late 1930s, a rector at an Arabic school in Karachi believed that ʿUthmānī's lectures on *Ṣaḥīḥ al-Bukhārī* were "so fresh and original and his language so lucid, elegant and exalting that no other previous exposition could equal it."[13] During these live lessons, one of ʿUthmānī's closest students took extensive notes and showed them to ʿUthmānī.[14] Apparently, ʿUthmānī wanted to organize these notes and arrange to have them published after he migrated to the nascent Pakistan, but he passed away before he was able to do so.[15] These notes, which had been left to ʿUthmānī's brother in manuscript form,[16] were, according to his brother, sketchy and disorganized. Some thought the notes should be published as is, but academic and religious presses did not want to publish such a work unrevised, since it would not be able to reach a broad audience.[17] According to ʿUthmānī's brother, however, anyone who looked at the notes was intimidated by the "awe-inspiring magnitude" of the revisions necessary to publish it.[18]

At last a little-known Deobandi scholar and judge named ʿAbd al-Raḥmān undertook this task and began to prepare the work for publication in Urdu and English, under the patronage of Muḥammad Ṭayyib (d. 1983) the rector of the Dār al-ʿUlūm in Deoband.[19] Considering the state of ʿUthmānī's notes when he acquired them, ʿAbd Raḥmān must have played a creative role in the revision, redaction, and annotation of this work. "I have left the language and exposition of these drafts as they were," he wrote, "but I have rearranged and adjusted the subject-matter of the exegesis. So the reader will find in it a concordance of the lectures and the recordings thereof."[20]

ʿAbd Raḥmān's labor as an editor and translator was not only intellectual but also bureaucratic. He wrote:

> The English translation might appear to be an easy job but in fact it is not. In the first place, the translated passages have to be compared with the original and the typescripts are sent to the members of the Board who examine the translation. The staff of the Idārah-i-ʿUlūm-i-Sharʿiyya [*sic*] then consults the translator who gives the scripts the final touch. Great pains have to be taken by the staff to ensure correct transliteration without which the English renderings of Arabic words and names cannot be pronounced correctly.[21]

While a written work in the manuscript age would have been proofed by a second reader, usually a qualified teacher, ʿAbd Raḥmān's printed edition involved a larger and more anonymous staff that micromanaged translation and transliteration choices.

According to ʿUthmānī's son-in-law, the revisions took years to complete.[22] For advice on the revision process, ʿAbd Raḥmān visited his mentor in Medina, Muḥammad Zakariyyā al-Kāndhlawī (d. 1982), a master hadith scholar and commentator who, among other works, composed multivolume commentaries on *Ṣaḥīḥ al-Bukhārī* and Mālik's *Muwaṭṭaʾ*. Sick with a fever, Kāndhlawī told ʿAbd Raḥmān not to overly concern himself with fully reproducing ʿUthmānī's marginal notes and references, lest it overly delay production.[23] Thus, in the English edition, ʿAbd Raḥmān omitted the portions of ʿUthmānī's commentary that would only appeal to specialists, but he preserved them in the Urdu edition.[24]

When the revisions of volume 1 were complete, ʿAbd Raḥmān recorded the date and the time as if the revisions themselves had been a devotional achievement: "Praise be to Allāh that he enabled me to go through a final proof the last pages of the First Volume of *Faḍl al-Bārī* . . . during the late hours of night, this twenty-seventh day of September 1975 (C.E.) corresponding to 20th of Ramaḍān 1395 A.H." Following its publication, ʿAbd Raḥmān took a few copies of the printed but not yet bound *Faḍl al-bārī* to Medina "to consecrate them to the resting place of the Holy Prophet so that these could be enshrined there."[25] While this would be the only volume in English Rahman would complete, he finished two volumes of the work in Urdu.[26]

What prompted ʿAbd Raḥmān to undertake this project? The available evidence tells a complicated story. Although ʿAbd Raḥmān was clearly well connected within the Deobandi scene through family and study, he left little to posterity other than these three volumes of ʿUthmānī's *Faḍl al-bārī* in Urdu and English. Nevertheless, Raḥmān was remembered for his political activism. He was imprisoned for his involvement with the Finality of [Muhammad's] Prophethood Movement (*taḥrīk-i khatm-i nubūwwat*), which branded the Ahmadiyya as heretics and sought to remove them from military and political positions within the Pakistani government. After five or six years of involvement in protests, Raḥmān was eventually arrested, following the civil unrest in 1953 and the imposition of martial law.[27] A related threat, for ʿAbd Raḥmān, was the influence of secular thought.[28] It is possible that ʿUthmānī's commentary, which marshals the hadith against the Ahmadiyya and secularism, appealed to ʿAbd Raḥmān's political and sectarian sensibilities and offered him a credible mouthpiece through which to advance his own ambitions and reputation.

ʿAbd Raḥmān's expressed motivation, however, is located in a different space and appeals to an order of interpretive ends internal to the commentary tradition. Apparently, ʿAbd Raḥmān was studying hadith in Medina with his mentor, Muḥammad Zakariyyā, and heard verse 34:28 from the Qur'an recited: "And We have not sent thee (O Muḥammad) save as a bringer of good tidings and a warner unto all mankind, but most of mankind know not."[29] ʿAbd Raḥmān portrayed his intention in this way to draw on the prestige of both the Qur'an and Medina to sacralize the labor of translation, editing, publication, and distribution. My point is not to frame ʿAbd Raḥmān's political motivations or his normative commitments as mutually exclusive or to suggest that ʿAbd Raḥmān's religious rhetoric was actually sectarian politics in disguise, or vice versa. On the contrary, ʿAbd Raḥmān's translation emerged in a context in which social and material rewards as well as interpretive excellences were intertwined, and in a context that linked local and global spaces and histories.

CONNECTING PAST AND PRESENT

As we saw in the preceding chapter, Deobandi scholars spoke to their present by maintaining a connectedness with a conception of the Islamic past. This was partly an issue of constructing a genealogy to the Arab lands. In ʿUthmānī's case, the genealogy his biographers attributed to him traced his ancestry to ʿUthmān ibn ʿAffān (r. 23–35/644–56), the third caliph, who presided over the collection and standardization of the Qur'an.[30] Again, whether this genealogy is apocryphal or not is beside the point. What matters for our purposes is that his readers and students saw his authority to be rooted in the rise of Islam in the Arabian Peninsula.

Another way the translation maintained a connection with the past is through Arabic and Arabic literary conventions. Even though the work was a translation, intended for audiences who could not speak or read Arabic, Raḥmān included the hadith in Arabic prior to ʿUthmānī's commentary. He also included, in the work's introduction, an Arabic panegyric (*taqrīẓ*), composed by a scholar and poet at the Prophet's Mosque in Medina who himself had migrated from an Uzbek-speaking community of Ṭarāz on the border of Kazakhstan and Kyrgyzstan.[31]

بسم الله الرحمن الرحيم

In the Name of Allāh, Who is Excessively Compassionate, Extremely Merciful

PANEGYRIC

By

The Learned Scholar, Sincere Friend, and Excellent Poet

Al-Shaykh Al-Sayyid Mahmud bin Nazir Al-Tarazi Al-Madani

(Lecturer at the Masjid-e-Nabawi, Madinah Munawwarah)

(May Allāh prolong his life to enable the scholars to benefit from him and may He continue to shower His blessings on the Muslims. Amen!)

صَحِيحُ إِمَامِ الْكُلِّ أَعْنِي مُحَمَّدًا — كِتَابٌ سَيَبْقَى فِي الْعُصُورِ مُخَلَّدًا

1. The book, the *Ṣhaīḥ Bukhārī*, by Imām al-Kul (Imām of all Imāms) Muḥammad Ibn Ismā'īl, is one that will endure for ever.

كِتَابٌ أَرَادَ اللهُ كَوْنَ مَقَامِهِ — بُعَيْدَ كِتَابِ اللهِ فِي الْفَضْلِ وَالْهُدَى

2. It ranks second only to the Holy Book in authority and guidance.

كِتَابٌ بِهِ يَزْهُو النَّبِيُّ رَسُولُنَا — وَيُرْشِدُ أَنْ يُنْمَى إِلَيْهِ وَيُسْنَدَا

3. It is such that the Holy Prophet (صلى الله عليه وسلم) spoke highly of it[2] in a dream[1] and directed to repose trust in it and to turn to it for guidance.

لَقَدْ رَزَقَ اللهُ الْبُخَارِيَّ جَمْعَهُ — فَأَبْدَاهُ عَمَّا لَمْ يَصِحَّ مُجَرَّدَا

4. God bestowed upon Imām Bukhārī the distinction of collecting *Aḥadīth*. He excluded from this collection all the sayings that did not bear proper testimony or authority.

أَئِمَّةُ دُنْيَا الْمُسْلِمِينَ جَمِيعُهُمْ — بِهِ عَرَفُوهُ الْيَوْمَ شَيْخًا مُمَجَّدَا

5. Because of this, the scholars of the Muslim world to-day acknowledge Imām Bukhārī (رحمة الله عليه) as their leader and the foremost authority on the Tradition.

FIGURE 9. English (above) and Urdu (opposite) translation of a panegyric written by Maḥmūd Nadhīr al-Ṭarāzī (d. 1990), commissioned for the purpose of lauding the publication of ʿUthmānī's commentary in English and Urdu translations. The total length of the poem is forty couplets. See ʿUthmānī, *Faḍl al-bārī* (in English, 1975), 1:44; (in Urdu, 1973), 1:30.

The original Arabic of the panegyric was preserved, and, like the Urdu edition, Raḥmān's translation was printed between the lines (see fig. 9). It may be the only panegyric on *Ṣaḥīḥ al-Bukhārī* published in English translation.

Arabic panegyrics were typically recited aloud at the closing (*khatm*) of a month-long (or months-long) reading or study of the work, accompanied by a celebratory feast. Although the printed translation could not create the communal celebration that a formal *khatm* could, the

بسم الله الرحمن الرحيم

تقريظ العلامة الاديب الاريب المشفق الحبيب صاحب القريحة النابغة والنظم العجيب

الشيخ السيد محمود بن نذير الطرازي المدني المدرس بالمسجد النبوي الشريف

متع الله الطلبة والمستفيدين بطول حياته وأعاد الله على المسلمين من بركاته آمين

اس منظوم تقریظ کا اردو ترجمہ الحاج حضرت مولینا عبد الملک صاحب مفتش تحفیظ القرآن مدینہ منورہ نے کیا۔

صحيح امام الكل اعني محمدا　　كتاب سيبقى في العصور مخلدا

امام الکل یعنی امام محمد ابن اسماعیل بخاری کی کتاب صحیح البخاری ایک ایسی کتاب ہے جو ہمیشہ ہمیشہ باقی رہے گی۔

كتاب اراد الله كون مقامه　　بعيد كتاب الله في الفضل والهدى

یہ ایک ایسی کتاب ہے جس کو اللہ تعالے نے صحت اور ہدایت ورہبری کے لحاظ سے قرآن مجید کے بعد کا درجہ دیا ہے۔

كتاب به يزهو النبي رسولنا　　ويرشد ان ينمى اليه ويسندا

یہ ایک ایسی کتاب ہے کہ خواب میں حضور صلی اللہ علیہ وسلم نے اس پر فخر کا اظہار فرمایا اور اسناد حدیث میں اس پر اعتماد اور اس کی طرف مراجعت کی ہدایت فرمائی

لقد رزق الله البخاري جمعه　　فابداه عما لم يصح مجردا

اللہ تعالے نے امام بخاری کو احادیث نبوی کے جمع کرنے کی توفیق بخشی، آپ نے ہر وہ حدیث جو معیار صحت پر نہ پہنچی اس کو اس کتاب سے الگ کر دیا

ائمة دنيا المسلمين جميعهم　　به عرفوه اليوم شيخا ممجدا

اسلامی دنیا کے سارے علماء آج اس کتاب کی وجہ سے امام بخاری کو بلند مرتبہ پیشوا اور علم حدیث میں امام تسلیم کرتے ہیں

panegyric Raḥmān commissioned nevertheless aimed to recreate some of these feelings of connection to a transtemporal and transregional community. As was convention, the panegyric began by praising the Prophet, *Ṣaḥīḥ al-Bukhārī,* its compiler, and its commentaries "in every age," including the work of recent Deobandi scholars such as Shaykh al-Hind Maḥmūd al-Ḥasan. ʿUthmānī himself was then praised, particularly for his eloquence in oratory and his commentary's accessible language. The delays in printing and ʿAbd Raḥmān's struggles to revise and verify the commentary were also lauded.[32]

ʿAbd Raḥmān echoed this sense of a transregional and transtemporal community in his introduction, writing that "thousands of miles intervene between us and them, nevertheless, the unity of purpose has removed all geographical distances and it seems as if we were members of the same fraternity living in different places and co-operating in the completion of this task."[33]

This connectedness across time and space was so vital to the function of the text and the authority of its exegetes that, through the medium of the commentary, temporal and spatial difference appeared to collapse. A great example of this transregional and transtemporal communal conversation is ʿUthmānī's contribution to the internal debate over the definition of faith (*īmān*).

FAITH: RECASTING A MILLENNIUM OF DEBATE

You may recall from chapter 7 that Ibn Ḥajar disagreed with Bukhārī, within the medium of the commentary, over the distinction between *islām* and faith (*īmān*). At stake was whether faith alone defined a true believer, as Bukhārī was likely suggesting, or whether it also required action, as Ibn Ḥajar maintained. Apparently, the Ḥanafī definition of *faith* also had a role to play in this controversy. According to ʿUthmānī, even though Ḥanafīs define *islām* as both faith and action, they were taken to task for certain statements of the school's eponymous founder, Abū Ḥanīfa. Opponents charged that Abū Ḥanīfa set the lowest possible bar for action: the only act truly required to complete one's faith was a verbal utterance of belief in God and his messenger.

In an extended discussion of the matter, ʿUthmānī condensed and reconstructed the complicated and multifaceted conversation that took place over roughly twelve hundred years.[34] Beginning with hadith, Qur'anic verses, and early Islamic differences in theology among groups like the Murjiʾa, the Khawārij, and others, he wound his way to the opinions of Abū Ḥanīfa and other key eponyms of schools of Islamic law. He then addressed what he understood to be Bukhārī's definition of *faith,* based on his editorial decisions and chapter headings in his *Ṣaḥīḥ.* Before turning to the modern period, he consulted a number of late classical and post-classical Muslim scholars, including Ibn Ḥajar. What is preserved in these discussions is a bitter polemic against Abū Ḥanīfa from the early hadith scholars who defined *faith* in a way that would require rather than recommend that one observe Islamic law more broadly to complete one's faith.[35]

Before delivering his own opinion, ʿUthmānī first consulted Deobandi scholars who attempted to resolve the debate in their own way. First among them was Shaykh al-Hind, who argued that the current opponents of the Ḥanafīs lack knowledge of the debate's historical context. In fact, Shaykh al-Hind argued that latter-day polemics against Ḥanafīs emerged from hadith scholars' attacks against an early Islamic religio-political movement called the Murjiʾa, who are often lambasted for not requiring that actions follow from faith. Shaykh al-Hind contended that contemporary opponents have misplaced their attacks on the Ḥanafīs, who, in his view, actually agree with them. Thus the medium of the commentary, which can narrativize these creedal disputes in their proper historical context, is especially well positioned to resolve them.[36]

ʿUthmānī also turned to Kashmīrī, who had undertaken a kind of source-criticism on Abū Ḥanīfa's statements.[37] Kashmīrī reasoned that because many of the problematic statements from Abū Ḥanīfa were preserved only in the words of polemicists attacking him, there was cause to wonder if Abū Ḥanīfa actually said them. Even though, after rigorous research, Kashmīrī could find no text directly attributing the problematic statements to Abū Ḥanīfa, he did find similar quotations preserved in what he believed to be reliable sources. The probability that Abū Ḥanīfa uttered those statements, for Kashmīrī, was more likely than not.

ʿUthmānī built on both of these Deobandi scholars' approaches to synthesize his own opinion, which he believed would "put an end to the whole controversy."[38] In his opinion, one needs to understand both the historical context and the full text of what Abū Ḥanīfa actually uttered. Relying on a renowned classical Ḥanafī scholar, al-Ṭaḥāwī (d. 321/933), ʿUthmānī closely analyzed what he believed was "the most dependable reproduction of Imām Abū Ḥanīfah's strand of belief."[39] The quote, as Ṭaḥāwī had it, defined *faith* as "an oral affirmation and attestation by the heart and (belief in) the command of the Holy Prophet."[40] According to ʿUthmānī, later scholars "mutilated" this quotation by leaving out the phrase that requires belief in the Prophet's command. In this way, ʿUthmānī used Kashmīrī's method of returning to the earliest sources to prove his teacher Shaykh al-Hind's point: that both the Ḥanafīs and the hadith folk already agree that actions and faith are constituitive of one another.

Two key points emerge from this case study that characterize ʿUthmānī's interpretive approach to the cumulative tradition. First, when the Ḥanafī position was called into question, ʿUthmānī and his teachers returned to the earliest foundations of their knowledge to respond. According to him and his teachers, both prooftexts and transmitted opinions can be textually corrupted over time, and scholars must do the necessary source-critical work to struggle against this. Moreover, when defending the position of Abū Ḥanīfa, no scholarly authority, not even Bukhārī, is above reproach. After all, when Bukhārī abridged a hadith that defined *faith* in a way contrary to the conception of the Ḥanafīs, ʿUthmānī challenged him on it, holding that Bukhārī's abridgement obscured the hadith's true meaning.[41]

Second, ʿUthmānī exploited the commentary's ability to tell an exegetical history of a topic's reception across time and place. In doing so, ʿUthmānī embedded himself and his teachers at Deoband in the cumulative tradition of the preceding millennium. Surely this brought him and his teachers prestige and constructed their authority as interpreters.

But offering audiences an exegetical history also helped to defuse polemics against the Ḥanafīs and settle a vital question about the meaning of *islām*. In other words, both social rewards and the achievement of interpretive excellences were at stake in ʿUthmānī's deployment of exegetical history.

SCIENTISTS, SECULARISTS, AND THOSE WITHOUT ARABIC

The printed translation was a new medium that allowed Muslim scholars to reach students who could not study in live settings in classical Islamicate languages. This included the Muslim English- and Urdu-reading public, for whom there were many commentaries on the Qur'an, but few on collections of hadith.[42] But in addition to addressing Muslim audiences, ʿUthmānī's commentary appealed to non-Muslims in the service of propagating Islam while simultaneously challenging secular opponents and Orientalist critics.[43] Muḥammad Ṭayyib, the patron of the printing house that published the commentary, wrote that one of the central founders of Dār al-ʿUlūm in Deoband, Muḥammad Qāsim al-Nānūtvī (d. 1880)

> had expressed the wish that he might learn the English language and go to Europe to tell the Western scholars that wisdom was not that which they held to be wisdom, but it lay in the instruction imparted to mankind by the Final Prophet of God, Muḥammad. . . . It is very much gratifying that Mawlānā Qāḍī ʿAbd al-Raḥmān has undertaken to give a practical shape to the wish of Mawlānā Qāsim [al-Nānūtvī]. . . . I am confident that not only Muslims will benefit spiritually from this work of everlasting value, but the people in the European countries in general and the Westernized people in particular, who are not in the grip of materialism, also will find spiritual solace and guidance.[44]

Although this is surely not the first commentary on a foundational Islamic text marshaled in the service of addressing non-Muslims, it is one of the first instances of a commentary on *Ṣaḥīḥ al-Bukhārī* functioning in this way. While the history of the Qur'an's origins necessitated that it address both nonbelievers and believers, hadith collections like *Ṣaḥīḥ al-Bukhārī* were primarily intended to address multiple audiences of believers, and those initiated with the modes of reasoning within the Sunni tradition recognized its authenticity. The only precedent for hadith commentary addressing nonbelievers was one produced by a missionary from the Ahmadiyya Movement on a British translation of a popular collection of hadith in the early part of the twentieth century.[45] Ṭayyib and ʿAbd Raḥmān may have recognized the need for a competing commentary composed and edited by Deobandi scholars.

Although the text of his commentary engages in polemics with the beliefs of other religious traditions—Christians, Jews, Sikhs, and various Hindu groups[46]—another target for ʿUthmānī was atheism and Western cultural assumptions. When explaining a hadith on the specific penalties (*ḥudūd*) for theft ordained by God in the Qur'an, he took the opportunity to challenge his critics in the West: "The people of Western culture and modern views generally criticize Islamic Ḥudūd on the ground that the punishments are uncivilized. Such critics ought to realise that theft is a cruel and barbarous act, and for suppressing it some sort of harsh punishment is essential."[47]

Since the nineteenth century, British legal observers had expressed anxiety about the severity of *ḥudūd* penalties, and amputation for theft served as a prime example. ʿUthmānī keenly perceived that there was more than a legal debate at stake in the case of the *ḥudūd,* but it was intertwined with a complex cultural matrix in which notions of civility and barbarity were constructed and contested.

Oddly, ʿUthmānī goes on to defend the *ḥudūd* by directing an extensive wave of verbal attacks against the "atheist poet" Abū ʿAlāʾ al-Maʿarrī, an eleventh- and twelfth-century Syrian litterateur who once doubted the wisdom of the *ḥudūd.*[48] Why quote Maʿarrī, who was neither Western nor modern? The reason he did so was that modernist voices in India contemporary to ʿUthmānī had taken up Maʿarrī as a freethinking model of a latent secular tradition within Islamic thought.[49] Orientalist scholars were likewise fascinated with Maʿarrī.[50] By slighting and refuting Maʿarrī, ʿUthmānī was pulling the rug from under his opponents while making a claim on the proper interpretation of the Islamic legal tradition.

While ʿUthmānī appeared to reject secular materialism, he seemed to accept or even find valuable metaphors from scientific methods. He drew on them to appeal not only to European audiences but also to local audiences trained in secular schools. In this way, he was not unlike other nineteenth- and twentieth-century thinkers who resisted colonial power while viewing science and modern technology as a constituitive element of Islamic thought and practice.[51] Nevertheless, these kinds of scientific analogies were unprecedented in the cumulative tradition of commentary on *Ṣaḥīḥ al-Bukhārī.* Take, for example, the following passage from this hadith commentary:

> Modern science has discovered a wire which when set on buildings, acts as an insulator and protects it against lightening. If not equipped with it, even the strongest building would be utterly destroyed. The reason is obvious that though the first type of building may be weak but it is equipped with a kind of wire or conductor rod which absorbs the electricity coming with the lightning and no harm is caused to the building. In the other building, however, there is no arrangement of this type. Therefore lightning destroys it. Similarly, in the present case also the Divine Light was the Light Absolute and Prophet Mūsā (*ʿalayhi al-salām*) had a part of this very Light in him. This is why he was able to withstand the shock of Divine manifestation. Although he did lose consciousness, still he remained alive.[52]

In this passage, Moses's withstanding of the power of divine inspiration (*waḥy*) is analogized to a lightning rod atop a modern building that conducts electricity safely to the ground when struck. The use of these kinds of scientific analogies in commentary on hadith must have been common in ʿUthmānī's scholarly milieu, considering that ʿUthmānī attributed the source of this explanation to an anonymous preacher from Delhi who was fielding questions from a layperson. ʿUthmānī used a number of such examples in crafting his commentary, weaving in references to X-rays; buttons, wires, and electric currents; and medical science.[53] In some cases, these analogies were marshaled in support of crucial points:

> Today scientists agree that the earth is bouncing away at the rate of thousands of miles per minute, which gives rise to the phenomena of night and day, rising and setting of the sun. However sharp-sighted a person might be his eyes will tell him that the earth is stationary. No one since the dawn of the world, has actually seen the earth move. Hence the scientists say that our sense of sight is at fault and its observations are rectified by the intellect. . . . It is, therefore, evident that all the methods and modes of acquiring knowledge and ratiocination adopted by all the [legal] schools are liable to errors.[54]

In this passage, ʿUthmānī suggested that human senses, no matter how sharp, cannot observe the rotation of the earth, which must be deduced by scientific reasoning. In relating this to Islamic law, ʿUthmānī went a step further—even modes of reasoning are prone to errors, and this explains the inevitability of differences of opinion among the legal schools.

ʿUthmānī's fraught relationship with the West is also captured in one of his explanations of a hadith in which the Prophet is remembered to have addressed Heraclius, a Byzantine emperor. Here, in the text of his commentary on a hadith, he even mentioned a British colonial administrator by name. After several pages of discussing how Muhammad interacted with various emperors of his time, he concluded with a modern anecdote:

> Once the Governor of the United Provinces (now Utter Paradesh [*sic*]) Mr. Marston, visited Deoband and the authorities of the Dār al-ʿUlūm arranged a reception for him because of certain considerations. ʿAllāmah Sayyid Anwar Shāh [al-Kashmīrī], was asked to say a few words of welcome as the Chairman of the Reception Committee. He was at a loss what to say, as Marston was the man who had ordered firing on a mosque in Kānpūr. But now he had gone there as the Chief Guest and the authorities of Deoband had to present an address. The Mawlānā [al-Kashmīrī] says he instantly thought of this *ḥadīth* [of Heraclius] and used this very word "ʿ*aẓīm.*" Because of this precedent in the *ḥadīth* he felt his heart at ease.[55]

Thus, the Deobandi commentator's relationship with a British official and political opponent is placed at the end of a broader Islamic history that parallels how Muhammad addressed the Byzantine emperor of his time: with "extreme courtesy towards enemies."[56] Although we do not typically think of the commentary as a genre of history, passages like these certainly function as a kind of exegetical history that connects the audiences' current social and historical context to the past.

COMMENTARY IN CONTEMPORARY HYDERABAD

Although contemporary hadith commentaries continue at Deobandi institutions, our study now turns to a contemporary Urdu commentary on *Ṣaḥīḥ al-Bukhārī* at another institution whose history is rooted in the diverse reformist landscape of the late nineteenth century: the Niẓāmiyya College in Hyderabad, India.[57] The author of this commentary is the Shaykh al-Ḥadīth at the Niẓāmiyya, Muḥammad Khʷāje Sharīf, whose reading certificate for *Ṣaḥīḥ al-Bukhārī* claims a chain of transmission to Bukhārī that includes Shāh Walī Allāh. Although Sharīf has been invited to Kuwait to give lectures on hadith, he is obscure in comparison to scholars like Ibn Ḥajar or even ʿUthmānī. His written commentary, published by his own Niẓāmiyya College, is limited to local distribution. The work is short and inexpensively produced. Two volumes published thus far are about eighty pages, bound between glossy multicolored paper covers with two metal staples. Sharīf's local audience, however, reveres him. He serves as the rector for the Niẓāmiyya College's Arabic school for middle school–aged students, and when students greet him in the courtyard of the school, they bow and kiss his hand, which he humbly demurs.

In the Niẓāmiyya, *Ṣaḥīḥ al-Bukhārī* is the capstone of a student's religious education and can only be approached after students have read and heard commentary on the Qur'an and three other hadith compilations. In childhood, students study the Qur'an. At the age of fourteen, they spend a year devoted to studying Muḥammad al-Khaṭīb al-Tabrīzī's (d. 741/1340–41) hadith compilation, *Mishkāt al-maṣābīḥ*. At fifteen, they spend a year devoted to the Niẓāmiyya's own Sayyid ʿAbdallāh Shāh's (d. 1964) modern and more Ḥanafī-leaning hadith compilation, *Zujājat al-maṣābīḥ*. At sixteen and seventeen, they study *Sunan Tirmidhī*, a two-year proposition.[58] Only then can a student undertake the two-year course on *Ṣaḥīḥ al-Bukhārī*. According to Sharīf, this is twice the length of time typically required in other madrasas in India.[59]

The space in which he explains *Ṣaḥīḥ al-Bukhārī* is thus neither a center of state power nor a mosque, but, like the case of Kashmīrī's and ʿUthmānī's commentaries, a school (see fig. 10). The lessons on *Ṣaḥīḥ al-Bukhārī* take place in a classroom filled with fifty to seventy students.[60] The students in attendance predominantly identify as Ḥanafī, but since there is a minority of students who are Shāfiʿī, Sharīf declares that his commentary is neutral with respect to legal affiliation.[61]

In terms of content and approach, however, Sharīf writes that the derivation of Ḥanafī rulings from the hadith is one of the explicit concerns of his commentary.[62] In this way, his method is similar to Kashmīrī and ʿUthmānī. Likewise, he also aims to elucidate Sufi and contemporary concerns if relevant to the hadith.[63] Unlike ʿUthmānī, however, Sharīf's commentary is largely free of any explicit sectarian or anti-secular polemics, reflecting the nonconfrontational attitude of the current Niẓāmiyya College. Of the three approaches he claimed that Shāh Walī Allāh identified in the study of hadith—speed recitation (*sard*), researching and grading authenticity (*baḥath wa-ḥāl*), and deep reflection (*imʿān wa-taʿammuq*)—Sharīf emphasizes the last.[64] While speed recitation may be impressive, the curriculum at the Nizamiyya claims to be focused on deep reflection and consideration of the meaning of the hadith.

At certain moments, Sharīf contributes new opinions of his own to the many layers of commentary. We saw in part 2 how commentators struggled to understand why Bukhārī omitted a key phrase from the text of the first hadith in *Ṣaḥīḥ al-Bukhārī*. The hadith is popularly transmitted as, "Actions are by intention, and every person receives what he intends. Whoever's migration (*hijra*) was for the sake of God and his messenger, his migration was for the sake of God and his messenger. Whoever's migration was aimed toward gaining the world or

FIGURE 10. The bookshelves of Muḥammad Khʷaje Sharīf in the library of the Arabic school in which he is a rector, in Hyderabad. Ibn Ḥajar's *Fatḥ al-bārī* sits on the top shelf, and the commentaries of Qasṭallānī, Ibn Baṭṭāl, and ʿAynī rest on the second and third shelves. Urdu commentaries on *Ṣaḥīḥ al-Bukhārī* are placed on the second lowest shelf. Immediately to the left of the second shelf (not pictured) are Arabic and Urdu commentaries on other hadith compilations, as well as Wensinck's *Concordance et Indices de la Tradition Musulmane.* (Author's photograph.)

marrying a woman, his migration was for whatever he migrated."[65] Instead, Bukhārī transmitted simply, "Actions are by intention, and every person receives what he intends. Whoever's migration was aimed toward gaining the world or marrying a woman, his migration was for whatever he migrated."[66]

While early critics and commentators supposed it was a scribal error, others, like Ibn Ḥajar, thought it was an intentional mark of Bukhārī's humility, who was loathe to appear to his audience as if he were arrogantly claiming his intentions were with God and his messenger alone. ʿAynī dismissed such accounts as pure speculation. Sharīf, however, over five centuries later, made new sense out of this omission in order to resolve the debate: the omission was intentional, but Bukhārī was not seeking to guard his own reputation. Instead, for Sharīf, Bukhārī wanted to impart a lesson of tough love to his students: omitting the potential reward of sincere intention forces students to contemplate more seriously the penalty of intending toward worldly gain.[67]

In composing his commentary, Sharīf made use of the Andalusian Ibn Baṭṭāl's commentary as well as a number of Mamluk-era sources in Arabic. He preferred ʿAynī's to Ibn Ḥajar's commentary, partly because ʿAynī was trained as a Ḥanafī. This is reflected in his list of sources, in which he listed ʿAynī's commentary prior to Ibn Ḥajar's, and in the fact that he includes an obscure and nonextant Ḥanafī commentary upon which ʿAynī's was based in his list of "well-known commentaries" (*mashhūr shurūḥāt*) in Arabic.[68] He denied any suggestion that ʿAynī had borrowed from Ibn Ḥajar, and he thought that accounts of their personal and intellectual conflicts were exaggerated.[69] In addition to citing commentators from South Asia, Sharīf also made use of a concordance of hadith compiled by the Dutch orientalist A. J. Wensinck (d. 1939), which is included among the Islamic commentaries on his bookshelves (see fig. 10). In this subtle way, his bookshelves are a reflection of his and his institution's syncretic origins in nineteenth-and twentieth-century colonial India.

On the day the commentary comes to a close (*khatm*) echoes the spectacle of the large Mamluk recitations. Some five hundred students and teachers, regionally and nationally, gather and recite the final hadith of *Ṣaḥīḥ al-Bukhārī,* hear its commentary, and recite an ode (*qaṣīda*) in classical Arabic marking the occasion.[70] The *qaṣīda* is then published with the Urdu commentary.[71]

The publication process for Sharīf is rooted in his live lessons. During these lessons, students take copious notes and then produce a written document of his oral commentary on *Ṣaḥīḥ al-Bukhārī* in Urdu. Sharīf then proofreads it. When the text is to his liking, he sends it to the Niẓāmiyya College's press for publication.[72] This distribution of labor—master as dictator, student as writer—is constituitive of a differential in power and status. In my own participant observation with him, I mistakenly transgressed this implicit commentarial etiquette when I requested that he write down the name of source he cited so that I might

FIGURE 11. A still from a YouTube video of a television broadcast of line-by-line lessons on *Ṣaḥīḥ al-Bukhārī* by Muḥammad Khʷāje Sharīf on Hyderabad's local channel 4, March 2009.

consult it myself. The problem, for the Shaykh al-Ḥadīth, was not my question or its aim, but rather the fact that I had asked him to write during the commentarial session.[73]

Sharīf's commentarial practice has also entered the age of television and online video (see fig. 11). Sharīf accepted an invitation to present his commentary on channel 4, a local Hyderabad television station, in March of 2009. Sharīf delivered his commentary sitting in front of a green screen, and the show was broadcast at a time chosen by the channel 4 executives to a mixed-age and mixed-gender local audience at home, perhaps sitting in their parlors or bedrooms. In theory, non-Muslims living in Hyderabad could also partake as audiences in the commentary—or at least flip through—since language would be a barrier for Telegu-speaking television viewers. Questions or live interactions with Sharīf were not entertained in this broadcast, although one could imagine that interaction could now be facilitated through social media applications. The spaces and times of this televised commentary thus marked a radical departure from the other premodern and modern commentaries discussed early in this book.

Yet the spaces and times of Sharīf's television appearance are fragmented further in the virtual world. The broadcast was recorded by an anonymous individual who took a digital video of a television set, probably using a cell phone, and then uploaded the recordings to YouTube.[74] The video clip, despite its grainy quality, fragmentation, and distorted audio, steadily attracted 4,438 views over the course of three years and was accessible from any networked computer until it was taken down for unknown reasons. The text and argument of the commentary itself was inaudible: only the live, moving image of the commentator in the act of commenting is transmitted.

. . .

In two chapters we have covered nearly five hundred years of history. As fast paced as this survey has been, such a large scope has been necessary to track change and continuity in the slow-moving, cumulative tradition of commentary on *Ṣaḥīḥ al-Bukhārī*. In doing so, we observed how the deepening of Western cultural and legal hegemony, globalization, new technologies, and the expansion of literacy, among other things, broadened the composition of hadith scholars' patrons and audiences, and changed how commentators communicated with them. In the midst of these radical changes—the influence of British colonialism and print foremost among them—commentators found new strategies of maintaining a connection with their past and mediating the moral, legal, and political challenges of their present through that connection. This included employing Arabic literary conventions, claiming blood genealogies to the Arab world, reading the foundational sources of knowledge anew, and writing an exegetical history that progressed from religious authorities in premodern Arabia to modern South Asia.

Although these strategies of preserving continuity with the commentary tradition clothed modern South Asian commentators in prestige, the commentators did not merely preserve the tradition as a symbolic license to speak to contemporary social issues. Nor did they merely project contemporary social issues back onto the past, claiming to "repeat" what was, in fact, a contemporary idea. Instead, they engaged in a reciprocal hermeneutic motion that allowed the standards, norms, and excellences of the cumulative tradition they inherited to shape them and speak to the social and political contexts of their present.

In the epigraph that commences this chapter, Nietzsche celebrated how the ancient Romans "naively" and "recklessly" translated the ancient Greek literary tradition they inherited.[75] This kind of translation, for Nietzsche, in which Romans replaced Greek names with their own, was best likened to "a form of conquest."[76] Nietzsche's description might be apt, with some exceptions, to the formation of Anglo-Muhammadan Law, which "translated" the Islamic legal tradition into languages and norms intelligible and acceptable to the British. But the English and Urdu commentaries in the mid-twentieth and twenty-first centuries tell a different story about translation. ʿUthmānī's and Sharīf's works were not, after all, translations undertaken by representatives of colonial powers, but by English-speaking and Urdu-speaking Muslims in India and Pakistan. Although their works could have only emerged in the syncretic worlds and technologies of post-colonial South Asia and made incursions onto the past at certain junctures, these cases also illustrate how contemporary commentators and their translators remained open to and formed by more than a millennium of commentary, and how they sought to achieve interpretive ends within the standards of excellence they inherited from their near and distant pasts.

Epilogue

Islamism, ISIS, and the Politics of Interpretation

This storm is what we call progress.

—Walter Benjamin

It is not uncommon for some academic publishers to urge their authors to avoid making references to current events in their books. The point of the convention is not to make the author's work irrelevant to the present, but to achieve an appearance of timelessness that will allow the work to serve as an authority for contemporary readers and to endure for audiences in the near and distant future. This aspiration toward timelessness can be found in many scholarly discourses of the past and present, and the tradition of hadith commentary is no exception. But one facet of my larger aim in this book has been to show that even when the excellences of hadith commentaries' interpretive achievements resonate for audiences across eras and oceans, commentaries are also always composed in particular times and settings and are always read in the particular times and settings of their later readerships.

In some cases, a commentator's impulse toward timelessness is itself, ironically, a timely marker of a commentary's function in a given social and historical setting. We can find numerous examples of this impulse in both the premodern and modern hadith commentary tradition. But the commentarial impulse toward timeliness—the foregrounding of current social and political events in one's interpretation—while glimpsed in certain corners of the premodern hadith commentary tradition, comes to be elevated to an unprecedented degree by commentators and readers of the modern Islamic world. We have already seen evidence of this in part 3 of this book, where the realities of daily life under

British colonialism surfaced in the lines of Kashmīrī's and ʿUthmānī's hadith commentaries.

In making references in my epilogue to contemporary politics, I am no doubt contributing to this modern turn toward timeliness rather than timelessness to address my present and future audiences. But, returning briefly to Borges's *mise en abyme,* it should be clear by now that the book you hold in your hands—or that you view on your electronic screen—is, like the very hadith commentary tradition it has been analyzing, a product of its own time, even as it aspires to engage audiences of the future. May my own book's datedness thus help me make my point, rather than detract from it.

ISIS, HADITH COMMENTARY, AND THE "REVIVAL OF SLAVERY"

The most notable contemporary movement to take up hadith commentary for its own ends is a Salafi-inspired militant group that is well known at present, alternately termed the Islamic State (IS), the Islamic State in Iraq and Syria (ISIS), the Islamic State in Iraq and the Levant (ISIL), as well as al-Dawlā al-Islāmiyya fī al-ʿIrāq wa'l-Shām (Daʿish, sometimes transliterated as Daesh).[1] Although this group dominates current newspapers, it is too early to say whether it will be remembered over the long haul. Whether this particular group endures or flickers out, they are nevertheless illustrative of some broader trends in Salafism in the early twenty-first century, as well as some new ones, especially in their deployment of the Sunni hadith commentary tradition.

Before ISIS, twentieth-century Salafi movements had largely concerned themselves with reviving the study of hadith criticism. The iconoclastic scholar Nāṣir al-Dīn al-Albānī (d. 1999) published a series of articles that reassessed the reliability of the chains of transmission of hadith long thought to be authentic, and later republished them as hadith compendia in printed volumes. He sometimes offered spare commentary on the meaning of the hadith with notes about how they ought to be applied in practice, but the major contribution of Albānī's scholarship was his reevaluation of the reliability of the hadith, not his novel interpretation of their meaning.[2]

Those Salafi scholars prior to ISIS who did undertake commentaries on hadith collections were highly deferential to Mamluk-era commentators like Nawawī and Ibn Ḥajar, and in this way they echoed the late nineteenth-century efforts of Ṣiddīq Ḥasan Khān. One Salafi scholar of high stature among the senior Saudi scholars, Muḥammad ibn al-ʿUthaymīn (d. 2001), delivered a live commentary on *Ṣaḥīḥ al-Bukhārī* that was largely a compilation of Mamluk-era works.[3] Likewise, another Salafi scholar among the senior Saudi scholars, ʿAbd al-ʿAzīz ibn Bāz (d. 1999, also known as Bin Bāz), wrote brief notes (*taʿlīqāt*) to Ibn Ḥajar's *Fatḥ al-bārī* that readers could depend on in moments where the Mamluk-era Shāfiʿī chief judge's explanations were insufficient. Even as Bin Bāz critiqued Ibn Ḥajar's work, he simultaneously affirmed his predecessor's centrality.[4] Since these texts and scholars focused on issues of purity, dress, and creed that seemingly transcended contemporary political circumstances, a quietist and depoliticized strain of Salafism was able take root in places as disparate as South East Asia, Europe, and North America.[5]

The militant strain of Salafism, often termed Jihadi-Salafism, put the hadith commentary tradition into conversation with contemporary events, but in a way that appeared to affirm the timelessness of the Mamluk-era tradition. Consider Osama bin Laden's (d. 2011) former deputy Ayman al-Ẓawāhirī (b. 1951)—the current head of the Sunni militant group al-Qaeda—who published a book called *al-Ḥaṣād al-murr* (*The bitter harvest*) in 1988 that was reprinted multiple times in the 1990s. In this work, Ẓawāhirī reproduced, verbatim, several pages from Ibn Ḥajar's hadith commentary on *Ṣaḥīḥ al-Bukhārī*. He used the lengthy excerpts as evidence that Muslims are obligated to rebel against any leader of a Muslim majority country who manifested Ẓawāhirī's definition of infidelity (*kufr*).[6] Here Ẓawāhirī claimed to be merely repeating the classical commentary on the hadith by diligently quoting Ibn Ḥajar's *Fatḥ al-bārī* at length, while concealing the fact that his reading was deeply influenced by his own historical and political moment, as was Ibn Ḥajar's.

We find a contrasting and novel use of Ibn Ḥajar's *Fatḥ al-bārī* in ISIS's English language propaganda magazine, *Dabiq*. In the issue "The Failed Crusade," an anonymous propagandist-cum-commentator for ISIS attempted to justify the revival of slavery by commenting on a hadith that suggests that "one of the signs of the Hour" is that "the slave girl gives birth to her master."[7] This koan-like hadith, found in *Ṣaḥīḥ al-Bukhārī*, was commented upon extensively since the formation of the commentary tradition in the fourth/tenth century.

Rather than bluntly abstracting the hadith from its tradition of commentarial disagreement, it is remarkable that the anonymous propagandist placed the meaning of this hadith in the context of a difference of opinion among distinguished Mamluk-era hadith commentators—

Nawawī in his commentary on *Ṣaḥīḥ Muslim,* Ibn Rajab al-Ḥanbalī in his commentary on Nawawī's *Arbaʿūn,* and Ibn Ḥajar in his commentary on *Ṣaḥīḥ al-Bukhārī*—each of whom debated but never fully closed the debate on the meaning of this hadith. Here the propagandist recounted the exegetical history of the hadith despite the fact that it would seem to complicate ISIS's novel solution.

Some medieval Muslim hadith commentators interpreted the hadith by its apparent meaning, devising an Oedipus-like scenario in which the estranged son of the slave becomes king, unknowingly purchases his own mother, and conceives a child with her. Ibn Ḥajar understood the koan-like phrase in this hadith to be a metaphor for the general depravity in which the social hierarchies of the family and the society at large are perversely overturned.

While the ISIS propagandist disagreed with Ibn Ḥajar's metaphorical reading, he did not think Ibn Ḥajar failed to understand the proper meaning of the hadith because of a deficiency in his reasoning. Rather, the ISIS propagandist contended, Ibn Ḥajar was unable to understand the hadith outside the limits of his historical context. In the propagandist's mind, Ibn Ḥajar lived in an era in which the institution of slavery was routine and the apparent meaning of the hadith—a slave giving birth to her master—could not have been a herald of the apocalypse. For this reason, the propagandist argued, Ibn Ḥajar could have only understood this hadith metaphorically.

By contrast, the propagandist maintained, for those who live in the present era of the abolition of slavery, the apparent meaning of the hadith—a slave giving birth to her master—is truly anomalous. Thus, the propagandist claimed, ISIS's "revival of slavery" can be treated literally as "one of the signs of the Hour."[8] Far from representing his interpretation as a timeless repetition of this puzzling hadith, this propagandist for ISIS argued that the meaning is revealed only in the context of a world in which abolition is hegemonic. For this ISIS propagandist-cum-commentator, timeliness, not timelessness, was key to this hadith's interpretation.

Theorist Talal Asad once argued that a discursive tradition is "not the apparent repetition of an old form," but a reflection of practitioners' conceptions of "how the past is related to present practices."[9] In an Asadian framework, neither the ISIS propagandist nor Ẓawāhirī is merely repeating an old form. However, there is a deliberate choice on the part of the interpreter to reveal or conceal this interplay between conceptions of the past and present. While Ẓawāhirī's interpretive approach claimed to apply the opinions of the premodern tradition to the present regardless of change across time, the scriptural hermeneutics of the anonymous ISIS interpreter, by contrast, drew attention to the contingency of their ability to interpret upon the present. This serves the double role of maintaining the authority of traditional opinions while introducing the possibility that present readers can appreciate the meaning of hadith in ways past interpreters could not.

TIMELY AND TIMELESS INTERPRETATIONS OF THE TREATMENT OF SLAVES

Apropos of ISIS's revival of slavery, another hadith from *Ṣaḥīḥ al-Bukhārī* has made a recent appearance in ISIS's foreign-language propaganda, as well as in an Arabic document on the rulings concerning slavery released by ISIS's Office of Research and Fatwas. It was transmitted on the authority of Abū Dharr al-Ghifārī, a well-known companion of Muhammad who died around 653. According to this hadith, Abū Dharr was once spotted alongside his slave dressed in nearly identical garments. When asked to explain this unusual practice, Abū Dharr confessed that he used to abuse his slave until Muhammad scolded him, stating, "those whom God has placed under your authority are your brothers. He who possesses his brother feeds him what he feeds himself and dresses him in what he dresses himself." Within this hadith are two layers of narrative: first, the Prophet's injunction to feed and clothe slaves as you would feed and clothe yourself; and second, Abū Dharr's application of its apparent meaning, in which he dressed himself and his slave in matching outfits.

How has ISIS made sense of this hadith, at the intersection of their justification of the revival of slavery and the deep and multilayered history of the hadith commentary tradition? And what might this case have to teach us about contemporary interpretive strategies and the politics of hadith commentary more broadly, from Umayyad Andalusia to Mamluk Egypt to modern India and the twenty-first-century Middle East?

Abū Dharr's approach first came under scrutiny among the earliest known community of hadith commentators in fifth-/eleventh-century Andalusia, Mālikī judges who may have been girding themselves against the rise of Ẓāhirism that was nascent in Córdoba in the final years of the Umayyad caliphate there. The Mālikī commentator Muhallab ibn Abī Ṣufra, contra the apparent meaning of the hadith, ridiculed the notion that the hadith enjoined slave masters to dress their slaves in clothes like their own, and feed them as they fed themselves. Slave masters, in his opinion, were required only to meet their slaves' basic necessities: cover their nakedness and feed them when they are hungry.[10] It would be absurd, he contended, for any legal scholar to require a slaveholder who ate rare fowl and Persian bread made from the finest flour, who dressed himself in elegant garments from far-away Nishapur, to feed and dress his slave in that same fashion.[11] This opinion must have played well in the wealthy courtly context of late Umayyad Córdoba.

But Muhallab's position was about more than just placating his patrons—it was contingent on the differences between a conception of his own time and place and the time and place in which the hadith was first thought to have been circulated. Muhallab contended that the early companions to whom this hadith was addressed never ate such rich foods and delicacies. Their diet was, according to Muhallab, mostly dates and barley.[12] How, then, could they expand the meaning of this hadith to enjoin slave masters to feed their slaves with rich foods they themselves never tasted?

Whether Muhallab's understanding of history is accurate or not, my point here is that his interpretation was expressly tied to a conception of how fashion and diet reflect status and power in his own historical context as well as to the historical context in which the hadith was first thought to have been circulated. In this case, Muhallab's reading, informed by his conception of history, worked against both the apparent meaning of the hadith and the apparent interpretation modeled by one of Muhammad's companions, to allow slave owners broad discretion concerning how kindly and how austerely they cared for their slaves.

As the regional center of hadith commentarial activity largely shifted in the seventh, eighth, and ninth centuries (thirteenth, fourteenth, and fifteenth CE) to Egypt and Syria, Mamluk-era commentators disagreed with Muhallab's interpretation, preferring to read and apply the hadith closer to its apparent meaning. After a dissection of the phrase "feed them from what you eat," Ibn Ḥajar conceded that the phrase only required a general parity between masters and slaves, not parity in every regard.[13] However, for Ibn Ḥajar, absolute parity in every regard was the ideal, as modeled by Abū Dharr's dressing himself and his slave in matching outfits.

Ibn Ḥajar, therefore, rejected Muhallab's historical argument about the early companions' diet as pure speculation. Even if it were true that the companions only ate dates and barley, it would not have negated the plain meaning of the hadith for Ibn Ḥajar: that each slave owner should attempt to approximate absolute parity with their slaves if they had the means to do so.[14] Although we can see Ibn Ḥajar weave in global politics at other points in his commentary, with respect to Abū Dharr's hadith he turned away from the vagaries of global and regional politics, as well as the changes in the institution of slavery across time. Instead, he interpreted the hadith by way of grammatical features and by reference to other hadith.

The locus of hadith commentary moved a third time to South Asia, amid the rise of modern globalization and the deepening of Western political, cultural, and legal hegemony. As we saw in the preceding chapters, commentators in India found new strategies of maintaining a connection with their past and mediating the moral, legal, and political challenges of their present through that connection. These strategies included employing Mamluk-era Arabic literary conventions, claiming blood genealogies to the companions of the Prophet, reading the foundational sources anew, and writing themselves into an exegetical history that progressed from religious authorities in premodern Arabia to modernity.

But the modern period in India also gave rise to new media and the expansion of literacy, which broadened the composition of hadith commentators' patrons and audiences and changed how commentators communicated with them. In this era, we witnessed democratized modes of reading and a deskilling of hadith commentary, in which the status and authority of the interpreter and the exercise of rarified techniques were no longer strict prerequisites for interpretation. These new voices saw in hadith commentary a venue for discussing global and regional politics, in ways both subtle and explicit.

When we revisit our hadith on Abū Dharr and the treatment of slaves in this period, we find it commented upon in a widely distributed 1999 commentary in Urdu and English on a popular Mamluk-era hadith collection titled *Riyāḍ al-Ṣāliḥīn*. The commentary was penned by an obscure Salafi commentator from Pakistan named Salahuddin Yusuf. Yusuf conceded that slavery had now been abolished as an institution but nevertheless argued that Abū Dharr's hadith was more than "mere ink on a dusty page," to borrow a phrase from Wael Hallaq.[15] Instead, Yusuf contended that the hadith ought be interpreted to "establish equality in the true sense of the word" between the capitalists and the "labourers who work in factories, shops and homes."[16]

Both Yusuf and Ibn Ḥajar aimed for absolute parity between master and slave as the ideal, although for Yusuf, *slave* was a broad metaphor for any laborer. But while Ibn Ḥajar insulated this hadith's interpretation away from the contingencies of history, Yusuf explicitly based his interpretation of the hadith on the present social and political circumstances, as Muhallab had done in Umayyad Andalusia, to arrive at the opposite ruling. Moreover, Yusuf maintained that this hadith presented a clearer conception of equality than is currently on offer by competing ideologies. Yusuf saw this hadith as maintaining a slave's humanity, the very thing that human rights discourses would contend the practice of slavery denies by definition.

At last we turn to a later issue of ISIS's English-language magazine *Dabiq,* for whom this metaphorical reading of "slavery" as exploitative wage labor does not go far enough. In this issue, an ISIS propagandist who goes by the female nom de guerre Umm Sumayyah outlined the benefits of reviving slavery for both Muslims and non-Muslims.[17] For Muslims, she argued that slavery allows Muslim men a licit opportunity for sexual gratification beyond marriage without committing the grave sin of an extramarital affair. She lampooned "politically 'correct'" Muslim scholars who, in her view, are hypocritically silent on the moral abuses of "prostitution" while invoking feminist and human-rights discourses against ISIS's practices of "slavery." Here her definition of *prostitution* included sex work but stood more broadly for the kind of Western economic, political, and cultural depravity.[18] For Umm Sumayyah, reestablishing slavery as an institution was the proper remedy.

Slavery was also, in her view, a divine tool to humiliate ISIS's enemies. Not simply was it tool against its regional targets, like the Iraqi Yazīdī community, whose women and children consequently suffered abduction, sale, and forced sex, but also its global ideological foes, who have made the abolition of slavery a metaphorical and literal foundation of their moral commitments and progressive narratives since the enlightenment. However, Umm Sumayyah stipulated an important caveat to her argument: God may have intended enslavement to be humiliating, but masters must treat their slaves with kindness, in accordance with a well-known prophetic hadith transmitted on the authority of Abū Dharr concerning the treatment of slaves: "feed them of what you eat, dress them of what you wear. . . ."[19]

In her commentary on this hadith, Umm Sumayyah went further than the classical commentary tradition by holding that this kindness may eventually guide enslaved unbelievers to their salvation. According to Umm Sumayyah, then, there was a hidden aim in God's will: He "made their liberation from the lands of *kufr* [or unbelief] a way for their salvation and guidance towards the straight path."[20] Liberation, for this ISIS propagandist, was paradoxically to be found in the revival of slavery.

Echoing Yusuf's claim that through this hadith, Islam establishes "equality in the true sense of the word," Umm Sumayyah expressly read the hadith as a champion of liberation, posing an alternative to human rights discourses that offer mere slogans of "freedom" and "equality."[21]

But what Yusuf took for granted—a post-abolition world—Umm Sumayyah did not abide. The term *slavery* must be understood by its apparent meaning, not as a metaphor for wage laborers, domestic servants, and the like. In the very same breath, however, Umm Sumayyah was not concerned with applying the hadith by its apparent meaning as Abū Dharr did. Rather, she read the text as merely enjoining Muslims to treat their slaves with "kindness," but not equality, as the hadith's apparent meaning stipulated.

This approach may be echoing the recent publication in Arabic from ISIS's Office of Research and Fatwas under the heading "The Command to Treat Slaves Kindly."[22] While omitting the discussion of human rights discourses that Umm Sumayyah included, the ISIS Office of Research and Fatwas reproduced a discussion of the hadith from al-Qurṭubī's seventh-/thirteenth-century Qur'an commentary, which largely echoed Muhallab's original position: the hadith, Qurṭubī argued, should only be taken as a general encouragement to be kind to one's slaves. There is no difference of opinion, Qurṭubī asserted, that slave owners are allowed to treat slaves as inferiors as long as their slaves' basic necessities are provided for. In this case, ISIS's Office of Research and Fatwas overlooks the apparent meaning of the Prophet's statement and a companion's model behavior based on it, in favor of a commentarial opinion from the postclassical scholarly tradition.

CONTINUITY OR CHANGE? LIBERAL OR LITERALIST?

Let us return once again to Asad's insight that tradition is "not the apparent repetition of an old form," but a reflection of practitioners' conceptions of "how the past is related to present practices." From this perspective, none of these interpreters are repeating a timeless tradition in which Muslims practiced and regulated slavery. Rather, they are strategically reading, as all interpreters do to some extent, the Islamic tradition with their present and future contexts in mind. On these grounds, ISIS's interpretive methods are not fundamentally different from that of their predecessors', although they share more in common with those who have explicitly engaged their history than those commentators who attempted to transcend it.

ISIS propagandists' novel conception of time is key. While Ibn Ḥajar crafted his work as an encyclopedic monument that could endure as a resource for the community, ISIS propagandists interpreted the hadith as if they were living near the end of time. For this reason, their present circumstances were their key to unlocking the meaning of cryptic hadith. This illustrates the extent to which the practice of commentary is not only backward looking but is always anticipating relatively near or distant futures.

This point may prove instructive to discourses in both academia and the public square. ISIS's approach to hadith is often described as scriptural literalism, but is this accurate? Literalism implies a certain kind of rigidity, a strict commitment to the letter rather than the spirit of a canonical text and, above all, a retrograde and willful refusal to assimilate the meaning of that text in the face of historical change. A literal translation is reputed to be awkward precisely because its language has not yet been adapted to fit its new cultural and temporal setting.

And yet ISIS's interpretive approach has absolutely assimilated the meanings of these hadith to speak fluently to a modern vernacular: a globalized post-abolition world in which human rights discourses are hegemonic and English is the lingua franca; where YouTube videos, spectacles, and images speak as loudly as or louder than texts; where readerships have been democratized by free access to online media; and where interpretation has been deskilled, eschewing the rarified credentials that have served as prerequisites for scholarly commentary for over a millennium.

In light of the shocking brutality of this group, there is an understandable resistance in the academy to understanding ISIS's propagandists as participating in the rich tradition of hadith commentary in any way other than to bring about its ruin. But if scholarly inquiry is to differ from the work of counter-propagandists, we must seek to analyze the strategies of ISIS's interpretive approach in the context of the cumulative tradition rather than to caricature them. Should we choose to keep the term *literalism* to describe ISIS's approach—and it arguably obscures more than it reveals—it is a literalism of a highly flexible variety, one that does not always bypass or oversimplify the postclassical tradition, and one that sometimes even airs the tradition's internal disagreements in order to arrive at novel solutions in the present social and political context.

• • •

A year after that balmy evening in 2009 when I first visited al-Īmān Mosque in Damascus, I returned to ʿIrqsūsī's live commentary on *Ṣaḥīḥ al-Bukhārī* that had been delivered weekly for a local, transregional, and transgenerational audience. Shoeless and cross-legged, I scribbled on my notepad while others captured the event with their clamshell cellphones or camcorders, in the margins of printed editions, and in their memories.

Midway through the session, ʿIrqsūsī turned back to a hadith that, at first blush, may have appeared relatively banal, a report in which Muhammad was alleged to have authorized more than one procedure for performing the lesser and greater pilgrimages to Mecca and Medina in conjunction.[23] At first he appeared to insulate his explanation from contemporary politics, by appealing to traditional scholarly authorities of grammar, rhetoric, and hadith across a millennium, offering his conception of the hadith's exegetical history. He then brought the hadith to present practices by peppering the students nearest him with questions. What were their own pilgrimage practices and experiences? Did they have more than one procedure for performing those pilgrimages? And did those multiple practices line up with the hadith under discussion? Eager for the shaykh's affirmation, the students competed to respond to his queries in detail. Off microphone, the broader audience could hardly hear them.

After moving across a range of opinions from wide expanses of time and space to the narrower discussion of the practices of the current students in attendance at al-Īmān, ʿIrqsūsī enlarged his scope yet again to the broader political circumstances facing the Sunni community in the Middle East and other parts of the globe. The fact that this hadith in *Ṣaḥīḥ al-Bukhārī* authorized multiple pilgrimage practices served as an opportunity for ʿIrqsūsī to make a point about Sunni identity and its tolerance of internal differences. He followed it up with a heavy-handed jab at his Salafi opponents who, he alleged, propagated a narrower understanding of Sunnism. Pointing to the text, ʿIrqsūsī argued that the Prophet wanted to accommodate multiple constituencies of the community, contra those Salafis who, in ʿIrqsūsī's opinion, were willing to hereticize anyone who failed to follow a singular model for correct Islamic practice. This may not be a fair depiction of Salafism, but ʿIrqsūsī's condemnation would have appealed to his supporters, as well as to the Syrian Baʿthist state who viewed Salafis as propagators of a militant sectarianism that was subversive to the state's power.

The Syrian president did not attend the commentary session, as numerous sultans or emirs had in the premodern Muslim world. But al-Īmān sat in the shadow of the Baʿth party headquarters, and ʿIrqsūsī's hadith commentary was widely assumed to be subject to state surveillance. In 2013, the mosque's political significance became all too apparent when it served as the site for a high-profile assassination and massacre during the ongoing Syrian civil war.[24] Muḥammad Saʿīd Ramaḍān al-Būṭī, one of the most prominent and prolific Sunni scholars in Syria at the time, was killed alongside fifty or so of his students following an explosion during a live line-by-line commentary on the Qur'an and the hadith. He had been a supporter of the regime.

The 2013 blast, which marked the epitome of a deskilled *riposte* to the commentator, was caught on a video camera that had been set up to record the commentary session. Rather than being distributed for an audience of students, the video circulated as footage for journalists and correspondents documenting a new low in the war. Sadly, that moment in which violence burst into the commentary session and silenced a commentator and his students may constitute the most widely observed Islamic commentary session by non-Muslims in the West.

In spite of all the drastic changes that have taken place from the manuscript age to the age of video, social media, and high-tech explosives, the hadith commentary has endured as an arena for competition for power and capital as well as the skilled achievement of interpretive excellences and commitment to norms. Like the Bājī affair in Andalusia, Ibn Ḥajar's rivalries in the presence of the Mamluk sultan, and the Gujarati sultan's interventions in the hadith commentary tradition, the live commentary today is still a place where politics intersect with interpretive reasoning in a creative and sometimes destructive spectacle. Although this history lies just below the surface of the written commentary tradition, shedding light on the times and settings in which hadith were explained live brings the social, political, and embodied aspects of interpretive culture and experience to the fore.

To this end, this book has endeavored to understand both live and written hadith commentary within its local and global contexts, as well as extended across the phases of its long history. To do so, I have offered a thick history of the cyclical commentary sessions and the long processes of composition and revision in which local and global social pressures were at work, as well as attending to the practice of reasoned debate over hadith across a millennium. In these settings, power and reason are mutually constitutive but are not ultimately reducible to one another. If we are to understand interpretive traditions as a social practice, we must keep both the social and material rewards on offer as well as the interpretive excellences internal to the tradition in full view.

When viewing the hadith commentary tradition as a social practice, it becomes evident that the medium of commentary is simultaneously creative and derivative, concerned as much with innovation as it is with preservation. But the ideals and standard-bearers of the tradition did not pursue preservation for the sake of preservation, or innovation for the sake of innovation. To be sure, Bājī, Ibn Ḥajar, Kashmīrī, and others were sometimes able to offer original syntheses after rehearsing the hadith and the history of exegetical debate it inspired. But it was, just as often, the way they framed and reframed each hadith's exegetical history—their choices of which voices to include and exclude, how they would be organized, abbreviated, and to what effect—that could be most revealing. In other words, commentators paradoxically sought preservation through innovation, and innovation through preservation. Here Foucault's axiom, the epigraph that opened this book, rings true: the task of the commentary is to tirelessly repeat that which has never been said before, and to say for the first time what has already been said countless times.[25]

This is not to say that hadith commentators were only concerned with surreptitiously reading their own interests into the text and the cumulative tradition. The power of an intellectual tradition that has endured over long periods of time is that is presses interpreters to open their present commitments and activities to the possibility of being formed by the texts and opinions they inherit. In this way, commentary may be better seen as the product of long negotiations and renegotiations of interpreters' and interpretive communities' reciprocal relationships with their pasts, presents, and futures.

As a central hub of Islamic social and intellectual life, the story of how Muslims interpreted and reinterpreted hadith across a millennium has been a missing piece in the academy's patchwork understanding of Islam and Islamic history. In complicating and enriching our knowledge of this tradition, we are also complicating and enriching our present, in which hadith are still being defined and redefined for living audiences. In the spirit of the tradition's many commentaries left unfinished, then, I will not presume that this epilogue offers an ending, but merely an introduction to further debate, questions, and commentary.

Acknowledgments

Over the past seven years, many scholars, teachers, colleagues, friends, family members, and institutions from Princeton to Damascus to Hyderabad have generously contributed to the making of this book. I hope the final product is worthy of their breath, their beating hearts, and their pocketbooks. If there is anything of value to be found in these pages, you have them to blame. I will take full credit for any errors.

I would like to single out in particular a number of scholars who inspired, challenged, and mentored me along the way: Muhammad Qasim Zaman, who supervised this project when it was in its infancy, alongside Michael Cook, Shaun Marmon, and Jeff Stout. Jonathan A. C. Brown and Issam Eido invited me into the world of hadith through stimulating conversations, fruitful suggestions, and learned scholarship. When navigating the toughest problems raised by a project of this size, I have often leaned on the friendship and good counsel of Nathaniel Deutsch, Steven Hopkins, and Mairaj Syed. Taken together, these teachers, colleagues, and friends have helped me fashion this book into a reality.

I would like to recognize the excellent staff at the University of California Press, and especially my editor, Eric Schmidt, who saw promise in this work and shepherded it into print with style. I likewise thank Asma Sayeed, Walid Saleh, and the anonymous readers who offered incisive suggestions on a late draft of this manuscript.

A book not only requires good footnotes but also good food, and Scott Kugle and Subah Dayal helped me find both while I was undertaking a research stint in Hyderabad, India. I am especially indebted to Scott for introducing me to Muhammad Khʷāje al-Sharīf at the Niẓamiyya, as I am to Youshaa Patel, who first invited me to ʿIrqsūsī's live commentary on *Ṣaḥīḥ al-Bukhārī* in Damascus.

Early and late material from this book was presented at a number of conferences and scholarly forums, including the Annual Conferences for the American

Academy of Religion, the Middle East Studies Association, the American Historical Association, and the School of Mamluk Studies; the Mellon Sawyer Conference on Islamic Intellectual History at the University of California, Berkeley; and a number of graduate conferences at the McGill Institute for Islamic Studies, Stanford University, and Leiden University. I am grateful to the hosts, organizers, and audiences of these talks, and I am especially grateful to John Dagenais, Ahmed El Shamsy, Hester Gelber, and Ebrahim Moosa, who took the time to read and publically respond to my chapters-in-progress.

I am also grateful to Asad Ahmed, Margaret Larkin, Antonella Ghersetti, Seth Richardson, and the anonymous reviewers who carefully read excerpts of this book and offered suggestions for improvements prior to their publication as articles in scholarly volumes. I thank Brill and the University of Chicago Press for allowing me to reprint with modifications those prior contributions: "Revision in the Manuscript Age: New Evidence of Early Versions of Ibn Ḥajar's *Fatḥ al-Bārī,*" *Journal of Near Eastern Studies* 76, no. 1 (2017): 39–51; "'Usefulness without Toil': Al-Suyūṭī and the Art of Concise *Ḥadīth* Commentary," in *Al-Suyūṭī, A Polymath of the Mamlūk Period,* ed. Antonella Ghersetti (Lieden: Brill, 2016): 182–200; and "Ḥadīth Commentary in the Presence of Patrons, Students and Rivals: Ibn Ḥajar's *Fatḥ al-Bārī* in Mamlūk Cairo," *Oriens* 42 (4–2), (2013).

I credit Claudia Smelser for designing the cover, the background of which is a photograph I took of a dome at Golconda Fort in Hyderabad, India. I credit Bill Nelson for drawing up the maps, Jennifer Eastman for her attentive copy-editing, and Amron Gravett for indexing. Dore Brown and Maeve Cornell-Taylor at UC Press were indispensable in supervising the book manuscript's production. I also tip my cap to Kevin Bell, Nate Hodson, and Jacob Olidort, for guiding me to the book's title, after many other friends (especially Brandon County), colleagues (especially Elias Muhanna), and family members helped me brainstorm. Naz Yucel and Fadi Khubbaz provided valuable research assistance. I would also like to thank my colleagues Usaama al-Azmi, Alex Bevilacqua, David Decosimo, Rozaliya Garipova, Susan Gunasti, Lance Jenott, Cameron Moore, Helen Pfeifer, Geoff Smith, Amin Venjara, Moulie Vidas, and Luke Yarbrough, who read, commented, or offered material advice on sections of the book manuscript. To be sure, there are many others—colleagues, teachers, students, and staff—too numerous to name who provided me with feedback and assistance at Princeton University, Oberlin College, Washington & Lee University, and George Washington University.

Several libraries and their staffs were also critical in the making of this project, and I am especially grateful to those libraries who granted me permission to publish photographs of select manuscript folios from their collections: the Cadbury Research Library and Special Collections at the University of Birmingham; the Rare Books and Special Collections at Princeton University; and the Süleymaniye Library in Istanbul. I also thank the staffs of the Salar Jung Library and the Osmania University Manuscript Library in Hyderabad, India; the National Library of Syria in Damascus; and the National Library of Tunisia in Tunis.

My research abroad, in Syria, India, and Turkey, was made possible in part by the U.S. Department of Education's Foreign Language and Area Studies grant, the U.S. Department of State's Critical Language Scholarship Alumni Development Fund, the Princeton Institute for International and Regional Studies, and the Lenfest Fund at Washington and Lee University. The department of history and the Institute for Middle East Studies at the George Washington University also provided generous support for this book's publication.

• • •

Lastly, I have benefited from the company of loved ones who kept me grounded when I was most absorbed in reading Arabic and Urdu texts. They offered me shelter, music, and broad smiles. Rondo, Starship, and the Perfection!sts, the West Philly folks, the Oberlin gang, the Thursday night Dreams, the Telluride crew, and many, many others. I thank little Milo, who dutifully accompanied me on long jogs through the Blue Ridge Mountains while I contemplated the book's many details, great and small.

I thank my extended family, especially my grandparents, Doris, Murray, and Ruthe, who turned ninety-six at the time this book was published. I thank Sara, Solmon, and Naomi for their love and support. I thank Saul, who passed away when this book was but a seedling of an idea, and Hannah, who tragically passed away as the book's final page proofs were sent off.

But some loved ones cannot be thanked enough with ink on a dusty page. Marc, Sharon, Ian, Jacob—and dearest Summer. This one's for you.

Joel Blecher
Washington DC, 2017

Notes

INTRODUCTION

1. Fuat Sezgin, who catalogs the number of hadith commentaries in his *Geschichte des aribischen Schrifttums* (*GAS*), defines the end of the classical period at the year 430/1038. His accounting of commentaries includes 56 commentaries on the canonical Sunni work *Ṣaḥīḥ al-Bukhārī* (*GAS*, 1:116–26), 9 commentaries on its adaptations (*GAS*, 1:128), and 7 on its headings (*GAS*, 1:129). It also includes other canonical Sunni collections: 27 commentaries for *Ṣaḥīḥ Muslim* (*GAS*, 1:136–40), 12 for *Sunan Abī Dāwūd* (*GAS*, 1:150–51), 12 for *Jāmiʿ al-Tirmidhī* (*GAS*, 1:155–56), 8 for *Sunan Ibn Māja* (*GAS*, 1:148), 4 for *Sunan al-Nasāʾī* (*GAS*, 1:168), and 5 on collections that combined *Ṣaḥīḥ al-Bukhārī* with *Ṣaḥīḥ Muslim* (*GAS*, 1:132). As for hadith compendia compiled by eponyms of the Sunni legal schools, *al-Muwaṭṭaʾ* of Mālik ibn Anas (d. 179/796) attracted at least 27 commentaries (*GAS* 1:460–63), *Musnad al-Shāfiʿī* attracted at least 9 (*GAS*, 1:488–89), and *Musnad Aḥmad* at least 2 (*GAS*, 1:506). *Al-Shamāʾil al-Muḥammadiyya*, a popular collection of hadith on Muhammad's moral qualities, appearance, and manners, received at least 31 commentaries (*GAS*, 1:158–59). Concerning Imāmī Shi'i works, *al-Kāfī* garnered at least 16 commentaries (*GAS*, 1:542), and *Kitāb man lā yaḥḍuruh al-faqīh* accumulated at least 7 (*GAS*, 1:546–7). Although these numbers are inexact, they represent the proportion of commentarial activity on each work.

2. This would include commentaries on collections of "forty hadith" (*arbaʿīniyyāt*) and Shi'i hadith collections, as well as lost, uncatalogued, or otherwise inaccessible commentaries that are referenced by the cumulative tradition or biographical dictionaries. For example, when lists of commentaries take at least some of these other categories into account, the approximate number of works produced on *Ṣaḥīḥ al-Bukhārī* leaps from 72 to 390. See

Muḥammad ʿIṣām ʿArār Ḥasanī, *Itḥāf al-qārī bi-maʿrifat juhūd wa-aʿmāl al-ʿulamāʾ ʿalā Ṣaḥīḥ al-Bukhārī* (Damascus: al-Yamāma, 1987), 418–47.

3. Jonathan A. C. Brown, *The Canonization of al-Bukhārī and Muslim* (Leiden: Brill, 2007), 264.

4. Alphonse Mingana, *An Important Manuscript of the Traditions of Bukhari, with Nine Facsimile Reproductions* (Cambridge, England: W. Heffer and Sons, 1936), 11–12.

5. See Scott C. Lucas, "The Legal Principles of Muḥammad b. Ismāʿīl al-Bukhārī and Their Relationship to Classical Salafi Islam," *Islamic Law and Society* 13, no. 3 (2006): 289–324; Stephen Burge, "Reading between the Lines: The Compilation of 'Ḥadīṯ' and the Authorial Voice," *Arabica* 58, no. 3 (2011): 168–97.

6. For instance, Abū ʿAmr al-Shaybānī's (d. ca. 213/828) *Kitāb Gharīb al-ḥadīth* and Abū ʿUbay al-Qāsim ibn al-Sallām's (d. 224/838) collection, *Gharīb al-ḥadīth*.

7. Muḥammad ibn Jarīr al-Ṭabarī, *Sharḥ ḥadīth Umm Zarʿ* (Köprülü Library Istanbul), MS 1080–83; *EI2*, s.v. "Sharḥ," (Claude Gilliot); Claude Gilliot, *Exégèse, langue et théologie* (Paris: Librairie Philosophique J. Vrin, 1990), 67.

8. Among others, Ibn Fūrak al-Iṣbahānī's (d. 406/1015) *Kitāb Mushkil al-ḥadīth* and Abū Jaʿfar al-Ṭaḥāwī's (d. 321/933) *Sharḥ Mushkil al-āthār.*

9. Vardit Tokatly, "The Aʿlām al-ḥadīth of al-Khaṭṭābī: A Commentary on al-Bukhārī's *Ṣaḥīḥ* or a Polemical Treatise?" *Studia Islamica,* no. No. 92 (2001): 53–91. Al-Khaṭṭābī also composed an important commentary on Abū Dāwūd's *Sunan,* which arguably enjoyed a higher status than *Ṣaḥīḥ al-Bukhārī* at the time.

10. Commentary on Mālik's *Muwaṭṭaʾ* flourished in particular, due to the foundational importance of the work to the Mālikī legal school. Notable examples include Ibn ʿAbd al-Barr's (d. 463/1071) *Kitāb al-tamhīd* and Abū al-Walīd al-Bājī's (d. 474/1081) *al-Muntaqā.* Meanwhile, scholars from the Muslim West produced influential commentaries on celebrated Sunni collections: Ibn Baṭṭāl of Córdoba (d. ca. 449/1057) commented on *Ṣaḥīḥ al-Bukhārī;* Abū ʿAbdallāh al-Māzarī (d. 536/1141–42) and Qāḍī ʿIyāḍ ibn Mūsa (d. 544/1149) composed celebrated commentaries on *Ṣaḥīḥ Muslim;* and Abū Bakr ibn al-ʿArabī (d. 543/1148) did so on *Sunan Tirmidhī.* Commentary on collections that combined selected hadith from *Ṣaḥīḥ al-Bukhārī, Ṣaḥīḥ Muslim,* and the *Muwaṭṭaʾ* were also popular, such as Qāḍī ʿIyāḍ's *Mashāriq al-anwār ʿalā ṣiḥāḥ al-āthār.* For a full catalog of Andalusian hadith scholars, see Ibn Khayr al-Ishbīlī, *Fihrisa,* ed. Muḥammad Fuʾād Manṣūr (Beirut: Dār al-Kutub al-ʿIlmiyya, 1998).

11. As we will see in part 1 of this book, Abū al-Walīd al-Bājī's (d. 474/1081) live hadith commentary in Dénia was the setting for a transregional controversy concerning his explication of a hadith from *Ṣaḥīḥ al-Bukhārī*'s "Book of Expeditions" (*Kitāb al-Maghāzī*). The Mālikī commentator Ibn Rushayd al-Sabtī (of Cueta, d. 761/1321) was also reported to have explained two hadith from *Ṣaḥīḥ al-Bukhārī* per day to his students at a mosque in Granada. See Abū al-Walīd al-Bājī, *Taḥqīq al-madhhab,* ed. Abū ʿAbd al-Raḥmān ibn ʿAqīl (Riyadh: ʿĀlam al-kutub, 1983), 115–18; Abū ʿAbd Allāh Ibn Rushayd, *Tarjumān al-tarājim ʿalā abwāb Ṣaḥīḥ al-Bukhārī* (Beirut: Dār al-Kutub al-ʿIlmiyya, 2008), 17. Meanwhile, Abū ʿAbdallāh al-Māzarī's renowned commentary on *Ṣaḥīḥ Muslim*

consists of notes dictated to his law students during study sessions (*majālis*) in Tunis during Ramadan of 499/1106. ʿAbdallāh al-Māzarī, "al-Muʿallim bi-fawāʾid Muslim" (Bibliothèque nationale de Tunisie, 499/1106), MS 7539, f. 1a.

12. Many examples abound, but the renowned Ibn Baṭūṭa (d. 770/1368–69), in his book of travels, recalled one such event in 726/1326, where he and a large audience gathered at the Umayyad mosque to hear *Ṣaḥīḥ al-Bukhārī* recited and explained in fourteen sittings in the latter part of Ramadan. See Muḥammad Ibn Baṭūṭa, *Tuḥfat al-Nuẓẓār fī gharāʾib al-amṣār* (Cairo: al-Maṭbaʿat al-Khayriyya, 1904), 1:78–82.

13. One oft-quoted chronicle reports that, during the late seventh / late thirteenth centuries, as the Mongols were advancing upon Syria, a governor ordered the Shāfiʿī chief justice (*qāḍī al-quḍāt*) of Mamluk Cairo, Ibn Daqīq al-ʿĪd (d. 702/1302), to gather the hadith scholars to quickly recite each volume of the *Ṣaḥīḥ* with the expectation of bringing about a miracle. Kamāl al-Dīn al-Udfuwī, *Al-Ṭāliʿ al-saʿīd: al-jāmiʿ li-asmāʾ al-fuḍalāʾ waʾl-ruwāh bi-aʿla al-ṣaʿīd*, 1st ed. (Egypt: al-Maṭbaʿa al-Jamāliyya, 1914), 323–4; ʿAbd al-ʿAzīz al-Dihlawī, *Bustān al-muḥaddithīn*, trans. Muḥammad Akram al-Nadwī (Beirut: Dār al-Gharb al-Islāmī, 2002), 252.

14. See Brown, *The Canonization of al-Bukhārī and Muslim*, 335–58. Of course, other genres of Islamic literature also functioned apotropaically, namely, the Qur'an and works containing descriptions (*ḥilya*) of Muhammad's appearance. The difference is of degree and perhaps that the *Ṣaḥīḥ* is unusual among multivolume hadith compilations in functioning regularly in such a way.

15. While some have translated *Fatḥ al-bārī* as "Victory of the Creator," my less literal translation captures the unlocking of multiple meanings for the reader.

16. Shams al-Dīn al-Safīrī's (d. 956/1549) *Sharḥ ʿiddat aḥādīth Ṣaḥīḥ al-Bukhārī* and Yūsuf-zāde's (d. 1167/1754) *Najāḥ al-Qārī* are notable examples. Hadith commentary also thrived on popular postclassical amalgamations of selections from multiple classical collections. Examples include ʿAlī ibn Sulṭān Muḥammad al-Qārī's (d. 1014/1606) *Mirqāt al-mafātīḥ* and Zayn al-Dīn al-Munāwī's (d. 1031/1622) *Fayḍ al-qadīr.* For more on the importance of *majālis* in the Ottoman context, see Helen Pfeifer, "Encounter after the Conquest: Scholarly Gatherings in 16th-century Ottoman Damascus," *International Journal of Middle East Studies* 47, no. 2 (2015): 219–39.

17. In the eleventh/seventeenth century alone, some fifteen Shi'i scholars are known to have written commentaries on *al-Kāfī*. See Rizwan Arastu's introduction to *al-Kāfī* (Dearborn: Taqwa Media, 2012), *xxxvi-xxxvii*. This activity was spurred in part by the dominance of an Imāmī Shi'i scripturalist movement that held that an apparentist reading of hadith and *akhbār,* rather than *ijtihād* (juristic interpretation), was the best method for obtaining certain and probable knowledge in matters of law and theology. Participants in this movement came to be known as the Akhbāriyya (the traditionists), and their opponents were later called the Uṣūliyya (the rationalists). The Akhbāriyya's methodological reliance on hadith and *akhbār* brought about unprecedented demand for new Imāmī Shiʿi hadith compilations and commentaries.

Most notable amongst the commentaries on Shi'i collections from this period are Muḥammad Bāqir al-Majlisī's (d. 1110/1698–99) commentaries on *al-Kāfī* and *Tahdhīb al-aḥkām* and Muḥsin Fayḍ al-Kashānī's (d. 1091/1680) commentary on a digest of the four canonical Imāmī Shi'i hadith collections. Shi'i commentators explained not only hadith attributed to Muhammad but also those attributed to Shi'i imams. Ṣafavid-era Shi'i collections have also been taken up again in the modern period. Al-Qummī's (d. 1940) *Safīnat al-biḥār* (The ship of the seas), for example, was composed to help readers navigate al-Majlisī's massive Ṣafavid-era hadith collection *Biḥār al-anwār* (Oceans of light).

18. For early legal and theological commentary on Shi'i hadith, see Andrew Newman, *The Formative Period of Twelver Shī'ism: Ḥadīth as Discourse between Qum and Baghdad* (London: Routledge, 2000); Robert Gleave, "Between Ḥadīth and Fiqh: The 'Canonical' Imāmī Collections of Akhbār," Islamic Law and Society 8, no. 3 (2001): 350–82. For discussion of hadith commentary in the Ṣafavid period, especially on Muḥammad Ṣadr al-Dīn al-Shirāzī (d. 1050/1640), a Ṣafavid-era philosopher and theologian who famously used the medium of hadith commentary as a means to explore complex themes in Sufi thought, see Armin Eschraghi, "'I Was a Hidden Treasure': Some Notes on a Commentary Ascribed to Mullā Ṣadrā Shīrāzī," in *Islamic Thought in the Middle Ages,* ed. Anna Akasoy and Wim Raven (Leiden: Brill, 2008), 91–99; Mohammad Reza Hemyari, "Understanding *'Aql* in Readings of *Uṣūl al-Kāfī:* Early Shi'ite Hadith and Its Later Interpreters" (MA thesis, George Washington University, 2014).

19. Joel Blecher, "Commentaries and Compendia of the Late Medieval Periods," in *The Oxford Handbook of Hadith Studies* (Oxford: Oxford University Press, forthcoming).

20. See Asma Sayeed, *Women and the Transmission of Religious Knowledge in Islam* (Cambridge: Cambridge University Press, 2013).

21. See Jonathan Berkey, "Women and Islamic Education in the Mamluk Period," in *Women in Middle Eastern History: Shifting Boundaries in Sex and Gender,* ed. Nikki R. Keddie and Beth Baron (New Haven, CT: Yale University Press, 2008), 143–58.

22. See Saba Mahmood, *Politics of Piety: The Islamic Revival and the Feminist Subject* (Princeton, NJ: Princeton University Press, 2005), 83–90.

23. 'Irqsūsī is a leader of the Jama'at Zayd movement. See Pierret and Selvik, "Limits of 'Authoritarian Upgrading' in Syria: Private Welfare, Islamic Charities, and the Rise of the Zayd Movement," *IJMES,* 41 (2009): 595–614.

24. Observed by Thomas Pierret, *Religion and State in Syria: The Sunni Ulama from Coup to Revolution* (Cambridge: Cambridge University Press, 2013), 116. A description of the live recitation sessions of *Ṣaḥīḥ al-Bukhārī* can also be found in Thomas Pierret, "Les oulémas syriens aux XXe–XXIe siècles" (PhD diss., IEP de Paris 2009), 414–25. Some of al-'Irqsūsī's lessons are posted on YouTube, such as "Hadith of the Shaykh on the Festival Prayer," YouTube video, 7:19, posted by "m11m11b," July 27, 2007, www.youtube.com/watch?v=AiCe1osK89I.

25. For the classical Sunni tradition of hadith commentary, Vardit Tokatly has shown how early written commentary on hadith served theological apologetics, as noted above. Tokatly has also produced an unpublished doctoral thesis in Hebrew on three early commentators on the *Ṣaḥīḥ al-Bukhārī:* al-Khaṭṭābī, Ibn

Baṭṭāl, and al-Nawawī. See Vardit Tokatly, "The Early Commentaries on al-Bukhārī's *Ṣaḥīḥ*" (PhD diss. Hebrew University of Jerusalem, 2003). Likewise, Norman Calder investigated how a notable Mamluk-era hadith commentator was influenced by legal aims and other genre-specific concerns of legal writing. See Norman Calder, *Islamic Jurisprudence in the Classical Era* (Cambridge: Cambridge University Press, 2010), 74–115. For the modern period, M.R. Woodward and Muhammad Qasim Zaman shed light on the practice of commentary in Indonesia and India, respectively, and the extent to which hadith commentary has responded to the concerns of modern societies. Zaman's work has been particularly influential in shedding light on the construction of commentarial authority in the age of colonialism and print. See M.R. Woodward, "Textual Exegesis as Social Commentary: Religious, Social, and Political Meanings of Indonesian Translations of Arabic Ḥadīth Texts," *Journal of Asian Studies* 52, no. 3: 565–53; Muhammad Qasim Zaman, "Commentaries, Print and Patronage: 'Ḥadīth' and the Madrasas in Modern South Asia," *Bulletin of the School of Oriental and African Studies* 62, no. 1 (1999): 60–81. For further reading, consult *Oxford Bibliographies On-line,* s.v. "Hadith Commentary" (Joel Blecher).

26. Ignaz Goldziher, *Muslim Studies (Muhammedanische Studien),* ed. S.M. Stern, trans. C.R. Barber and S.M. Stern., 2 vols. (London: Allen and Unwin, 1968); Joseph Schacht, *Origins of Muhammadan Jurisprudence* (Oxford: Clarendon Press, 1966); G.H.A. Juynboll, *Muslim Tradition* (Cambridge: Cambridge University Press, 1983). See also the more recent work of Harald Motzki, ed., *Hadith: Origins and Developments* (Aldershot, England: Ashgate Publishing, 2004).

27. This recent generation of academic studies has drawn on a range of sources: hadith criticism, biographies of transmitters, audition records (*samāʿāt*), legal works, and the hadith collections themselves. Jonathan A.C. Brown, for instance, documented how the collections of *Ṣaḥīḥ al-Bukhārī* and *Ṣaḥīḥ Muslim* came to be awarded a canonical status over time and, in doing so, illuminated how Muslim scholars themselves constructed and deconstructed the authority of these works. Likewise, Aisha Y. Musa examined how it was that hadith came to serve as an authority prior to the canonization of key collections and how their authority was leveraged in later discourses explaining the Qur'an and Islamic law. Meanwhile, Asma Sayeed's recent work has shed much needed light on the shifting fortunes of female hadith transmitters from the rise of Islam to the end of the Mamluk period. Brown, *The Canonization of al-Bukhārī and Muslim;* Aisha Y. Musa, *Hadith as Scripture: Discussions on the Authority of Prophetic Traditions in Islam* (New York: Palgrave Macmillan, 2008); Asma Sayeed, *Women and the Transmission of Religious Knowledge in Islam* (Cambridge: Cambridge University Press, 2013).

28. For a greater theoretical discussion of why these three aspects of religious traditions and social practices—experience, power, and meaning-making—can and should be brought together rather than treated separately, see Stephen Bush, *Visions of Religion: Experience, Meaning, and Power* (Oxford: Oxford University Press, 2014).

29. Hans Ulrich Gumbrecht, "Fill Up Your Margins! About Commentary and *Copia,*" in *Commentaries—Kommentare,* ed. Glenn Most (Göttingen:

Vandenhoeck and Ruprecht, 1999). John Dagenais, in a path-breaking and theoretically nuanced study of a fourteenth-century Iberian work's commentaries, laments the overemphasis on written practices but saw no other avenue forward: "Clearly, the nature of oral reading is lost to us for all time, given the ephemeral contingency of time and place, the perishability of the oral medium." For this reason, he observed that scholars cannot begin their investigation with oral readings, but rather with "individual readings carried out with the physical text in hand." John Dagenais, *The Ethics of Reading in Manuscript Culture: Glossing the "Libro de buen amor"* (Princeton, NJ: Princeton University Press, 1994), 27. John Henderson's *Scripture, Canon, Commentary* relies exclusively on written commentaries on canonical texts in order to examine and compare commentarial strategies and assumptions across religious traditions. John Henderson, *Scripture, Canon, Commentary* (Princeton, NJ: Princeton University Press, 1991). Even Foucault, in making the point that certain forms of commentaries can eclipse the base text upon which they comment, cites only written examples: a translation, a textual explication, and a novel. Foucault writes: "One and the same literary work can give rise simultaneously to very distinct types of discourse: the 'Odyssey' as a primary text is repeated, in the same period, in the translation by Bérard, and in the endless 'explications de texte,' and in Joyce's *Ulysses*." Michel Foucault, "The Order of Discourse (1970)," in *Untying the Text: A Post-Structuralist Reader,* ed. Robert Young (London: Routledge, 1981), 57.

30. *Tafsīr* studies developed in earnest in the mid-1970s with the publication of John Wansborough, *Quranic Studies: Sources and Methods of Scriptural Interpretation* (Oxford: Oxford University Press, 1977), which was followed by a bevy of monographs and collected volumes, including Andrew Rippin, ed., *Approaches to the History of the Interpretation of the Qur'an* (Oxford: Oxford Univeristy Press, 1988); Andrew Rippin, *The Qur'an and Its Interpretive Tradition* (Aldershot, England: Ashgate, 2001); Walid Saleh, *The Formation of the Classical Tafsīr Tradition: the Qur'ān Commentary of Tha'labī* (Leiden: Brill, 2004); and Karen Bauer, ed., *Aims, Methods and Contexts of Qur'anic Exegesis (2nd/8th–9th/15th C.)* (Oxford: Oxford University Press, 2013).

31. Contemporary scholar of Tibetan Buddhism, José Cabezón has called for a "sociocultural analysis" of scholastic commentary that would give a sense of the day-to-day pressures of interpreters, "the political, economic and material factors that influence and are influenced by scholasticism . . . the lived lives of scholastics as individuals, their influence on the broader communities in which they are located, and in turn the pressures exerted on, and the rewards offered to them, by those communities." José Ignacio Cabezón, ed., *Scholasticism: Cross-Cultural and Comparative Perspectives* (Albany: State University of New York Press, 1998), 248. Although this call has largely gone unanswered in studies of Islamic commentary, there are a number of medievalists who have undertaken studies of Islamic education more broadly. Their studies have drawn on reading certificates (*samā'āt*), library catalogues, endowment deeds (*awqāf*), legal *responsa* (*fatāwā*), and manuscript art. See Konrad Hirschler, *The Written Word in the Medieval Arabic Lands: A Social and Cultural History of Reading Practices* (Edinburgh: Edinburgh University Press, 2012); Jonathan Berkey, *The*

Transmission of Knowledge in Medieval Cairo (Princeton, NJ: Princeton University Press, 1992); Michael Chamberlain, *Knowledge and Social Practice in Medieval Damascus* (Cambridge: Cambridge University Press, 1994); Sayeed, *Women and the Transmission of Religious Knowledge in Islam.*

Likewise, anthropologists such as Brinkley Messick have investigated commentary as both an oral lesson and a written composition in the Yemeni context: "The 'dictation' relationship involved both a dictating teacher and note-taking students, but it was the oral recitation-like activity of the teacher and the listening of the students rather than his reading and their writing that were taken to be of consequence." See Brinkley Messick, *The Calligraphic State: Textual Domination and History in a Muslim Society* (Berkeley: University of California Press, 1993), 30–31. Following Messick, Saba Mahmood's ethnographic work documents how a contemporary female preacher at the upper-middle-class ʿUmar Mosque in Cairo employed rhetorical strategies to maintain her audience's interest during a commentarial lesson. Saba Mahmood, *Politics of Piety: The Islamic Revival and the Feminist Subject* (Princeton, NJ: Princeton University Press, 2005), 83–90.

32. A similar objection could be raised against sociocultural analyses that take Foucault's statement—"discourse is not simply that which translates struggles or systems of domination, but is the thing for which and by which there is struggle, discourse is the power which is to be seized"—to mean that intellectual debates are nothing more than an instrument of and trophy of power. Foucault, "The Order of Discourse (1970)," 52–53.

33. This concept of a reciprocal hermeneutic motion across time has been articulated by a number of scholars in translation studies: George Steiner, *After Babel: Aspects of Language and Translation* (Oxford: Oxford University Press, 1975), 296–303; Walter Benjamin, "The Task of the Translator," in *Illuminations* (New York: Schocken, 1968), 69–82; and Ebrahim Moosa, "Contrapuntal Readings in Muslim Thought: Translations and Transitions," *Journal of the American Academy of Religion* 74, no. 1 (March 2006): 107–18. While these studies offer explicitly normative claims about how to undertake the task of a reciprocal interpretation, these works are also invaluable for historians attempting to understand the predicament of hadith commentators and other interpreters of scripturalized texts.

34. Scholar of religion Wilfred Cantwell Smith first described Islamic legal commentary as accumulative over time, since commentators not only preserved the base text but also the layers of traditional opinions interpreting those base texts. Wilfred Cantwell Smith, *The Meaning and End of Religion* (Minneapolis, MN: Fortress Press, 1962), 154–69. Patterns of consensus on a hadith's meaning, if reached within these cumulative layers of commentary, were a real burden for novel interpretations to overcome. The cumulative tradition could thus serve to check outlying opinions.

35. As Islamicist Norman Calder has pointed out, at some point these many layers become unwieldy, and certain commentators took steps to pare down the cumulative tradition to extend its meaning for the present. Norman Calder, "Tafsīr from Ṭabarī to Ibn Kathīr: Problems in the Description of a Genre, Illustrated with Reference to the Story of Abraham," in *Approaches to the*

Qur'ān, ed. G.R. Hawting and Abdul-Kader Shareef (New York: Routledge, 1993), 101–4.

36. At stake in Bourdieu's conception of a social practice was "symbolic capital, a transformed and thereby disguised form of physical 'economic' capital, produces its proper effect inasmuch, and only inasmuch, as it conceals the fact that it originates in 'material' forms of capital which are also, in the last analysis, the source of its effects." Pierre Bourdieu, *Outline of a Theory of Practice,* trans. Richard Nice (Cambridge: Cambridge University Press, 1977), 183.

37. In the case of Islamic history, social historian Michael Chamberlain, informed by Weber and Bourdieu, framed knowledge as a social practice in medieval Damascus in which Muslim scholars broadly "acquired and used the rare symbolic capital by which they claimed power, resources, and social honor and passed them on within lineages." See Chamberlain, *Knowledge and Social Practice,* 22. Chamberlain's influence on the field—and, by extension, Bourdieu's concept of a social practice—is evident in the major monographs on the social history of Islamic societies published since then.

For a deeper discussion of this concept of a social practice—and a critique of Bourdieu's—see the introduction to Bush, *Visions of Religion: Experience, Meaning, and Power,* 1–22. Although Bush urges scholars to take into account experience, meaning, and power, the present book will attend largely to the workings of meaning-making and power, while offering leads to any future scholars interested in exploring the experiential dimension of commentary.

38. Alisdair MacIntyre, *After Virtue,* 3rd ed. (Notre Dame: University of Notre Dame Press, 2007), 187. MacIntyre is rightfully taken to task by critics for his assertion that moderns have lost touch with excellences "internal" to premodern traditions of ethics. However, one does not need to subscribe to MacIntyre's larger normative argument to benefit from his framework.

39. MacIntyre defines a *tradition* as "an historically extended, socially embodied argument, an argument precisely in part about the goods which constitute that tradition." In Talal Asad, "The Idea of an Anthropology of Islam," in *Occasional Papers* (Washington, DC: Center for Contemporary Arab Studies, Georgetown University, 1986), 14–15; MacIntyre, *After Virtue,* 222.

40. We should, however, be careful not to assume that the domain of meaning is found only internal to the tradition, or to assume that the domains of capital and power are only found outside of it. To be sure, the meanings and norms of the hadith can also be constructed outside the practice of the commentary tradition, and certain kinds of material and social rewards can only be obtained internal to the practice of the tradition—stature and recognition from one's commentarial peers, for instance. Nevertheless, MacIntyre's sensitivity to ends internal to the tradition is useful for shedding light on the standards of excellence that are defined by and defining of the interpretive tradition itself. See MacIntyre, *After Virtue,* 175–76.

41. I conceive of "orthodoxy" as a dynamic and always contested product of networks seeking the maintenance of power rather than a fixed set doctrines. This approach is informed by Bourdieu, *Outline of a Theory of Practice,* 159–70. For greater discussion and critiques of the use of "orthodoxy" in Islamic studies, see Asad, "The Idea of an Anthropology of Islam," 15–16; M. Brett

Wilson, "The Failure of Nomenclature: The Concept of 'Orthodoxy' in the Study of Islam," *Comparative Islamic Studies* 3, no. 2 (2007): 169–94; and Robert Langer and Udo Simon, "Dynamics of Orthodoxy and Heterodoxy: Dealing with Divergence in Muslim Discourses and Islamic Studies," *Die Welt des Islams* 48 (2008): 273–88. As for recent thematic legal studies upon which my diachronic case studies are modeled, see Behnam Sadeghi, *The Logic of Law Making in Islam: Women and Prayer in the Legal Tradition,* Cambridge Studies in Islamic Civilization (Cambridge: Cambridge University Press, 2013); and Mairaj U. Syed, *Coercion and Responsibility in Classical Islamic Thought* (Oxford: Oxford University Press, 2017).

1. THE PERILS OF PUBLIC COMMENTARY

1. Ibn Ḥajar al-ʿAsqalānī, *Fatḥ al-bārī,* ed. ʿAbd al-ʿAzīz ibn Bāz, 13 vols. (Beirut: Dār al-Maʿrifa, 1970), 7:499 (Kitāb al-Maghāzī: Bāb ʿUmrat al-Qaḍāʾ).

2. Norman Calder has argued that the "philological-historical examination of the three Qurʾanic terms *ummī, ummiyyun,* and *umma* does not confirm the popular interpretation of *ummī,* which focuses exclusively on illiteracy. Rather, this interpretation seems to reflect a post-Qurʾanic approach that evolved in circles of Muslim learning (possibly not before the first half of the 2nd/8th century)." This much longer debate is summarized and analyzed in Norman Calder, "The Ummī in Early Islamic Juristic Literature," *Der Islam* 67 (1990): 111–23, esp. 15–16; *EQ,* s.v. "Ummī" (Sebastian Günther).

3. Qur'an, 29:48. The Arabic for "inscribe it" is *takhuṭṭuhu.*

4. Al-Bājī, *Taḥqīq al-madhhab,* 170.

5. Maribel Fierro, "Local and Global in Ḥadīth Literature: The Case of al-Andalus," in *The Transmission and Dynamics of the Textual Sources of Islam: Essays in Honour of Harald Motzki,* ed. Nicolet Boekhoff-van der Voort, Kees Versteegh, and Joas Wagemakers (Leiden: Brill, 2011), 82.

6. See David J. Wasserstein, *The Caliphate in the West: An Islamic Political Institution in the Iberian Peninsula* (Oxford: Clarendon Press, 1993); David J. Wasserstein, *The Rise and Fall of the Party-Kings: Politics and Society in Islamic Spain, 1002–1086* (Princeton: Princeton University Press, 1985); P.C. Scales, *The Fall of the Caliphate of Córdoba: Berbers and Andalusis in Conflict* (Leiden: Brill, 1994).

7. Fierro, "Local and Global in Ḥadīth Literature," 81; Munīra bint ʿAbd Raḥmān Sharqī, *ʿUlamāʾ al-Andalus fī al-qarnayn al-rābiʿ waʾl-khāmis al-hijrīyayn: dirāsa fī awḍāʿihim al-iqtiṣādiyya wa-āthārihā ʿalā mawāqifihim al-siyāsiyya* (Riyadh: Maktabat al-Malik Fahd al-Waṭaniyya, 2002), 268–69.

8. See Munīra bint ʿAbd Raḥmān Sharqī, *ʿUlamāʾ al-Andalus,* 263–64, 268–69.

9. See Fierro, "Local and Global in Ḥadīth Literature," 72; Muḥammad ibn Zayn al-ʿĀbidīn Rustam, "al-Madrasa al-Andalusiyya fī sharḥ *al-Jāmʿi al-ṣaḥīḥ* min al-qarn al-khāmis ilā al-qarn al-thāmin al-hijrī," *Majallat Jāmiʿat Umm al-Qura li-ʿUlūm al-Sharīʿa waʾl-Lugha al-ʿArabiyya wa-Ādābihā* 15, no. 27 (1424/2003): 6. Some hadith scholars of this time, including al-Khaṭṭābī, favored Abū Dāwūd's *Sunan* during this time, as is discussed in Goldziher,

Muslim Studies, 2:235–56. The authoritative station of Abū Dāwūd's *Sunan* is also reflected in the fact that it was Abū Bakr al-Jaṣṣāṣ's (d. 370/981) preferred source for hadith in his *Aḥkām al-Qur'ān.* See Abū Bakr Aḥmad ibn ʿAlī al-Rāzī al-Jaṣṣāṣ, *Kitāb Aḥkām al-Qur'ān,* 3 vols. (Beirut: Dār al-Kitāb al-ʿArabī, 1978). My thanks to Michael Cook for this reference.

10. The earliest systematic commentary on *Ṣaḥīḥ al-Bukhārī* was penned in the Islamic West by the Mālikī Jurist Abū Jaʿfar al-Dāwūdī (d. 402/1011–12) of Tripoli. Ḥasanī, *Itḥāf al-qārī,* 98. Tokatly suggests that al-Dāwūdī's was the second earliest, following al-Khaṭṭābī's, but we do not have precise enough information to order these works chronologically. Tokatly, "The Early Commentaries on al-Bukhārī's *Ṣaḥīḥ,*" xvii. Jonathan Brown credits al-Muhallab ibn Abī Ṣufra of Almería (d. ca. 435/1044) as the earliest commentator in the West. See Brown, *The Canonization of al-Bukhārī and Muslim,* 376.

11. Among them were Ibn Barṭāl (d. 394/1003–4) and ʿAbd Allāh al-Juhanī (d. 395/1004–5), who, after traveling east, propagated recitations of the *Ṣaḥīḥ* on the authority of Ibn al-Sakan (353/964), a student of renowned hadith transmitter al-Firabrī (320/932), considered and later revered as one of al-Bukhārī's most reliable students. Rustam, "al-Madrasa al-Andalusiyya," 5–6.

12. Fierro, "Local and Global in Ḥadīth Literature," 76.

13. Abū ʿAmr al-Ṣafāqisī (d. 440/1048–49), who returned to Córdoba in 436/1044–45, after acquiring some of the highest chains of transmission in circulation abroad. He was known not only for his prodigious memory but also for his ability to discern, critique, and explicate hadith and their transmitters. Ibn Bashkuwāl, *al-Ṣila,* 3 vols. (Beirut: Dār al-Kitāb al-Lubnānī, 1990), 2:595–97, no. 885.

14. For a brief account of al-Bājī's travels, *EI2,* s.v. "al-Bādjī" (D.M. Dunlop).

15. Ḥasanī, *Itḥāf al-qārī,* 358; Tokatly, "The Early Commentaries on al-Bukhārī's *Ṣaḥīḥ,*" 163–176. Once thought lost, a transmission of al-Muhallab's commentary on *Ṣaḥīḥ al-Bukhārī* has recently surfaced and has been made available for researchers in a printed edition: *al-Mukhtaṣar al-naṣīḥ fī tahdhīb al-Jāmʿ al-ṣaḥīḥ,* ed. al-Sharīf Walad Ābāh, 4 vols. (Ribat, Morocco: Dār al-Qalam, 2007).

16. Ḥasanī, *Itḥāf al-qārī,* 197; Tokatly, "The Early Commentaries on al-Bukhārī's *Ṣaḥīḥ,*" 182–222.

17. A student of al-Bājī's, Abū ʿAlī Ibn Sukkara al-Ṣadafī (d. 514/1120) traced his *isnād* through al-Bājī back to al-Firabrī by way of Abū Dharr's three shaykhs in one of the earliest known manuscripts of the *Ṣaḥīḥ* in 493/1100. Ibn Sukkara's transmission, which was copied by Ibn Saʿāda (d. 565/1170), was then used as the basis for later manuscripts for Muslim scholars in the West for the centuries that followed. É. Lévi-Provençal, "La recension maghribine du *Ṣaḥīḥ* d'al-Bukhārī," *Journal Asiatique* (1923): 233; *EI2,* s.v. "Ibn Saʿāda" (J. Robson). The renowned Mālikī scholar and commentator on *Ṣaḥīḥ Muslim* Qāḍī ʿĪyāḍ was among Ibn Sukkara's students, *EI2,* s.v. "al-Ṣadafī" (M. Fierro).

18. Among al-Bājī's students were Abū ʿAlī al-Jayyānī (d. 498/1105), a master of *isnād* criticism, and Ibn ʿAbd al-Barr (463/1071) in Andalusia. Ḥasanī, *Itḥāf al-qārī,* 117; Brown, *The Canonization of al-Bukhārī and Muslim,* 376;

Johann Fück, "Beiträge zur Überlieferungsgeschichte von Bukhārī's Traditionssammlung," *Zeitschrift der deutschen Morgenländischen Gesellschaft* 92 (1938): 67–68.

19. Abū al-Walīd al-Bājī, *al-Muntaqā: Sharḥ Muwaṭṭa' Mālik,* 9 vols. (Beirut: Dār al-Kutūb al-'Ilmiyya, 1999).

20. "Fa-akhadha rasūl Allāh al-kitāba wa-laysa yuḥsinu yaktubu *fa-kataba* hādha: 'mā qāḍā Muḥammad ibn 'Abd Allāh . . . '" al-'Asqalānī, *Fatḥ al-bārī,* 7:499 (Kitāb al-Maghāzī: Bāb 'Umrat al-qaḍā'). Emphasis mine.

21. This anecdote is attributed to Muslim historian Ibn al-Ḥasan al-Bunnāhī (d. 798/1389–90). See the editor's introduction to al-Bājī, *Taḥqīq al-madhhab,* 117–18. Emphasis mine, and pronouns referring to al-Bājī have been made explicit in my translation.

22. The death date for Abū Bakr ibn al-Ṣā'igh is unknown, but he is surely not the better-known philosopher and *wazīr* Abū Bakr ibn al-Ṣā'igh Ibn Bājja, who died young in 533/1139.

23. Al-Bājī, *Taḥqīq al-madhhab,* 115.

24. Ibid., 116.

25. Ibid.

26. The emir was most likely 'Alī ibn Mujāhid, Iqbāl al-Dawla (r. 436 to 468/1044–45 to 1075–76). See Wasserstein, *The Rise and Fall of the Party-Kings.*

27. For a number of *responsa* on this matter, consult al-Bājī, *Taḥqīq al-madhhab,* 241–344.

28. Ibid., 127–28.

29. This can also be found, among other places, in *Ṣaḥīḥ Muslim.* See al-'Asqalānī, *Fatḥ al-bārī,* 6:282 (Kitāb al-Jizya wa'l-muwāda'a: Bāb al-Muṣālaḥa 'alā thalāthat ayyām aw waqt ma'lūm); Muslim ibn al-Ḥajjāj al-Qushayrī and Abū Zakariyyā al-Nawawī, *Ṣaḥīḥ Muslim bi-sharḥ Nawawī,* 18 vols. (Cairo: al-Maṭba'a al-Miṣriyya bi'l-Azhar, 1930), 12:134–36 (Kitāb al-Jihād wa'l-siyar: Bāb Ṣulḥ al-Ḥudaybiyya). In another narration, also found in *Ṣaḥīḥ al-Bukhārī,* Muhammad scrubbed out the designation in question but the report left it ambiguous who actually wrote the treaty. Al-'Asqalānī, *Fatḥ al-bārī,* 5:303 (Kitāb al-Ṣulḥ: Bāb Kayf yuktabu hādha mā ṣālaḥ . . .).

30. In a narration in *Ṣaḥīḥ Muslim,* not found in *Ṣaḥīḥ al-Bukhārī,* Muhammad ordered someone else to write and then to emend the treaty, but it was ambiguous who satisfied the order. See Muslim ibn al-Ḥajjāj and Abū Zakariyyā al-Nawawī, *Ṣaḥīḥ Muslim bi-sharḥ Nawawī,* 12:138–39 (Kitāb al-Jihād wa'l-siyar: Bāb Ṣulḥ al-Ḥudaybiyya). In another account from *Ṣaḥīḥ Muslim,* not found in *Ṣaḥīḥ al-Bukhārī,* Muhammad, incapable of reading or writing, was directed to the line of text in which to scrub his own name, and 'Alī made the emendation "son of 'Abd Allāh" after having refused. Ibid., 12:136–38 (Kitāb al-Jihād wa'l-siyar: Bāb Ṣulḥ al-Ḥudaybiyya). The *Sunan* of Dārimī and the *Musnad* of Aḥmad ibn Ḥanbal contain similar traditions, although Mālik's *Muwaṭṭa'* is silent on the matter.

31. Al-Bājī, *Taḥqīq al-madhhab,* 207.

32. Ibid., 198–99.

33. Ibid., 199.

34. Ibid., 218–19.

35. Ibid., 220.

36. Ibid., 233.

37. Abū ʿAbd Allāh al-Anṣārī of Almería (d. 532/1137–38), a Ẓāhirī expert on *ʿilm al-rijāl,* was one of the earliest to produce an abridged compilation combining select hadith from al-Bukhārī and Muslim's compilations. Bashkuwāl, *al-Ṣila,* 3:845–46, no. 1288; Samir Kaddouri, "Refutations of Ibn Ḥazm by Mālikī Authors from al-Andalus and North-Africa," in *Ibn Ḥazm of Cordoba: The Life and Works of a Controversial Thinker,* ed. Camilla Adang, Maribel Fierro, and Sabine Schmidtke (Leiden: Brill, 2013), 574. Ibn Ḥazm, as we will see in the next chapter, also turned to *Ṣaḥīḥ al-Bukhārī* in order to bolster support for his position.

38. Brown, *The Canonization of al-Bukhārī and Muslim,* 225.

39. Ibn al-Munayyir, *al-Mutawārī ʿalā abwāb al-Bukhārī* (Beirut: Maktab al-Islāmī, 1990), 36.

40. Ibn Ḥajar al-ʿAsqalānī, *Hady al-sārī,* ed. ʿAbd al-Qādir Shayba al-Ḥamad (Riyadh: Maktabat al-Malik Fahd al-Waṭaniyya, 2000), 13.

41. For discussion of "apparentism," or what had recently been termed "textualism" in Ẓāhirism, see Amr Osman, "The History and Doctrine of the Ẓāhirī *Madhhab*" (PhD diss., Princeton University, 2010), 226–93; Intisar Rabb, "Doubt's Benefit: Legal Maxims in Islamic Law (7th–16th Centuries)" (PhD diss., Princeton University, 2009), 355–73.

42. Al-ʿAsqalānī, *Fatḥ al-bārī,* 7:504 (Kitāb al-Maghāzī: Bāb ʿUmrat al-Qaḍāʾ).

43. Anwar Shāh al-Kashmīrī, *Fayḍ al-bārī* (Beirut: Dār Iḥyāʾ al-Turāth al-ʿArabī, 2005), 4:108–9 (Kitāb al-Maghāzī: Bāb ʿUmrat al-Qaḍāʾ).

2. THE INNER WORLD OF THE INTERPRETIVE TRADITION

1. Mundhir al-Ballūṭī (d. 355/966). See Ignaz Goldziher, *Ẓāhirīs: Their Doctrine and Their History: A Contribution to the History of Islamic Theology* (Boston: Brill, 2007), 107–8.

2. Maribel Fierro, *ʿAbd al-Rahman III: The First Cordoban Caliph* (Oxford: Oneworld, 2005), 130–31; Kaddouri, "Refutations of Ibn Ḥazm," 542–43.

3. For an example of a disagreement between Abū Zinād ibn Sirāj of Córdoba (d. 422/1030–31) and al-Muhallab ibn Abī Ṣufra of Almería (d. ca. 435/1044) see ʿAlī ibn Khalaf Ibn Baṭṭāl, *Sharḥ Saḥīḥ al-Bukhārī,* 11 vols. (Riyadh: Maktabat Rushd, 2003), 88; Rustam, "al-Madrasa al-Andalusiyya," 21.

4. Maribel Fierro, "The Polemic about the *karāmat al-awliyāʾ* and the Development of Sufism in al-Andalus (Fourth/Tenth–Fifth/Eleventh Centuries)," *Bulletin of the School of Oriental and African Studies* 55 (1992): 236–49.

5. José Miguel Puerta Vílchez, "Ibn Ḥazm: A Biographical Sketch." In *Ibn Ḥazm of Cordoba: The Life and Works of a Controversial Thinker,* edited by Camilla Adang, Maribel Fierro, and Sabine Schmidtke (Leiden: Brill, 2013), 13; Kaddouri, "Refutations of Ibn Ḥazm," 549.

6. This might have been around the time of al-Bājī's return to Andalusia in 439/1047–48, after which he wrote the first systematic refutation of Ibn Ḥazm

and Ẓāhirism in a volume titled *Firāq al-fuqahā'*. See Kaddouri, "Refutations of Ibn Ḥazm," 557; Ḥasanī, *Itḥāf al-qārī,* 130. Other evidence, such as the burning of Ibn Ḥazm's books, sometime between 445/1053 and his death in 456/1064, likewise suggests that the polemical disputes over Ẓāhirism reach a fever pitch with a later wave of scholars, after Abū Zinād's and al-Muhallab's deaths, and probably after Ibn Baṭṭāl's as well. Vílchez, "Ibn Ḥazm: A Biographical Sketch," 19.

7. This next wave of Andalusian commentators was transmitted, in part, by Ibn Rushayd al-Sabtī and was later quoted by Mamluk commentators such as Ibn Ḥajar and Ibn al-Mulaqqin.

8. Al-ʿAsqalānī, *Fatḥ al-bārī,* 12:175 (Kitāb al-Ḥudūd: Bāb Kam al-taʿzīr wa'l-adab).

9. Ibn Baṭṭāl, *Sharḥ Saḥīḥ al-Bukhārī,* 8:485.

10. Ibid. This list also includes al-Layth ibn Saʿd (d. 175/791–92).

11. Zayd ibn Thābit (d. 42 to 56 / 662–63 to 675–76). Ibid.

12. Ibid.

13. Ibid.

14. Ibid.

15. Ibn Abī Layla (d. 148/765) and Abū Yūsuf (d. 182/798). Ibid.

16. Arabic: *idhā addā al-imām ijtihāduhu ilā dhālika.* Ibid.

17. Muḥammad ibn Fattūḥ al-Ḥumaydī, *Jadhwat al-muqtabis fī dhikr wulāt al-Andalus* (Cairo: al-Dār al-Miṣriyya, 1966), 257. ʿAbd Allāh ibn Muḥammad Ibn al-Faraḍī, *Tārīkh al-ʿulamāʾ wa'l-ruwāh lil-ʿilm bi'l-Andalus* (Cairo: ʿIzzat al-ʿAṭṭār al- Ḥusaynī, 1954), 1:290; Brown, *The Canonization of al-Bukhārī and Muslim,* 366–67; Rustam, "al-Madrasa al-Andalusiyya," 6.

18. Al-Faraḍī, *Tārīkh al-ʿulamāʾ wa'l-ruwāh,* 1:290. A diagram of early transmissions of the *Ṣaḥīḥ,* including al-Aṣīlī's, can be found in Fück, "Beiträge zur Überlieferungsgeschichte von Bukhārī's Traditionssammlung," 79; Mingana, *An Important Manuscript of the Traditions of Bukhari.*

19. Al-Ḥumaydī, *Jadhwat al-muqtabis,* 258. Among al-Aṣīlī's students was Abū Aṣbagh Ibn Sahl (d. 486/1093) from Jaén, who claimed that he transmitted the *Ṣaḥīḥ* on the authority of al-Aṣīlī. He delivered a commentary clarifying matters of difficulty (*ishkhāl*) in the *Ṣaḥīḥ* at the request of his colleagues in the year 456/1063–64, the same year he rose to prominence as a judge in Córdoba. Samir Kaddouri, "al-Faqīh al-Qāḍī ʿIsā ibn Sahl al-Asadī al-Jayyānī (d. 486/1093)," *Majallat al-Tārīkh al-ʿArabī* 37 (Summer 2006): 307–32.

20. Eerick Dickinson's translation of *muḍṭarib min al-ḥadīth* is a "disrupted hadith," but a "disrupted" *isnād* is a more precise characterization than al-Aṣīlī's *iḍṭaraba* implies. See Ibn al-Ṣalāḥ al-Shahrazūrī, *An Introduction to the Science of Ḥadīth: Kitāb Maʿrifat anwāʿ ʿilm al-ḥadīth,* trans. Eerik Dickinson (Reading: Garnet, 2006), 71–72.

21. Ibn Baṭṭāl, *Sharḥ Saḥīḥ al-Bukhārī,* 8:485–86. Ibn Baṭṭāl recalled that the Shāfiʿī jurist Ibn al-Mundhir (d. 318/930–31) of Nishapur also thought the chain that included Jābir was unreliable (*maqāl*). He did not elaborate further.

22. ʿUmar Ibn al-Mulaqqin, *al-Tawḍīḥ li-sharḥ al-Jāmiʿ al-Ṣaḥīḥ* (Qaṭar: Dār al-Falāḥ, 2009), 31:274–75; and al-ʿAsqalānī, *Fatḥ al-bārī,* 12:176–77 (Kitāb al-Ḥudūd: Bāb Kam al-taʿzīr wa'l-adab).

23. Al-ʿAsqalānī, *Fatḥ al-bārī,* 12:176–77 (Kitāb al-Ḥudūd: Bāb Kam al-taʿzīr wa'l-adab). Al-Jayyānī claimed that al-Aṣīlī confused *ibn* (son of) with *ʿan* (on the authority of). Both words' orthography is similar in Arabic. Al-Jayyānī had become a master of hadith through his studies with al-Bājī and others. He is often quoted as an authority on *isnād* criticism by Mamluk-era commentators on the *Ṣaḥīḥ.*

24. Ibid.

25. According to Ibn Ḥajar, both Jābir and Abū Burda were from the *anṣār,* so either of them could be the anonymous man from the *anṣār.*

26. Al-Shahrazūrī, *Introduction to the Science of Ḥadīth,* 71–72.

27. For a greater discussion of *matn* criticism, see Jonathan A.C. Brown, "How We Know Early Ḥadīth Critics Did *Matn* Criticism and Why It's So Hard to Find" *Islamic Law and Society* 15 (2008): 143–84; idem, "The Rules of *Matn* Criticism: There Are No Rules," *Islamic Law and Society* 19, no. 4 (2012): 356–96.

28. This was a companion report on Ibn Shihāb al-Zuhrī's (d. 124/741–42) authority. Ibn Baṭṭāl, *Sharḥ Saḥīḥ al-Bukhārī,* 8:486. Ibn Baṭṭāl did not list which title of al-Ṭaḥāwī's he relied upon, but al-Ṭaḥāwī's opinion on this matter can be found in a number of his works, including his *Sharḥ Maʿānī al-āthār.*

29. Ibid.

30. Ibid., 8:486–87. Ibn Mulaqqin later cast doubt on whether this was ʿUmar ibn al-Khaṭṭāb, the second caliph, or another ʿUmar.

31. Ibid., 8:487.

32. Ibid., 8:484.

33. Ibid., 8:485.

34. Ibid., 8:487.

35. Al-ʿAsqalānī, *Fatḥ al-bārī,* 12:179 (Kitāb al-Ḥudūd: Kam al-taʿzīr wa'l-adab).

36. Abū Muḥammad Ibn Ḥazm, *Ṭawq al-ḥamāma* (Damascus: Maktabat ʿArafa, 1981), 136.

37. Arabic: *lā yajibu al-qatl ʿalā aḥad.* Ibid.

38. Ibn al-Mulaqqin, *al-Tawḍīḥ,* 31:279 (Kitāb al-Rajm: Bāb Kam al-taʿzīr wa'l-adab).

39. Ibn Ḥazm, *Ṭawq al-ḥamāma,* 138–39. This, despite the fact that "according to a well known Prophetic saying, fire was a punishment reserved uniquely for the hereafter," Christian Lange, *Justice, Punishment and the Medieval Muslim Imagination* (Cambridge: Cambridge University Press, 2008), 67–69.

40. Ibn Ḥazm, *Ṭawq al-ḥamāma,* 138.

41. For a larger critique of this position, see Camilla Adang, "Ibn Ḥazm on Homosexuality: A Case-Study of Ẓāhirī Legal Methodology," *Al-Qanṭara* 24, no. 1 (2003): 5–31. Adang engages Louis Crompton, who has since tempered his position. See Louis Crompton, *Homosexuality and Civilization* (Cambridge, MA: Harvard University Press, 2006), 166.

42. See Abū Muḥammad Ibn Ḥazm, *al-Muḥallā,* 11 vols. (Damascus: Idārat al-Ṭibāʿa al-Munayriyya, 1933–34), 11:380.

43. See Ibn Ḥazm, *Ṭawq al-ḥamāma,* 138. It should be pointed out that in his legal work, *al-Muḥallā,* Ibn Ḥazm drew on a different prooftext and linked

it to the Ḥanafī position (*al-Muḥallā,* 11:383); Adang, "Ibn Ḥazm on Homosexuality," 18.

44. Gadamer called this an "effective history," *Wirkungsgeschichte,* while Jauss called it *Rezeptionsgeschichte.* Hans-Georg Gadamer, *Truth and Method,* trans. W. Glen-Doepel, 2nd, rev. ed. (New York: Continuum, 2004), 299–300; Hans Jauss, "Literary History As a Challenge to Literary Theory," *New Literary History* 2 (1970): 7–37. For a more detailed discussion of these terms, consult Robert Evans, *Reception History, Tradition and Biblical Interpretation: Gadamer and Jauss* (London: Bloomsbury, 2014), xvii–xviii, 1–19.

45. This is consistent with the findings in Tokatly, "Early Commentaries on al-Bukhārī's *Ṣaḥīḥ,*" 219–22.

3. FOR SULTANS, STUDENTS, AND SCHOLARS

1. ʿAbd al-Raḥmān ibn Muḥammad Ibn Khaldūn, *Muqaddima* (Beirut: Dār al-Fikr, 2001), 560; Ibn Khaldūn, *The Muqaddimah,* trans. Franz Rosenthal, 3 vols. (Princeton, NJ: Princeton University Press, 1967), 2:457–59.

2. Calder, *Islamic Jurisprudence in the Classical Era,* 115.

3. Since the Mamluk period witnessed a popularization of "writerly culture and reading practices," made possible by the transformative growth of institutions of learning in Damascus and Cairo, we can reconstruct a detailed account of the place of manuscript culture and live study sessions within the Mamluk-era commentarial writing process. For a monographic treatment of this phenomenon, see Hirschler, *Written Word,* 3.

Moreover, because of the fame of Ibn Ḥajar's *Fatḥ al-bārī* in particular, later biographers, such as Ibn Ḥajar's closest student, Shams al-Dīn al-Sakhāwī (d. 902/1497), preserved specifics on the process of composing this commentary in greater detail than had been done for previous commentaries on *Ṣaḥīḥ al-Bukhārī.* Al-Sakhāwī relied heavily on Ibn Ḥajar's autobiographical description of his writing process in the introduction to a work called *Intiqāḍ al-iʿtirāḍ,* which Ibn Ḥajar wrote after he had formally completed writing *Fatḥ al-bārī.* This autobiographical passage was not without an ulterior motive. Ibn Ḥajar had sought to prove that Badr al-Dīn al-ʿAynī (d. 855/1451), a commentarial rival who was simultaneously producing a commentary on *Ṣaḥīḥ al-Bukhārī* in Cairo, had "borrowed without attribution" from Ibn Ḥajar's *Fatḥ al-bārī.* Due to the polemical motivations behind the introduction to *Intiqāḍ al-iʿtirāḍ,* it may not be possible to extrapolate based on Ibn Ḥajar's and al-Sakhāwī's accounts alone, and I will try, wherever possible, to draw on other sources, including chronicles, biographical dictionaries, authorial introductions, and manuscript evidence.

4. A prolegomenon to and commentary on *Ṣaḥīḥ al-Bukhārī* was one of the last works the Syrian scholar Muḥyī al-Dīn Abū Zakariyyā al-Nawawī composed before his death in 676/1277. Abū Zakariyyā Yaḥyā al-Nawawī, *al-Talkhīṣ [fī] sharḥ al-Jāmiʿ al-ṣaḥīḥ lil-Bukhārī,* 2 vols. (Riyadh: Dār al-Ṭayba lil-Nashr wa'l-Tawziʿ, 2008), 1:146. For more biographical information on al-Nawawī, see Ibn al-ʿAṭṭār, *Tuḥfat al-ṭālibīn fī tarjamat al-Imām Muḥyī Dīn* (Riyadh: Dār al-Ṣumayʿī 1994). Likewise, the Cairene scholar ʿUmar ibn ʿAlī ibn al-Mulaqqin composed his commentary on *Ṣaḥīḥ al-Bukhārī,* called *al-Tawḍīḥ,* late in life; see

Ibn al-Mulaqqin, *al-Tawḍīḥ*, 1:341. The renowned Shāfiʿī jurist and Sufi paragon Zakariyyā al-Anṣārī (d. 926/1520) composed his commentary on *Ṣaḥīḥ al-Bukhārī* after he had retired from his chief judgeship. Najm al-Dīn al-Ghazzī, *Al-Kawākib al-sāʾira bi-aʿyān al-miʾa al-ʿāshira*, ed. Jibrāʾīl Sulaymān Jabbūr (Beirut: Dār al-Āfāq al-Jadīda, 1979), 1:199. My thanks to Matthew Ingalls for this reference; see Matthew B. Ingalls, "Subtle Innovation within Networks of Convention: The Life, Thought, and Intellectual Legacy of Zakariyyā al-Anṣārī (d. 926/1520)" (PhD diss., Yale University, 2011), 97–98.

5. *EI2*, s.v. "Ibn Ḥa*dj*ar al-ʿAsḳalānī" (Franz Rosenthal). Ibn Ḥajar had been teaching hadith since 808/1406 at the Shaykhūniyya and taught in several prominent centers of learning throughout Cairo, including al-Khānqāh al-Baybarsiyya, al-Madrasa al-Jamāliyya, al-Jāmiʿ al-Ṭūlūnī, al-Qubba al-Manṣ ūriyya, and al-Madrasa al-Maḥmūdiyya, as well as in the Dār al-Ḥadīth al-Ashrafiyya in Damascus in 836/1433. See Shams al-Dīn al-Sakhāwī, *al-Jawāhir wa'l-durar* (Beirut: Dār Ibn Ḥazm, 1999), 2:591–96.

6. Al-Nawawī's works on hadith transmitters, language, and law were titled *Tahdhīb al-asmāʾ wa'l-lughāt* and *Minhāj al-ṭālibīn*. Ibn Ḥajar's work was called *Taʿlīq al-taghlīq*. For a longer discussion of this work and its warm reception by his teachers and peers, see Sabri Kawash, "Ibn Ḥajar al-Asqalānī: A Study of the Background, Education, and Career of a ʿĀlim in Egypt" (PhD diss., Princeton University, 1968), 196–97.

7. Abū Zakariyyā Yaḥyā al-Nawawī, *Ṣaḥīḥ Muslim bi-sharḥ al-Nawawī*, 18 vols. (Cairo: al-Maṭbaʿa bi'l-Azhar 1969), 1:4–5, translation by Calder, *Islamic Jurisprudence in the Classical Era*, 107.

8. Al-Nawawī, *Ṣaḥīḥ Muslim bi-sharḥ al-Nawawī*, 1:4–5, translation by Calder, *Islamic Jurisprudence in the Classical Era*, 107.

9. Norman Calder translates al-Nawawī's description of the process: "[al-Nawawī's] commentary [on Muslim's *Ṣaḥīḥ*] would be of intermediate size avoiding excessive concision and excessive expansion (neither *mukhtaṣar* nor *mabsūṭ*)." See Calder, *Islamic Jurisprudence in the Classical Era*, 107.

10. Al-Sakhāwī, *al-Jawāhir wa'l-durar*, 2:675–76.

11. Hans Ulrich Gumbrecht, *The Powers of Philology: Dynamics of Textual Scholarship* (Urbana: University of Illinois Press, 2003), 44.

12. Al-ʿAsqalānī, *Fatḥ al-bārī*, 1:5. At certain moments during the commentary, Ibn Ḥajar laments this constraint. See, for instance, ibid., 2:431. For a comparative perspective, see Ivan Illich's work on the relationship between gloss and base text in the layout of works of medieval Christian scholasticism; Ivan Illich, *In the Vineyard of the Text* (Chicago: University of Chicago Press, 1993), 87–88 and 106–7. Thanks to Jeff Kosky for the reference.

13. See Ibn Ḥajar al-ʿAsqalānī, *Intiqāḍ al-iʿtirāḍ* (Riyadh: Maktabat Rushd, n.d.), 1:7. Ibn Ḥajar's unfinished mega-commentary on the *Ṣaḥīḥ* may have initially been titled *Hudā al-sārī*, a voluminous commentary to match a voluminous prolegomenon. See al-Dihlawī, *Bustān al-muḥaddithīn*, 234.

14. Al-ʿAsqalānī, *Intiqāḍ al-iʿtirāḍ*, 1:7.

15. Al-Sakhāwī, *al-Jawāhir wa'l-durar*, 2:675–76.

16. Shams al-Dīn al-Sakhāwī, *al-Ḍawʾ al-lāmiʿ li-ahl al-qarn al-tāsiʿ* (Beirut: Dār al-Jīl, 1992), 1:45.

17. Ibid., 2:675; al-ʿAsqalānī, *Intiqāḍ al-iʿtirāḍ,* 1:7.

18. The commentary was completed on a Thursday, Rajab 1, 842 (December 12, 1438), and it would be unusual if the final session of his commentary on the *Ṣaḥīḥ* had been delivered at any time other than the regularly appointed time. Ibn Ḥajar had a highly regular teaching schedule during this period, instructing hadith at the *khānqāh* of Baybars each week on Tuesday with little interruption. See al-Sakhāwī, *al-Jawāhir wa'l-durar,* 2:675. For a greater description of Ibn Ḥajar's weekly routine, see Kawash, "Ibn Ḥajar al-Asqalānī," esp. 126 and 144–46. Hirschler also points out that "Thursday also had strong religious connotations on which fasting was enjoined and the gates of paradise were said to be opened. Accordingly, normative treatises particularly encouraged scholars to study *ḥadīth*" on Thursday. Hirschler, *Written Word,* 39. However, an early dictated copy of *Fatḥ al-bārī,* dated 822/1419, was completed on a Monday, so there may have been some exceptions to this schedule. See Ibn Ḥajr al-ʿAsqalānī, *Fatḥ al-bārī* (Süleymaniye Library Istanbul, 1419), MS Mahmud Paşa 79, f. 317a.

19. Shams al-Dīn al-Sakhāwī, *al-Ḍawʾ al-lāmiʿ li-ahl al-qarn al-tāsiʿ* (Beirut: Dār al-Jīl, 1992), 1:43–45.

20. Ibid., 1:45.

21. See al-Sakhāwī, *al-Jawāhir wa'l-durar,* 2:675; al-ʿAsqalānī, *Intiqāḍ al-iʿtirāḍ,* 1:7.

22. For a prominent example of this phenomenon, see Abū ʿAbd Allāh Muḥammad ibn Idrīs al-Shāfiʿī, *al-Risāla* (Beirut: Dār al-Kitāb al-ʿArabī, 2006), 315–18.

23. "[*T*]*aḥrīr hādhā al-sharḥ.*" See al-Sakhāwī, *al-Jawāhir wa'l-durar,* 2:675–76.

24. This change in the editing process may explain some stylistic differences between the first quarter of the work and the last three quarters.

25. Al-Sakhāwī, *al-Jawāhir wa'l-durar,* 2:38 and 2:675–76; al-ʿAsqalānī, *Intiqāḍ al-iʿtirāḍ,* 1:7. For relative values of dinars, consult Wan Kamal Mujani, "The Fineness of Dinar, Dirham and Fals during the Mamluk Period," *Journal of Applied Sciences Research* 7, no. 12 (2011): 1895–900.

26. Kawash, "Ibn Ḥajar al-Asqalānī," 234.

27. *Farāgh:* al-Sakhāwī, *al-Jawāhir wa'l-durar,* 2:675–76; al-ʿAsqalānī, *Intiqāḍ al-iʿtirāḍ,* 1:7. *Khatm:* al-Sakhāwī, *al-Ḍawʾ al-lāmiʿ,* 2:38.

28. Gumbrecht writes: "[Commentary] appears to be a discourse which, almost by definition, never reaches its end. Whereas an interpreter cannot help extrapolating an author-subject as a point of reference for his or her interpretation (and while he cannot help giving shape to this reference as the interpretation progresses), a commentator is never quite sure of the needs (i.e., of the *lacunae* in knowledge) of those who will use the commentary." See Gumbrecht, *The Powers of Philology,* 42.

29. These transregional requests for *Fatḥ al-bārī* arrived in 833/1429–30. Ibn Ḥajar al ʿAsqalānī, *Inbāʾ al-ghumr bi-abnāʾ al-ʿumr fī al-tārīkh,* ed. Ḥasan Ḥabashī, 4 vols. (Cairo: al-Majlis al-Aʿlā lil-Shuʾūn al-Islāmiyya, 1969), 3:434; al-ʿAsqalānī, *Intiqāḍ al-iʿtirāḍ,* 1:8.

30. See al-ʿAsqalānī, *Intiqāḍ al-iʿtirāḍ,* 1:8.

31. Ibid. For a biography of al-Birishkī, see al-Sakhāwī, *al-Ḍaw' al-lāmi'*, 4:132–33.

32. This is the same Ibn al-Jazarī who was known as the renowned expert on the various recitations of the Qur'an (*qirā'āt*). See al-'Asqalānī, *Intiqāḍ al-i'tirāḍ*, 1:8; *EI2*, s.v. "Ibn al-DJazarī, Shams al-Dīn" (M. Bencheneb).

33. Al-'Asqalānī, *Intiqāḍ al-i'tirāḍ*, 1:8. For an account of the controversy concerning this gift giving, consult Anne Broadbridge, "Academic Rivalries and the Patronage System in Fifteenth-Century Egypt: al-'Aynī, al-Maqrīzī, and Ibn Ḥajar al-'Asqalānī," *Mamlūk Studies Review* 3 (1999): 85–107.

34. Al-Sakhāwī, *al-Ḍaw' al-lāmi'*, 2:38; Mujani, "Fineness of Dinar, Dirham and Fals," 1895–900.

35. Adam Sabra, *Poverty and Charity in Medieval Islam: Mamluk Egypt, 1250–1517* (Cambridge: Cambridge University Press, 2000), 123–27 and 131.

36. For a fuller discussion, see R. Kevin Jaques, *Ibn Hajar* (New Delhi: Oxford University Press, 2009), 11–12.

37. See al-'Asqalānī, *Fatḥ al-bārī*, 3:458–60 (Kitāb al-Ḥajj: Bāb Kiswat al-Ka'ba).

38. Ibid., 3:460 (Kitāb al-Ḥajj: Bāb Kiswat al-Ka'ba).

39. Ibid., 3:448–49 (Kitāb al-Ḥajj: Bāb Faḍl makkā wa-bunyānihā).

40. Ibid., 3:437 (Kitāb al-Ḥajj: Bāb Min ayna yakhruju min makka).

41. Ibid., 2:399 (Kitāb al-Jum'a: Bāb al-Khuṭba 'alā al-minbar).

42. Ibid., 3:460 (Kitāb al-Ḥajj: Bāb Kiswat al-Ka'ba).

43. Al-Sakhāwī, *al-Jawāhir wa'l-durar*, 2:616–17.

44. Ibid.

45. See Jaques, *Ibn Hajar*, 106.

46. See G.E. von Grunebaum, "The Concept of Plagiarism in Arabic Theory," *Journal of Near Eastern Studies* 3 (1944): 234–53; Franz Rosenthal, *The Technique and Approach of Muslim Scholarship*, Analecta Orientalia 24 (Rome: Pontificium Institutum Biblicum, 1947), 46–48.

47. Vardit Tokatly briefly discusses this accusation near the end of her dissertation. See Tokatly, "Early Commentaries on al-Bukhārī's *Ṣaḥīḥ*," 242–49.

48. See Yossef Rapoport, "Legal Diversity in the Age of Taqlīd: The Four Chief Qāḍīs under the Mamluks," *Islamic Law and Society* 10, no. 2 (2003): 210. For a monographic treatment of Islamic legal authority in practice during the Burjī period, see Kristen Stilt, *Islamic Law in Action: Authority, Discretion, and Everyday Experiences in Mamluk Egypt* (Oxford: Oxford University Press, 2011). For theoretical discussions of the status of Shāfi'ī judges in the Baḥrī Mamluk period, see Sherman Jackson, *Islamic Law and the State: The Constitutional Jurisprudence of Shihāb al-Dīn al-Qarāfī* (Leiden: Brill, 1996), 53–56; Joseph H. Escovitz, "Patterns of Appointment to the Chief Judgeships of Cairo during the Baḥrī Mamlūk Period," *Arabica* 30, no. 2 (1983): 165ff.

49. Michael Winter, "'Ulama' between the State and Society in Pre-modern Sunni Islam," in *Guardians of Faith in Modern Times: 'Ulama' in the Middle East*, ed. Meir Hatina (Leiden: Brill, 2009), 34ff.

50. See Broadbridge, "Academic Rivalries," 85–107.

51. Ibid., 98–99.

52. See al-ʿAsqalānī, *Inbāʾ al-ghumr,* 7:280. Ibn Taghrībīrdī recounted this narrative under the events of 821 rather than 820, which is perhaps why Anne Broadbridge overlooked Ibn Ḥajar's own account of the exchange in her article, cited above. See Yūsuf Ibn Taghrībirdī, *al-Nujūm al-zāhira fī mulūk Miṣr wa'l-Qāhira,* 16 vols. (Beirut: Dār al-Kutub al-ʿIlmiyya, 1992), 13:225. I use Ibn Ḥajar's date, not only because he was personally involved in the events, but also because he included many chronological details that Ibn Taghrībīrdī lacks regarding the events, such as the detail that the events unfolded in the last days of the month Dhū al-Ḥijja. The later Syrian historian Ibn Asbāṭ (d. ca. 926/1520) adds to the confusion by dating the event to 816. See Ibn Asbāṭ, *Ṣidq al-akhbār* (Tripoli, Lebanon: Jurūs Burs, 1993), 2:775.

53. Ibn Taghrībirdī, *al-Nujūm al-zāhira,* 13:225.

54. Ibid.

55. Ibid.; al-ʿAsqalānī, *Inbāʾ al-ghumr,* 7:281.

56. Ibn Taghrībirdī, *al-Nujūm al-zāhira,* 15:287. The 1971 printed edition goes so far as to make the connection explicit by printing "al-ʿAynī" rather than "al-ʿayn[i]." See Ibn Taghrībirdī, *al-Nujūm al-zāhira fī mulūk Miṣr wa'l-Qāhira,* 16 vols. (Cairo: al-Muʾassasa al-Miṣriyya al-ʿĀmma lil-Taʾlīf wa'l-Ṭibāʿa wa'l-Nashr, 1971), 14:75–76. All references in this book will be to the 1992 edition, unless indicated otherwise.

57. Al-ʿAsqalānī, *Inbāʾ al-ghumr,* 7:281.

58. Ibn Taghrībirdī, *al-Nujūm al-zāhira,* 13:225.

59. Ibn Asbāṭ, *Ṣidq al-akhbār,* 2:775–76.

60. Kawash, "Ibn Ḥajar al-Asqalānī," 167.

61. The dates in which al-ʿAynī's commentary was completed are documented in a colophon transcribed in Rashīd Aḥmad Gangohī and Muḥammad Zakariyyā al-Kāndhlawī, *Lāmiʿ al-darārī ʿalā Jāmiʿ al-Bukhārī,* 10 vols. (Mecca: al-Maktaba al-Imdādiyya, 1975), 1:404. See also al-ʿAsqalānī, *Intiqāḍ al-iʿtirāḍ,* 1:10.

62. Many examples in which al-ʿAynī takes Ibn Ḥajar's original phrasing not found in earlier commentaries, such as al-Kirmānī's—without acknowledging a citation can be found. For one example in which al-ʿAynī quoted himself (*qultu*) but instead offered Ibn Ḥajar's opinion, without attribution, compare Badr al-Dīn al-ʿAynī, *ʿUmdat al-qārī fī sharḥ Ṣaḥīḥ al-Bukhārī* (Beirut: Dār al-Kutub al-ʿIlmiyya, 2001), 24:35 (Kitāb al-Muḥāribīn min ahl al-kufr wa-ridda: Bāb Kam al-taʿzīr wa'l-adab); al-ʿAsqalānī, *Fatḥ al-bārī,* 12:177 (Kitāb al-Ḥudūd: Bāb Kam al-taʿzīr wa'l-adab). As Vardit Tokatly has pointed out, al-ʿAynī incorporated without attribution huge swaths of text from al-Nawawī's prolegomenon to the *Ṣaḥīḥ* in the prolegomenon to his *ʿUmdat al-Qārī;* compare al-ʿAynī's prolegomenon with al-Nawawī, *al-Talkhīṣ,* 1:183–285; Tokatly, "Early Commentaries on al-Bukhārī's *Ṣaḥīḥ,*" 242–49.

63. See Rosenthal, *Technique and Approach of Muslim Scholarship,* 41–45.

64. "Fa-lam yaʿud ilā al-kitāba fīh[i] hattā shārif *Fatḥ al-bārī* al-farāgh fa-ṣār yastaʿīr min baʿḍ man katab[a] li-nafsih[i] min al-ṭalaba," al-ʿAsqalānī, *Intiqāḍ al-iʿtirāḍ,* 1:10.

65. Ibid.

66. Ibid., 1:12–13.
67. Ibid., 1:9–10.
68. Ibid.
69. See al-ʿAsqalānī, *Hady al-sārī,* 489ff.
70. Ibid.
71. See Michael Cook, "On Islam and Comparative Intellectual History," *Daedalus* 135, no. 4 (Fall 2006); Rosenthal, *Technique and Approach of Muslim Scholarship,* 48–53.
72. Al-Sakhāwī, *al-Jawāhir wa'l-durar,* 1:390–92.
73. Ibid.
74. Ibn al-Mulaqqin, *al-Tawḍīḥ,* 1:289.
75. Al-Sakhāwī, *al-Jawāhir wa'l-durar,* 1:390–92.
76. Hirschler notes that there was an explosion in the usage of the phrase *qirāʾa bi-nafsihi* between the ninth and tenth centuries (fourteenth and fifteenth CE). See Hirschler, *Written Word,* 14–15. It is possible that this phenomenon allowed more sources to be read and cited in commentaries, such as Ibn Ḥajar's *Fatḥ al-Bārī* and al-ʿAynī's *ʿUmdat al-Qārī.*
77. Al-Dihlawī, *Bustān al-muḥaddithīn,* 241.
78. Ibid. Also mentioned in Chase Robinson, *Islamic Historiography* (Cambridge: Cambridge University Press, 2003), 186. Lest I overlook my own acknowledgment, I thank Jonathan Brown for first mentioning this anecdote to me.
79. E.M. Sartain, *Jalāl al-Dīn al-Suyūṭī: Biography and Background,* 2 vols. (Cambridge: Cambridge University Press, 1975), 1:72.
80. Ibid., 1:75–76. See also Goldziher, *Muslim Studies,* 2:245n3.
81. Sartain, *Jalāl al-Dīn al-Suyūṭī,* 1:76.
82. Ibid.
83. For discussion of another plagiarism dispute concerning Ibn Ḥajar and al-Sakhāwī, see Frédéric Bauden, "Should al-Maqrīzī Be Thrown Out with the Bath Water? The Question of His Plagiarism of al-Awḥadī's *Khiṭaṭ* and the Documentary Evidence," *Mamlūk Studies Review* 14 (2010): 159–232.
84. See G.E. von Grunebaum, "Concept of Plagiarism," 234–53; Michiko Kakutani, "Texts without Context," *New York Times,* March 17, 2010.

4. RIVALRY AND REVISION IN THE MANUSCRIPT AGE

1. This is the state of the field, despite Rosenthal's urging of studies that address the "progressive development within individual" premodern Muslim authors almost seven decades ago. See Rosenthal, *The Technique and Approach of Muslim Scholarship,* 66–68.
2. For a critique of this approach from a medieval Europeanist's perspective, see Dagenais, *Ethics of Reading in Manuscript Culture.*
3. Frédéric Bauden, "Maqriziana II: Discovery of an Autograph Manuscript of al-Maqrīzī: Towards a Better Understanding of His Working Method Analysis," *Mamlūk Studies Review* 12, no. 1 (2008): 51–118; Li Guo, "Ibn Dāniyāl's 'Dīwān': In Light of MS Ayasofya 4880," *Quaderni di Studi Arabi* 5/6 (2011): 163–76; and

Sami G. Massoud, "Ibn Qāḍī Shuhba's 'al-Dhayl al-Muṭawwal': The Making of an All Mamluk Chronicle," *Quaderni di Studi Arabi* 4 (2009): 61–79.

4. My transcription of the colophon reads, "ʿ[A]llaqahu li-nafsih min imlāʾ sayyidī wa-mufīdī al-Imām al-Ḥāfiẓ al-ʿAlīm Abī al-Faḍl Aḥmad al-Maḥmūd Abī al-Ḥasan ʿAlī ibn Ḥajar amtaʿ Allāh bi-hayātihi afqar ʿibād Allāh wa-aḥwājuhum ilā maghfiratihi wa-ʿafwihi Muḥammad ibn Abī al-Ḥayāt al-Khiḍr ibn Abī Sulaymān Dāwūd al-Miṣrī ʿafā Allāh ʿanhum ijmaʿīn. Wa-wāfiq al-farāgh min hādhā al-mujallad fī ṣabīḥat nahār al-ithnayn sābiʿ ʿishrīn shaʿbān muʿaẓẓam ʿām ithnayn wa-ʿishrīn wa-thamānī miʾa bi'l-madrasa al-Nāṣiriyya Bayn al-Qaṣrayn bi'l-Qāhira al-Maḥrūsa ḥamāha Allāhu taʿālā wa-sā'ir bilād al-Muslimīn." See Süleymaniye Library Istanbul, MS Mahmud Paşa 79, f. 317a.

5. Al-Sakhāwī, *al-Jawāhir wa'l-durar,* 2:675–6; al-ʿAsqalānī, *Intiqāḍ al-iʿtirāḍ.*

6. My transcription of the marginal note reads, "[A]l-ḥamdullilāh. Balagha muqābalatan bi-ḥasab al-ṭāqa wa-kitābat al-zawāʾid alladhīna al-muʾallaf abqāhu Allāhu taʿāllā wa mataʿ Allāh bi-ḥayātihi ʿalā nuskhat al-Shaykh Burhān al-Dīn Ibn Khiḍr fī shahr Ramaḍān sanat khamsīn wa-thamānī miʾa aḥsan Allāhu ʿāqabahā." See Süleymaniye Library Istanbul, MS Mahmud Paşa 79, f. 317a.

7. See Bauden, "Discovery of an Autograph Manuscript of al-Maqrīzī," 56.

8. Like many great works of Islamic literature, there is neither a known holograph nor a critical edition of *Fatḥ al-bārī.* Early copies of the work that were based on Ibn Ḥajar's exemplar have, however, survived (see, for example, a copy collated against an *aṣl ṣaḥīḥ* in 856/1452 at Princeton University Library's Rare Books and Special Collections, shelved under 87Yq, and a possible autograph copy at El Escorial shelved under 1451, see *GAS,* 121). One of the earliest printed editions of *Fatḥ al-bārī,* the Būlāq edition of 1882–83, does not describe the manuscript sources used to establish the printed text. Bin Bāz's edition, dated to 1950, represents some improvement, in that he checked the Būlāq edition against two manuscripts, one of which was collated in 1234/1819. Unfortunately, these manuscripts' prestige is not derived from any special connection to Ibn Ḥajar's *aṣl,* but from an ownership statement in which one of the manuscripts was endowed to the Saudi ruler Fayṣal ibn Turkī (d. 1865). These manuscripts' authority was maintained in the library of one of the descendants of Muḥammad ibn ʿAbd al-Wahhāb, which may have brought further esteem to them in Bin Bāz's view. Shayba al-Ḥamad's 2000 edition of *Fatḥ al-bārī* is more visually appealing but offers no indication of how he established the text of *Fatḥ al-bārī* (the manuscripts pictured in the editor's introduction under the misleading title "description of manuscripts" are of *Ṣaḥīḥ al-Bukhārī,* a work not originally included in *Fatḥ al-bārī*). Nevertheless, in the absence of a critical edition in print, we can use Bin Bāz's edition as an example of a version of *Fatḥ al-bārī* based on a later recension of the text. Bin Bāz saw few variants between his nineteenth-century manuscripts and the Būlāq edition, which may be indicative of the extent to which *Fatḥ al-bārī* was conservatively transmitted after Ibn Ḥajar's death. See al-ʿAsqalānī, *Fatḥ al-bārī,* 1:3–4; al-ʿAsqalānī, *Fatḥ al-bārī,* ed. Shayba al-Ḥamad (Riyadh: Ibn ʿAbd al-ʿAzīz Āl Saʿūd, 2000), 1:21–26.

9. Süleymaniye Library Istanbul, MS Mahmud Paşa 79, f. 317a.

10. See al-ʿAsqalānī, *Inbāʾ al-ghumr,* 4:86. As might be expected, there are some minor discrepancies between the names of Ibn al-Miṣrī's ancestors. Among them, the colophon appears to read Ibn *Abī* Sulaymān Dāwūd whereas Ibn Ḥajar recalls Ibn *Akhī* Sulaymān Dāwūd. This discrepancy notwithstanding, the broader evidence removes any doubt concerning this match. It is possible that the confusion between Abī and Akhī was the result of a scribal error or an accident of memory.

11. Ibid. "[S]amiʿa minnī wa-kataba fī al-imlāʾ min sharḥ *al-Bukhārī.*"

12. Süleymaniye Library Istanbul, MS Mahmud Paşa 79, f. 317a.

13. This is what is sometimes termed a *scholar's copy.* See Adam Gacek, *Arabic Manuscripts: A Vademecum for Readers* (Leiden: Brill, 2009), 78.

14. Süleymaniye Library Istanbul, MS Mahmud Paşa 79, f. 317a.

15. See al-ʿAsqalānī, *Fatḥ al-bārī,* 1:5. At certain moments during the commentary, Ibn Ḥajar laments this constraint. See, for instance, ibid., 2:431.

16. The collation note in the margin states: "Balagha Ṣāḥibuhu Shaykh Shams al-Dīn samāʿan wa-muqābalatan min awwal abwāb al-adhān katabahu muʾallifuhu," or "[The copy's] owner, Shaykh Shams al-Dīn [a *laqab* of Ibn al-Miṣrī's] completed the audition and collation from the beginning of the chapters on the *adhān.* Signed by its author [Shams al-Dīn]." See Süleymaniye Library Istanbul, MS Mahmud Paşa 79, f. 2a.

17. Compare with Muḥammad ibn Yūsuf al-Kirmānī, *Ṣaḥīḥ Abī ʿAbd Allāh al-Bukhārī bi-Sharḥ,* 2nd ed., 25 vols. (Beirut: Dār Iḥyāʾ al-Turāth al-ʿArabī, 1981), 5:47.

18. Süleymaniye Library Istanbul, MS Mahmud Paşa 79, f. 30a. Bin Bāz's edition currently has *al-dhikr* (remembrance). Perhaps Ibn Ḥajar revised it a third time, but most likely *al-dhākir* is the reading Ibn Ḥajar preferred, as he was listing actors, not actions. See al-ʿAsqalānī, *Fatḥ al-bārī,* 2:143–4.

19. For examples of Ibn Ḥajar's and al-Sakhāwī's handwriting, consult A. J. Arberry, *The Chester Beatty Library: A Handlist of the Arabic Manuscripts,* 8 vols. (Dublin, 1955), vol. 2: plates 59, 64, and 65.

20. For Ibn al-Miṣrī's son Khiḍr's biography, consult al-Sakhāwī, *al-Ḍawʾ al-lāmiʿ,* 3:179–80.

21. This debate continues to this day to be the subject of many Shi'i, Salafi, and legal school polemics questioning the authenticity of the practice.

22. Süleymaniye Library Istanbul, MS Mahmud Paşa 79, f. 136b–137a.

23. Copyists would often omit marginal notes, so "the publishing technique of the manuscript age thus made no allowance for marginal notes and footnotes. However, the need for such notes was felt, and a substitute invented. Beginning in the thirteenth, or rather the fourteenth century, authors increasingly used the device of inserting additional remarks, which often were lengthy excursus, in the context, but separating them from it by an introductory expression, such as *tanbīh,* or *fāʾidah,*'note.'" Rosenthal, *Technique and Approach of Muslim Scholarship,* 40.

24. Al-ʿAsqalānī, *Fatḥ al-bārī,* 2:394–95.

25. This could be described as a form of Mamluk-era *matn* criticism. For more on the history of this technique, see Brown, "How We Know Early Ḥadīth Critics Did *Matn* Criticism"; and Brown, "The Rules of *Matn* Criticism."

26. Ibn al-Mulaqqin, *al-Tawḍīḥ,* 7:514–521; Badr al-Dīn al-ʿAynī, *ʿUmdat al-qārī fī sharḥ Ṣaḥīḥ al-Bukhārī,* 25 vols. (Beirut: Idārat al-Ṭabāʿat al-Muniriyya, 1970), 6:210–12.

27. Calder, "Tafsīr from Ṭabarī to Ibn Kathīr," 103–4.

28. Al-Sakhāwī, *al-Ḍawʾ al-lāmiʿ,* 2:38.

29. See al-ʿAsqalānī, *Intiqāḍ al-iʿtirāḍ,* 7–11.

30. "Thubita lafẓ hādhihi al-tarjama fī ḥadīth marfūʿ akhrajahu Abū Dāwūd wa'l-Nasāʾī, wa-ṣaḥḥaḥahu Ibn Khuzayma wa-ghayruhu min ḥadīth Ibn ʿUmar." See Süleymaniye Library Istanbul, MS Mahmud Paşa 79, f. 3b.

31. "Thubita lafẓ hādhihi al-tarjama fī ḥadīth li-Ibn ʿUmar marfūʿ akhrajahu Abū Dāwūd al-Ṭayālisī fī musnadihi, fa-qāla fīhi 'mathnā, mathnā.' Wahuwa ʿind Abī Dāwūd wa'l-Nasāʾī, wa-ṣaḥḥaḥahu Ibn Khuzayma wa-ghayruhu min hādhā al-wajh lākin bi-lafẓ 'maratayn, maratayn.'" See al-ʿAsqalānī, *Fatḥ al-bārī,* 2:82. Emphasis mine.

32. See al-ʿAsqalānī, *Intiqāḍ al-iʿtirāḍ,* 1:354.

33. Ibid.

34. Ibid.

35. Like *Fatḥ al-bārī,* there is no critical edition of *ʿUmdat al-qārī.* Although the Dār al-Kutub al-ʿIlmiyya edition makes no mention of any manuscript sources, the Muniriyya edition claims that its text was "compared with a number of manuscripts" but offers no details about the provenance of the manuscripts they consulted. Nevertheless, we should assume that the modern editions broadly reflected a later manuscript tradition, likely from the late Islamic period.

36. "Laysa lafẓ al-ḥadīth al-madhkhūr wa-innamā rawāhu Abū Dāwūd ʿan Ibn ʿUmar bi-lafẓ 'Innamā kān al-adhān ʿalā ʿahd rasūl Allāh maratayn maratayn.'" See al-ʿAynī, *ʿUmdat al-qārī,* 5:109.

37. "Hādhā bāb yudhkar fīhi al-adhān mathnā mathnā, wa mathnā hākadhā mukarraran riwāyāt al-Kushmihānī, wa-fī riwāyāt ghayrihi mathnā mufaradan, wa mathnā mathnā maʿdūl min ithnayn ithnayn." Ibid.

38. Joel Blecher, "Ḥadith Commentary in the Presence of Students, Patrons, and Rivals: Ibn Ḥajar and *Ṣaḥīḥ al-Bukhārī* in Mamluk Cairo," *Oriens* 41, no. 3–4 (2013): 275–76.

39. For a comparative discussion of this trans-scriptural commentarial assumption and others, see Henderson, *Scripture, Canon, Commentary,* 140–55.

40. Ibn Khaldūn (d. 808/1406) had heard many shaykhs of his time say that "'commenting on Bukhārī's text remains an outstanding debt (*dayn*) over the community (*umma*),' meaning that a scholar (*ʿālim*) of the community has not [yet] fully taken on the requirements of commentary in this [full] sense." Ibn Khaldūn, *Muqaddima,* 560; Ibn Khaldūn, *The Muqaddimah,* 2:457–59.

41. Michael Baxandall, *Patterns of Intention: On the Historical Explanation of Pictures* (New Haven, CT: Yale University Press, 1985), 62. My thanks to Michael Cothren for the reference.

42. Ibid., 63.

5. ORATORY IN THE SHADE OF THE SULTAN'S GARDEN

1. Hirschler, *Written Word,* 27. Or, as R. Kevin Jaques recently put it, "the sponsorship of the reading of the *Sahih* at court under the gaze and authority of the sultan transferred some of the power of the image of the Prophet to the throne and helped legitimize the sultan as a religious figure. . . . Reading the text in the presence of the sultan was also thought to sanctify him and his office and to create a 'sacred centre' during which phenomenal time and space were interrupted. The reading thus caused a sense of 'stepping back through time,' and created a bridge between the sultan and the Prophet, the former functioning as a stand-in for the latter." See Jaques, *Ibn Hajar,* 95.

2. Hirschler, *Written Word,* 27.

3. Jaques, *Ibn Hajar,* 94.

4. For more on the social dimension of seating order at text-reading sessions, see Hirschler, *Written Word,* 46–51.

5. Al-Sakhāwī, *al-Ḍaw' al-lāmi',* 4:108ff.

6. Ibid., 6:34–36.

7. Al-'Asqalānī, *Inbā' al-ghumr,* 3:306.

8. Ibid.

9. Ibid.

10. Ibid.

11. Since al-'Aynī often translated historical texts from Arabic into Turkish when lecturing Sultan Barsbāy, it is possible that live translators were also present to aid him, although our chroniclers do not mention them in their accounts. Broadbridge, "Academic Rivalries," 90.

12. For an extended account of al-Harawī's dramatic corruption scandal, see Jaques, *Ibn Hajar,* 77–83. Jaques argues that al-Harawī served as "a scapegoat to blame for the punishment that God was exacting on the Mamluk state" by way of the plague.

13. Al-Sakhāwī, *al-Ḍaw' al-lāmi',* 8:151. The scholarly relationship is entirely plausible but is not reported in any other accounts.

14. Al-'Asqalānī, *Inbā' al-ghumr,* 3:377.

15. Carl Petry, *The Civilian Elite of Cairo in the Later Middle Ages* (Princeton, NJ: Princeton University Press, 1981), 65.

16. Ibid., 34–36. See also Anne Broadbridge, *Kingship and Ideology in the Islamic and Mongol Worlds* (Cambridge: Cambridge University Press, 2008), 168–97.

17. Aḥmad ibn 'Alī al-Maqrīzī, *Kitāb al-Sulūk li-ma'rifat duwal al-mulūk,* 4 vols. (Cairo: Lajnat al-Ta'līf wa'l-Tarjama wa'l-Naṣr, 1956), 1:448.

18. Ibid., 2:670–71. For more on Mamluk-era costume, see L. A. Mayer, *Mamluk costume: a survey* (Geneva: Albert Kundig, 1952).

19. Al-Maqrīzī, *Kitāb al-Sulūk,* 2:670–71.

20. Ibid., 1:448.

21. Ibid.

22. Al-'Asqalānī, *Inbā' al-ghumr,* 3:377.

23. Ibn Taghrībirdī, *al-Nujūm al-zāhira,* 15:136.

24. Ibid.

25. Ibid., 14:307–8.

26. Ibid., 15:136.
27. Al-ʿAsqalānī, *Inbāʾ al-ghumr*, 7:309.
28. Ibid.
29. Al-Sakhāwī, *al-Ḍawʾ al-lāmiʿ*, 8:152.
30. Al-ʿAsqalānī, *Inbāʾ al-ghumr*, 7:309.
31. Ibid.
32. Ibid.
33. Ibid.
34. Al-Sakhāwī, *al-Ḍawʾ al-lāmiʿ*, 4:108ff.
35. Ibid. To my knowledge, al-Bulqīnī's commentary *al-Ifhām bi-mā fī al-Bukhārī min al-Afhām* is not extant save for its partial preservation in later commentaries.
36. Al-ʿAsqalānī, *Inbāʾ al-ghumr*, 7:309; al-Sakhāwī, *al-Ḍawʾ al-lāmiʿ*, 4:108ff.
37. Ibn al-Mughulī became known for these inter-*madhhab* debates at live recitation and commentary sessions of *Ṣaḥīḥ al-Bukhārī*. He had drawn out a long debate with al-Tafahnī, the Ḥanafī chief justice, during the completion (*khatm*) of Ramadan in 823/1420 and initiated clamorous debates during the recitation of *Ṣaḥīḥ al-Bukhārī* during Ramadan of 826/1423. See al-ʿAsqalānī, *Inbāʾ al-ghumr*, 3:224 and 3:306.
38. Al-Sakhāwī, *al-Ḍawʾ al-lāmiʿ*, 4:108ff.
39. Ibid.
40. Al-ʿAsqalānī, *Inbāʾ al-ghumr*, 3:63–64.
41. Chamberlain, *Knowledge and Social Practice*.
42. Broadbridge, "Academic Rivalries," 107.
43. Al-ʿAsqalānī, *Inbāʾ al-ghumr*, 3:56–7.
44. Ibid., 3:62.
45. Death date unknown.
46. Al-ʿAsqalānī, *Inbāʾ al-ghumr*, 3:62.
47. Ibid.
48. Ibid.
49. Al-Dihlawī, *Bustān al-muḥaddithīn*, 235.
50. Shams al-Dīn al-Mawṣilī, "Lawāmiʿ al-anwār ʿalā ṣiḥāḥ al-āthār," Garrett Collection MS 1731, Princeton University Library, MS 1731).
51. Dwight F. Reynolds, ed., *Interpreting the Self: Autobiography in the Arabic Literary Tradition* (Berkeley: University of California Press, 2001), 82–83. This finding ought to encourage future research on autobiographical material in Arabic literature to be sought in chronicles in addition to biographical dictionaries.
52. Al-ʿAsqalānī, *Inbāʾ al-ghumr*, 3:63.
53. See al-ʿAsqalānī, *Fatḥ al-bārī*, 2:143–44 (Kitāb al-Adhān: Bāb Man jalasa fī al-masjid yantaẓiru al-ṣalāt, wa-faḍl al-masājid).
54. See ibid. Corrected against Süleymaniye Library Istanbul, MS Mahmud Paşa 79, f. 29b.
55. Süleymaniye Library Istanbul, MS Mahmud Paşa 79, f. 30a.
56. See al-ʿAsqalānī, *Fatḥ al-bārī*, 2:144 (Kitāb al-Adhān: Bāb Man jalasa fī al-masjid yantaẓiru al-ṣalāt, wa-faḍl al-masājid).

57. Mālik ibn Anas and Jalāl al-Dīn al-Suyūṭī, *Muwaṭṭa' al-Imām Mālik: wa-sharḥuhu Tanwīr al-ḥawālik*, 2 vols. (Egypt: Sharikat Maktaba wa-Maṭba'at Muṣṭafā al-Bābī al-Ḥalabī, 1951), 2:234–36.

58. Ibid., 2:236.

59. Sartain, *Jalāl al-Dīn al-Suyūṭī*, 1:75–76.

60. Muḥammad Zakariyyā al-Kāndhlawī, *Awjaz al-masālik ilā Muwaṭṭa' Mālik*, 18 vols. (U.A.E.: n.p., 2003), 17:78. For more on Muḥammad Zakariyyā, his background and context, see Zaman, "Commentaries, Print and Patronage," 65–68.

6. GATEKEEPERS OF THE LAW

1. Foucault, "The Order of Discourse (1970)," 61–62.

2. Ibid., 62–63.

3. Ibid., 63.

4. Franz Kafka, *The Metamorphosis, In the Penal Colony, and Other Stories*, trans. Anne Rice (New York: Schocken Books, 1995), 148.

5. For the growing interest of Shāfi'ī scholars in analyzing and criticizing *isnād*s, see Brown, *The Canonization of al-Bukhārī and Muslim*, ch. 4. For an overview of this phenomenon, see William A. Graham, "Traditionalism in Islam: An Essay in Interpretation," *The Journal of Interdisciplinary History* 23, no. 3 (Winter 1993).

6. Al-Nawawī, *al-Talkhīṣ*, 1:190ff.

7. Ibid.

8. Al-'Asqalānī, *Fatḥ al-bārī*, 1:9; al-'Asqalānī, *Hady al-sārī*, 516.

9. Arabic: *an asūqahā 'alā namaṭ mukhtari'*. See al-'Asqalānī, *Fatḥ al-bārī*, 1:7.

10. Ibid., 1:7–11. A partial diagram of Ibn Ḥajar's chain of transmission to the *Ṣaḥīḥ* can be found in Fück, "Beiträge zur Überlieferungsgeschichte von Bukhārī's Traditionssammlung," 97. A larger diagram can be found in Mingana, *An Important Manuscript of the Traditions of Bukhari*.

11. For a deeper discussion of al-Firabrī's importance to the transmission of the *Ṣaḥīḥ*, see Brown, *The Canonization of al-Bukhārī and Muslim*, 121. If a manuscript dated 711/1311 is any indication, Abū Dharr's recitation was so distinguished among the late Mamluk-era scholars that scribes were still copying and circulating the prayer which al-Kushmihānī (d. 389/998), one of Abū Dharr's three teachers, dictated to him on the occasion of the *khatm* (conclusion) of al-Bukhārī's *Ṣaḥīḥ*; see al-Kushmihānī, "Prayer and Index to *Ṣaḥīḥ al-Bukhārī*" (Khuda Bakhsh Library), MS 152.

12. See the translator's introduction to Ibn Khaldūn, *The Muqaddimah*, 1:xlii.

13. A list of some common abbreviations can be found in Fück, "Beiträge zur Überlieferungsgeschichte von Bukhārī's Traditionssammlung," 80; Gacek, *Arabic Manuscripts*, 272.

14. Al-'Asqalānī, *Fatḥ al-bārī*, 1:13 (Kitāb Bad' al-waḥy: Bāb Kayf kān bad' al-waḥy).

15. For another discussion of *ʿan* as it relates to *Ṣaḥīḥ al-Bukhārī,* see Brown, *The Canonization of al-Bukhārī and Muslim,* 283–85.

16. Ḥasanī, *Itḥāf al-qārī,* 171–72.

17. Al-Sakhāwī, *al-Jawāhir wa'l-durar,* 1:380.

18. Brown, *The Canonization of al-Bukhārī and Muslim,* 237.

19. A complete diagram of al-ʿAynī's scholarly genealogy to the *Ṣaḥīḥ* can be found in Fück, "Beiträge zur Überlieferungsgeschichte von Bukhārī's Traditionssammlung," 95.

20. Al-ʿAynī, *ʿUmdāt al-qārī,* 1:23–24 (Kitāb Badʾ al-waḥy: Bāb Kayf kān badʾ al-waḥy).

21. Tokatly, "Early Commentaries on al-Bukhārī's *Ṣaḥīḥ,*" 242–49.

22. While this topic has generated a great deal of scholarly debate, a general overview can be found in ʿAbd al-Wahhāb Khallāf, *ʿIlm uṣūl al-fiqh* (Damascus: n.p., 1992), 140–91. A more detailed discussion can be found in Wael Hallaq, *A History of Islamic Legal Theories* (Cambridge: Cambridge University Press, 1997), 40–58.

23. For further discussion, see Brown, *The Canonization of al-Bukhārī and Muslim,* 257–58.

24. Rapoport, "Legal Diversity in the Age of Taqlīd," 227.

25. Ibid.

26. Ibid.; see also Lutz Wiederhold, "Legal Doctrines in Conflict: The Relevance of Madhhab Boundaries to Legal Reasoning in the Light of an Unpublished Treatise on Taqlīd and Ijtihād," *Islamic Law and Society* 3, no. 2 (1996): 234–304.

27. "There is one prejudice of the enlightenment that defines its essence: the fundamental prejudice of the enlightenment is the prejudice against prejudice itself, which denies tradition of its power." See Hans-Georg Gadamer, *Truth and Method,* 272–73.

28. Al-Kirmānī, *al-Kawākib al-darārī,* 3.

29. Al-Sakhāwī, *al-Jawāhir wa'l-durar,* 1:381.

30. Calder, *Islamic Jurisprudence in the Classical Era,* 74–116.

31. See Brown, *The Canonization of al-Bukhārī and Muslim,* 333.

32. See ibid.

33. Rapoport, "Legal Diversity in the Age of Taqlīd," 221.

34. Ibid.

35. Al-ʿAsqalānī, *Fatḥ al-bārī,* 12:177 (Kitāb al-Ḥudūd: Bāb Kam al-taʿzīr wa'l-adab).

36. For more on al-Ismāʿīlī's *Mustakhraj,* see Brown, *The Canonization of al-Bukhārī and Muslim,* 109–11.

37. Al-ʿAsqalānī, *Fatḥ al-bārī,* 12:177 (Kitāb al-Ḥudūd: Bāb Kam al-taʿzīr wa'l-adab).

38. Ibid.

39. The activity of sourcing the hadith in this way is called *takhrīj,* and it is a common practice of hadith scholars. Ibn al-Mulaqqin remarked that the ten lashes hadith was found in Muslim's *Ṣaḥīḥ* and "the four" (*al-arbaʿ*), meaning the four *Sunan*s of Abū Dāwūd, Tirmidhī, Nasāʾī, and Ibn Māja. He then

adduced Ṭabarānī, Dāraquṭnī, and Bayhaqī as authorities in evaluating the veracity of the ten lashes hadith's chain of transmission. He preserved the dissent of Aṣīlī by way of Jayyānī, but this dissent's force is diminished when placed next to the opinions aforementioned and better-known hadith scholars. Ibn al-Mulaqqin, *al-Tawḍīḥ,* 31: 273–4 (Kitāb al-Rajm: Bāb Kam al-taʿzīr wa'l-adab).

40. Al-ʿAsqalānī, *Fatḥ al-bārī,* 12:177–8 (Kitāb al-Ḥudūd: Bāb Kam al-taʿzīr wa'l-adab); Ibn al-Mulaqqin, *al-Tawḍīḥ,* 31: 280 (Kitāb al-Rajm: Bāb Kam al-taʿzīr wa'l-adab).

41. Al-ʿAsqalānī, *Fatḥ al-bārī,* 12:178 (Kitāb al-Ḥudūd: Bāb Kam al-taʿzīr wa'l-adab). In *Fatḥ al-Bārī,* Ibn Ḥajar speculates that this opinion is Ibn Taymiyya's, but he relies on a statement from Ibn Taymiyya's student Ibn al-Qayyim al-Jawziyya (d. 751/1350). Ibn Taymiyya did indeed hold this position, however. For the full text and translation, consult Taqī al-Dīn Aḥmad Ibn Taymiyya, *al-Siyāsa al-Sharʿiyya,* ed. Muḥammad ʿAbdallāh al-Sammān (Cairo: Anṣār al-Sunna, 1961), 112–27; Bernard Lewis, *Islam: From the Prophet Muhammad to the Capture of Constantinople* (Oxford: Oxford University Press, 1987), 35–39. See also a discussion of this hadith in a commentary composed for an audience of Ḥanbalī jurists in training in eighth-/fourteenth-century Damascus, in Zayn al-Dīn Abū al-Faraj Ibn Rajab, *Jāmiʿ al-ʿulūm wa'l-ḥikam: sharḥ khamsīn ḥadīthan min jawāmʿ al-kalim* (Damascus: Dār Ibn Kathīr, 2008), 62.

42. Al-ʿAsqalānī, *Fatḥ al-bārī,* 12:178 (Kitāb al-Ḥudūd: Bāb Kam al-taʿzīr wa'l-adab).

43. Ibid.

44. Ibid.

45. Rapoport, "Legal Diversity in the Age of Taqlīd," 221.

46. This Dāwūdī was likely not the earliest commentator, Dāwūdī of Tripoli, since Ibn Baṭṭāl does not quote him. Most likely, it the Abū Jaʿfar al-Dāwūdī, a later Mālikī judge whose opinions were preserved in the commentaries of Ibn al-Tīn al-Ṣafāqisī (d. 611/1214–15), Ibn Rushayd, Ibn al-Mulaqqin, and Ibn Ḥajar. See Ḥasanī, *Itḥāf al-qārī,* 63 and 191; al-ʿAsqalānī, *Fatḥ al-bārī,* 12:179 (Kitāb al-Ḥudūd: Bāb Kam al-taʿzīr wa'l-adab).

47. Ibn al-Mulaqqin, *al-Tawḍīḥ,* 31:279 (Kitāb al-Rajm: Bāb Kam al-taʿzīr wa'l-adab).

48. "[L]aw balaghah[u] mā ʿadala ʿanhu fa-yajib[u] ʿalā man balaghah[u] an yaʾkhudh[a] bih[i]." al-ʿAsqalānī, *Fatḥ al-bārī,* 12:179 (Kitāb al-Ḥudūd: Bāb Kam al-taʿzīr wa'l-adab).

49. Al-ʿAynī, *ʿUmdāt al-qārī,* 24:35 (Kitāb al-Muḥāribīn min ahl al-kufr wa-ridda: Bāb Kam al-taʿzīr wa'l-adab).

50. He ruled against his own school in the introduction to his commentary on Marghīnānī's *Hidāya* and on the issue of group prayers. Sadeghi, *Logic of Law Making in Islam,* 89–91, 137.

51. Al-ʿAynī, *ʿUmdāt al-qārī,* 24:35 (Kitāb al-Muḥāribīn min ahl al-kufr wa-ridda: Bāb Kam al-taʿzīr wa'l-adab); al-ʿAsqalānī, *Fatḥ al-bārī,* 12:177 (Kitāb al-Ḥudūd: Bāb Kam al-taʿzīr wa'l-adab).

52. Al-ʿAynī, *ʿUmdāt al-qārī,* 24:35 (Kitāb al-Muḥāribīn min ahl al-kufr wa-ridda: Bāb Kam al-taʿzīr wa'l-adab).

53. Ibid., 24:36 (Kitāb al-Muḥāribīn min ahl al-kufr wa-ridda: Bāb Kam al-ta'zīr wa'l-adab).

54. Ibid., 24:35 (Kitāb al-Muḥāribīn min ahl al-kufr wa-ridda: Bāb Kam al-ta'zīr wa'l-adab).

7. MYSTERIES OF THE THRESHOLDS

1. Gérard Genette's book, *Seuils,* appears in English as *Paratexts: Thresholds of Interpretation,* trans. Jane Lewin (Cambridge: Cambridge University Press, 1997), 1–2.

2. Goldziher, *Muslim Studies,* 2:217–18; Goldziher, *Ẓāhirīs,* 97–101.

3. Later scholars have built on this insight. See, for instance, Lucas, "Legal Principles of Muḥammad b. Ismā'īl al-Bukhārī," 306.

4. See Goldziher, *Muslim Studies,* 2:217; al-Khaṭīb al-Qasṭallānī, *Irshād al-sārī,* 10 vols. (Būlāq: al-Maṭba'a al-Kubra al-Amīriyya, 1905), 3:156 (Kitāb al-Ḥajj: Bāb Qawl Allāh "ja'ala Allāh al-ka'bata . . ."); Muhammad Fadel, "Ibn Ḥajar's *Hady al-Sārī:* A Medieval Interpretation of the Structure of al-Bukhārī's *al-Jāmi' al-Ṣaḥīḥ:* Introduction and Translation," *Journal of Near Eastern Studies* 54 (1995): 173–74.

5. Goldziher, *Ẓāhirīs,* 97. Repeated in Tokatly, "A'lām al-ḥadīth of al-Khaṭṭābī," 55–57.

6. For one fascinating case in which social and historical context pushed some readers to consult Abū Dāwūd's *Sunan* rather than *Ṣaḥīḥ al-Bukhārī* because al-Bukhārī's chapter headings were more limiting than Abū Dāwūd's, see Judith Pfeiffer, "'Faces Like Shields Covered with Leather': Keturah's Sons in the Post-Mongol Islamicate Eschatological Traditions," in *Horizons of the World: Festschrift for İsenbike Togan,* ed. İlker Evrim Binbaş and Nurten Kılıç-Schubel (Istanbul: İthaki, 2011), 580–81 and n72.

7. Burge, "Reading between the Lines," 168–97; Lucas, "Legal Principles of Muḥammad b. Ismā'īl al-Bukhārī."

8. See al-'Asqalānī, *Fatḥ al-bārī,* 1:10–11. Al-Ismā'īlī's opinion is found in his *mustakhraj* (a text concerned with displaying chains of transmission for a collection of hadith), rather than a *sharḥ* proper.

9. Mingana, *An Important Manuscript of the Traditions of Bukhari;* Brown, "Canonization of al-Bukhārī and Muslim," 523–24; Norman Calder, *Studies in Early Muslim Jurisprudence* (Oxford: Clarendon Press, 1993), 194.

10. Al-Khaṭṭābī, for instance, sought to defend the compiler of the *Ṣaḥīḥ* from the objection that he was a proponent of anthropomorphizing God (*tashbīh*). See Tokatly, "A'lām al-ḥadīth of al-Khaṭṭābī," 53–91. Tokatly has recently gone further to argue that his commentary "shows a fundamental lack of interest in the renowned framework of al-Bukhārī's work." This is primarily because al-Khaṭṭābī presented the commentary as an apologetic treatise in defense of hadith folk (*ahl al-ḥadīth*), and secondarily because the *Ṣaḥīḥ* "did not yet occupy the exceptional place which it later attained." Ibid., 57–58.

11. Brown, *Canonization of al-Bukhārī and Muslim,* 230–34. A later scholar, Aḥmad Ibn Rashīq (d. post-440/1048) of Córdoba also believed that the problems of Bukhārī's chapter headings merited discussion, but his work did not

survive long enough to circulate in the layers of later commentaries. Al-Ḥumaydī, *Jadhwat al-muqtabis,* 122–23; Abū ʿAbd Allāh Ibn Rushayd, *Tarjumān al-tarājim ʿalā abwāb Ṣaḥīḥ al-Bukhārī* (Beirut: Dār al-Kutub al-ʿIlmiyya, 2008), 7.

12. See Ibn Baṭṭāl, *Sharḥ Saḥīḥ al-Bukhārī,* (Kitāb al-Ḥajj: Bāb Qawl Allāh "jaʿala Allāh al-Kaʿbata . . .") 4:274–78; al-ʿAsqalānī, *Fatḥ al-bārī,* (Kitāb al-Ḥajj: Bāb Qawl Allāh "jaʿala Allāh al-Kaʿbata . . .") 3:454.

13. Tokatly, "Early Commentaries on al-Bukhārī's *Ṣaḥīḥ.*" 219–22.

14. Rustam, "al-Madrasa al-Andalusiyya," 34.

15. Ibn Khaldūn, *Muqaddima,* 560.

16. See Goldziher, *Ẓāhirīs,* 97–98; Goldziher, *Muslim Studies,* 2:227.

17. Al-Nawawī, *al-Talkhīṣ,* 1:230–31.

18. Ibid., 230. Al-Nawawī similarly burnished al-Bukhārī's biography, leading readers "to believe that Bukhārī's decision to compile a collection of authentic hadith was no longer a radical departure from tradition," according to Brown, *Canonization of al-Bukhārī and Muslim,* 276–78.

19. Ibn al-Munayyir, *al-Mutawārī,* 35. N.b.: I am relying on an edition (Beirut, 1990) that corrected typographical errors present in an earlier edition (Kuwait, 1987). The two editions depart frequently.

20. Ibid. For a description of Ibn Ḥajar al-Haytamī's (d. 974/1567) reception of this same quote, see Marion Holmes Katz, "The 'Corruption of the Times' and the Mutability of the Shari'a," *Cardozo Law Review* 28, no. 1 (October 2006): 179. Katz writes that although "the maxim is generally attributed to the Umayyad caliph ʿUmar ibn ʿAbd al-ʿAziz (reigned 99–101 A.H. / 717–720 C.E.), it was endorsed by Mālik."

21. Ibn al-Munayyir, *al-Mutawārī,* 35–36.

22. Ibid., 38–39.

23. Ibid., 39.

24. Ibid., 38. Ibn al-Munayyir's introduction also represents the earliest extant attempt to list the functions of the titles systematically. Many of the basic functions will be repeated by later commentators, as we will observe below.

25. Ibid., 36.

26. Ibid., 36–37.

27. The other scholar is Ibn Daqīq al-ʿĪd (d. 702/1302), who served as Shāfiʿī chief justice in Cairo. The contemporary who said this was ʿIzz al-Dīn ibn ʿAbd al-Salām al-Sulamī (d. 660/1262), another much revered scholar of Egypt. Ibid., 12.

28. Ibid., 39.

29. Ibid., 51.

30. Ibid., 17. This is much to the dismay of the work's modern editors, who are committed to contemporary Ḥanbalī theology.

31. Ibid.

32. Qur'an 51:58 at ibid., 421; 20:39 and 54:14 at ibid., 426.

33. Ibid., 51.

34. Qur'an 5:97.

35. Ibn al-Munayyir, *al-Mutawārī,* 142–43.

36. Ibid.

37. Badr al-Dīn Ibn al-Jamāʿa, *Munāsabāt tarājim al-Bukhārī,* ed. Muḥammad Isḥāq Muḥammad Ibrāhīm (Bombay: al-Dār al-Salafiyya, 1984), 25–28.

38. Abū ʿAbd Allāh Ibn Rushayd, *Tarjamān al-tarājim,* 39.

39. Ibid., 23–34.

40. An incomplete manuscript of this work is available at Princeton University's Rare Books collection. Ibn ʿUrwa al-Zaknūn, *al-Kawākib al-darārī fī tartīb Musnad al-Imām Aḥmad ʿalā abwāb al-Bukhārī* (Garrett Collection MS 2604, Princeton University Library). My thanks to Jonathan Brown for drawing my attention to this work.

41. Ibn Khaldūn, *Muqaddima,* 560; Ibn Khaldūn, *The Muqaddimah,* 2:457–59.

42. While Ibn Khaldūn mentions the titles and elaborates on them briefly in Rosenthal's edition, I have not found any edition in Arabic that makes use of additional material located in the manuscript 1936 of the Atif Effendi library in Istanbul (identified as "C" in Franz Rosenthal's translation of the work), which I have not been able to access. According to Rosenthal, the text of C is "superior. . . . [It] contains many of the additions and corrections that constitute the later stages of the text of the *Muqaddimah,*" in Ibn Khaldūn, *The Muqaddimah,* 1:xci–xcvii. I have resigned myself to using Rosenthal's translation for those passages yet to be edited in Arabic. While it is difficult to draw any broader conclusions from the fact that Ibn Khaldūn added more information about al-Bukhārī's *tarājim* in later versions, it is not insignificant that he felt the point required elaboration.

43. See Ibn Khaldūn, *The Muqaddimah,* 2:457–58; Ibn Khaldūn, *Muqaddima,* 560.

44. Ibn al-Munayyir, *al-Mutawārī,* 142–43.

45. Ibn Khaldūn, *The Muqaddimah,* 2:458.

46. See ibid., 1:xlii.

47. Ibid., 2:458.

48. Ibn Khaldūn recalled that the puzzle arose in a chapter heading in the "Book of Trials (*fitan*)" that claimed that "the Kaʿba will be destroyed by the one who has little stick-legs from Ethiopia" followed by the Qur'anic verse 2:125. No mention of such a heading, hadith, or verse exists in this book. It would have been many years since Ibn Khaldūn studied this material in Fez, although, as we know from our study of the early Andalusian commentators, there were several recensions of *Ṣaḥīḥ al-Bukhārī* circulating, some of which may have transmitted certain portions of the text differently. Whether he misremembered the correct hadith or correctly recalled a variant text, Rosenthal points us to a virtually identical problem in the "Book of Pilgrimage (*Ḥajj*)" that contained a Qur'anic verse that corresponds in meaning to 2:125 (5:97) followed by the hadith on the prophecy of the "stick-legged Ethiopian." Ibid., 1:xlii and 2:458n144.

49. Al-ʿAsqalānī, *Hady al-sārī,* 13.

50. Ibid. For an annotated translation of Ibn Ḥajar's section on the *tarājim* and *ikhtiṣār,* consult Fadel, "Ibn Ḥajar's *Hady al-Sārī,*" 180–85.

51. Al-ʿAsqalānī, *Hady al-sārī,* 13–14.

52. Ibid.

53. Ibid. For example, according to Ibn Ḥajar, the title "An imām's use of a *siwāk* [a teeth-cleaning twig] in front of his attendants" may break a reader's assumption that such behavior is poor etiquette; or, for example, the titles "Quraysh are commanders" and "a group is two or more" betray al-Bukhārī's legal positions on those issues, even when the hadith included below the titles do not necessarily or directly provide evidence for those positions.

54. See Ibn Baṭṭāl, *Sharḥ Saḥīḥ al-Bukhārī,* 4:274–78 (Kitāb al-Ḥajj: Bāb Qawl Allāh "ja'ala Allāh al-Ka'bata . . ."); al-'Asqalānī, *Fatḥ al-bārī,* 3:454 (Kitāb al-Ḥajj: Bāb Qawl Allāh "ja'ala Allāh al-Ka'bata . . .").

55. See Ibn Baṭṭāl, *Sharḥ Saḥīḥ al-Bukhārī,* 4:274–78 (Kitāb al-Ḥajj: Bāb Qawl Allāh "ja'ala Allāh al-Ka'bata . . ."); al-'Asqalānī, *Fatḥ al-bārī,* 3:454 (Kitāb al-Ḥajj: Bāb Qawl Allāh "ja'ala Allāh al-Ka'bata . . .").

56. See al-'Asqalānī, *Fatḥ al-bārī,* 1:10 (Kitāb Bad' al-waḥy: Bāb Kayf kān bad' al-waḥy).

57. See ibid.

58. See ibid., (Kitāb Bad' al-waḥy: Bāb Kayf kān bad' al-waḥy) 1:10.

59. Arabic: "hādha al-su'āl sāqiṭ." See al-'Aynī, *'Umdāt al-qārī,* (Kitāb Bad' al-waḥy: Bāb Kayf kān bad' al-waḥy) 1:52.

60. Ibid.

61. Al-'Asqalānī, *Fatḥ al-bārī,* 12:176 (Kitāb al-Ḥudūd: Bāb Kam al-ta'zīr wa'l-adab).

62. Ibid.

63. The full title of the chapter is "The Chapter of Jibrīl's Question to the Prophet concerning *īmān, islām, iḥsān,* knowledge of the [final] hour, and the explanation of the Prophet [concerning those subjects] to him, then saying, 'Jibrīl came to teach your religion (*dīn*), so he made all of that a *dīn,*' and what the Prophet explained regarding *īmān* to the delegation of 'Abd al-Qays, and his saying, may he be exalted: 'Whosoever follows a *dīn* other than *islām,* [his *dīn*] will not be accepted from Him.'" See Muḥammad ibn Ismā'īl al-Bukhārī, *Ṣaḥīḥ al-Bukhārī,* 3 vols. (Germany: Thesaurus Islamicus Foundation, 2000), 1:15 (Kitāb al-Īmān: Bāb Su'āl Jibrīl lil-nabī . . .); al-Bukhārī, *Fatḥ al-bārī,* 1:114 (Kitāb al-Īmān: Bāb Su'āl Jibrīl lil-nabī . . .).

64. Arabic: "bi'l-ta'wīl ilā ṭarīqatihi." See al-Bukhārī, *Fatḥ al-bārī,* 1:114–45 (Kitāb al-Īmān: Bāb Su'āl Jibrīl lil-nabī . . .).

65. Arabic: "muḥaṣṣal kalāmihi." See ibid., (Kitāb al-Īmān: Bāb Su'āl Jibrīl lil-nabī . . .) 1:114.

66. For more on the principle of charity with respect to the canonization of *Ṣaḥīḥ al-Bukhārī,* see Brown, *Canonization of al-Bukhārī and Muslim,* 42–46, 262–99. On theories of the principle of charity and the process of canonization more broadly, Brown consults Moshe Halbertal, *People of the Book: Canon, Meaning and Authority* (Cambridge, MA: Harvard University Press, 1997), 28–29.

67. See Goldziher, *Muslim Studies,* 2:223. Goldziher discusses how lacunae, places where words were missing in the *matn,* were left as a blank space (*bayāḍ*) or sometimes filled or recited with the word *bayāḍ*. See ibid., 2:219.

68. Ibid.

69. Al-'Asqalānī, *Hady al-sārī,* 15–16.

70. Yaḥyā ibn Sharf al-Dīn al-Nawawī, *Sharḥ matn al-Arbaʿīn al-Nawawiyya* (Beirut: al-Maktaba al-Islāmī, 1984), 6.

71. Al-ʿAsqalānī, *Fatḥ al-bārī,* 1:9 (Kitāb Badʾ al-waḥy: Bāb Kayf kān badʾ al-waḥy).

72. Ibid., 1:15–16 (Kitāb Badʾ al-waḥy: Bāb Kayf kān badʾ al-waḥy). See Abū Bakr ibn Zubayr al-Ḥumaydī, *Musnad al-Ḥumaydī* (Damascus: Dār al-Saqqā, 1996). A *musnad* is another kind of hadith collection, which preserves and displays a hadith transmitter's chain of transmission.

73. See al-ʿAsqalānī, *Fatḥ al-bārī,* 1:10–11. Al-Ismāʿīlī's opinion is found in his *mustakhraj* (a text concerned with displaying chains of transmission for a collection of hadith), rather than a *sharḥ* proper.

74. Ibid., 1:15–6 (Kitāb Badʾ al-waḥy: Bāb Kayf kān badʾ al-waḥy). Although, as Dr. Issam Eido suggested to me, the act of removing "God and his messenger" from a hadith could itself be read as an expression of arrogance.

75. Naʿīm al-ʿIrqsūsī, *Sharḥ Ṣaḥīḥ al-Bukhārī,* DVD (Damascus: Maktabat al- Īmān, 2002), audio recording on DVD 1.

76. Halbertal, *People of the Book,* 32.

8. THE ART OF CONCISION

1. Al-Suyūṭī is far better known and studied for his commentary on the Qur'an; his serial hadith commentaries are virtually overlooked in the current scholarly literature. For instance, see Andrew Rippin, "Al-Zarkashī and al-Suyutī [*sic*] on the Function of the 'Occasion of Revelation' Material," *Islamic Culture* 59, no. 3 (1985): 243–58; Stephen Burge, "Scattered Pearls: Exploring al-Suyūṭī's Hermeneutics and Use of Sources in *Al-Durr al-manthūr fī'l-tafsīr bi'l-ma'thūr,*" *Journal of the Royal Asiatic Society* 24, no. 2 (2014): 251–96.

2. For a discussion of the fourteenth-century boom in encyclopedic and compilatory literature, see Elias Muhanna, "Why Was the Fourteenth Century a Century of Arabic Encyclopaedism?" in *Encyclopaedism from Antiquity to the Renaissance,* ed. Jason König and Greg Woolf (Cambridge: Cambridge University Press, 2013): 343–56.

3. Sartain, *Jalāl al-Dīn al-Suyūṭī,* 48 and 50; Jalāl al-Din al-Suyūṭī, *al-Taḥadduth biniʿmat Allah* (Cambridge: Cambridge University Press, 1975), 157–59.

4. Jonathan A.C. Brown, *Hadith* (Oxford: Oneworld, 2009), 53.

5. Muḥammad Ḥayāt al-Sindī (d. 1163/1750). See Aḥmad ibn Shuʿayb al-Nasāʾī, Jalāl al-Dīn al-Suyūṭī, and Muḥammad Ḥayāt al-Sindī, *Sunan al-Nasāʾī: bi-sharḥ al-Suyūṭī wa'l-Sindī* (Cairo: Dār al-Ḥadīth, 1999).

6. Saudi presses have been especially active in printing these works, two of which have been used in the making of this chapter: Jalāl al-Dīn al-Suyūṭī, *al-Tawshīḥ sharḥ Jāmiʿ al-ṣaḥīḥ al-Bukhārī: sharḥ Ṣaḥīḥ al-Bukhārī,* ed. Raḍwān Jāmiʿ Raḍwān, 9 vols. (Riyadh: Maktabat al-Rushd, 1998); Jalāl al-Dīn al-Suyūṭī, *al-Dībāj ʿalā Ṣaḥīḥ Muslim ibn Ḥajjāj,* ed. Abū Isḥaq al-Ḥawaynī al-Atharī, 6 vols. (al-Khabar: Dār ibn ʿAffān, 1991). The latter work, *al-Dībāj,* was edited by Abū Isḥāq al-Ḥawaynī, an Egyptian student of al-Albānī and a celebrity hadith scholar among Salafi audiences.

7. Marlis Saleh, "Al-Suyūṭī and His Works: Their Place in Islamic Scholarship from Mamluk Times to the Present," *Mamlūk Studies Review* 5 (2001): 87–88. Al-Suyūṭī, *al-Taḥadduth bini'mat Allah,* 107 and 130.

8. Al-Suyuṭī, *al-Tawshīḥ,* 42; 'Abd al-'Azīz ibn Aḥmad Dihlawī, *The Garden of the Hadith Scholars: Bustān al-Muḥadithīn,* trans. Muḥammad Akram Nadwī and Aisha Abdurrahman Bewley (London: Turath, 2007), 341.

9. See al-Qasṭallānī, *Irshād al-sārī.*

10. See Anas and al-Suyūṭī, *Muwaṭṭa' al-Imām Mālik.* To compare this work with an important earlier commentary on the *Muwaṭṭa'*, see al-Bājī, *al-Muntaqā: Sharḥ Muwaṭṭa' Mālik.*

11. See the author's introduction to Jalāl al-Dīn al-Suyūṭī and Aḥmad ibn Ḥanbal, *'Uqūd al-zabarjad fī i'rāb al-ḥadīth al-nabawī,* ed. Salmān Quḍāh (Beirut: Dār al-Jīl, 1994).

12. See Jaques, *Ibn Hajar,* 94.

13. The readings took place during Ramadan. See Jalāl al-Dīn al-Suyūṭī, *Ḥusn al-muḥāḍara fī tārīkh Miṣr wa'l-Qāhira* (Cairo: Dār Iḥyā' al-Kutub al-'Arabīya, 1967), 2:304.

14. Sartain, *Jalāl al-Dīn al-Suyūṭī,* 41.

15. 'Abd al-Qādir al-'Aydarūs, *Tārīkh al-Nūr al-sāfir 'an akhbār al-qarn al-'āshir* (Beirut: Dār Ṣādir, 2001), 413. For manuscript evidence of live commentary sessions in sixteenth-century Ottoman Syria, see Shams al-Dīn al-Safīrī, "'Iddat aḥādīth *Ṣaḥīḥ al-Bukhārī*" (Cadbury Research Library: Special Collections, University of Birmingham, eighteenth century), MS Mingana IA 938. Mawlā Luṭfī's (d. 900/1494) *Sharḥ al-Bukhārī* and Yūsuf Zāde's (d. 1167/1754) *Najāḥ al-Qārī* are two Ottoman commentaries on the *Ṣaḥīḥ* that survive in manuscript form, which may have been dictated live.

16. Al-Suyūṭī, *al-Taḥadduth bini'mat Allah,* 130.

17. Sartain, *Jalāl al-Dīn al-Suyūṭī,* 31.

18. He studied a number of collections with Muḥyī al-Dīn al-Kāfiyajī (d. 879/1474) and much of *Ṣaḥīḥ Muslim* with Shams al-Dīn Muḥammad ibn Mūsā al-Sīrāmī (d. 871/1466–67). 'Alam al-Dīn Ṣāliḥ al-Bulqīnī (d. 868/1464), with whom al-Suyūṭī studied Shāfi'ī *fiqh,* could be added to this list of possible influences, as al-Suyūṭī was often referenced as an authority on the legal benefits of the hadith. Ibid., 26–28.

19. Ibid., 26. It was not unusual for children to attend auditions of hadith, and an elevated status was conferred on adults who had been fortunate enough to attend auditions with master hadith transmitters as children. See Garrett Davidson, "Carrying on the Tradition: An Intellectual and Social History of Post-Canonical Hadith Transmission" (PhD diss., University of Chicago, 2014), 95–106 and 174–78.

20. See Rippin, "Al-Zarkashī and al-Suyutī," 243–58.

21. Al-Zarkashī, Badr al-Dīn, *al-Tanqīḥ l'ilfāẓ al-Jāmi' al-Ṣaḥīḥ,* ed. Yaḥyā ibn Muḥammad 'Alī al-Ḥakamī, 3 vols. (Riyadh: Maktabat Ibn Rushd, 2003), 1:1–2; Dihlawī, *The Garden of the Hadith Scholars,* 313.

22. Al-Nawawī, *Ṣaḥīḥ Muslim bi-sharḥ al-Nawawī,* 1:4–5. Translation by Calder, *Islamic Jurisprudence in the Classical Era,* 107.

23. See Ibn Ḥajar al-ʿAsqalānī, *Ḥawāshī Tanqīḥ al-Zarkashī ʿalā al-Bukhārī* (Beirut: ʿĀlam al-Kutub, 2008); Badr al-Dīn al-Damāmīnī, *Taʿaqqubāt al-ʿAllāmah Badr al-Dīn al-Damāmīnī fī kitābihi Maṣābīḥ al-Jāmiʿ al-ṣaḥīḥ ʿalā al-Imām Badr al-Dīn al-Zarkashī fī kitābihi al-Tanqīḥ li-alfāẓ al-Jāmiʿ al-ṣaḥīḥ fī al-qaḍāyā al-naḥwīyah wa'l-ṣarfīyah wa'l-lughawīyah,* ed. ʿAlī ibn Sulṭān al-Ḥakamī (Medina: Dār al-Bukhārī, 1995), 150–1; al-Damāmīnī, *Maṣābīḥ al-Jāmiʿ*, ed. Nūr al-Dīn Ṭālib, 10 vols. (Qatar: Wizārat al-Awqāf, 2009), 1:54–64.

24. For more biographical information on al-Damāmīnī, see, Ḥasanī, *Itḥāf al-qārī,* 245–46; Muhammad Ishaq, *India's Contribution to the Study of Hadith Literature* (Dhakha: University of Dhakha (Dacca) Press, 1955), 87–88.

25. See al-Damāmīnī, *Taʿaqqubāt al-ʿAllāmah Badr al-Dīn al-Damāmīnī,* 16–17. Testifying to this trend, an extant copy of *Ṣaḥīḥ al-Bukhārī* from the fourteenth century contains numerous marginal references to al-Zarkashī's *al-Tanqīḥ l'ilfāẓ al-Jāmiʿ al-ṣaḥīḥ.* See Muḥammad ibn Ismāʿīl al-Bukhārī, *Ṣaḥīḥ al-Bukhārī* (Garrett Collection 341 Bq, Princeton University Library, ca. fourteenth century), f. 36b and passim.

26. Al-Suyūṭī, *al-Tawshīḥ,* 1:41–42.

27. Arabic: "al-nafʿ bilā taʿab wa'l-arab bilā naṣab." Ibid., 42; Dihlawī, *The Garden of the Hadith Scholars,* 341. Emphasis mine.

28. See, for instance, Ibn Rushayd, *Tarjamān al-tarājim;* Ibn al-Munayyir, *al-Mutawārī;* ʿUmar ibn Raslān al-Bulqīnī, *Kitāb Tarājim al-Bukhārī: al-musammā Munāsabāt abwāb Ṣaḥīḥ al-Bukhārī li-baʿḍihā baʿḍan,* ed. Aḥmad ibn Fāris Sallūm (Riyadh: Maktabat al-Maʿārif lil-Nashr wa'l-Tawzīʿ, 2010).

29. Although there is some overlap between the two works in the lemmata upon which they clarify, al-Suyūṭī did not always choose to clarify the same lemmata in his *Tawshīḥ.* For example, compare al-Zarkashī, *al-Tanqīḥ,* 3:1212; and al-Suyūṭī, *al-Tawshīḥ,* 9:3982.

30. Al-ʿAsqalānī, *Hady al-sārī,* 13–14. For an annotated translation of Ibn Ḥajar's section on the *tarājim* and *ikhtiṣār,* consult Fadel, "Ibn Ḥajar's *Hady al-Sārī,*" 180–85.

31. Compare al-Suyūṭī, *al-Tawshīḥ,* 1:128; and al-ʿAsqalānī, *Fatḥ al-bārī,* 1:15–16 (Kitāb Badʾ al-waḥy: Bāb Kayf kān badʾ al-waḥy)

32. Compare al-Suyūṭī, *al-Tawshīḥ,* 1:134; and al-ʿAsqalānī, *Fatḥ al-bārī,* 1:19 and 1:22 (Kitāb Badʾ al-waḥy: Bāb Kayf kān badʾ al-waḥy)

33. Compare al-Suyūṭī, *al-Tawshīḥ,* 3:1266; and al-ʿAsqalānī, *Fatḥ al-bārī,* 3:458–60 (Kitāb al-Ḥajj: Bāb Kiswat al-Kaʿba).

34. See al-Suyūṭī, *al-Tawshīḥ,* 3:1267.

35. Al-ʿAsqalānī, *Fatḥ al-bārī,* 3:461 (Kitāb al-Ḥajj: Bāb Hadm al-Kaʿba).

36. Al-Suyūṭī, *al-Tawshīḥ,* 6:2638.

37. Al-Bājī, *Taḥqīq al-madhhab,* 115–18; Fierro, "Local and Global in Ḥadīth Literature," 82.

38. See al-ʿAsqalānī, *Fatḥ al-bārī,* 7:504 (Kitāb al-Maghāzī: Bāb ʿUmrat al-Qaḍāʾ).

39. Al-Suyūṭī, *al-Tawshīḥ,* 3:879–902. For a similar trend, see "Kitāb al-jazāʾ al-ṣayyid" in ibid., 4:1373–97.

40. Ibid., 1:217–21 and 9:4361–63.

41. Ibid., 2:689; Anas and al-Suyūṭī, *Muwaṭṭa' al-Imām Mālik,* 2:234–36.

42. Al-Suyūṭī, *al-Tawshīḥ,* 4:1486.

43. See al-Suyūṭī, *al-Dībāj,* 1:6.

44. Ignaz Goldziher once described him as "the talented scholar offended in his vanity who is moved to an extravagant assertion of his own worth." See Michael Barry and J. O. Hunwick, "Ignaz Goldziher on al-Suyūṭī," *The Muslim World* 68, no. 2 (1978): 12.

45. Al-Suyūṭī, *al-Tawshīḥ,* 9:4017.

46. Al-Zarkashī, *al-Tanqīḥ,* 3:1213.

47. Al-Suyūṭī, *al-Tawshīḥ,* 9:4017.

48. Al-Suyūṭī, *al-Dībāj,* 4:308.

49. Saleh, "Al-Suyūṭī and His Works," 86; al-Suyūṭī, *al-Taḥadduth bini'mat Allah,* 105. In 1871, Goldziher wrote that "al-Suyūṭī constantly attaches great importance to blazing new trails in his works, trails never trodden by others." See Barry and Hunwick, "Ignaz Goldziher on al-Suyūṭī," 94.

50. Sartain, *Jalāl al-Dīn al-Suyūṭī,* 31.

9. TRUSTEES ACROSS THE OCEAN

1. For more on early trade networks across the Indian Ocean, see Janet Abu Lughod, *Before European Hegemony: The World System A.D. 1250–1350* (Oxford: Oxford University Press, 1989), 251–90; George Fadlo Hourani, *Arab Seafaring in the Indian Ocean in the Ancient and Early Medieval Times* (Princeton, NJ: Princeton University Press, 1995).

2. These seafarers presumably consisted of wealthy merchants and traders with access to a library, possibly scholars themselves who traveled as merchants. al-'Asqalānī, *Hady al-sārī,* 15. Jonathan Brown has highlighted some similar examples of the use of al-Bukhārī's *Ṣaḥīḥ* in Islamic supplicatory, medicinal, calendrical, and political rituals across geographic regions and historical periods. See Brown, *Canonization of al-Bukhārī and Muslim,* 335–49.

3. To be sure, hadith scholarship in India predated the arrival of these Mamluk-era Egyptian hadith scholars. Perhaps the earliest example would be the Indian hadith scholar al-Ḥasan ibn Muḥammad al-Ṣaghānī's (d. 650/1252) *Mashāriq al-anwār* (The source of light), a popular compilation that combined select hadith from *Ṣaḥīḥ al-Bukhārī* and *Ṣaḥīḥ Muslim.* Al-Ṣaghānī was born in Lahore, studied in Mecca, and settled in Baghdad. *EI2,* s.v. "al-Ṣaghānī" (R. Baalbaki). For secondary sources on the origins of the Gujarati sultanate, see Samira Sheikh, *Forging a Region: Sultans, Traders, and Pilgrims in Gujarat, 1200–1500* (Oxford: Oxford University Press, 2010), 186–93; Jyoti Gulati Balachandran, "Texts, Tombs and Memory: The Migration, Settlement, and Formation of a Learned Muslim Community in Fifteenth-Century Gujarat" (PhD diss., UCLA, 2012), 1–32; *EI2,* s.v. "Gudjarāt" (J. Burton Page).

4. See *EI2,* s.v. "Gudjarāt" (J. Burton Page); 'Abd Allāh Ulugkhānī, *Zafar ul wālih bi Muzaffar wa ālihi [sic]: An Arabic History of Gujarat,* trans. M. F. Lokhandwala, 2 vols. (Baroda: Oriental Institute, 1970), 2:754.

5. Engseng Ho, "The Two Arms of Cambay: Diasporic Texts of Ecumenical Islam in the Indian Ocean," *Journal of the Economic and Social History of the Orient* 50, no. 2/3 (2007): 353.

6. For more on Aḥmad Shāh's patronage of scholars, see Sheikh, *Forging a Region,* 205–6.

7. See al-Damāmīnī, *Maṣābīḥ al-Jāmiʿ,* 1:5–12. For more biographical information, see Ḥasanī, *Itḥāf al-qārī,* 245–46; Ishaq, *India's Contribution,* 87–88.

8. Aḥmad Shāh was also presented with a collection of hadith compiled by the Syrian hadith scholar and Qur'an scholar Ibn Jazarī. Sheikh, *Forging a Region,* 206.

9. In 887/1482 Maḥmūd Shāh was said to have executed a non-Muslim enemy who refused to convert, and in 906/1501 he pushed back against a growing movement that held that a Muslim scholar named Muḥammad Jaunpūrī (d. 910/1505) was the *Mahdī,* "the guided one," who was prophesized to rule prior to the end of time. Ulugkhānī, *Zafar ul wālih,* 1:29 and 32; Sikandar ibn Muḥammad Manjhū ibn Akbar, *Mirāt-i Sikandirī* (Baroda, India: University of Baroda Press, 1961). Political calculations enframed these decisions, as Sheikh has argued, "apart from the over protection and patronage to the Sunni orthodoxy and the Sufi orders, there was little state discrimination between other groups," who "were put down only when they became a political threat." Sheikh, *Forging a Region,* 218. On circumcision, see Manjhū ibn Akbar, *Mirāt-i Sikandirī,* 101. On Maḥmūd Shāh's prohibition of interest and usury, see Akbar, *Mirāt-i Sikandirī,* 104.

10. Al-ʿAydarūs, *al-Nūr al-sāfir,* 150–51. For more on Wajīh al-Dīn, see Ishaq, *India's Contribution,* 93–94. While al-Sakhāwī's lessons in Mecca were most influential in training students in hadith who were on their way to or had just returned from India, scholars in Egypt continued to play an important role. Ibn Ḥajar al-Haytamī (d. 974/1566–67) and Zakariyyā al-Anṣārī played an important role in this regard. Ishaq, *India's Contribution,* 80–86. ʿAbd al-Muʿtī ibn al-Ḥasan al-Ḥaḍramī (d. 989/1581), a Meccan scholar who later migrated to Gujarat in the middle of the tenth/sixteenth century to instruct students in hadith, studied *Ṣaḥīḥ al-Bukhārī* with Zakariyyā al-Anṣārī. ʿAbd al-Muʿtī's father was employed as al-Anṣārī's recitation assistant. Ishaq, *India's Contribution,* 97.

11. Sheikh, *Forging a Region,* 215; Manjhū ibn Akbar, *Mirāt-i Sikandirī,* 110.

12. A version of this hadith is preserved in Abū Dāwūd's *Sunan,* in "The Book of Prayer," under the chapter heading "Mā yaqṭaʿu al-ṣalāt." See Abū Dāwūd, *Sunan,* 2 vols. (Germany: Thesaurus Islamicus Foundation, 2000), 1:120–21. For the Persian account of the anecdote, see Manjhū ibn Akbar, *Mirāt-i Sikandirī,* 110.

13. See Manjhū ibn Akbar, *Mirāt-i Sikandirī,* 110.

14. Ulugkhānī, *Zafar ul wālih,* 1:107.

15. al-ʿAydarūs, *al-Nūr al-sāfir,* 211; Ishaq, *India's Contribution,* 94.

16. The copy was gifted to the sultan by Mukhāṭib ʿAlī Khān (d. ca. tenth/sixteenth century), who had received it from Wajīh al-Dīn. See Ulugkhānī, *Zafar ul wālih,* 1:106; Ishaq, *India's Contribution,* 93–94.

17. Ulugkhānī, *Zafar ul wālih,* 1:106.
18. Manjhū ibn Akbar, *Mirāt-i Sikandirī,* 207–8.
19. Ho, "The Two Arms of Cambay," 356.
20. Arabic: "min ayāt Allāh al-Kubrā." See al-ʿAydarūs, *al-Nūr al-sāfir,* 39.
21. Ibid., 413.
22. Arabic: "bi'l-ʿayn al-shaḥmiyya," (lit. "with the white eye"). Ibid. This is the only recorded claim of an appearance of the Prophet at a live commentary session on hadith.
23. Gangohī and al-Kāndhlawī, *Lāmiʿ al-darārī,* 1:458; Ḥasanī, *Itḥāf al-qārī,* 130; Ishaq, *India's Contribution,* 121–22.
24. Gangohī and al-Kāndhlawī, *Lāmiʿ al-darārī,* 1:458.
25. ʿUthmān ibn ʿĪsā al-Ḥanafī al-Sindī (d. 1008/1600) trained in Gujarat and compiled his own commentary using Zaydpūrī's *Fayḍ al-bārī,* in addition to Ibn Ḥajar's, Kirmānī's, and Qasṭallānī's (see Ishaq, *India's Contribution,* 135–36). Another student of Zaydpūrī's born near Gujarat, Ibn Yūsuf al-Sindī al-Burhānpūrī (d. 1004/1595), wrote a supercommentary on Qasṭallānī's *Irshād al-sārī* (see Ishaq, *India's Contribution,* 133; Ḥasanī, *Itḥāf al-qārī,* 134–35).
26. Ibn Ḥajar al-ʿAsqalānī, *Fatḥ al-bārī,* Arabic Manuscripts MS 165, Khuda Bakhsh Library, Hyderabad, India (sixteenth century), fol. 1a; Ishaq, *India's Contribution,* 105–6. For more on Nawras's book collection, see Keelan Hall Overton, "A Collector and His Portrait: Book Arts and Painting for Ibrahim 'Adil Shah II of Bijapur (r. 1580–1627)" (PhD diss., University of California, Los Angeles, 2011), 44–102.
27. George Michell and Mark Zebrowski, *Art and Architecture of the Deccan Sultanates* (Cambridge: Cambridge University Press, 1999), 88–89.
28. Documented in Bashīr al-Dīn Aḥmad, *Wāqiʿāt-i Mamlakat-i Bijāpūr* (Agra: Muḥammad Qādir ʿAlikhān, 1915), 2:25, 28–31. Also cited in Ishaq, *India's Contribution,* 105n4.
29. Nawras's identity, like that of many figures, is more complicated than can be captured in passing mention. A more sensitive portrait can be glimpsed in Deborah Hutton, *Art of the Court of Bijapur* (Bloomington: Indiana University Press, 2006), 14–15; Overton, "A Collector and His Portrait," esp. 37ff. and 48ff.
30. Jaʿfar Badr-i-ʿĀlam's (d. 1085/1675) *Fayḍ al-ṭārī,* the *Khayr al-jārī* of Abū Yūsuf al-Bayānī of Lahore (d. 1098/1687), Ibn Sayf al-Dīn al-Sirhindī's (d. 1114/1702) *Fayḍ al-bārī,* Nūr al-Dīn ibn Ṣāliḥ al-Aḥmadābādī (d. 1155/1742)'s *Nūr al-qārī,* and Mir Azād Bilgrāmī's (d.1200/1785) *Ḍawʾ al-dārī.* Gangohī and al-Kāndhlawī, *Lāmiʿ al-darārī,* 1:454–68. Bilgrāmī's drew heavily on al-Qasṭallānī's commentary, and the other works were likely based on one or more late Mamluk-era commentaries as well.
31. For a brief but detailed summary of these changes, consult Ira Lapidus, *A History of Islamic Societies,* 1st ed. (Cambridge: Cambridge University Press, 1988), 718–736.
32. Francis Robinson, *Islam and Muslim History in South Asia* (Delhi: Oxford University Press, 2000), 105–21.
33. For an overview of these groups, consult the Lapidus, *A History of Islamic Societies.* For a more substantive treatment, consult Barbara Metcalf,

Islamic Revival in British India: Deoband, 1860–1900 (Princeton, NJ: Princeton University Press, 1982); Muhammad Qasim Zaman, *The 'Ulama in Contemporary Islam: Custodians of Change* (Princeton, NJ: Princeton University Press, 2002).

34. The Deobandi movement, however, has begun to receive careful attention in the secondary literature, both as a South Asian and transregional movement. In addition to the texts by Metcalf and Zaman already noted above, see Brannon Ingram, "Deobandis Abroad: Sufism, Ethics and Polemics in a Global Islamic Movement" (PhD diss., University of Chapel Hill, North Carolina, 2011).

35. Metcalf, *Islamic Revival in British India,* 248–58 and 262–63.

36. Zaman, "Commentaries, Print and Patronage," 71.

37. Metcalf, *Islamic Revival in British India;* Lapidus, *A History of Islamic Societies,* 725.

38. Zaman, "Commentaries, Print and Patronage," 73–74.

39. Metcalf, *Islamic Revival in British India,* 105 and 126; Lapidus, *A History of Islamic Societies,* 726.

40. Robinson, *Islam and Muslim History in South Asia,* 66–104; Messick, *The Calligraphic State,* 231–50.

41. Qur'an 47:38.

42. Translated in Muhammad Qasim Zaman, "Commentaries, Print and Patronage," 71. For the original Arabic in the edition of *Fayḍ al-bārī* referenced in my study, see al-Kashmīrī, *Fayḍ al-bārī,* 15–16.

43. See al-Kashmīrī, *Fayḍ al-bārī,* 1:17. For a discussion of other modern and premodern Indian "memories or myths of origin of somewhere" in "the Arab Middle East," see Muhammad Qasim Zaman, "Arabic, the Arab Middle East, and the Definition of Muslim Identity in Twentieth Century India," *Journal of the Royal Asiatic Society* 8, no. 1 (1998): 59–60.

44. Zaman writes, "Those to whom such a demonstration [of a mastery of Arabic] needed to be made included British colonial officials themselves, who saw Arabic as one of the 'classical languages of India'; and W. D. Arnold, who in 1856 was appointed as the first Director of Public Instruction in the Punjab, thought that 'Urdu is as offensive to a learned Arabic scholar as vernacular English in connection with English subjects would have been to a scholar of the age of Erasmus.' Yet English officials also complained that most Indian Muslim scholars lacked the ability to converse or write properly in the Arabic language." Zaman, "Arabic, the Arab Middle East," 65.

45. Ibid., 64–65.

46. Ibid.

47. See Zaman, "Commentaries, Print and Patronage," 63.

48. Al-Kashmīrī, *Fayḍ al-bārī,* 32; Muhammad Qasim Zaman, "Studying in a Madrasa in the Early Twentieth Century," in *Islam in South Asia,* ed. Barbara Metcalf (Princeton, NJ: Princeton University Press, 2009), 229.

49. See Zaman, "Commentaries, Print and Patronage," 63.

50. Aḥmad Riḍā Bajnūrī, *Anwār al-bārī: urdū sharḥ Ṣaḥīḥ al-Bukhārī* (Delhi: Rabbānī Book Depot, n.d.), 427–28. For more on the use of Urdu in this context, see Metcalf, *Islamic Revival in British India,* 206–10.

51. See Bajnūrī, *Anwār al-bārī.* An exception to this general rule was the Urdu translation of the Qur'ān by Shāh 'Abd al-Qādir (d. 1815). This translation was thought so highly of by Deobandi scholars that the Shaykh al-Hind Maḥmūd Ḥasan (d. 1920) averred that "had the Qur'ān been revealed in Urdu instead of Arabic, its language would have been the same or nearly the same as in this translation." Shabbīr Aḥmad 'Uthmānī, *Faḍl al-Bārī: Commentary on the Ṣaḥīḥ al-Bukhārī,* ed. Qāḍī 'Abd al-Raḥmān, trans. Qāḍī 'Abd al-Raḥmān (Karachi: Idārah 'Ulūm-i-shary'iyyah and Javed and Anjuman Press, 1975), 153. Such a claim is quite bold, considering the lengthy debates over translation in other parts of the modern world, including Egypt and Turkey. See Brett Wilson, *Translating the Qur'an in an Age of Nationalism* (Oxford: Oxford University Press, 2014), esp. ch. 6.

52. Zaman, "Commentaries, Print and Patronage," 63.

53. The work was titled *Lāmi' al-darārī.* Ibid., 69–71. For a glimpse into the role of commentators' students in the production of Arabic and Urdu commentary on *Ṣaḥīḥ al-Bukhārī,* see Taqī 'Uthmānī, *In'ām al-bārī: durūs-i Bukhārī sharīf* (Gujarat: Maktaba Haqqaniyya, 2006), 1:146–48. 'Uthmānī's text is itself based on oral lessons.

54. Manāẓir Aḥsan Gīlānī, *Ihata-yi Dar al-'Ulum main bite huwe din* (Deoband: Matkab-yi tayyiba, n.d.), 155–56; translated in Zaman, "Studying in a Madrasa," 233–34.

55. Shaykh al-Hind had his analyses of Bukhārī's chapter headings published in a short printed volume. See Maḥmūd Ḥasan, *al-Abwāb wa'l-tarājim* (Nagīnah: Maṭba' al-Amān Akhbār, [1920?]).

56. Gīlānī, *Ihata-yi Dar al-'Ulum main bite huwe din,* 155–56; translated in Zaman, "Studying in a Madrasa," 233–34.

57. Anwar Shāh al-Kashmīrī and 'Abd al-Fattāh Abū Ghudda, *al-Taṣrīḥ bi-mā tawātar fī nuzūl al-masīḥ*, 5th ed. (Beirut: Maktab al-Matbū'āt al-Islāmiyya bi-Ḥalab, 1992), 25; al-Kashmīrī, *Fayḍ al-bārī,* 1:31.

58. See al-Kashmīrī, *Fayḍ al-bārī,* 26–30.

59. Ibid., 1:30.

60. Aḥmad Riḍā Bijnūrī, *Anwār al-bārī: urdū sharḥ Ṣaḥīḥ al-Bukhārī* (Delhi: Rabbānī Book Depot, n.d.), 1:430.

61. Zaman, "Studying in a Madrasa," 225–26.

62. See Zaman, "The 'Ulamā': Scholarly Tradition and New Public Commentary," in *The New Cambridge History of Islam,* ed. Robert Hefner (Cambridge: Cambridge University Press, 2010), 340–41.

63. Al-Kashmīrī, *Fayḍ al-bārī,* 1:38. Muḥammad Zakariyyā (d. 1982), in his introduction to Rashīd Aḥmad Gangohī's (d. 1905) commentary on Bukhārī's *Ṣaḥīḥ, Lāmi' al-darārī,* notes the current Ḥanafī preference of 'Aynī's *'Umdat al-qārī,* a preference still noted by contemporary commentators in South Asia. See Gangohī and al-Kāndhlawī, *Lāmi' al-darārī,* 1:401. This was also suggested in a lesson with Shaykh al-Ḥadīth Muḥammad Khʷāje Sharīf at the Niẓamiyya College, July 26, 2011.

64. Al-Kashmīrī, *Fayḍ al-bārī,* 1:38. Banūrī claims he read the work in manuscript form.

65. Robinson, *Islam and Muslim History in South Asia,* 124.

66. Ebrahim Moosa, "Colonialism and Islamic Law," in *Islam and Modernity*, ed. Muhammad Khalid Masud, Armando Salvatore, and Martin van Bruinessen (Edinburgh: Edinburgh University Press, 2010), 158–81; Wael Hallaq, *Sharīʿa: Theory, Practice, Transformations* (Cambridge: Cambridge University Press, 2009), 371–95.

67. Scott Kugle, "Framed, Blamed and Renamed: The Recasting of Islamic Jurisprudence in Colonial South Asia," *Modern Asian Studies* 35, no. 2 (May 2001): 257–313.

68. Roland Wilson, *Anglo-Muhammadan Law: A Digest* (London: W. Thacker and Co., 1903), 71.

69. Furqan Ahmad, "Contribution of Maulana Ashraf ʿAli Thanavi to the Protection and Development of Islamic Law in the Indian Subcontinent," *Islamic and Comparative Law Quarterly* 6, no. 1 (1986): 71–79.

70. Al-Kashmīrī, *Fayḍ al-bārī,* 4:456–57 (Kitāb al-Muḥāribīn: Bāb Kam al-taʿzīr wa'l-adab).

71. References to opinions from competing schools appeared only in the footnotes provided by his students. Ibid., 4:456–58 (Kitāb al-Muḥāribīn: Bāb Kam al-taʿzīr wa'l-adab).

72. Ibid., 4:456–57 (Kitāb al-Muḥāribīn: Bāb Kam al-taʿzīr wa'l-adab).

73. Ibid., 4:457 (Kitāb al-Muḥāribīn: Bāb Kam al-taʿzīr wa'l-adab).

74. Ibid., 4:458 (Kitāb al-Muḥāribīn: Bāb Kam al-taʿzīr wa'l-adab).

75. Ibid.

76. Ibid., 4:108–9 (Kitāb al-Maghāzī: Bāb ʿUmrat al-Qaḍāʾ).

77. For al-Kashmīrī's views on Ibn Taymiyya and some of his controversial positions, see Bijnūrī, *Anwār al-bārī,* 1:318–19. For Ibn Taymiyya's controversial critique of visitation of Sufi saint shrines, see Christopher S. Taylor, *In the Vicinity of the Righteous: Ziyāra and the Veneration of Muslim Saints in Late Medieval Egypt* (Leiden: Brill, 1998), 168–94.

78. An excellent overview of the roots of these polemics can be found in Ingram, "Deobandis Abroad," 32–64. The reform movement inspired by Muḥammad ibn ʿAbd al-Wahhāb (d. 1206/1792) in central Arabia also bitterly opposed certain saint-shrine practices.

79. While the studies of the Ahl-i Ḥadīth remain a *desideratum,* an overview is provided in Metcalf, *Islamic Revival in British India,* 268–96. Claudia Preckel's dissertation on Ṣiddīq Ḥasan Khān provides a useful overview of the scholarly networks and trends in interpretation. See Claudia Preckel, "Islamische Bildungsnetzwerke und Gelehrtenkultur im Indien des 19. Jahrhunderts. Muḥammad Ṣiddīq Ḥasan Khān (st. 1890) und die Entstehung der Ahl-e Ḥadīth-Bewegung in Bhopal" (PhD diss., Ruhr-University Bochum, 2005). For a basic overview of Ḥasan Khān's life, see *EI3,* s.v. "Ahl-i Ḥadīth" (Claudia Preckel); Gangohī and al-Kāndhlawī, *Lāmiʿ al-darārī,* 1:466–67.

80. *EI2,* s.v. "Nawwāb Sayyid Ṣiddīḳ Ḥasan Ḵẖān" (Ẓafarul-Islām Khān); Metcalf, *Islamic Revival in British India,* 268.

81. For outline of some of these disagreements, *EI3,* s.v. "Ahl-i Ḥadīth" (Claudia Preckel).

82. Bernard Haykel, *Revival and Reform in Islam: The Legacy of Muhammad al-Shawkānī* (Cambridge: Cambridge University Press, 2003), 76–108. For

a comparative discussion of Shawkānī's and the Ahl-i Ḥadīth's positions on *taqlīd,* see Zaman, "The 'Ulamā'" 339–40.

83. Narrated in Ṣiddīq Ḥasan Khān, *al-Ḥiṭṭa fī al-ṣiḥāh al-sitta* (Beirut: Dār al-Jīl, 1987), 131–32.

84. Ṣiddīq Hasan Khān, *'Awn al-bārī* (Beirut: Dār al-Kutub al-'Ilmiyya, 2008), 1:11–12.

85. Zaman, "Commentaries, Print and Patronage," 63.

86. See Metcalf, *Islamic Revival in British India,* 205–6.

87. Muḥammad ibn 'Alī al-Shawkānī and Muḥammad Ṣiddīq Ḥasan Khān, *Nayl al-awṭār min asrār Muntaqā al-akhbār wa-bi-hāmishihi Kitāb 'Awn al-bārī,* 7 vols. (Būlāq: [s.n.], 1880).

88. Ḥasan Khān may have been harsher and more argumentative in other venues. See Metcalf, *Islamic Revival in British India,* 278–80.

89. Ibid., 278–80, 293.

90. Khān, *'Awn al-bārī,* 6:270; al-'Asqalānī, *Fatḥ al-bārī,* 12:178 (Kitāb al-Muḥāribīn: Bāb Kam al-ta'zīr wa'l-adab).

91. Khān, *'Awn al-bārī,* 6:271 (Kitāb al-Muḥāribīn: Bāb Kam al-ta'zīr wa'l-adab).

92. Khān, *'Awn al-bārī,* 6:270 (Kitāb al-Muḥāribūn: Bāb Kam al-ta'zīr wa'l-adab); al-'Asqalānī, *Fatḥ al-bārī,* 12:178 (Kitāb al-Ḥudūd: Bāb Kam al-ta'zīr wa'l-adab).

93. Khān, *'Awn al-bārī,* 6:271 (Kitāb al-Muḥāribīn: Bāb Kam al-ta'zīr wa'l-adab).

94. "Lā yanbaghī li-muṣnif al-ta'wīl[u] 'alā qawl al-āḥād 'ind qawl rasūl Allāh," al-Shawkānī and Khān, *Nayl al-awṭār wa-bi-hāmishihi Kitāb 'Awn al-bārī,* 7:61 (Kitāb al-Ḥudūd: Bāb Ma jā' fī qadr al-ta'zīr).

95. Metcalf, *Islamic Revival in British India,* 283–84.

10. LOST IN TRANSLATION

1. Anwār al-Ḥasan Shērkūtī in 'Uthmānī, *Faḍl al-bārī,* 56.

2. Ibid.

3. Ibid., 57.

4. Ibid., 58. Al-Kashmīrī died in 1933, and 'Uthmānī returned to Deoband in 1936.

5. Ibid., 59.

6. Ibid., 57; Muhammad Miyan, *Silken Letters Movement* (New Delhi: Manak Publications, 2012), 50.

7. Shērkūtī in 'Uthmānī, *Faḍl al-bārī,* 58. For an overview of the Jam'iyyat al-'Ulamā'-yi Hind (The Muslim Scholars of India Association), see Yohanan Friedmann, "The Attitude of the Jam'iyyat-i 'Ulama'-i Hind to the Indian National Movement and the Establishment of Pakistan," in *The 'Ulama' in Modern History: Studies in Memory of Professor Uriel Heyd,* ed. G. Baer (Jerusalem: Israeli Oriental Society, 1971), 157–83; Robinson, *Islam and Muslim History in South Asia,* 196–99.

8. Shērkūtī in 'Uthmānī, *Faḍl al-bārī,* 59.

9. Shērkūtī in ibid., 59–60.

10. Muhammad Ali Jinnah, "First Presidential Address August 11, 1947," in *Pakistan Movement Historical Documents,* ed. G. Allana (Karachi: Department of International Relations, University of Karachi, 1969), 407–11.
11. Shērkūtī in 'Uthmānī, *Faḍl al-bārī,* 60.
12. Muḥammad Yaḥyā Ṣiddīqī in ibid., 38.
13. Muḥammad Yūsuf Banūrī in ibid., 50.
14. Ishtiyāq Ḥusayn Qurashī in ibid., 25.
15. Qāḍī 'Abd al-Raḥmān in ibid., 35.
16. Shērkūtī in ibid., 67.
17. Ibid., 39.
18. Ishtiyāq Qurashī in ibid., 25.
19. Muḥammad Ṭayyib in ibid., 26.
20. Qāḍī 'Abd al-Raḥmān in ibid., 34.
21. Ibid., 37.
22. Muḥammad Yaḥyā Ṣiddīqī in ibid., 38.
23. Muḥammad Zakariyyā al-Kāndhlawī in ibid., 43.
24. Qāḍī 'Abd al-Raḥmān in ibid., 32.
25. Muḥammad Zakariyyā in ibid., 43.
26. See Shabbīr Aḥmad Uthmānī, *Faḍl al-bārī sharḥ urdū Ṣaḥīḥ al-Bukhārī,* ed. Qāḍī 'Abd al-Raḥmān, 2 vols. (Karachi: Idārat 'Ulūm Shar'iyyah, 1973).
27. Ali Usman Qasmi, *The Ahmadis and the Politics of Exclusion in Pakistan* (New York: Anthem Press, 2014), 1–10, 65–118.
28. Qāḍī 'Abd al-Raḥmān in 'Uthmānī, *Faḍl al-bārī,* 35.
29. Ibid.
30. Ibid., 56.
31. The panegyric was written by Maḥmūd Nadhīr al-Ṭarāzī (d. 1990), who himself had published works on Arabic panegyrics.
32. Maḥmūd Nadhīr al-Ṭarāzī in 'Uthmānī, *Faḍl al-bārī,* 44–48.
33. Qāḍī 'Abd al-Raḥmān in ibid., 36.
34. Ibid., 274–86.
35. 'Uthmānī called the opponents of Abū Ḥanīfa *muḥaddithūn* and followers of the *salāf.* Current academic conventions typically refer to this group as the "hadith folk," or *ahl al-ḥadīth.*
36. 'Uthmānī, *Faḍl al-bārī,* 286.
37. Ibid., 286–87.
38. Ibid., 292.
39. Ibid., 293.
40. Ibid., 294.
41. Ibid., 293.
42. Muḥammad Salīm Allāh Khān and Muḥammad Yaḥyā Ṣiddīqī in ibid., 40 and 55.
43. Qāḍī 'Abd al-Raḥmān in ibid., 33–34. Also see Shērkūtī in ibid., 67.
44. Muḥammad Ṭayyib in ibid., 27.
45. F.K. Khan Durrani, *Mishkat-ul-masabeeh,* trans. F.K. Khan Durrani and Capt. A.N. Matthews (Lahore: Tabligh Literature Company, 19[—]).
46. 'Uthmānī, *Faḍl al-Bārī,* 433–35.
47. Ibid., 394.

48. Ibid.

49. See M. Ziauddin, "Maʿarri the Free-Thinker," *Visva-Bharati Quarterly* (1935): 34–42.

50. Ibid., 34 and 37.

51. For example, Jamāl al-Dīn al-Afghānī (d. 1897) and the prominent thinkers he influenced. See Albert Hourani, *Arabic Thought in the Liberal Age, 1798–1939* (Cambridge: Cambridge University Press, 1983), 103–39.

52. ʿUthmānī, *Faḍl al-bārī,* 199.

53. Ibid., 543, 546, and 551.

54. Ibid., 165.

55. Ibid., 257.

56. Ibid., 256.

57. For a historical and contemporary description of the Niẓāmiyya, see Gregory C. Kozlowski, "Loyalty, Locality and Authority in Several Opinions (*Fatāwā*) Delivered by the Muftī of the Jamiʿah Niẓāmiyyah Madrasah, Hyderabad, India," *Modern Asian Studies* 29, no. 4 (October 1995): 893–927.

58. Muḥammad Khwāje Sharīf, lesson at the Niẓāmiyya College, July 26, 2011.

59. Muḥammad Khwāje Sharīf, lesson at the Niẓāmiyya College, July 26, 2011. I was unable to verify the shaykh's claim. It nevertheless indicates that the Niẓamiyya values students who devote time to studying the *Ṣaḥīḥ*.

60. Muḥammad Khwāje Sharīf, lesson at the Niẓāmiyya College, July 26, 2011.

61. Muḥammad Khwāje Sharīf, lesson at the Niẓāmiyya College, July 26, 2011.

62. See Muḥammad Khwāje Sharīf, *Tharwat al-qārī min anwār al-Bukhārī* (Hyderabad, India: Markaz Taḥqīqāt Islāmiyya, Jāmiʿa Niẓāmiyya, 2000), 1:5.

63. Ibid.

64. See Muḥammad Khwāje Sharīf, *Muqaddimat Tharwat al-qārī min anwār al-Bukhārī* (Hyderabad, India: Markaz Taḥqīqāt Islāmiyya, Jāmiʿa Nizāmiyya, 2000), viii–ix.

65. al-Nawawī, *Sharḥ matn al-Arbaʿīn al-Nawawiyya,* 6.

66. al-ʿAsqalānī, *Fatḥ al-bārī,* 1:9 (Kitāb Badʾ al-waḥy: Bāb Kayf kān badʾ al-waḥy).

67. Khwāje Sharīf, *Tharwat al-qārī,* 1:35.

68. Ibid., 1:41.

69. Muḥammad Khwāje Sharīf, lesson at the Niẓāmiyya College, July 26, 2011.

70. Muḥammad Khwāje Sharīf, lesson at the Niẓāmiyya College, July 26, 2011.

71. See Khwāje Sharīf, *Tharwat al-qārī,* 2:74–75.

72. Ibid.

73. Participant observation at Niẓāmiyya College, July 23, 2011.

74. It was at www.youtube.com/watch?v = DrpY9bhbJDs&feature = channel&list = UL. The video has has been taken down.

75. Friedrich Nietzsche, *The Gay Science,* trans. Walter Kaufmann (New York: Vintage, 1974), 136–38.

76. Ibid.

EPILOGUE

1. For more on the history of ISIS, see Cole Bunzel, "From Paper State to Caliphate: The Ideology of the Islamic State," *The Brookings Project on U.S. Relations with the Islamic World* 19 (2015): 1–42. For more on their conception of time, which is pertinent to this chapter, see Shahzad Bashir, "Islam and the Politics of Temporality: The Case of ISIS," in *Time, Temporality and Global Politics,* ed. Andrew Hom, Christopher McIntosh, Alasdair McKay, and Liam Stockdale (Bristol: E-International Relations, 2016). With respect to Salafism, Jonathan A.C. Brown has defined it as a modern reformist movement that seeks "to rejuvenate the Muslim community by reviving the primordial greatness of Islam" and recreating "the Prophet's sunna by making the classical study of *ḥadīth* and the ways of the early community paramount." Brown, *The Canonization of al-Bukhārī and Muslim,* 305. For a more detailed genealogy of the evolving definition of Salafism, see Henri Lauzière, "The Construction of *Salafiyya:* Reconsidering Salafism from the Perspective of Conceptual History," *IJMES* 42 (2010): 369–89.

2. Brown, *The Canonization of al-Bukhārī and Muslim,* 321–34.

3. Audio recordings of it circulated online. See "Sharḥ Ṣaḥīḥ al-Bukhārī: al-Shaykh Ṣāliḥ Muḥammad ibn al-ʿUthaymīn," posted by Islamway.net, https://ar.islamway.net/collection/903/.

4. ʿAbd al-ʿAzīz ibn Bāz, *Ṭabʿa jadīda li-Fatḥ al-bārī (Būlāq)* (Cairo: Maktabat Ibn Taymiyya, 2008), 11–109.

5. For an example of a case in North America, see Joel Blecher and Josh Dubler, "Overlooking Race and Secularism in Muslim Philadelphia," in *Race and Secularism in America,* ed. Vincent Lloyd and Jonathan S. Kahn (New York: Columbia University Press, 2016), 122–50. For more on this strain of transnational Salafism, see Laurent Bonnefoy, "How Transnational Is Salafism in Yemen?" in *Global Salafism: Islam's New Religious Movement,* ed. Roel Meijer (Oxford: Oxford University Press, 2009), 321–41.

6. Aymān al-Ẓawāhirī, *al-Ḥasād al-Murr* (Markaz al-Fajr, 1991?), 31.

7. Anonymous, "The Revival of Slavery before the Hour," *Dabiq* 4 (2014): 16. For a more elaborate discussion of this piece and the history of this hadith, see Younus Mirza, "'The Slave Girl Gives Birth to Her Master': Female Slavery from the Mamlūk Era (1250–1517) to the Islamic State (2014–)," *Journal of the American Academy of Religion* (2017): https://doi.org/10.1093/jaarel/lfx001.

8. Ibid.

9. Asad, "The Idea of an Anthropology of Islam," 14–15.

10. Ibn Baṭṭāl, *Sharḥ Saḥīḥ al-Bukhārī,* 7:64.

11. Ibid.

12. Ibid.

13. The Arabic term Ibn Ḥajar uses to discuss parity here is *al-musāwā.*

14. Al-ʿAsqalānī, *Fatḥ al-bārī,* 5:207.

15. Hallaq, *Sharīʿa,* 390.

16. Salahuddin Yusuf, *Riyād-us-Sāliheen* [*sic*] [*with*] *Commentary* (Lahore: Darussalam, 1999), 1011.

17. Umm Sumayyah al-Muḥājirah, "From Our Sisters: Slave Girls or Prostitutes?" *Dabiq* 9 (2015): 48.

18. That ISIS framed their November 2015 attack on Paris as an attack on the "capital of prostitution" is very much an extension of this rhetoric.

19. Al-Muḥājirah, "From Our Sisters," 48.

20. Ibid.

21. Ibid. In a recent study of textbooks approved for use in classrooms by ISIS, there are several passages that explicitly criticize human rights in some detail. See Jacob Olidort, "Inside the Caliphate's Classroom: Textbooks, Guidance Literature, and Indoctrination Methods of the Islamic State." (Washington, DC: Washington Institute for Near East Policy, 2016).

22. "*Al-Sabī: Aḥkām wa-masā'il,*" ed. Diwān al-Buḥūth wa'l-Iftā' (2014).

23. See *Ṣaḥīḥ al-Bukhārī,* 1:296 (Kitāb al-Ḥajj: Bāb al-Tamattu' wa'l-Iqrān, Ḥadīth 1592).

24. See "Syria Mosque Blast: Pro-Assad Cleric among Dozens Dead," *BBC News,* March 21, 2013, www.bbc.co.uk/news/world-middle-east-21887877.

25. Foucault, "The Order of Discourse (1970)," 58.

Works Cited

PRIMARY SOURCES

Abū ʿAbd Allāh Ibn Rushayd. *Tarjumān al-tarājim ʿalā abwāb Ṣaḥīḥ al-Bukhārī.* Beirut: Dār al-Kutub al-ʿIlmiyya, 2008.

Aḥmad, Bashīr al-Dīn. *Wāqiʿāt-i Mamlakat-i Bijāpūr.* Agra, India: Muḥammad Qādir ʿAlikhān, 1915.

Anas, Mālik ibn, and Jalāl al-Dīn al-Suyūṭī. *Muwaṭṭaʾ al-Imām Mālik: wa-sharḥuhu Tanwīr al-ḥawālik.* 2 vols. Egypt: Sharikat Maktaba wa-Maṭbaʿat Muṣṭafā al-Bābī al-Ḥalabī, 1951.

Anonymous. "The Revival of Slavery before the Hour." *Dabiq* 4 (2014): 14–17.

ʿAsqalānī, Ibn Ḥajar al-. "Fatḥ al-bārī." Arabic Manuscripts MS 165, Khuda Bakhsh Library, Hyderabad, India.

———. "Fatḥ al-bārī." Mahmud Paşa MS79, Süleymaniye Library, Istanbul.

———. *Fatḥ al-bārī.* Edited by ʿAbd al-ʿAzīz ibn Bāz. 13 vols. Beirut: Dār al-Maʿrifa, 1970.

———. *Fatḥ al-bārī.* Edited by Shayba al-Ḥamad. Riyadh: Ibn ʿAbd al-ʿAzīz Āl Saʿūd, 2000.

———. *Hady al-sārī.* Edited by ʿAbd al-Qādir Shayba al-Ḥamad. Riyadh: Maktabat al-Malik Fahd al-Waṭaniyya, 2000.

———. *Ḥawāshī Tanqīḥ al-Zarkashī ʿalā al-Bukhārī.* Beirut: ʿĀlam al-Kutub, 2008.

———. *Inbāʾ al-ghumr bi-abnāʾ al-ʿumr fī al-tārīkh.* Edited by Ḥasan Ḥabashī. 4 vols. Cairo: al-Majlis al-Aʿlā lil-Shuʾūn al-Islāmiyya, 1969.

———. *Intiqāḍ al-iʿtirāḍ.* Riyadh: Maktabat Rushd, n.d.

ʿAṭṭār, Ibn al-. *Tuḥfat al-ṭālibīn fī tarjamat al-Imām Muḥyī Dīn.* Riyadh: Dār al-Ṣumayʿī, 1994.

ʿAydarūs, ʿAbd al-Qādir al-. *Tārīkh al-Nūr al-sāfir ʿan akhbār al-qarn al-ʿāshir.* Beirut: Dār Ṣādir, 2001.

ʿAynī, Badr al-Dīn al-. *ʿUmdat al-qārī fī sharḥ Ṣaḥīḥ al-Bukhārī*. 25 vols. Beirut: Idārat al-Ṭabāʿat al-Muniriyya, 1970.

———. *ʿUmdat al-qārī fī sharḥ Ṣaḥīḥ al-Bukhārī*. Beirut: Dār al-Kutub al-ʿIlmiyya, 2001.

Bājī, Abū al-Walīd al-. *al-Muntaqā: Sharḥ Muwaṭṭaʾ Mālik*, 9 vols. Beirut: Dār al-Kutūb al-ʿIlmiyya, 1999.

———. *Taḥqīq al-madhhab*, ed. Abū ʿAbd al-Raḥmān ibn ʿAqīl. Riyadh: ʿĀlam al-kutub, 1983.

Bashkuwāl, Ibn. *al-Ṣila*. 3 vols. Beirut: Dār al-Kitāb al-Lubnānī, 1990.

Bāz, ʿAbd al-ʿAzīz ibn. *Ṭabʿa jadīda li-Fatḥ al-bārī (Būlāq)*. Cairo: Maktabat Ibn Taymiyya, 2008.

Bijnūrī, Aḥmad Riḍā. *Anwār al-bārī: urdū sharḥ Ṣaḥīḥ al-Bukhārī*. Delhi: Rabbānī Book Depot, n.d.

Birmāwī, Muḥammad ibn ʿAbd al-Dāʾim al-. "al-Lāmiʿ al-ṣaḥīḥ bi-sharḥ al-Jāmiʿ al-ṣaḥīḥ." Garrett Collection MS 2372Yq, Princeton Univerity Library.

Bukhārī, Muḥammad ibn Ismāʿīl al-. *Ṣaḥīḥ al-Bukhārī*. 3 vols. Stuttgart, Germany: Thesaurus Islamicus Foundation, 2000.

———. "Ṣaḥīḥ al-Bukhārī." Garrett Collection 341 Bq, Princeton University Library.

Bulqīnī, ʿUmar ibn Raslān al-. *Kitāb Tarājim al-Bukhārī: Al-musammā Munāsabāt abwāb Ṣaḥīḥ al-Bukhārī li-baʿḍihā baʿḍan*. Edited by Aḥmad ibn Fāris Sallūm. Riyadh: Maktabat al-Maʿārif lil-Nashr wa'l-Tawzīʿ, 2010.

Damāmīnī, Badr al-Dīn al-. *Maṣābīḥ al-Jāmiʿ*. Edited by Nūr al-Dīn Ṭālib. 10 vols. Qatar: Wizārat al-Awqāf, 2009.

———. *Taʿaqqubāt al-ʿAllāmah Badr al-Dīn al-Damāmīnī fī kitābihi Maṣābīḥ al-Jāmiʿ al-ṣaḥīḥ ʿalā al-Imām Badr al-Dīn al-Zarkashī fī kitābihi al-Tanqīḥ li-alfāẓ al-Jāmiʿ al-ṣaḥīḥ fī al-qaḍāyā al-naḥwīyah wa'l-ṣarfīyah wa-al-lughawīyah*. Edited by ʿAlī ibn Sulṭān al-Ḥakamī. Medina: Dār al-Bukhārī, 1995.

Dāwūd, Abū. *Sunan*. 2 vols. Stuttgart, Germany: Thesaurus Islamicus Foundation, 2000.

Dihlawī, ʿAbd al-ʿAzīz al-. *Bustān al-muḥaddithīn*. Translated by Muḥammad Akram al-Nadwī. Beirut: Dār al-Gharb al-Islāmī, 2002.

———. *The Garden of the Hadith Scholars: Bustān al-Muḥadithīn*. Translated by Muḥammad Akram Nadwī and Aisha Abdurrahman Bewley. London: Turath, 2007.

Durrani, F.K. Khan. *Mishkat-ul-Masabeeh*. Translated by F.K. Khan Durrani and Capt. A.N. Matthews. Lahore: Tabligh Literature Company, 19[—].

Faraḍī, ʿAbd Allāh ibn Muḥammad ibn al-. *Tārīkh al-ʿulamāʾ wa'l-ruwāh lil-ʿilm bi'l-Andalus*. Cairo: ʿIzzat al-ʿAṭṭār al-Ḥusaynī, 1954.

Gangohī, Rashīd Aḥmad, and Muḥammad Zakariyyā al-Kāndhlawī. *Lāmiʿ al-darārī ʿalā Jāmiʿ al-Bukhārī*. 10 vols. Mecca: al-Maktaba al-Imdādiyya, 1975.

Ghazzī, Najm al-Dīn al-. *Al-Kawākib al-sāʾira bi-aʿyān al-miʾa al-ʿāshira*. Edited by Jibrāʾīl Sulaymān Jabbūr. Beirut: Dār al-Āfāq al-Jadīda, 1979.

Ḥasan, Maḥmūd. *al-Abwāb wa'l-tarājim*. Nagīnah: Maṭbaʿ al-Amān Akhbār, [n.d., 1920s].

Ḥasanī, Muḥammad ʿIṣām ʿArār. *Itḥāf al-qārī bi-maʿrifat juhūd wa-aʿmāl al-ʿulamāʾ ʿalā Ṣaḥīḥ al-Bukhārī.* Damascus: al-Yamāma, 1987.

Ḥumaydī, Abū Bakr ibn Zubayr. *Musnad al-Ḥumaydī* (Damascus: Dār al-Saqqā, 1996).

Ḥumaydī, Muḥammad ibn Fattūḥ al-. *Jadhwat al-muqtabis fī dhikr wulāt al-Andalus.* Cairo: al-Dār al-Miṣriyya, 1966.

Ibn Asbāṭ. *Ṣidq al-akhbār.* Tripoli, Lebanon: Jurūs Burs, 1993.

Ibn Baṭṭāl, ʿAlī ibn Khalaf. *Sharḥ Saḥīḥ al-Bukhārī.* 11 vols. Riyadh: Maktabat Rushd, 2003.

Ibn Baṭūṭa, Muḥammad. *Tuḥfat al-Nuẓẓār fī gharāʾib al-amṣār.* Cairo: al-Maṭbaʿat al-Khayriyya, 1904.

Ibn Ḥazm, Abū Muḥammad. *al-Muḥallā.* 11 vols. Damascus: Idārat al-Ṭibāʿa al-Munayriyya, 1933–34.

———. *Ṭawq al-ḥamāma.* Damascus: Maktabat ʿArafa, 1981.

Ibn al-Jamāʿa, Badr al-Dīn. *Munāsabāt tarājim al-Bukhārī.* Edited by Muḥammad Isḥāq Muḥammad Ibrāhīm. Bombay: al-Dār al-Salafiyya, 1984.

Ibn Khaldūn, ʿAbd al-Raḥmān Ibn Muḥammad. *Muqaddima.* Beirut: Dār al-Fikr, 2001.

———. *The Muqaddimah.* Translated by Franz Rosenthal. 3 vols. Princeton, NJ: Princeton University Press, 1967.

Ibn al-Mulaqqin, ʿUmar. *al-Tawḍīḥ li-sharḥ al-Jāmiʿ al-Ṣaḥīḥ.* Qaṭar: Dār al-Falāḥ, 2009.

Ibn al-Munayyir. *al-Mutawārī ʿalā abwāb al-Bukhārī.* Beirut: Maktab al-Islāmī, 1990.

Ibn Rajab, Zayn al-Dīn Abū al-Faraj. *Jāmiʿ al-ʿulūm wa'l-ḥikam: sharḥ khamsīn ḥadīthan min jawāmʿ al-kalim.* Damascus: Dār Ibn Kathīr, 2008.

Ibn Rushayd, Abū ʿAbd Allāh. *Tarjumān al-tarājim ʿalā abwāb Ṣaḥīḥ al-Bukhārī.* Beirut: Dār al-Kutub al-ʿIlmiyya, 2008.

Ibn Taghrībirdī, Yūsuf. *al-Nujūm al-zāhira fī mulūk Miṣr wa'l-Qāhira.* 16 vols. Cairo: al-Muʾassasa al-Miṣriyya al-ʿĀmma lil-Taʾlīf wa'l-Ṭibaʿa wa'l-Nashr, 1971.

———. *al-Nujūm al-zāhira fī mulūk Miṣr wa'l-Qāhira.* 16 vols. Beirut: Dār al-Kutub al-'Ilmiyya, 1992.

Ibn Taymiyya, Taqī al-Dīn Aḥmad. *al-Siyāsa al-Sharʿiyya.* Edited by Muḥammad ʿAbdallāh al-Sammān. Cairo: Anṣār al-Sunna, 1961.

ʿIrqsūsī, Naʿīm al-. *Sharḥ Ṣaḥīḥ al-Bukhārī.* DVD. Damascus: Maktabat al-Īmān, 2002.

Ishbīlī, Ibn Khayr al-. *Fihrisa.* Edited by Muḥammad Fuʾād Manṣūr. Beirut: Dār al-Kutub al-ʿIlmiyya, 1998.

Islamic State (IS) Office of Research and Responsa (*Diwān al-Buḥūth wa'l-Iftāʾ*). *al-Sabī: Aḥkām wa-masāʾil.* Syria or Iraq: [s.n.], 2014.

Jaṣṣāṣ, Abū Bakr Aḥmad ibn ʿAlī al-Rāzī al-. *Kitāb Aḥkām al-Qurʾān.* 3 vols. Beirut: Dār al-Kitāb al-ʿArabī, 1978.

Jinnah, Muhammad Ali. "First Presidential Address August 11, 1947." In *Pakistan Movement Historical Documents*, edited by G. Allana, 407–11. Karachi: Department of International Relations, University of Karachi, 1969.

Kāndhlawī, Muḥammad Zakariyyā al-. *Awjaz al-masālik ilā Muwaṭṭa' Mālik.* 18 vols. U.A.E.: n.p., 2003.
Kashmīrī, Anwar Shāh al-. *Fayḍ al-bārī.* Beirut: Dār Iḥyā' al-Turāth al-'Arabī, 2005.
Kashmīrī, Anwar Shāh al-, and 'Abd al-Fattāḥ Abū Ghudda. *al-Taṣrīḥ bi-mā tawātar fī nuzūl al-masīḥ.* 5th ed. Beirut: Maktab al-Matbū'āt al-Islāmiyya bi-Ḥalab, 1992.
Khallāf, 'Abd al-Wahhāb. *'Ilm uṣūl al-fiqh* Damascus: n.p., 1992.
Khān, Ṣiddīq Ḥasan. *'Awn al-bārī.* Beirut: Dār al-Kutub al-'Ilmiyya, 2008.
———. *al-Ḥiṭṭa fī al-ṣiḥāh al-sitta.* Beirut: Dār al-Jīl, 1987.
Khwāje Sharīf, Muḥammad. *Muqaddimat Tharwat al-qārī min anwār al-Bukhārī.* Hyderabad, India: Markaz Taḥqīqāt Islāmiyya, Jāmi'a Niẓāmiyya, 2000.
———. *Tharwat al-qārī min anwār al-Bukhārī.* Hyderabad, India: Markaz Taḥqīqāt Islāmiyya, Jāmi'a Niẓāmiyya, 2000.
Kirmānī, Muḥammad ibn Yūsuf al-. [*Kawākib al-Darārī:*] *Ṣaḥīḥ Abī 'Abd Allāh al-Bukhārī bi-Sharḥ al-Kirmānī.* 2nd ed. 25 vols. Beirut: Dār Iḥyā' al-Turāth al-'Arabī, 1981.
Kushmihānī. "Prayer and Index to *Ṣaḥīḥ al-Bukhārī.*" Arabic Manuscripts MS 152, Khuda Bakhsh Library, Hyderabad, India.
Manjhū ibn Akbar, Sikandar ibn Muḥammad. *Mirāt-i Sikandirī.* Baroda, India: University of Baroda Press, 1961.
Maqrīzī, Aḥmad ibn 'Alī al-. *Kitāb al-Sulūk li-ma'rifat duwal al-mulūk.* 4 vols. Cairo: Lajnat al-Ta'līf wa'l-Tarjama wa'l-Naṣr, 1956.
Mawṣilī, Shams al-Dīn al-. "Lawāmi' al-anwār 'alā ṣiḥāḥ al-āthār."Garrett Collection MS 1731, Princeton University Library.
Māzarī, 'Abdallāh al-. "al-Mu'allim bi-fawā'id *Muslim.*" MS 7539, Bibliothèque nationale de Tunisie, Tunis, Tunisia.
Muḥājirah, Umm Sumayyah al-. "From Our Sisters: Slave Girls or Prostitutes?" *Dabiq* 9 (2015): 44–49.
Nasā'ī, Aḥmad ibn Shu'ayb al-, Jalāl al-Dīn al-Suyūṭī, and Muḥammad Ḥayāt al-Sindī. *Sunan al-Nasā'ī: bi-sharḥ al-Suyūṭī wa'l-Sindī.* Cairo: Dār al-Ḥadīth, 1999.
Nawawī, Abū Zakariyyā Yaḥyā al-. *al-Talkhīṣ [fī] sharḥ al-Jāmi' al-ṣaḥīḥ lil-Bukhārī.* 2 vols. Riyadh: Dār al-Ṭayba lil-Nashr wa'l-Tawzī', 2008.
———. *Ṣaḥīḥ Muslim bi-sharḥ al-Nawawī.* 18 vols. Cairo: al-Maṭba'a bi'l-Azhar, 1969.
———. *Sharḥ matn al-Arba'īn al-Nawawiyya.* Beirut: al-Maktaba al-Islāmī, 1984.
Qasṭallānī, al-Khaṭīb al-. *Irshād al-sārī.* 10 vols. Būlāq, Cairo, Egypt: al-Maṭba'a al-Kubra al-Amīriyya, 1905.
Qushayrī, Muslim ibn al-Ḥajjāj al-, and Abū Zakariyyā al-Nawawī. *Ṣaḥīḥ Muslim bi-sharḥ Nawawī.* 18 vols. Cairo: al-Maṭba'a al-Miṣriyya bi'l-Azhar, 1930.
Safīrī, Shams al-Dīn al-. "'Iddat aḥādīth *Ṣaḥīḥ al-Bukhārī.*" MS Mingana IA 938, Cadbury Research Library, University of Birmingham Library.
Sakhāwī, Shams al-Dīn al-. *al-Ḍaw' al-lāmi' li-ahl al-qarn al-tāsi'.* Beirut: Dār al-Jīl, 1992.
———. *al-Jawāhir wa'l-durar.* Beirut: Dār Ibn Ḥazm, 1999.

Shāfiʿī, Abū ʿAbd Allāh Muḥammad ibn Idrīs al-. *al-Risāla*. Beirut: Dār al-Kitāb al-ʿArabī, 2006.

Shahrazūrī, Ibn al-Ṣalāḥ al-. *An Introduction to the Science of Ḥadīth: Kitāb Maʿrifat anwāʿ ʿilm al-ḥadīth*. Translated by Eerik Dickinson. Reading, England: Garnet, 2006.

Shawkānī, Muḥammad ibn ʿAlī al-, and Muḥammad Ṣiddīq Ḥasan Khān. *Nayl al-awṭār min asrār Muntaqā al-akhbār wa-bi-hāmishihi Kitāb ʿAwn al-bārī*. 7 vols. Būlāq: [s.n.], 1880.

Suyūṭī, Jalāl al-Din al-. *al-Taḥadduth biniʿmat Allah*. Cambridge: Cambridge University Press, 1975.

———. *al-Dībāj ʿalā Ṣaḥīḥ Muslim ibn Ḥajjāj*. Edited by Abū Isḥaq al-Ḥawaynī al-Atharī. 6 vols. al-Khabar, Saudi Arabia: Dār ibn ʿAffān, 1991.

———. *Ḥusn al-muḥāḍara fī tārīkh Miṣr wa'l-Qāhira*. 2 vols. Cairo: Dār Iḥyāʾ al-Kutub al-ʿArabīya, 1967.

———. *al-Tawshīḥ sharḥ Jāmiʿ al-ṣaḥīḥ al-Bukhārī: sharḥ Ṣaḥīḥ al-Bukhārī*. Edited by Raḍwān Jāmiʿ Raḍwān. 9 vols. Riyadh: Maktabat al-Rushd, 1998.

Suyūṭī, Jalāl al-Dīn al-, and Aḥmad ibn Ḥanbal. *ʿUqūd al-zabarjad fī iʿrāb al-ḥadīth al-nabawī*. Edited by Salmān Quḍāh. Beirut: Dār al-Jīl, 1994.

Ṭabarī, Muḥammad ibn Jarīr al-. "Sharḥ ḥadīth Umm Zarʿ." Köprülü Library, Istanbul, Turkey.

Udfuwī, Kamāl al-Dīn al-. *Al-Ṭāliʿ al-saʿīd: Al-jāmiʿ li-asmāʾ al-fuḍalāʾ wa'l-ruwāh bi-aʿla al-ṣaʿīd*. 1st ed. Cairo, Egypt: al-Maṭbaʿa al-Jamāliyya, 1914.

Ulugkhānī, ʿAbd Allāh. *Zafar ul wālih bi Muzaffar wa ālihi [sic]: An Arabic History of Gujarat*. Translated by M.F. Lokhandwala. 2 vols. Baroda, India: Oriental Institute, 1970.

ʿUthmānī, Shabbīr Aḥmad. *Faḍl al-bārī sharḥ urdū Ṣaḥīḥ al-Bukharī*. Edited by Qāḍī ʿAbd al-Raḥmān. 2 vols. Karachi: Idārat ʿUlūm Sharʿiyyah, 1973.

———. *Faḍl al-Bārī: Commentary on the Ṣaḥīḥ al-Bukhārī*. Translated by Qāḍī ʿAbd al-Raḥmān. Edited by Qāḍī ʿAbd al-Raḥmān. Karachi: Idārah ʿUlūm-i-sharyʿiyyah and Javed & Anjuman Press, 1975.

ʿUthmānī, Taqī. *Inʿām al-bārī: durūs-i Bukhārī sharīf*. Gujarat, India: Maktaba Haqqaniyya, 2006.

Wilson, Roland. *Anglo-Muhammadan Law: A Digest*. London: W. Thacker and Co., 1903.

Yusuf, Salahuddin. *Riyād-us-Sāliheen [sic] [with] Commentary*. Lahore, Pakistan: Darussalam, 1999.

Zaknūn, Ibn ʿUrwa al-. "al-Kawākib al-darārī fī tartīb Musnad al-Imām Aḥmad ʿalā abwāb al-Bukhārī." Garrett Collection MS 2604, Princeton University Library.

Zarkashī, Badr al-Dīn al-. *al-Tanqīḥ l'ilfāẓ al-Jāmiʿ al-Ṣaḥīḥ*. Edited by Yaḥyā ibn Muḥammad ʿAlī al-Ḥakamī. 3 vols. Riyadh: Maktabat Ibn Rushd, 2003.

Ẓawāhirī, Aymān al-. *al-Ḥasād al-Murr*. N.p.: Markaz al-Fajr, [n.d., 1990s].

Ziauddin, M. "Maʿarri the Free-Thinker." *Visva-Bharati Quarterly* (1935): 34–42.

SECONDARY SOURCES

Abu Lughod, Janet. *Before European Hegemony: The World System A.D. 1250–1350*. Oxford: Oxford University Press, 1989.
Adang, Camilla. "Ibn Ḥazm on Homosexuality: A Case-Study of Ẓāhirī Legal Methodology." *Al-Qanṭara* 24, no. 1 (2003): 5–31.
Ahmad, Furqan. "Contribution of Maulana Ashraf ʿAli Thanavi to the Protection and Development of Islamic Law in the Indian Subcontinent." *Islamic and Comparative Law Quarterly* 6, no. 1 (1986): 71–79.
Arastu, Rizwan. *Al-Kafi: The Earliest and Most Important Compilation of Traditions from Prophet Muhammad and His Successors*. Dearborn: Taqwa Media, 2012.
Arberry, A.J. *The Chester Beatty Library: A Handlist of the Arabic Manuscripts*. 8 volumes. Dublin: E. Walker, 1955.
Asad, Talal. "The Idea of an Anthropology of Islam." In *Occasional Papers*. Washington, DC: Center for Contemporary Arab Studies, Georgetown University, 1986.
Bajnūrī, Aḥmad Riḍā. *Anwār al-bārī: urdū sharḥ Ṣaḥīḥ al-Bukhārī*. Dehli: Rabbānī Book Depot, n.d.
Balachandran, Jyoti Gulati. "Texts, Tombs and Memory: The Migration, Settlement, and Formation of a Learned Muslim Community in Fifteenth-Century Gujarat." PhD diss., UCLA, 2012.
Barry, Michael, and J.O. Hunwick. "Ignaz Goldziher on al-Suyūṭī." *The Muslim World* 68, no. 2 (1978): 79–99.
Bashir, Shahzad. "Islam and the Politics of Temporality: The Case of ISIS." In *Time, Temporality and Global Politics,* edited by Andrew Hom, Christopher McIntosh, Alasdair McKay, and Liam Stockdale, 134–49. Bristol: E-International Relations, 2016.
Bauden, Frédéric. "Maqriziana II: Discovery of an Autograph Manuscript of al-Maqrīzī: Towards a Better Understanding of His Working Method Analysis." *Mamlūk Studies Review* 12, no. 1 (2008): 51–118.
———. "Should al-Maqrīzī Be Thrown Out with the Bath Water? The Question of His Plagiarism of al-Awḥadī's *Khiṭaṭ* and the Documentary Evidence." *Mamlūk Studies Review* 14 (2010): 159–232.
Bauer, Karen, ed. *Aims, Methods and Contexts of Qurʾanic Exegesis (2nd/8th–9th/15th C.)*. Oxford: Oxford University Press, 2013.
Baxandall, Michael. *Patterns of Intention: On the Historical Explanation of Pictures*. New Haven, CT: Yale University Press, 1985.
Bearman, P., Th. Bianquis, C.E. Bosworth, E. van Donzel, and W.P. Heinrichs, eds. *Encyclopaedia of Islam*. 2nd ed. Leiden: Brill, 1960–2005.
Ben Cheneb, M. "Ibn al-DJazarī, *Sh*ams al-Dīn." In Bearman, Bianquis, Bosworth, van Donzel, and Heinrichs, *Encyclopaedia of Islam*. dx.doi.org/10.1163/1573-3912_islam_SIM_3141.
Benjamin, Walter. "The Task of the Translator." *Illuminations,* 69–82. New York: Schocken, 1968.
Berkey, Jonathan. *The Transmission of Knowledge in Medieval Cairo*. Princeton, NJ: Princeton University Press, 1992.

———"Women and Islamic Education in the Mamluk Period." In *Women in Middle Eastern History: Shifting Boundaries in Sex and Gender,* edited by Nikki R. Keddie and Beth Baron, 143–160. New Haven, CT: Yale University Press, 2008.

Blecher, Joel. "Commentaries and Compendia of the Late Medieval Periods." In *The Oxford Handbook of Hadith Studies,* edited by Mustafa Shah. Oxford: Oxford University Press, forthcoming.

———. "Hadith Commentary." In *Oxford Bibliographies On-line,* edited by Andrew Rippin. Oxford: Oxford University Press, 2016.

———. "Ḥadith Commentary in the Presence of Students, Patrons, and Rivals: Ibn Ḥajar and *Ṣaḥīḥ al-Bukhārī* in Mamluk Cairo." *Oriens* 41, no. 3–4 (2013): 261–87.

———. "Revision in the Manuscript Age: New Evidence of Early Versions of Ibn Ḥajar's *Fatḥ al-bārī.*" *Journal of Near Eastern Studies* 79, no. 1 (2017): 39–51.

———. "'Usefulness without Toil': Al-Suyūṭī and the Art of Concise Ḥadīth Commentary." *Al-Suyūṭī, A Polymath of the Mamluk Period,* 182–200. Leiden: Brill, 2016.

Blecher, Joel, and Josh Dubler. "Overlooking Race and Secularism in Muslim Philadelphia." In *Race and Secularism in America,* edited by Vincent Lloyd and Jonathan S. Kahn, 122–50. New York: Columbia University Press, 2016.

Bonnefoy, Laurent. "How Transnational Is Salafism in Yemen?" In *Global Salafism: Islam's New Religious Movement,* edited by Roel Meijer, 321–41. Oxford: Oxford University Press, 2009.

Bourdieu, Pierre. *Outline of a Theory of Practice.* Translated by Richard Nice. Cambridge: Cambridge University Press, 1977.

Broadbridge, Anne. "Academic Rivalries and the Patronage System in Fifteenth-Century Egypt: Al-ʿAynī, al-Maqrīzī, and Ibn Ḥajar al-ʿAsqalānī." *Mamlūk Studies Review* 3 (1999): 85–107.

———. *Kingship and Ideology in the Islamic and Mongol Worlds.* Cambridge: Cambridge University Press, 2008.

Brown, Jonathan A. C. *The Canonization of al-Bukhārī and Muslim.* Leiden: Brill, 2007.

———. "The Canonization of al-Bukhārī and Muslim." PhD diss., University of Chicago, 2006.

———. *Hadith.* Oxford: Oneworld, 2009.

———. "How We Know Early Ḥadīth Critics Did *Matn* Criticism and Why It's So Hard to Find." *Islamic Law and Society* 15 (2008): 143–84.

———. "The Rules of *Matn* Criticism: There Are No Rules." *Islamic Law and Society* 19, no. 4 (2012): 356–96.

Bunzel, Cole. "From Paper State to Caliphate: The Ideology of the Islamic State." *The Brookings Project on U.S. Relations with the Islamic World* 19 (2015): 1–42.

Burge, Stephen. "Reading between the Lines: The Compilation of 'Ḥadīṯ' and the Authorial Voice." *Arabica* 58, no. 3 (2011): 168–97.

———. "Scattered Pearls: Exploring al-Suyūṭī's Hermeneutics and Use of Sources in *Al-Durr al-manthūr fī'l-tafsīr bi'l-ma'thūr.*" *Journal of the Royal Asiatic Society* 24, no. 2 (2014): 251–96.

Burton-Page, J. "Gudjarāt." In Bearman, Bianquis, Bosworth, van Donzel, and Heinrichs, *Encyclopaedia of Islam.* dx.doi.org/10.1163/1573-3912_islam_COM_0242

Bush, Stephen. *Visions of Religion: Experience, Meaning, and Power.* Oxford: Oxford University Press, 2014.

Cabezón, José Ignacio, ed. *Scholasticism: Cross-Cultural and Comparative Perspectives.* Albany: State University of New York Press, 1998.

Calder, Norman. *Islamic Jurisprudence in the Classical Era.* Cambridge: Cambridge University Press, 2010.

———. *Studies in Early Muslim Jurisprudence.* Oxford: Clarendon Press, 1993.

———. "Tafsīr from Ṭabarī to Ibn Kathīr: Problems in the Description of a Genre, Illustrated with Reference to the Story of Abraham." In *Approaches to the Qur'ān,* edited by G.R. Hawting and Abdul-Kader Shareef, 101–40. New York: Routledge, 1993.

———. "The Ummī in Early Islamic Juristic Literature." *Der Islam* 67 (1990): 111–23.

Chamberlain, Michael. *Knowledge and Social Practice in Medieval Damascus.* Cambridge: Cambridge University Press, 1994.

Cook, Michael. "On Islam and Comparative Intellectual History." *Daedalus* 135, no. 4 (Fall 2006): 108–11.

Crompton, Louis. *Homosexuality and Civilization.* Cambridge, MA: Harvard University Press, 2006.

Dagenais, John. *The Ethics of Reading in Manuscript Culture: Glossing the "Libro de buen amor."* Princeton, NJ: Princeton University Press, 1994.

Davidson, Garrett. "Carrying On the Tradition: An Intellectual and Social History of Post-Canonical Hadith Transmission." PhD diss., University of Chicago, 2014.

Dunlop, D.M. "al-Bādjī." In Bearman, Bianquis, Bosworth, van Donzel, and Heinrichs, *Encyclopaedia of Islam.* dx.doi.org/10.1163/1573-3912_islam_SIM_1009.

Eschraghi, Armin. "'I Was a Hidden Treasure': Some Notes on a Commentary Ascribed to Mullā Ṣadrā Shīrāzī." In *Islamic Thought in the Middle Ages,* edited by Anna Akasoy and Wim Raven, 91–99. Leiden: Brill, 2008.

Escovitz, Joseph H. "Patterns of Appointment to the Chief Judgeships of Cairo during the Baḥrī Mamlūk Period." *Arabica* 30, no. 2 (1983): 147–68.

Evans, Robert. *Reception History, Tradition and Biblical Interpretation: Gadamer and Jauss.* London: Bloomsbury, 2014.

Fadel, Muhammad. "Ibn Ḥajar's *Hady al-Sārī:* A Medieval Interpretation of the Structure of al-Bukhārī's *al-Jāmiʿ al-Ṣaḥīḥ:* Introduction and Translation." *Journal of Near Eastern Studies* 54 (1995): 161–95.

Fierro, Maribel. "al-Ṣadafī." In Bearman, Bianquis, Bosworth, van Donzel, and Heinrichs, *Encyclopaedia of Islam.* dx.doi.org/10.1163/1573-3912_islam_SIM_6408

———. *ʿAbd al-Rahman III: The First Cordoban Caliph.* Oxford: Oneworld, 2005.

———. "Local and Global in Ḥadīth Literature: The Case of al-Andalus." In *The Transmission and Dynamics of the Textual Sources of Islam: Essays in Honour of Harald Motzki,* edited by Nicolet Boekhoff-van der Voort, Kees Versteegh, and Joas Wagemakers, 63–90. Leiden: Brill, 2011.

———. "The Polemic about the *karāmat al-awliyāʾ* and the Development of Sufism in al-Andalus (Fourth/Tenth–Fifth/Eleventh Centuries)." *Bulletin of the School of Oriental and African Studies* 55 (1992): 236–49.

Foucault, Michel. "The Order of Discourse (1970)." In *Untying the Text: A Post-Structuralist Reader,* edited by Robert Young, 48–78. London: Routledge, 1981.

Friedmann, Yohanan. "The Attitude of the Jamʿiyyat-i ʿUlamaʾ-i Hind to the Indian National Movement and the Establishment of Pakistan" In *The ʿUlamaʾ in Modern History: Studies in Memory of Professor Uriel Heyd,* edited by G. Baer, 157–83. *Asian and African Studies* 7. Jerusalem: Israeli Oriental Society, 1971.

Fück, Johann. "Beiträge zur Überlieferungsgeschichte von Bukhārī's Traditionssammlung." *Zeitschrift der deutschen Morgenländischen Gesellschaft* 92 (1938): 60–82.

Gacek, Adam. *Arabic Manuscripts: A Vademecum for Readers.* Leiden: Brill, 2009.

Gadamer, Hans-Georg. *Truth and Method.* Translated by W. Glen-Doepel. Second, revised ed. by Joel Weinsheimer, and Donald G. Marshall. New York: Contiuum, 2004.

Genette, Gérard. *Paratexts: Thresholds of Interpretation.* Translated by Jane Lewin. Cambridge: Cambridge University Press, 1997.

Gīlānī, Manāẓir Aḥsan. *Ihata-yi Dar al-ʿUlum main bite huwe din.* Deoband: Matkab-yi tayyiba, n.d.

Gilliot, Claude. *Exégèse, langue et théologie.* Paris: Librairie Philosophique J. Vrin, 1990.

———. "Sharḥ." In Bearman, Bianquis, Bosworth, van Donzel, and Heinrichs, *Encyclopaedia of Islam.* dx.doi.org/10.1163/1573-3912_islam_COM_1039.

Gleave, Robert. "Between Ḥadīth and Fiqh: The 'Canonical' Imāmī Collections of Akhbār." *Islamic Law and Society* 8, no. 3 (2001): 350–82.

Goldziher, Ignaz. *Muslim Studies (Muhammedanische Studien).* Translated by C.R. Barber and S.M. Stern. Edited by S.M. Stern. 2 vols. London: Allen & Unwin, 1968.

———. *Ẓāhirīs: Their Doctrine and Their History: A Contribution to the History of Islamic Theology.* Boston: Brill, 2007.

Graham, William A. "Traditionalism in Islam: An Essay in Interpretation." *The Journal of Interdisciplinary History* 23, no. 3 (Winter 1993): 495–522.

Grunebaum, G.E. von. "The Concept of Plagiarism in Arabic Theory." *Journal of Near Eastern Studies* 3 (1944): 234–53.

Gumbrecht, Hans Ulrich. "Fill Up Your Margins! About Commentary and *Copia.*" In *Commentaries—Kommentare,* edited by Glenn Most, 443–54. Göttingen: Vandenhoeck and Ruprecht, 1999.

———. *The Powers of Philology: Dynamics of Textual Scholarship*. Urbana: University of Illinois Press, 2003.
Günther, Sebastian. "Ummī." *Encyclopedia of the Qur'an,* ed. Jane Dammen McAulliff. Leiden: Brill, 2006.
Guo, Li. "Ibn Dāniyāl's 'Dīwān': In Light of MS Ayasofya 4880." *Quaderni di Studi Arabi* 5/6 (2011): 163–76.
Halbertal, Moshe. *People of the Book: Canon, Meaning and Authority*. Cambridge, MA: Harvard University Press, 1997.
Hallaq, Wael. *A History of Islamic Legal Theories*. Cambridge: Cambridge University Press, 1997.
———. *Sharīʿa: Theory, Practice, Transformations*. Cambridge: Cambridge University Press, 2009.
Haykel, Bernard. *Revival and Reform in Islam: The Legacy of Muhammad al-Shawkānī*. Cambridge: Cambridge University Press, 2003.
Hemyari, Mohammad Reza. "Understanding *ʿAql* in Readings of *Uṣūl al-Kāfī:* Early Shi'ite Hadith and Its Later Interpreters." Master's thesis, George Washington University, 2014.
Henderson, John. *Scripture, Canon, Commentary*. Princeton, NJ: Princeton University Press, 1991.
Hirschler, Konrad. *The Written Word in the Medieval Arabic Lands: A Social and Cultural History of Reading Practices*. Edinburgh: Edinburgh University Press, 2012.
Ho, Engseng. "The Two Arms of Cambay: Diasporic Texts of Ecumenical Islam in the Indian Ocean." *Journal of the Economic and Social History of the Orient* 50, no. 2/3 (2007): 347–61.
Hourani, Albert. *Arabic Thought in the Liberal Age, 1798–1939*. Cambridge: Cambridge University Press, 1983.
Hourani, George Fadlo. *Arab Seafaring in the Indian Ocean in the Ancient and Early Medieval Times*. Princeton, NJ: Princeton University Press, 1995.
Hutton, Deborah. *Art of the Court of Bijapur*. Bloomington: Indiana University Press, 2006.
Illich, Ivan. *In the Vineyard of the Text*. Chicago: University of Chicago, 1993.
Ingalls, Matthew B. "Subtle Innovation Within Networks of Convention: The Life, Thought, and Intellectual Legacy of Zakariyyā al-Anṣārī (d. 926/1520)." PhD diss., Yale University, 2011.
Ingram, Brannon. "Deobandis Abroad: Sufism, Ethics and Polemics in a Global Islamic Movement." PhD diss., University of Chapel Hill, North Carolina, 2011.
Ishaq, Muhammad. *India's Contribution to the Study of Hadith Literature*. Dhakha: University of Dhakha (Dacca) Press, 1955.
Jackson, Sherman. *Islamic Law and the State: The Constitutional Jurisprudence of Shihāb al-Dīn al-Qarāfī*. Leiden: Brill, 1996.
Jaques, R. Kevin. *Ibn Hajar*. New Delhi: Oxford University Press, 2009.
Jauss, Hans. "Literary History As a Challenge to Literary Theory." *New Literary History* 2 (1970): 7–37.

Juynboll, G.H.A. *Muslim Tradition.* Cambridge: Cambridge University Press, 1983.

Kaddouri, Samir. "al-Faqīh al-Qāḍī ʿIsā ibn Sahl al-Asadī al-Jayyānī (d. 486/1093)." *Majallat al-Tārīkh al-ʿArabī* 37 (Summer 2006): 307–32.

———. "Refutations of Ibn Ḥazm by Mālikī Authors from al-Andalus and North-Africa." In *Ibn Ḥazm of Cordoba: The Life and Works of a Controversial Thinker,* edited by Camilla Adang, Maribel Fierro, and Sabine Schmidtke, 539–600. Leiden: Brill, 2013.

Kafka, Franz. *The Metamorphosis, In the Penal Colony, and Other Stories.* Translated by Anne Rice. New York: Schocken Books, 1995.

Kakutani, Michiko. "Texts without Context." *The New York Times,* March 17, 2010.

Katz, Marion Holmes. "The 'Corruption of the Times' and the Mutability of the *Shari'a.*" *Cardozo Law Review* 28, no. 1 (October 2006).

Kawash, Sabri. "Ibn Ḥajar al-Asqalānī: A Study of the Background, Education, and Career of a ʿĀlim in Egypt." PhD diss., Princeton University, 1968.

Khān, Ẓafarul-Islām. "Nawwāb Sayyid Ṣiddīḳ Ḥasan K͟hān." In Bearman, Bianquis, Bosworth, van Donzel, and Heinrichs, *Encyclopaedia of Islam.*

Kozlowski, Gregory C. "Loyalty, Locality and Authority in Several Opinions (*Fatāwā*) Delivered by the Muftī of the Jamiʿah Niẓāmiyyah Madrasah, Hyderabad, India." *Modern Asian Studies* 29, no. 4 (October 1995): 893–927.

Kugle, Scott. "Framed, Blamed and Renamed: The Recasting of Islamic Jurisprudence in Colonial South Asia." *Modern Asian Studies* 35, no. 2 (May 2001): 257–313.

Lange, Christian. *Justice, Punishement and the Medieval Muslim Imagination.* Cambridge: Cambridge University Press, 2008.

Langer, Robert, and Udo Simon. "Dynamics of Orthodoxy and Heterodoxy. Dealing with Divergence in Muslim Discourses and Islamic Studies." *Die Welt des Islams* 48 (2008): 273–88.

Lapidus, Ira. *A History of Islamic Societies.* 1st ed. Cambridge: Cambridge University Press, 1988.

Lauzière, Henri. "The Construction of *Salafiyya:* Reconsidering Salafism from the Perspective of Conceptual History." *IJMES* 42 (2010): 369–89.

Lévi-Provençal, É. "La recension maghribine du *Ṣaḥīḥ* d'al-Bukhārī." *Journal Asiatique* (1923): 202–33.

Lewis, Bernard. *Islam: From the Prophet Muhammad to the Capture of Constantinople.* Oxford: Oxford University Press, 1987.

Lucas, Scott C. "The Legal Principles of Muḥammad b. Ismā'īl al-Bukhārī and Their Relationship to Classical Salafi Islam." *Islamic Law and Society* 13, no. 3 (2006): 289–324.

MacIntyre, Alisdair. *After Virtue.* 3rd ed. Notre Dame, IN: University of Notre Dame Press, 2007.

Mahmood, Saba. *Politics of Piety: The Islamic Revival and the Feminist Subject.* Princeton, NJ: Princeton University Press, 2005.

Massoud, Sami G. "Ibn Qāḍī Shuhba's *al-Dhayl al-Muṭawwal*: The Making of an All Mamluk Chronicle." *Quaderni di Studi Arabi* 4 (2009): 61–79.

Mayer, L.A. *Mamluk Costume: A Survey.* Geneva: Albert Kundig, 1952.

Messick, Brinkley. *The Calligraphic State: Textual Domination and History in a Muslim Society*. Berkeley: University of California Press, 1993.
Metcalf, Barbara. *Islamic Revival in British India: Deoband, 1860–1900*. Princeton, NJ: Princeton University Press, 1982.
Michell, George, and Mark Zebrowski. *Architecture and Art of the Deccan Sultanates*. Cambridge: Cambridge University Press, 1999.
Mingana, Alphonse. *An Important Manuscript of the Traditions of Bukhari, with Nine Facsimile Reproductions*. Cambridge, England: W. Heffer and Sons, 1936.
Mirza, Younus. "'The Slave Girl Gives Birth to Her Master': Female Slavery from the Mamlūk Era (1250–1517) to the Islamic State (2014–)," *Journal of the American Academy of Religion* (2017): doi.org/10.1093/jaarel/lfx001.
Miyan, Muhammad. *Silken Letters Movement*. New Delhi: Manak Publications, 2012.
Moosa, Ebrahim. "Colonialism and Islamic Law." In *Islam and Modernity,* edited by Muhammad Khalid Masud, Armando Salvatore, and Martin van Bruinessen, 158–81. Edinburgh: Edinburgh University Press, 2010.
———. "Contrapuntal Readings in Muslim Thought: Translations and Transitions." *Journal of the American Academy of Religion* 74, no. 1 (March 2006): 107–18.
Motzki, Harald, ed. *Hadith: Origins and Developments*. Aldershot, England: Ashgate Publishing, 2004.
Muhanna, Elias. "Why Was the Fourteenth Century a Century of Arabic Encyclopaedism?" In *Encyclopaedism from Antiquity to the Renaissance,* edited by Jason König and Greg Woolf, 343–56. Cambridge: Cambridge University Press, 2013.
Mujani, Wan Kamal. "The Fineness of Dinar, Dirham and Fals during the Mamluk Period." *Journal of Applied Sciences Research* 7, no. 12 (2011): 1895–900.
Musa, Aisha Y. *Hadith As Scripture: Discussions on the Authority of Prophetic Traditions in Islam*. New York: Palgrave Macmillan, 2008.
Newman, Andrew. *The Formative Period of Twelver Shīʿism: Ḥadīth as Discourse between Qum and Baghdad*. London: Routledge, 2000.
Nietzsche, Friedrich. *The Gay Science*. Translated by Walter Kaufmann. New York: Vintage, 1974.
Olidort, Jacob. "Inside the Caliphate's Classroom: Textbooks, Guidance Literature, and Indoctrination Methods of the Islamic State." Washington, DC: Washington Institute for Near East Policy, 2016.
Osman, Amr. "The History and Doctrine of the Ẓāhirī *Madhhab*." PhD diss., Princeton University, 2010.
Overton, Keelan Hall. "A Collector and His Portrait: Book Arts and Painting for Ibrahim 'Adil Shah II of Bijapur (r. 1580–1627)." Phd diss., University of California, Los Angeles, 2011.
Petry, Carl. *The Civilian Elite of Cairo in the Later Middle Ages*. Princeton, NJ: Princeton University Press, 1981.
Pfeifer, Helen. "Encounter after the Conquest: Scholarly Gatherings in 16th-century Ottoman Damascus," *International Journal of Middle East Studies,* 47, no. 2 (2015): 219–39.

Pfeiffer, Judith. "'Faces Like Shields Covered with Leather': Keturah's Sons in the Post-Mongol Islamicate Eschatological Traditions." In *Horizons of the World: Festschrift for İsenbike Togan,* edited by İlker Evrim Binbaş and Nurten Kılıç-Schubel, 557–94. Istanbul: İthaki, 2011.

Pierret, Thomas. "Les oulémas syriens aux XXe-XXIe siècles." PhD diss., IEP de Paris, 2009.

———. *Religion and State in Syria: The Sunni Ulama from Coup to Revolution.* Cambridge: Cambridge University Press, 2013.

Preckel, Claudia. "Ahl-i Ḥadīth." In *Encyclopedia of Islam,* edited by Kate Fleet, Gudrun Krämer, Denis Matringe, John Nawas, and Everett Rowson, 3rd ed. Leiden: Brill, 2007–. dx.doi.org/10.1163/1573-3912_ei3_COM_0107.

———. "Islamische Bildungsnetzwerke und Gelehrtenkultur im Indien des 19. Jahrhunderts. Muḥammad Ṣiddīq Ḥasan Khān (st. 1890) und die Entstehung der Ahl-e Ḥadīth-Bewegung in Bhopal." PhD diss., Ruhr-University Bochum, 2005.

Qasmi, Ali Usman. *The Ahmadis and the Politics of Exclusion in Pakistan.* New York: Anthem Press, 2014.

Rabb, Intisar. "Doubt's Benefit: Legal Maxims in Islamic Law (7th–16th Centuries)." PhD diss., Princeton University, 2009.

Rapoport, Yossef. "Legal Diversity in the Age of Taqlīd: The Four Chief Qāḍīs under the Mamluks." *Islamic Law and Society* 10, no. 2 (2003): 210–28.

Reynolds, Dwight F., ed. *Interpreting the Self: Autobiography in the Arabic Literary Tradition.* Berkeley: University of California Press, 2001.

Rippin, Andrew. "Al-Zarkashī and al-Suyutī [*sic*] on the Function of the 'Occasion of Revelation' Material." *Islamic Culture* 59, no. 3 (1985): 243–58.

———, ed. *Approaches to the History of the Interpretation of the Qur'an.* Oxford: Oxford University Press, 1988.

———. *The Qur'an and Its Interpretive Tradition.* Aldershot, England: Ashgate, 2001.

Robinson, Chase. *Islamic Historiography.* Cambridge: Cambridge University Press, 2003.

Robinson, Francis. *Islam and Muslim History in South Asia.* Delhi: Oxford University Press, 2000.

Robson, J. "Ibn Saʿāda." In Bearman, Bianquis, Bosworth, van Donzel, and Heinrichs, *Encyclopaedia of Islam.* dx.doi.org/10.1163/1573-3912_islam_SIM_3340.

Rosenthal, Franz. "Ibn ḤaDJar al-ʿAsḳalānī." In Bearman, Bianquis, Bosworth, van Donzel, and Heinrichs, *Encyclopaedia of Islam.* dx.doi.org/10.1163/1573-3912_islam_SIM_3178

———. *The Technique and Approach of Muslim Scholarship.* Analecta Orientalia. Rome: Pontificium Institutum Biblicum, 1947.

Rustam, Muḥammad ibn Zayn al-ʿĀbidīn. "al-Madrasa al-Andalusiyya fī sharḥ *al-Jāmʿi al-ṣaḥīḥ* min al-qarn al-khāmis ilā al-qarn al-thāmin al-hijrī." *Majallat Jāmiʿat Umm al-Qura li-ʿUlūm al-Sharīʿa wa'l-Lugha al-ʿArabiyya wa-Ādābihā* 15, no. 27 (1424/2003): 4–55.

Sabra, Adam. *Poverty and Charity in Medieval Islam: Mamluk Egypt, 1250–1517.* Cambridge: Cambridge University Press, 2000.

Sadeghi, Behnam. *The Logic of Law Making in Islam: Women and Prayer in the Legal Tradition.* Cambridge Studies in Islamic Civilization. Cambridge: Cambridge University Press, 2013.

Saleh, Marlis. "Al-Suyūṭī and His Works: Their Place in Islamic Scholarship from Mamluk Times to the Present." *Mamlūk Studies Review* 5 (2001): 73–89.

Saleh, Walid. *The Formation of the Classical Tafsīr Tradition: The Qur'ān Commentary of Thaʿlabī.* Leiden: Brill, 2004.

Sartain, E.M. *Jalāl al-Dīn al-Suyūṭī: Biography and Background.* 2 vols. Cambridge: Cambridge University Press, 1975.

Sayeed, Asma. *Women and the Transmission of Religious Knowledge in Islam.* Cambridge: Cambridge University Press, 2013.

Scales, P.C. *The Fall of the Caliphate of Córdoba: Berbers and Andalusis in Conflict.* Leiden: Brill, 1994.

Schacht, Joseph. *Origins of Muhammadan Jurisprudence.* Oxford: Clarendon Press, 1966.

Sharqī, Munīra bint ʿAbd Raḥmān. *ʿUlamāʾ al-Andalus fī al-qarnayn al-rābiʿ wa'l-khāmis al-hijrīyayn: dirāsa fī awḍāʿihim al-iqtiṣādiyya wa-āthārihā ʿalā mawāqifihim al-siyāsiyya.* Riyadh: Maktabat al-Malik Fahd al-Waṭaniyya, 2002.

Sheikh, Samira. *Forging a Region: Sultans, Traders, and Pilgrims in Gujarat, 1200–1500.* Oxford: Oxford University Press, 2010.

Smith, Wilfred Cantwell. *The Meaning and End of Religion.* Minneapolis, MN: Fortress Press, 1962.

Steiner, George. *After Babel: Aspects of Language and Translation.* Oxford: Oxford University Press, 1975.

Stilt, Kristen. *Islamic Law in Action: Authority, Discretion, and Everyday Experiences in Mamluk Egypt* Oxford: Oxford University Press, 2011.

Syed, Mairaj U. *Coercion and Responsibility in Classical Islamic Thought.* Oxford: Oxford University Press, 2017.

Taylor, Christopher S. *In the Vicinity of the Righteous: Ziyāra and the Veneration of Muslim Saints in Late Medieval Egypt.* Leiden: Brill, 1998.

Tokatly, Vardit. "The Aʿlām al-ḥadīth of al-Khaṭṭābī: A Commentary on al-Bukhārī's *Ṣaḥīḥ* or a Polemical Treatise?" *Studia Islamica* 92 (2001)c.

———. "The Early Commentaries on al-Bukhārī's *Ṣaḥīḥ*." PhD diss., Hebrew University of Jerusalem, 2003.

Vaux, B. Carra de. "Ḥadd." In Bearman, Bianquis, Bosworth, van Donzel, and Heinrichs, *Encyclopaedia of Islam.*

Vílchez, José Miguel Puerta. "Ibn Ḥazm: A Biographical Sketch." In *Ibn Ḥazm of Cordoba: The Life and Works of a Controversial Thinker,* edited by Camilla Adang, Maribel Fierro, and Sabine Schmidtke, 1–24. Leiden: Brill, 2013.

Wansborough, John. *Quranic Studies: Sources and Methods of Scriptural Interpretation.* Oxford: Oxford University Press, 1977.

Wasserstein, David J. *The Caliphate in the West: An Islamic Political Institution in the Iberian Peninsula.* Oxford: Clarendon Press, 1993.

———. *The Rise and Fall of the Party-Kings: Politics and Society in Islamic Spain, 1002–1086.* Princeton, NJ: Princeton University Press, 1985.

Wiederhold, Lutz. "Legal Doctrines in Conflict: The Relevance of Madhhab Boundaries to Legal Reasoning in the Light of an Unpublished Treatise on Taqlīd and Ijtihād." *Islamic Law and Society* 3, no. 2 (1996): 234–304.

Wilson, Brett. *Translating the Qur'an in an Age of Nationalism.* Oxford: Oxford University Press, 2014.

———. "The Failure of Nomenclature: The Concept of 'Orthodoxy' in the Study of Islam." *Comparative Islamic Studies* 3, no. 2 (2007): 169–94.

Winter, Michael. "'Ulama' between the State and Society in Pre-modern Sunni Islam." In *Guardians of Faith in Modern Times: 'Ulama' in the Middle East,* edited by Meir Hatina, 19–46. Leiden: Brill, 2009.

Woodward, M.R. "Textual Exegesis as Social Commentary: Religious, Social, and Political Meanings of Indonesian Translations of Arabic Ḥadīth Texts." *Journal of Asian Studies* 52, no. 3 (1993): 565–83.

Zaman, Muhammad Qasim. "Arabic, the Arab Middle East, and the Definition of Muslim Identity in Twentieth Century India." *Journal of the Royal Asiatic Society* 8, no. 1 (1998): 59–81.

———. "Commentaries, Print and Patronage: 'Ḥadīth' and the Madrasas in Modern South Asia." *Bulletin of the School of Oriental and African Studies* 62, no. 1 (1999): 60–81.

———. "Studying in a Madrasa in the Early Twentieth Century." In *Islam in South Asia,* edited by Barbara Metcalf, 225–39. Princeton, NJ: Princeton University Press, 2009.

———. *The 'Ulama in Contemporary Islam: Custodians of Change.* Princeton, NJ: Princeton University Press, 2002.

———. "The 'Ulamā': Scholarly Tradition and New Public Commentary." In *The New Cambridge History of Islam,* edited by Robert Hefner, 335–54. Cambridge: Cambridge University Press, 2010.

Index of Names and Titles

Index of Subjects and Terms